BRITISH POLITICS AND EUROPEAN ELECTIONS 1994

British Politics and European Elections 1994

David Butler
Fellow of Nuffield College, Oxford

and

Martin Westlake
Centre for Legislative Studies, University of Hull
Secretariat General, EC Commission, Brussels

St. Martin's Press

First published in Great Britain 1995 by
MACMILLAN PRESS LTD
Houndmills, Basingstoke, Hampshire RG21 2XS
and London
Companies and representatives
throughout the world

A catalogue record for this book is available
from the British Library.

ISBN 0–333–61736–3 hardcover
ISBN 0–333–64670–3 paperback

10   9   8   7   6   5   4   3   2   1
04 03 02 01 00 99 98 97 96 95

Printed and bound in Great Britain by
Antony Rowe Ltd
Chippenham, Wiltshire

First published in the United States of America 1995 by
Scholarly and Reference Division,
ST. MARTIN'S PRESS, INC.,
175 Fifth Avenue,
New York, N.Y. 10010

ISBN 0–312–12641–7

Library of Congress Cataloging-in-Publication Data
British politics and European elections 1994 / by David Butler
and Martin Westlake. — 1st ed.
p. cm.
Includes bibliographical references and index.
ISBN 0–312–12641–7
1. European Parliament—Elections, 1994.   2. Elections—Great
Britain.   3. Great Britain—Politics and government—1979–
I. Butler, David, 1924–   . II. Westlake, Martin.
JN36.B765 1995
324.94'0559'0941—dc20   95–8226
                                                  CIP

Contents

List of Tables

List of Figures, Cartoons and Plates

FIGURES

CARTOONS

PLATES

Acknowledgements

This book has two principal authors, but it is the product of much labour by many people. We are greatly indebted to the Warden and Fellows of Nuffield College, both officially and personally, for once more supporting an election study. Our thanks go also to the Nuffield Foundation for its vital support. We are also indebted to the European Commission and the European Parliament for their cooperation. However, the authors want to make it clear that any opinions expressed are entirely personal.

We have also to thank those in the political parties who gave us so much of their time. It would be impossible to produce this sort of study without the full cooperation of the participants, and we have been helped most generously by the candidates, the MEPs (old and new), MPs, ministers and frontbench spokesmen, and a large number of party officials. To them go our grateful thanks.

Those who contributed named sections to this study were punctual and perceptive. Important backroom contributions were made by Martin Range and Roger Mortimore. Our grateful thanks go to the polling organisations and to the cartoonists who have authorised us to reproduce their work here.

As well as contributing directly to this study, Lewis Baston gave us invaluable research assistance, and we are particularly indebted to him.

Thanks are due to *The Times*, the *Independent*, the *Sunday Telegraph* and the *Daily Telegraph* for permission to reproduce cartoon material.

Martin Westlake would like to thank Teresa and Bernard Westlake in London and Marion and Robert Rickman in Oxford for putting him up, during the election campaign and the writing of this study.

Last but by no means least, our grateful thanks go to our wives, Marilyn and Godelieve.

Nuffield College
31 October 1994

DAVID BUTLER
MARTIN WESTLAKE

Notes on Authors and Contributors

David Butler, Emeritus Fellow of Nuffield College, Oxford, has been associated with the Nuffield election studies since 1945 and has been the author or co-author of each one since 1951. His most recent publications include *British Political Facts* (with Gareth Butler, 1994), and *The British General Election of 1992* (with Dennis Kavanagh, 1992). He is well known for his election commentaries on BBC television and radio and has written widely on British, American and Australian politics.

Martin Westlake has worked in the European Policy Unit at the European University Institute, Florence, the Parliamentary Assembly of the Council of Europe, Strasbourg, and the Secretariat General of the EU Council of Ministers. He currently works in the Secretariat General of the EC Commission, where he is responsible for relations with the European Parliament. His most recent publications include *Britain's Emerging Euro-Elite? The British in the European Parliament, 1979–1992* (1994), *The Commission and the Parliament: Partners and Rivals in the European Policymaking Process* (1994), and *A Modern Guide to the European Parliament* (1994). He is an Associate Member of the Centre for Legislative Studies at the University of Hull, and was a visiting academic at Nuffield College, Oxford, in 1994.

Lewis Baston is researching London local government politics at Nuffield College, Oxford. He has worked at the Institute for Fiscal Studies in London and at Yale University and is currently principal research assistant on an academic biography of John Major.

John Curtice is Senior Lecturer in Politics at Strathclyde University and Deputy Director of the Centre for Research into Elections (CREST). He is co-author of *How Britain Votes* and *Understanding Political Change* (1985), and co-editor of *Labour's Last*

Chance? The 1992 Elections and Beyond (1994). He has contributed to every Nuffield election study since 1979.

John Fitzmaurice is Lecturer at the Institute of European Studies at the Free University of Brussels, and Head of Unit in the Secretariat General of the EC Commission (relations with the European Parliament). He has written widely on the European Parliament and on political parties. He stood for the House of Commons in 1987 and 1992 in the South-West.

Paul Furlong is Senior Lecturer in the Department of Political Science and International Studies at the University of Birmingham. He has written extensively on European politics. His most recent publication is *Modern Italy: Representation and Reform* (1993). His main area of research interest at present is the reform of public procurement in the European Union, and he is also working on a comparative project on legislative reponses to the Single European Act and the Maastricht Treaty.

John Greenaway is Lecturer in Politics, School of Economic and Social Studies, University of East Anglia. He is the author of *The Dynamics of Political Change* (1980 with R. A. Chapman), *Deciding Factors in British Politics* (1992, with S. M. Smith and J. R. Street) and numerous chapters and articles relating to the civil service and administrative reform.

Paul Hainsworth is Lecturer in the Department of Politics at the University of Ulster at Jordanstown. He is co-author of *Decentralisation and Change in Contemporary France* (1986) and *Northern Ireland in the European Community: An Economic and Political Analysis* (1989). He has published widely on French, European and Northern Ireland politics. He is co-founder and co-editor of the journal *Regional Politics and Policy*.

Simon Henig is a researcher at Nuffield College, Oxford. He specialises in the analysis of regional voting behaviour in British elections.

Stanley Henig is Professor and Head of Department of European Studies. He has been at the University of Central Lancashire (formerly Lancashire Polytechnic) since 1976, in a range of positions, including Dean of the Faculty of Health and Social Studies. He is a former Member of Parliament. He is a former editor of the *Journal of Common Market Studies*, a former Chairman of the University Association for Contemporary European Studies, and is a member of the Council of the Federal Trust for Education and Research. His published works include *Power and Decision in Europe*, *Political Parties in the European*

Community (1979), and *External Relations of the European Community* (1971). He is currently working on a book to be entitled *European Union: Gateway to a Federal Europe.*

David Millar, OBE, is Honorary Fellow at the Europa Institute, University of Edinburgh, and was previously a senior official in the European Parliament. His recent publications include 'European Political Cooperation' in *Parliament and International Relations* (eds. C. Carstairs and R. Warr, 1991), 'Local Government in Britain' in *La decentralisation française et l'Europe* (ed. H Portelli, 1993) and numerous articles on electoral reform, subsidiarity, and the European Community. David Millar was the Liberal Democrat candidate for the European constituency of the South of Scotland in the 1994 European Elections.

Duncan Mitchell is Jean Monnet Lecturer in EC Studies in the School of European Studies of the University of Wales, Cardiff. His recent publications include 'Wales and the Political Impact of "1992"' in *Contemporary Wales* (1992) and 'Wales and the European Community after Maastricht' (1994, Coleg Harlech Occasional Paper).

Philip Norton is Professor of Government, and Director of the Centre for Legislative Studies, at the University of Hull. His most recent publications include *The British Polity*, 3rd ed. (1993), *Does Parliament Matter?* (1993), *Back from Westminster* (with D. Wood, 1993), *Parliamentary Questions* (with M. Franklin, 1993), *New Directions in British Politics?* (ed., 1991), *Legislatures* (1990) and *Parliaments in Western Europe* (ed., 1990). He is the President of the Politics Association and a past President of the British Politics Group in the USA.

Michael Steed is now Honorary Lecturer in Politics and International Relations at the University of Kent at Canterbury and was a Lecturer in Government at the University of Manchester. He has contributed Statistical Appendices to every Nuffield election study since 1964.

List of Abbreviations

ARC	Rainbow Group (*ARC-EN-CIEL*)
CG	Communist Group
CSCE	Conference on Security and Co-operation in Europe
DR	European Right Group
DUP	Democratic Unionist Party
EC	European Communities
EEA	European Economic Area
ECOFIN	Economic and Finance Ministers Council
ECSC	European Coal and Steel Community
ECU	European Currency Unit
EDA	European Democratic Alliance
EDC	European Defence Community
EDG	European Democratic Group
EEC	European Economic Community
EFTA	European Free Trade Association
ELDR	European Liberal Democrat and Reformist Group/Party
EMI	European Monetary Institute
EMU	European Monetary Union
EPLP	European Parliamentary Labour Party
EPP	European People's Party
ERA	European Radical Alliance
ERM	Exchange Rate Mechanism
EU	European Union
EUL	European United Left
FE	Forza Europe
IGC	Intergovernmental Conference
MEP	Member of the European Parliament
NEC	National Executive Committee (Labour Party)
NI	Northern Ireland
NI	*Non-Inscrits* (MEPs unattached to a Group)
PC	Plaid Cymru
PES	Party of European Socialists
OMOV	One Member, One Vote
SDLP	Social Democratic and Labour Party
SF	Sinn Fein
SLD	Social and Liberal Democrats
SNP	Scottish National Party

SPD	Social Democratic Party (Germany)
TUC	Trades Union Congress
UKIP	United Kingdom Independence Party
UUP	Ulster Unionist Party
VAT	Value Added Tax

1 Background

Since 1979 there have been four sets of direct elections to the European Parliament. The first three had only a limited impact. Few voted, and little was read into the outcome. But the fourth Euro-elections seem, perhaps by chance, to have marked a turning point in British politics. The turnout and the media coverage were scarcely greater than before. However, the death of John Smith transformed not only the potential significance of the campaign, but the balance of political forces. Paradoxically, the outcome, in which the government narrowly avoided a near 'wipe-out', consolidated John Major's premiership. The Liberal Democrats won Euro-seats for the first time but were disappointed not to have broken through in the south of England. And the Labour Party, which had been expecting modest gains, saw its representation leap from 45 to 62 seats, as a new force – the 'Blair effect' – made itself felt in British politics.

The story of the Euro-election runs at many levels. There is the high politics of Brussels, with the competing forces of intergovernmentalism and federalism jostling in the run-up to the 1996 intergovernmental conference. There is the politics of the European Parliament itself, with its complicated calculations about the size and the power of political groups. There is the grand strategy of British party politics, involving policy stances and the fortunes of the party leaders. There is the tactical battle of the day-to-day campaign. There is also the minutiae of electioneering; boundary drawing, candidate selection, finance, media coverage, and all the diverse constituency business of contacting and mobilising voters.

In the following pages we try to set the 1994 contest in its longer European perspective, but we also seek to record in some detail an event which, coinciding with the death of John Smith, may have marked a sea change in British politics.

BRITAIN AND EUROPE

Post-war continental Europe has invariably seen Britain as an awkward and reluctant partner (see Chronology Tables 1.1 and 1.2). The years 1945 to 1994 can be divided into three distinct parts. The

Chronology Table 1.1   1948–1989: Events

17 Mar. 48	Brussels Treaty signed (B, F, Lux, NL and UK defence agreement)
4 Apr. 49	North Atlantic Treaty signed
5 May 49	Council of Europe established
3 Jun. 50	Britain declines participation in Schuman Plan
18 Dec. 51	Britain says it won't send army units to the planned European Defence Community
24 Jul. 52	European Coal and Steel Community (ECSC) established
10 Sep. 52	ECSC Parliamentary Assembly meets for the first time
30 Aug. 54	European Defence Community plans abandoned
23 Oct. 54	Western European Union established
2 May 55	Messina Conference opens – Britain declines to take part
25 Mar. 57	Treaties of Rome signed
19 Mar. 58	European Assembly meets for the first time
14 Jan. 63	De Gaulle vetoes Britain's first application to join the EC
29 Jan. 66	Luxembourg Compromise
29 Nov. 67	De Gaulle vetoes Britain's second application
30 Jun. 70	Britain reopens negotiations to join the EC
22 Jan. 72	Britain signs the Treaty of Rome
4 Oct. 72	Labour decides not to participate in the European Parliament until the terms of entry have been satisfactorily renegotiated
16 Jan. 73	First British MEPs (Conservative and Liberal) take their places in the Strasbourg hemicycle
10 Dec. 74	Paris Summit agrees to the principle of direct elections for 1978
1 Apr. 74	British government opens renegotiation of entry terms
11 Mar. 75	British renegotiation complete
5 Jun. 75	British referendum on continued EC membership – 67.2 per cent vote Yes
18 Jun. 75	First Labour delegates take their places in the European Parliament
17 Feb. 76	Government Green Paper on direct elections
20 Sep. 76	Council of Ministers signs European Assembly Elections Act
22 Mar. 77	Lib/Lab Pact
1 Apr. 77	Government White Paper on direct elections
5 May 78	Royal Assent to European Assembly Elections Bill

3 Jun. 79	General Election returns first Thatcher government
7 Jun. 79	First European elections (UK results in seats: Con. 60, Lab. 17, Lib. 0, others 4)
17 Jul. 79	First directly elected European Parliament meets in Strasbourg
1 Oct. 80	Labour Party Conference votes for British withdrawal from the EC
10 Nov. 80	Michael Foot beats Denis Healey to become Labour Leader
26 Mar. 81	SDP launched
1 Oct. 81	Labour Party Conference votes to withdraw from the EC without a referendum
9 Jun. 83	General Election returns second Thatcher government
1 Oct. 83	Neil Kinnock elected Labour Party Leader. Labour abandons opposition to EC membership
14 Feb. 84	European Parliament adopts draft Treaty establishing the European Union. Despite Margaret Thatcher's instructions to the contrary, 21 Conservative MEPs voted for the draft Treaty; 6 abstained and 28 were absent from the vote
14 Jun. 84	Second European elections (UK results in seats: Con. 45, Lab. 32, Lib. 0, others 4)
25–6 Jun. 84	The Fontainebleau European Council resolves the five-year running dispute about Britain's budgetary rebate
7 Jan. 85	The first Delors Commission takes office
28–9 Jun. 85	The Milan European Council decides, with Britain opposing, to convene an intergovernmental conference on treaty reform
2 Dec. 85	The IGC completes its work at the Luxembourg European Council
17 Feb. 86	The twelve Member State governments sign the Single European Act
11 Jun. 87	General Election returns third Thatcher government
1 Jul. 87	Single European Act comes into force
3 Mar. 88	Social and Liberal Democrat Party launched
27–8 Jun. 88	Hanover European Council establishes Delors Committee on EMU
8 Sep. 88	Jacques Delors addresses TUC
20 Sep. 88	Margaret Thatcher's Bruges speech
6 Jan. 89	The second Delors Commission takes office
15 Jun. 89	Third European elections (results in the UK in seats: Lab. 54, Con. 32, SLD 0, others 4, but Green Party wins 15 per cent of the vote)

Chronology Table 1.2   1946–94: Britain as an awkward, reluctant and idiosyncratic European

19 Nov. 46	In Zurich speech Winston Churchill calls for a 'United States of Europe', later explaining that he saw Britain as being 'with but not in' such an entity
17 Mar. 48	Brussels Treaty signed
5 May 49	Basically intergovernmental Council of Europe established
9 May 50	Schuman declaration – invitation extended to the UK
2 Jun. 50	Britain declines invitation
18 Apr. 51	European Coal and Steel Community is established with UK outside
18 Dec. 51	Foreign Secretary Eden says Britain will not send army units to proposed European Defence Community
23 Oct. 54	Basically intergovernmental Western European Union established
29 May 56	Foreign Ministers of the Six decide to begin negotiations to establish new communities. UK invited and declines
25 Mar. 57	European Economic Community and the European Atomic Energy Community are established with UK outside
3 May 60	European Free Trade Association established. UK a founder member
31 Jul. 61	UK applies for EEC membership
14 Jan. 63	De Gaulle's doubts lead to suspension of enlargement negotiations
11 May 67	UK reapplies for EEC membership, but because of de Gaulle's continued doubts, negotiations do not begin
2 Dec. 69	Hague summit gives green light to negotiations
30 Jun. 70	Negotiations begin
22 Jan. 72	Negotiations end
1 Jan. 73	UK joins the EC
28 Feb. 74	Labour government elected on platform which includes promise to renegotiate terms of entry
1 Apr. 74	Renegotiations commence
5 Jun. 75	Referendum in the UK
Spring 78	Labour government's problems lead to delay on direct elections legislation
10 Mar. 79	European Monetary System is established. Britain declines participation
7 Jun. 79	First European elections. 32 per cent turnout in the UK. 60 Conservative MEPs become third largest group in the European Parliament in their own right

26 Jun. 81	At various European Councils, culminating at Fontainebleau, the British government renegotiates Britain's budgetary rebate
29 Jun. 85	Intergovernmental conference launched despite British opposition
17 Feb. 86	Margaret Thatcher signs Single European Act
27 Jun. 89	Thatcher agrees to EMU IGC at Madrid
8 Oct. 90	Sterling unilaterally joins the ERM
28 Oct. 90	EMU IGC's terms agreed despite British opposition
15 Dec. 90	Two IGCs begin with John Major agreeing
8 Jan. 91	Britain publishes 'hard ECU' proposals
10 Dec. 91	Maastricht Treaty agreed, with British 'opt-out' on Social Chapter and 'opt-in' on EMU
16 Sep. 92	'Black Wednesday'. Britain leaves ERM
5 Nov. 92	Britain postpones parliamentary ratification of the Maastricht Treaty
2 Aug. 93	Britain deposits instruments of ratification the day the ERM collapses
27 Mar. 94	Blocking minority row leads to Ioannina compromise
25 Jun. 94	Britain vetos Dehaene as President of Commission

first, the 1940s and the 1950s, was a period in which Britain championed an intergovernmental approach and then, once the continental European countries seemed intent on going further, first refused to take part, and then established a rival grouping. The western Continent's first political organisation was the Council of Europe (set up on 5 May 1949), which was derived from an earlier and narrower five-power defence agreement, the 1948 Brussels Treaty. France and Belgium wanted the Council to be a supranational body, but Britain successfully insisted on a basically intergovernmental structure. When Britain was invited (May 1950) to take part in the negotiations leading to the creation of the European Coal and Steel Community, with its revolutionary pooling of industrial sovereignty, she declined. A year later (1951) Anthony Eden made it clear that British army units would not participate in the envisaged (and ultimately ill-fated) European Defence Community. When the EDC failed (1954) Eden championed the creation of the confederal Western European Union. In 1956 Britain declined participation in the talks that would lead to the 25 March 1957 creation of the European Economic Community (EEC) and the European Atomic Energy Community (EURATOM) but, rather, instigated the negotiations which led to the 3 May 1960 creation of the alternative European Free Trade Association (EFTA).

The second period, the 1960s, has been described as Britain's 'slow adjustment to a changed reality' (George, 1990). Whereas, in the 1950s, the arguments for deeper British involvement in the European supranational experiment had been basically political, by the 1960s there were increasingly powerful economic arguments for British accession. These led Britain (and Ireland and Denmark) to apply for membership of the EEC in the summer of 1961. However, de Gaulle's doubts about the depth of British commitment led him to stall the accession negotiations and effectively veto the British application (14 January 1963). Britain applied again in May 1967, but, after the November 1967 devaluation, a still doubtful de Gaulle refused to allow negotiations to proceed.

The third period began with Britain finally negotiating entry (1970–72) and acceding to the Community (1 January 1973), just as the Community's most successful and prosperous period was ending, and as a prolonged international recession began. Furthermore, by then the Community had developed in ways which were bound to suit its original six Member States more than any new arrivals. Thereafter Britain sought to renegotiate its terms of membership. This led to the 1975 referendum and, later, to the 1979–84 negotiations over the size of Britain's budgetary contribution, which culminated in the agreement reached at the June 1984 Fontainebleau European Council.

British membership was characterised by reluctance: Labour members did not take up their places in the European Parliament until after the 1975 referendum; legislation on the introduction of direct elections was delayed (see Chapter 3); Britain declined membership of the European Exchange Rate Mechanism (see Chapter 2); Britain objected to the holding of the 1985 intergovernmental conference (though signing the resulting Single European Act); Britain objected to the terms for the economic and monetary union part of the Maastricht intergovernmental conference (though allowing it to go ahead); Britain won an 'opt-out' on the Social Chapter and an 'opt in' on Economic and Monetary Union; Britain delayed its ratification of the Maastricht Treaty.

British membership has also become characterised by awkward idiosyncrasy: Britain championed enlargement ('widening') before constitutional reform ('deepening'); Britain was alone in not signing up to the Social Charter; Britain joined the ERM unilaterally and on its own terms (see Chapter 2); sterling was unilaterally forced out of the ERM; Britain championed its own 'hard ECU' proposals when the consensus lay elsewhere; Britain was against any increase in the size of the blocking minority in Council. Perhaps most idiosyncratic of all, Britain has insisted on maintaining an electoral system for European elections which, in the eyes of the other eleven Member States (which all practise forms of PR), seems unfair and little short of perverse in its distorting effects.

Since the Conservative Party has been in government for fifteen years, and since both Mr Major and his predecessor have had stormy relationships with 'Europe', it might be tempting to suppose that the Conservative Party is particularly predisposed to such problems. A former Conservative Chief Whip, for example, has described 'Europe' as the 'San Andreas fault of the Conservative Party'. But the 1974 Labour government of Harold Wilson was every bit as riven over Europe as John Major's government twenty years later. In truth, virtually every post-war British Prime Minister has been in a similar position and played a similar role, from Attlee to Churchill and Eden, from Macmillan to Wilson, and from Callaghan to Thatcher and Major. If there is a European 'problem' it is not restricted to one British political party, but more generally diffused throughout the British political and administrative establishment.

Numerous explanations have been advanced for Britain's awkwardness and reluctance. In the first place, Britain was a victor in 1945 and had successfully fought a war to preserve the independence of nation states, whereas most of the other defeated and/or devastated European countries saw the pre-eminence of the nation state as a prime cause of the war. Also, at the conceptual level, Britain remained a commercial and devoutly free-trading nation and looked disapprovingly on efforts, in the 1940s and, more successfully, in the 1950s and 1960s, to create a customs union (with a common external tariff). In the immediate post-war period, Britain remained an imperial power, with the (increasingly onerous) responsibilities and rights that go with empire. Even after the Empire had mostly been dissolved, the Commonwealth remained far more important, in economic terms, than Europe, a situation which did not change until the 1960s. Another fundamental consideration in British post-war foreign policy has been the 'special relationship' with the United States. British preoccupation with the 'special relationship' was a prime consideration in de Gaulle's 1963 and 1967 vetos of British accession to the Community. Succeeding generations of British politicians have invariably looked first to Washington, and only secondarily to Paris or Bonn or Brussels. What has been elegantly termed 'the force of prior assumptions' (George, 1990, p. 23) has been much at play; increasing difficulties with Britain's first two priorities, the 'special relationship' and the Commonwealth, led it to expend even more energy on those two priorities, when it might have been better served in pursuing the third, Europe. Last but not least, until May 1994 (when the Channel Tunnel was officially opened), Britain was an island and it continued to retain a very distinct culture. At the political level, this culture includes a particularly strong attachment to an ancient and unwritten constitution, to the one-member constituency link, to the adversarial style of government, to ageing political institutions, and to the alleged unsullied sovereignty and quasi-mythical role of the House of Commons.

All of these considerations, together with many more, have played in the minds of British politicians of both major parties over the past forty years. If they have retained their force, it is because they are either unresolvable, or resolvable only in the longer term. Yet changes are slowly taking place. *Eurobarometer* opinion polling shows that between 1981 and 1983 the number of UK citizens who believed EC membership to be a 'good thing' never rose above 30 per cent whereas, between 1987 and 1992, the figure only once fell below 50 per cent. The '1992' internal market programme caught people's imaginations in a way that Europe had never before achieved and was welcomed enthusiastically by the business community. Despite deep recession and high unemployment, more of the advantages of membership of a European Community were becoming apparent. The concept of 'Europe' has been particularly popular among the young.

Politicians, too, have gradually changed their opinions. Margaret Thatcher, champion of national sovereignty, signed the 1987 Single European Act, which led to the creation of the internal market, and also introduced majority decision-making in the Council of Ministers and an increase in the legislative role of the European Parliament. John Major brought home an 'opt-out' on social policy and an 'opt-in' on economic and monetary union from the 1991 Maastricht intergovernmental conference, but he also signed up to extensions of qualified majority decision-making and far-ranging extensions of the European Parliament's powers. However, a most striking phenomenon has been the retroactive nature of political debate in the United Kingdom. The House of Commons discussed membership of the Community long and hard in 1972, but the real national argument over membership only occurred in 1975, during the referendum campaign. Equally, the Commons debated the Single European Act at considerable length, but its consequences were only discussed in depth during parliamentary ratification of the Maastricht Treaty.

Perhaps above all, because 'Europe' remains an unsettled issue in British politics, it remains a political issue, and hence a political football, used within and between the political parties as a means of identification and differentiation. This goes some way towards explaining the paradoxical situation whereby, although European issues dominated the British political agenda for most of the 1989–95 period, as Chapter 2 shows, the 1994 European elections in the United Kingdom were largely fought on domestic political issues.

THE EUROPEAN PARLIAMENT

The European Parliament has been the Cinderella of the Community's institutions. Its envisaged development was almost immediately stymied by General Charles de Gaulle's accession to power in 1958. The 'founding fathers' had seen direct elections to the Parliament as the key to its evolution, yet such supranational concepts were anathema to de Gaulle, who cherished an alternative vision of intergovernmental cooperation. Throughout the 1960s, the Parliament remained a relatively inconsequential institution, with only the feeblest of consultative powers, whilst the Commission and the Council were fast consolidating their roles and powers. Walter Hallstein's 1965 attempt to reform the Community's finances in a way which would have centralised them, and given the Parliament some say, was crushed by de Gaulle, who ordered a boycott of the Community's institutions until the issue was resolved. De Gaulle's 1969 departure led to renewed talks about finance, culminating in the creation of the Community's 'own resources'. The April 1970 Luxembourg Treaty first granted the Parliament budgetary powers. These were later consolidated by the July 1975 Brussels Treaty, but the European Parliament did not have the political muscle to explore the full extent of its budgetary powers until after the first direct elections in 1979.

From the outset, the Parliament did have one very powerful weapon; it could censure (effectively sack) the Commission. But this power, which has been variously described as a 'blunderbuss' and a 'nuclear weapon', was too powerful and indiscriminate in its effects. Only seven censure motions have ever been tabled (the first in 1972), and none have come near to being adopted.

The key remained direct elections. Chapter 3 details the negotiations which ultimately led to the first direct elections in June 1979. Since then, the Parliament, aided and abetted by Court rulings, a sympathetic Commission, and friendly Council presidencies, has rapidly evolved into a major player in the Community system. Above all, the implementation of the Single European Act (1987) and of the Treaty on European Union, or 'Maastricht Treaty' (1993), has given the Parliament far-reaching legislative powers and created a far more even political balance between it and the Commission and the Council. In addition, such recent events as the vote on enlargement (May 1994) and the close vote on Jacques Santer's nomination (July 1994) hint at Parliament's burgeoning ratification and appointment powers.

But if the Parliament has at last begun to develop into the sort of political player the Community's founding fathers envisaged, it has so far largely failed in another, equally important, role; that of 'populariser' and 'democratiser'.

The so-called 'democratic deficit', part of a generalised, post-Cold War malaise in the Western body politic, is a many-faceted phenomenon affecting political institutions at both the national and the European level. In April 1994 *Eurobarometer* found that 53 per cent of EU citizens were dissatisfied with their own country's democracy, compared with 48 per cent with the state of the EU's democracy (the figures for the UK were 45 per cent and 39 per cent respectively). It might be supposed that the Euro-Parliament would be seen as a potential correction to the democratic deficit, and yet overall participation in European elections has gone down, and not up, since the first direct elections, from about 66 per cent in 1979 to 56 per cent in 1994, and turnout in some Member States, including the UK, has remained obstinately, and depressingly, low. Part of the problem is general unawareness of the institution. With just over a month to go to the 1994 European elections, only half (52 per cent) of all EU citizens had 'heard something recently about the EP' in the media (47 per cent in the UK). Three-quarters of EU citizens did not know the date of the forthcoming elections (59 per cent), or guessed wrongly (19 per cent). Only 9 per cent of UK respondents knew there were elections and got the date right. A reason for such low levels of awareness could be the shadow thrown by other, better-established, political events (such as the 5 May local government elections in the UK), but this is only a partial explanation. The various factors people say influence the way they vote are of more significance. Of those intending to vote, most felt national (55 per cent) rather than European (37 per cent) issues would be more important (63 per cent and 31 per cent respectively in the UK). The message that may be drawn from this is that the European

Parliament must somehow develop a higher, more distinct, and specifically European profile, sentiments expressed in the inaugural speech (20 July 1994) of Parliament's new President, the German Social Democrat Klaus Hänsch: 'During the election campaign, we have all learnt in a variety of ways that this Parliament and its work is still distant from the citizen. This is certainly not the citizen's fault . . . For our Parliament must not wait until 1999 before it tries to catch the eye and the ear of the electorate again.' But how?

At first sight, the *Eurobarometer* survey offered the European Parliament little encouragement in its role as democratic corrective; overall, only 44 per cent of respondents wanted to see the Parliament gain more power (only 27 per cent in the UK). But a more detailed breakdown gives a possible clue. Overall, 73 per cent of EU citizens would like the President and the members of the European Commission to have the support of a majority in the European Parliament or otherwise resign – 72 per cent in the UK!

In this light the Santer nomination process – the new President of the Commission was ultimately approved with just a 22-vote majority – takes on fresh significance. Here was a high profile and specifically European event that could rival in terms of intensity and theatricality the most intense events in any of the Member State parliaments. The European Parliament's supporters have always argued, chicken-and-egg style, that the Parliament could only be a popular institution if it became a relevant institution. The Single European Act and the Maastricht Treaty have given the European Parliament greatly enhanced powers and a central role in much of the European Community's legislative process. Because of this, the 1994–9 European Parliament may well prove to be the turning point.

2 1989–1994

INTRODUCTION

Throughout the five years leading up to the 1994 European elections, European matters dominated the British domestic political agenda as perhaps they had never done before (see Chronology Table 2.1). Within a week of the 1989 European elections, Mrs Thatcher was involved in the events at the Madrid European Council that were ultimately to lead to her downfall. In October 1990 sterling joined the Exchange Rate Mechanism. By November Mrs Thatcher was gone and in December her successor participated in the Rome European Council's decision to open two intergovernmental conferences. A troubled year of negotiations later, in December 1991, a triumphant John Major brought back the Maastricht Treaty, declaring it the best deal Britain could possibly have obtained. Six months after that, in June 1992, the Danes rejected the treaty and the now beleaguered British Prime Minister became embroiled in an extraordinary parliamentary process that almost brought down his government. In July 1992 the British government took over the EC Presidency, but ten weeks later sterling had to be ignominiously withdrawn from the ERM, and most of the rest of the British Presidency was spent trying to tailor solutions for sceptical Danes and rebellious Conservative back-benchers. The first half of 1993 was dominated by the government's tortured attempts to get the Maastricht Treaty through the Commons. In March 1994, as the enlargement negotiations with Austria, Finland, Norway and Sweden drew to a close, the British government became involved in a row over the arcane matter of blocking minorities in the Council and had to climb down embarrassingly at Ioannina. In April and May, a fresh Euro-row brewed over the appointment of the successor to Jacques Delors, and the UK again found itself in an awkward minority. As the Prime Minister's position came under threat, even his potential usurpers were distinguished primarily on the basis of their attitude to Europe, from the 'Thatcherite' Michael Portillo, through the newfound Euro-scepticism of Michael Heseltine, to the pro-European Kenneth Clarke.

Europe was itself in political and economic turmoil throughout the half-decade. A harbinger of change had come in the form of Austria's July 1989 application for EC membership. In November the Berlin Wall fell and thereafter the former Warsaw Pact, and the mighty Soviet Union itself, rapidly disintegrated. Within a year, Germany had unified, becoming easily the most populous and powerful of the Member States. The former sleeping giant began to take a more active stance in European and world affairs. The catharsis of German unification, the implications of the nearly complete single European market (particularly the freedom of capital movements) and the prospect of further enlargements accelerated the European Community's plans for economic and monetary union (EMU), and ultimately resulted in the Maastricht Treaty and the transformation of the Community into a European Union. But the terms of German monetary union, and the vast amount of investment sucked into the country, led a stern and cautious Bundesbank to raise and maintain high interest rates at a moment when the European economy was sliding into cyclical recession. High interest rates exacerbated and prolonged the recession. The Maastricht Treaty ratification process got caught up in an untimely combination of forces: the unpopularity of long-serving governments (in part due to the recession); the consequences of agricultural reform (itself bound up in a new attempt to liberalise world trade through the GATT Uruguay Round); and huge international speculative capital movements (as large investors played off the growing tensions between parities within the ERM against the fixed timetables of the Danish and French referendums). In the end, several currencies could not stand the strain and were forced out of the ERM, and the narrow bands had subsequently to be relaxed. The implementation of the Maastricht Treaty on 1 November 1993 was rapidly followed by the beginning of EMU stage II and the entry into force of the European Economic Area (1 January 1994), and by the conclusion of enlargement negotiations in March 1994. The net effect of all these changes was to consolidate the European Union's position as the central and pre-eminent European organisation.

In some large and many small ways, Europe came closer to the British people in the 1989–94 period. The spiral of increasing violence in the former Yugoslavia and Europe's inability to deal with this problem on its own doorstep underlined to many the potential advantages of having a truly common European foreign and defence policy. An April 1994 *Eurobarometer* survey showed that 55 per cent of British citizens favoured a common foreign policy and 70 per cent a

Chronology Table 2.1   1989–94: Events

15 Jun. 89	Third European elections (UK seats: Lab. 45, Con. 32, SLD 0, others 4, but Green Party wins 15 per cent of the vote)
26 Jun. 89	Madrid European Council – Britain conditionally agrees to join the ERM, and the Council agrees to establish an IGC on EMU
24 Jul. 89	Sir Geoffrey Howe reshuffled to leadership of the House. John Major appointed Foreign Secretary
17 Jul. 89	Austria applies for EC membership
26 Oct. 89	Nigel Lawson resigns. John Major becomes Chancellor of the Exchequer. Douglas Hurd becomes Foreign Secretary
11 Nov. 89	The Berlin Wall falls
5 Dec. 89	Thatcher defeats Sir Anthony Meyer 314 to 24 (31 abstentions)
14 Mar. 90	European Parliament adopts first Martin report urging treaty reform
17 May 90	European Court of Justice pension ruling (Barber case)
25–6 Jun. 90	Dublin European Council agrees to second IGC on political union
1 Jul. 90	First stage of EMU, not requiring treaty amendments, begins
11 Jul. 90	European Parliament adopts second Martin report setting out detailed draft treaty amendments
14 Jul. 90	Nicholas Ridley resigns over anti-German remarks in *Spectator* interview
2 Aug. 90	Iraq invades Kuwait
3 Oct. 90	German unification
8 Oct. 90	UK unilaterally joins the ERM at high parity
27–8 Oct. 90	At Rome I European Council Margaret Thatcher is isolated over anti-EMU views; other eleven governments agree main features of EMU
13 Nov. 90	Sir Geoffrey Howe makes resignation speech to the Commons
19 Nov. 90	Margaret Thatcher in Paris for CSCE summit
20 Nov. 90	Thatcher 204, Heseltine 152 (Thatcher withdraws on 22 November)
22 Nov. 90	European Parliament adopts third Martin report with proposals for IGCs
27 Nov. 90	Major 185, Heseltine 131, Hurd 56
27–30 Nov. 90	National parliaments and the European Parliament meet in Rome 'assizes' to discuss IGCs
28 Nov. 90	John Major becomes Prime Minister. Norman Lamont becomes Chancellor of the Exchequer

15 Dec. 90	Rome II European Council opens IGCs on EMU and political union
6 Jan. 91	Mrs Thatcher accepts presidency of the Bruges Group
8 Jan. 91	Norman Lamont announces detailed 'hard ECU' proposals to EMU IGC
11 Feb. 91	John Major describes his Bonn 'working visit' as marking the start of 'a new era of cooperation'
11 Mar. 91	During Bonn visit John Major describes vision of UK 'at the very heart of Europe'
19 Mar. 91	Bundesbank president Karl Otto Pohl tells EP's Monetary Affairs Sub-Committee that far more economic convergence is required
11 May 91	At informal Finance ministers meeting to discuss EMU Jacques Delors proposes insertion of clause leaving transition to stage 3 to a future UK parliament
16 May 91	Labour win Monmouth by-election from Conservatives
21 May 91	105 Conservative MPs sign resolution calling on the Prime Minister to reject moves towards EMU
9 Jun. 91	Kohl–Major summit results in agreement on no binding decisions at forthcoming Luxembourg European Council
11 Jun. 91	Leaked Bruges Group memorandum describes John Major as 'too frightened' to veto any EMU treaty
17 Jun. 91	Margaret Thatcher, in Chicago speech, attacks creation 'of a new artificial state'
18 Jun. 91	Margaret Thatcher, in New York speech, calls for 'Atlantic Economic Community'
24 Jun. 91	Major–Mitterrand talks result in agreement on no binding decisions at Luxembourg
28 Jun. 91	Mrs Thatcher announces she will not be seeking re-election
28–9 Jun. 91	Luxembourg European Council discusses political union draft treaty
1 Jul. 91	Sweden applies for EC membership
25 Jul. 91	European Court of Justice overrules UK legislation on fisheries quotas
9 Oct. 91	European Parliament calls for number of German MEPs to be raised from 81 to 99
21 Oct. 91	John Major expresses 'severe irritation' over Commissioner Ripa di Meana's blocking of seven UK transport projects on environmental grounds
7 Nov. 91	Conservatives lose Kincardine and Deeside by-election to the Lib Dems and Langbaurgh to Labour
9–10 Dec. 91	Maastricht European Council reaches conclusions on all outstanding points in IGCs. Major wins opt-out on social policy and opt-in on EMU

7 Feb. 92	Maastricht Treaty signed. Bundesbank expresses doubts about EMU timetable
18 Mar. 92	Finland applies for EC membership
7 Apr. 92	British Conservative MEPs dissolve their group in the EP and become 'allied members' of the Christian Democratic group, the EPP
9 Apr. 92	General Election returns Major government
13 Apr. 92	Neil Kinnock announces that he will resign
12 May 92	Queen Elizabeth addresses the European Parliament in Strasbourg
15 May 92	Margaret Thatcher says that 'the problem of German power has again surfaced'
21 May 92	House of Commons approves Maastricht Bill in second reading by 336 to 92
2 Jun. 92	Danish referendum rejects Maastricht Treaty by 50.7 to 49.3 per cent
3 Jun. 92	President Mitterrand announces a referendum in France
5 Jun. 92	Dissolution honours list contains peerages for Margaret Thatcher, Norman Tebbit and Cecil Parkinson
18 Jun. 92	Irish referendum approves Maastricht Treaty by 69 to 31 per cent
26–7 Jun. 92	Lisbon European Council
1 Jul. 92	UK Presidency of the EC begins
18 Jul. 92	John Smith (91 per cent of Electoral College votes) defeats Bryan Gould (9 per cent) to become leader of the Labour Party
31 Jul. 92	EC Commission drops legal action against the UK in five of seven alleged infringements of environmental impact assessment directives
5 Sep. 92	With ERM under growing pressure, Economic and Finance ministers meet in Bath, but Norman Lamont refuses to devalue sterling and the Bundesbank refuses to cut interest rates or revalue the Deutschmark
16 Sep. 92	'Black Wednesday'. Norman Lamont unilaterally withdraws sterling from the ERM. The lira also withdraws.
20 Sep. 92	French referendum approves Maastricht Treaty by 51 to 49 per cent
27 Sep. 92	Bryan Gould resigns from the shadow Cabinet *inter alia* over its support for the EMU process and the ERM
9 Oct. 92	John Major tells Conservative Party Conference non-ratification of the Maastricht Treaty would mean 'breaking Britain's future in Europe'
13 Oct. 92	British Coal announces imminent closure of 31 pits

16 Oct. 92	Birmingham European Council
19 Oct. 92	Michael Heseltine announces postponement and review of pit closures
4 Nov. 92	Commons narrowly votes (319 to 316) to resume consideration of the Maastricht Treaty
5 Nov. 92	John Major announces that completion of the ratification process would be delayed until after the second Danish referendum
10 Nov. 92	Government announces Matrix Churchill inquiry
22 Nov. 92	Renewed monetary turbulence leads to ERM realignment
25 Nov. 92	Norway applies for EC membership
11–12 Dec. 92	Edinburgh European Council adopts subsidiarity, transparency and openness package designed to help Danes
31 Dec. 92	British Presidency ends
1 Jan. 93	Single European market formally comes into being
3 Jan. 93	John Major states no imminent prospect of sterling's return to the ERM
6 Jan. 93	Third Delors Commission takes office
26 Jan. 93	Hoover simultaneously announces 600 redundancies in France and 400 new jobs at Cambuslang near Glasgow
10 Mar. 93	Commission orders British Aerospace to repay £44 million UK government aid it received when it took over Rover
13 Jan. 93	Danish government falls and is replaced by Social Democrat coalition
14 Jan. 93	Commons resumes consideration of Maastricht Bill (committee stage)
1 Feb. 93	Enlargement negotiations open with Austria, Finland and Sweden
8 Mar. 93	Government defeated over amendment in committee stage to Maastricht Treaty ratification bill
5 Apr. 93	Enlargement negotiations open with Norway
16 Mar. 93	Norman Lamont's budget introduces VAT on fuel and power, 8 per cent in 1994–5, and a planned rise to 17.5 per cent in 1995–6
6 May 93	Conservatives lose Newbury by-election to the Lib Dems on a 28.4 per cent swing. Government's majority cut to 19
18 May 93	Second Danish referendum approves Maastricht Treaty by 56.8 to 43.2 per cent
20 May 93	Commons approves Maastricht Bill (third reading) by 292 to 112
27 May 93	Government reshuffle. Norman Lamont refuses environment portfolio and leaves government. Kenneth Clarke becomes Chancellor of the Exchequer

1 Jun. 93	EC Labour ministers adopt 48 hour working week directive by qualified majority. UK granted ten year renewable exemption
9 Jun. 93	Norman Lamont's resignation speech criticises the Prime Minister, the government, and the Bundesbank
21 Jun. 93	Michael Heseltine suffers heart attack in Venice
21–2 Jun. 93	Copenhagen European Council
24 Jun. 93	Pauline Green elected European Parliamentary Labour Party leader
20 Jul. 93	Lords approves Maastricht Bill (third reading) by 141 to 29
22 Jul. 93	Commons ties on Labour amendment seeking UK adherence to Social Protocol. Amendment defeated 318 to 317. But resolution as a whole (accepting non-adherence) is defeated 324 to 316
23 Jul. 93	New vote on resolution, linked to motion of confidence in the government, is approved 339 to 299
29 Jul. 93	Conservatives lose Christchurch by-election to the Lib Dems
30 Jul. 93	UK High Court unanimously rejects Lord Rees-Mogg's claim that the Maastricht Treaty ratification process was 'flawed'
2 Aug. 93	The ERM effectively collapses. John Major says the Maastricht Treaty Monetary Union timetable now 'totally unrealistic'. Lord Rees-Mogg rules out any appeal to the High Court and the British government therefore deposits its instruments of ratification of the Maastricht Treaty in Rome
26 Aug. 93	German Chancellor Kohl and French Prime Minister Balladur meet in Bonn and confirm Franco-German commitment to European integration
9 Sep. 93	After two months of pressure and monetary turbulence, the Bundesbank finally cuts its interest rates
25 Sep. 93	Mr Major publishes *Economist* article with Euro-sceptical sentiments
1 Oct. 93	Labour Party Conference at Brighton billed as victory for John Smith. The Conference approves a series of modernising moves, including one-member, one-vote. John Prescott's support deemed crucial. Margaret Beckett prevaricates
5–8 Oct. 93	Conservative Party Conference in Blackpool. John Major makes Euro-sceptical speech. Peter Lilley accuses other Community nationals of abusing the benefits scheme
12 Oct. 93	German Constitutional Court delivers ruling enabling Germany to ratify the Maastricht Treaty – the last Member State to do so

29 Oct. 93	Brussels European Council agrees on the distribution of some EC institutions. Frankfurt gets the EMI – potential forerunner of a European Central Bank. London gets the European Agency for the Evaluation of Medicinal Products
1 Nov. 93	Maastricht Treaty comes into force
5–6 Nov. 93	John Smith signs European Socialist manifesto at Brussels Congress of European Socialist Parties
22 Nov. 93	European finance ministers discuss Jacques Delors' draft growth plan. The UK Chancellor dismisses some of its provisions as 'folly'
10–11 Dec. 93	Brussels European Council broadly endorses Jacques Delors' growth plan
15 Dec. 93	Anglo-Irish Downing Street declaration
1 Jan. 94	Stage 2 of EMU, including the creation of a European Monetary Institute, comes into force EEA agreement enters into force
2 Jan. 94	Bill Cash calls in the Commons for renegotiation of Maastricht Treaty
5 Jan. 94	Tim Yeo, Minister for the Environment, resigns after allegations about his private life
8 Jan. 94	Alan Duncan resigns as parliamentary private secretary
9 Jan. 94	The Earl of Caithness, Minister for Aviation and Shipping, resigns after the death of his wife
22 Jan. 94	Michael Portillo, Chief Secretary to the Treasury, attacks 'creeping Euro-federalism'
25 Jan. 94	Jimmy Boyce, Labour MP for Rotherham, dies
1 Feb. 94	Jo Richardson, Labour MP for Barking, dies. John Major dismisses backbench 92 Group rebels led by George Gardiner
3 Feb. 94	John Major 'gets tough' before 1922 Committee. European Christian Democratic parties sign European Christian Democrat manifesto in Brussels, allied British Conservative MEPs take no part
4–6 Feb. 94	Labour holds European Conference in Glasgow
4 Feb. 94	Michael Portillo makes 'foreigners' speech in Southampton
6 Feb. 94	Stephen Milligan, Conservative MP for Eastleigh, dies
8 Feb. 94	Norman Tebbit attacks 'corruption in EU' in Bruges Group speech. Paddy Ashdown launches 'making Europe work for us'
9 Feb. 94	Bryan Gould announces his forthcoming retirement from Parliament
10 Feb. 94	European Parliament adopts, with Conservative MEPs against, the Herman report on a European constitution
13 Feb. 94	Hartley Booth resigns as parliamentary private secretary after allegations about his private life

15 Feb. 94	Michael Portillo attacks EU's uncompetitiveness and protectionism in American Chamber of Commerce speech. John Major in Russia. Commons votes through Constituency Committees' recommendations
16 Feb. 94	The European Commission imposes a fine of 32 million ECU on British Steel for 'anti-competition activities'. Peter Lilley makes loyalist speech to 92 Group
23 Feb. 94	Sir Norman Fowler and David Hunt attack John Smith's adherence to the European Socialist manifesto
24 Feb. 94	Douglas Hurd letter to Conservative MEPs: 'go for victory'
25 Feb. 94	Malaya excludes British companies from any future government contracts
27 Feb. 94	John Major in US
28 Feb. 94	Ron Leighton, Labour MP for Newham North East, dies
1 Mar. 94	Enlargement negotiations concluded with Austria, Finland and Sweden. Gordon Brown visits Brussels
3 Mar. 94	Stephen Dorrell addresses TUC conference. Michael Heseltine Stockton lecture
7 Mar. 94	Douglas Hurd Brussels speech attacks 'fraud, waste and far-fetched idealism'. John Major, in Jimmy Young interview, says 'I've never run away from a challenge in my life. I am surely not doing so now'. Government launches legal challenge to 48-hour working week directive
8 Mar. 94	Kenneth Clarke tells the *Independent* 'I would like to be a contender but at a time of John Major's choosing'
9 Mar. 94	William Waldegrave embroiled in 'right to lie' row. *Guardian* reports Jean-Luc Dehaene candidature
16 Mar. 94	Enlargement negotiations concluded with Norway
22 Mar. 94	John Major dubs John Smith 'Monsieur Oui, the poodle of Brussels'
25–7 Mar. 94	Tory Central Council meeting in Plymouth
25 Mar. 94	Douglas Hurd tells Tories to stop 'scratching' at European wounds
26 Mar. 94	Michael Heseltine makes 'rousing' speech
27 Mar. 94	Douglas Hurd returns from Ioannina with effective ultimatum over blocking minority row
29 Mar. 94	British cabinet accepts Ioannina compromise. Tony Marlow, a Conservative backbencher, calls for the Prime Minister to resign
30 Mar. 94	A second Conservative backbencher, John Carlisle, calls for the Prime Minister to resign

31 Mar. 94	Commons rises for 12-day Easter recess. Mrs Thatcher does not favour an early leadership election.
1 Apr. 94	Douglas Hurd letter to Conservative MPs and MEPs setting out campaign themes
4 Apr. 94	Sir Nicholas Fairbairn calls for the Prime Minister to resign. Archbishop of Canterbury attacks 'shameful gap' between rich and poor
6 Apr. 94	Archbishop of Canterbury says Britain is 'an ordinary little nation'
8–9 Apr. 94	EC finance ministers and central bank governors decide against a return to a narrow-band ERM
12 Apr. 94	Bob Cryer, Labour MP for Bradford South, dies
13 Apr. 94	Douglas Hurd Mansion House speech ('our European policy is not an optional extra . . . It is essential')
14 Apr. 94	Speaker of the Commons rebukes PM for unparliamentary conduct. Conservative European election campaign press conference attended by Kenneth Clarke and Michael Heseltine
21 Apr. 94	D-Day celebrations controversy reaches climax. Prime Minister compromises on veterans' demands
22 Apr. 94	Michael Portillo's 'quiet majority' speech
27 Apr. 94	Unfruitful Chequers summit between the Prime Minister and Helmut Kohl. Lord Young says Britain 'wasting its time' in the EC. Labour NEC adopts European elections manifesto
1 May 94	Michael Portillo says Britain should never sign up to a single currency
2 May 94	Tory backbencher David Evans urges John Major to sack six of his cabinet
3 May 94	Downing Street 'calls in' Michael Portillo
4 May 94	European Parliament grants assent to accession treaties with Austria, Finland, Norway, and Sweden. Kenneth Clarke makes 'centrist' speech
5 May 94	Local government elections. The Conservatives poll 27 per cent. Their representation in contested seats falls by 429, and the party loses its majority in 18 Councils. Labour gain 88 seats. The Lib Dems gain 388 seats. Labour hold in Rotherham by-election. Conservative manifesto adopted by cabinet

common defence policy (the overall European figures were 68 per cent and 75 per cent respectively) (see also Figure 2.1). With British mortgage payers suffering as a direct result of the decisions of the Bundesbank, people were able to balance for themselves arguments about monetary sovereignty against the realities of high interest rates. The European institutions began to play a more direct role in domestic affairs. In July 1991 the European Court of Justice overruled UK legislation (on fisheries quotas) for the first time; here was proof positive of the pre-eminence of Community law and the erosion of parliamentary sovereignty. In the autumn of the same year, Italian Commissioner Carlo Ripa di Meana temporarily blocked seven UK transport projects, including Oxleas Wood and Twyford Down, on environmental grounds. His action provoked John Major into firing off an irritated letter to Jacques Delors, but it struck a chord among the British conservationist movement. In January 1993, Hoover simultaneously announced 600 redundancies in France and the creation of 400 jobs at Cambuslang near Glasgow, provoking a row between the French and British governments about the British opt-out from the Social Chapter. But Europe could also bite: on 10 March 1993 it ordered British Aerospace to repay £44 million of UK government aid it had received as an alleged 'sweetener' when it took over Rover, and on 16 February 1994 the European Commission imposed a 32 million ECU fine on British Steel for 'anti-competition activities'. Europe also came physically closer, with the official opening of the Channel Tunnel on 6 May 1994.

THE 1989 EUROPEAN ELECTIONS IN THE UNITED KINGDOM

The 1989 European elections in the United Kingdom had represented something of a watershed in British politics (see also Table 2.2). For the first, and last, time Mrs Thatcher lost a national election, and the Tories' defeat by Labour was their first since 1974. The election occurred in the mid-term of the Westminster Parliament's cycle, and it was always likely that the government would suffer from a high protest vote. Nevertheless, the scale of the defeat was primarily attributed to the Prime Minister's indifference, to public splits within the Conservative Party, and above all to a maladroit campaign. Labour won 13 Euro-seats at Conservative expense, and Conservative representation in Scotland and Wales was wiped out. For Labour, the result represented a consolidation of its recovery and was a vindication of Mr Kinnock's policy review process and the party's slow shift back towards the centre-left of British politics. The elections were devastating for the traditional third force in British politics. The Social

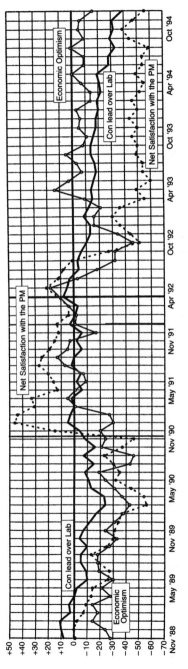

Figure 2.1   Opinion Poll Trends 1989–94

Source: MORI

Table 2.2   *European elections in Great Britain, 1984 and 1989*

	Votes	1989 % of poll	Seats	Votes	1984 % of poll	Seats
Labour	6,153,640	40.1	45	4,865,261	36.5	32
Conservative	5,331,077	34.7	32	5,426,821	40.8	45
Alliance				2,591,635	19.5	
Green	2,292,705	14.9				
SLD	986,292	6.2				
SNP	406,686	2.7	1	230,594	1.7	1
Plaid Cymru	115,062	0.8		103,031	0.8	
SDP	75,886	0.5				
Others	41,295	0.3		95,531	0.7	
Total	15,353,154		78	13,312,963		78

Electorate: 42,590,060 (1984: 41,917,313)
Votes cast: 15,353,154 (1984: 13,312,963)
Turnout: 35.9% (1984: 31.8%)

and Liberal Democrats, successors to the SDP/Liberal Alliance, were beaten into fourth place, taking just 6.2 per cent of the vote, compared with the Alliance's 19.5 per cent in 1984. The elections also marked the effective end of the SDP experiment. The rump party, led by Dr David Owen, managed to contest just 16 seats and won just 75,886 votes (0.5 per cent of the poll) nationwide (see Tables 2.3 and 2.4).

The 1989 elections were also remarkable for the sudden and unexpected rise of the Green Party, which had never previously saved a candidate's deposit in a Westminster election and which, in the 1987 General Election, had won 1.4 per cent of the vote in the constituencies where it stood. In the 1989 local government elections this had increased to 8.6 per cent, but their performance in June far surpassed this. The Party contested every British mainland seat, saved every deposit, and won almost 15 per cent of the vote – more than in any other Member State. An irony of the British electoral system, much

Key to Tables 2.3 and 2.4

ARC	Arc en Ciel (Rainbow Group)
CG	Communist Group
DR	Droit European (Democratic Right)
EDA	European Democratic Alliance
EDG	European Democratic Group
EPP	European People's Party
LDR	Liberal Democrat and Reformist Group
NI	Non-Attached Members

Table 2.3 Political Groups in the European Parliament before the 1989 European Elections

	Belgium	Denmark	France	Germany	Greece	Ireland	Italy	Luxembourg	Netherlands	Portugal	Spain	UK	Total
SOC	8	3	20	33	10	–	12	2	9	7	28	33	165
EPP	6	1	8	41	8	6	27	3	8	4	1	–	113
EDG	–	4	–	–	–	–	–	–	–	–	17	45	66
CG	–	2	10	–	4	–	26	–	–	3	3	–	48
LDR	5	2	14	–	–	1	6	1	5	10	2	–	46
EDA	–	–	19	–	1	8	–	–	–	–	–	1	29
ARC	4	4	–	7	–	–	2	–	2	–	1	–	20
DR	–	–	9	–	1	–	5	–	–	–	–	1	16
NI	1	–	1	–	–	–	3	–	1	–	8	1	15
Total	24	16	81	81	24	15	81	6	25	24	60	81	518

Table 2.4 Political Groups in the European Parliament after the 1989 European elections

	Belgium	Denmark	France	Germany	Greece	Ireland	Italy	Luxembourg	Netherlands	Porugal	Spain	UK	Total
SOC	8	4	22	31	9	1	14	2	8	8	27	46	180
EPP	7	2	6	32	10	4	27	3	10	3	16	1	121
LDR	4	3	13	4	–	2	3	1	4	9	6	–	49
EDG	–	2	–	–	–	–	–	–	–	–	–	32	34
Green	3	–	8	8	–	–	7	–	2	1	1	–	30
EUL	–	1	–	–	1	–	22	–	–	–	4	–	28
EDA	–	–	13	–	1	6	–	–	–	–	–	–	20
DR	1	–	10	6	–	–	–	–	–	–	–	–	17
CG	–	–	7	–	3	1	–	–	–	3	–	–	14
ARC	1	4	1	–	–	–	4	–	–	–	2	1	13
NI	–	–	1	–	–	1	4	–	1	–	4	1	12
Total	24	16	81	81	24	15	81	6	25	24	60	81	518

remarked upon on the Continent, was that despite this spectacular showing the Greens did not return a single MEP. As the 1992 General Election and the 1994 European elections were to show, the Green Party's success was a transitory phenomenon, a temporary repository for the traditional protest vote rather than the emergence of a new political force in British politics: the party was soon to be split and rendered ineffective by internal disputes. But the unexpected result did succeed in 'greening' the other mainstream parties. For example, one of the Greens' demands had been for the sacking of Nicholas Ridley, and in the July 1989 government reshuffle he was moved sideways, and the more ecologically conscious Chris Patten was appointed Environment Secretary. Labour also reacted swiftly, and one of its first moves in the European Parliament was to get Ken Collins elected as the Chairman of the powerful Environment Committee. As the Green's campaigns coordinator, Darren Johnson, pointed out in 1994, the absorption of traditional green concerns into the political agendas of the mainstream parties was the Green party's real success.

The 1989 results also far surpassed the Labour Party's initial expectations of a four- to six-seat overall gain. Labour's campaign strategists, Neil Kinnock, Peter Mandelson (the party's communications chief) and Bryan Gould (the campaign coordinator) had decided to use the European elections to convince a warming public that they were once again a potential party of government, and that there was a constructive and cooperative alternative to the Conservative Party's 'destructive and chauvinist' line on Europe. The party adopted a far more assertive campaign stance. There were daily press conferences in London with frontbench spokesmen (the Conservatives restricted theirs to three a week), and Mr Kinnock toured the country energetically. But on the substance of its European policies the party was not so far from the position of the Conservatives. The party's private polling had shown four chief worries among voters – the poll tax, water privatisation, the health service and interest rates, and Conservative politicians were openly airing their differences on economic policy issues. Under these circumstances it was not suprising that the Labour campaign focussed more on domestic issues. The campaign was judged to be well-coordinated and energetic. Labour recovered lost ground in the Midlands and London, but the Labour vote fell half a percent in Scotland, where the SNP almost doubled its share of the poll. The result was an important morale-booster for party activists and voters alike and encouraged the party to think that the next General Election was within its grasp.

Indisputably the chief political phenomenon of the 1989 European elections was the disastrous Tory campaign. Several aspects were to have consequences for the 1994 battle. First there was the Prime Minister's aloofness (she did not really become involved until the last week) and her thinly-veiled hostility towards matters European, in line with the sentiments expressed in her Bruges speech the previous autumn. Party activists were agreed that, whatever the merits of her stance, it was extraordinarily difficult to fight European elections on a negative basis (Labour had had a similar experience in 1979); above all, negativism discouraged turnout. A second aspect lay in the open divisions within the party. The Prime Minister, Mr Heath and various ministers turned the beginning of the campaign into a protracted slanging match, and the press made much of the increasing tensions between Mrs Thatcher and her Chancellor over the merits of ERM entry. These much-reported internal disputes were a welcome gift to the opposition.

A third aspect was the Conservative advertising campaign, said to have been personally sanctioned by the Prime Minister. This was generally adjudged to have been catastrophic. Sir Leon Brittan, ensconced in Brussels as a Commissioner, described it as 'quite extraordinarily negative, damaging and confusing'. The strategy had been to maximise Conservative turnout by warning the Tory faithful of the risks of letting Labour win by default, the object being to attribute Labour's newfound warmness to Europe to the party's hopes of getting its policies imposed on Britain via Brussels. But in its execution the strategy backfired. Two campaign posters were singled out for particular opprobrium. The first, a large photograph of the famous entry to Number 10 Downing Street, was accompanied by the motto 'Don't let Labour in by the back door'. This delighted the Labour Party, who considered it a tactical blunder, since it was seen as implicit Conservative recognition of the fact that Labour *might* get into government. But a second, more infamous poster told confused voters 'Stay at home on June 15 and you'll live on a diet of Brussels'. Fear of such ambiguous negativity loomed large among the 1994 Conservative candidates, and particularly incumbent MEPs.

The 1989 elections consolidated Labour's new, more pro-European stance, and were to have important consequences within the European Parliament. With 45 MEPs, the EPLP was now the largest contingent within the Socialist Group (the second largest was the German SPD, with 31 MEPs) which, in turn, was the largest and most influential group within the Parliament. The British contingent's numerical size entitled it to a number of important hierarchical positions within the Parliament. David Martin, a former leader of the EPLP, was elected a Vice President. Mel Read was elected a quaestor. As part of the party's 'greening' process, Ken Collins, a veteran from 1979, was elected Chairman of the increasingly powerful Environment Committee (a post he had held before). Christine Crawley (1984) was elected Chairwoman of the Women's Rights Committee, and Peter Crampton (1989) was elected Chairman of the Sub-Committee on Human Rights. At the administrative level, the post of Secretary General of the Socialist Group went to an Englishman, Julian Priestley. But nowhere was the party's new acceptability more in evidence than in some of the rapporteurships it held. Alan Donnelly, the new MEP for Tyne and Wear, was first appointed rapporteur on important EMU-connected legislation, and on the strength of this performance was appointed as rapporteur on German unification, a task he acquitted with such distinction that the German Republic made him a Knight Commander of its Order of Merit. David Martin became Parliament's rapporteur on three separate reports leading up to the Maastricht intergovernmental conference and played a vital role in asserting the Parliament's views and defending its prerogatives. John Tomlinson and Terry Wynn were rapporteurs on the 1990 and 1994 budgets respectively. Such roles, and the political attitudes behind them, would have been unthinkable in the 1984–1989 Parliament. Glyn Ford was re-elected leader of the European Parliamentary Labour Party (EPLP) from 1989 to 1993, when he was defeated by Pauline Green in a close vote (22 to 19 on a second ballot).

As Labour's star rose, that of the Conservatives fell. In the previous Parliament the 45 Conservative MEPs had enticed the 17 members of the Spanish Partido Popular into the European Democratic Group, and together they represented the third largest grouping within the Parliament – half as large as the European People's Party (EPP). Lord Plumb had been President, and Conservatives had chaired two important committees, but after the elections their numbers were much reduced, and the Partido Popular Members spurned European Democratic Group (EDG) membership, giving as a primary reason their unhappiness with Mrs Thatcher's anti-Community invective. The reduced size of the ED Group entitled the British Conservatives to just one committee chairmanship. Peter Price chaired the Budgetary Control Committee from 1989 to 1991, and Amédée Turner chaired the Civil Liberties Committee from 1992 to the end of the legislature. Few important rapporteurships came their way (an important exception was Sir Christopher Prout's role as rapporteur on the Parliament's post-Maastricht Treaty rules changes package, a role he had played after the implementation of the Single European Act, but this came after the dissolution of the EDG). Sir Fred Catherwood was elected as a Vice-President of the Parliament from 1989 to 1991, and Sir Jack Stewart Clark from 1992 to 1994. Anthony Simpson became a quaestor. As Sir Christopher Prout pointed out to journalists, it was clear that, with just 34 members in a 518-member Parliament, the EDG could hardly hope for much effective influence. He held a press conference together with the German leader of the Christian Democratic grouping, Egon Klepsch, at which he brought out into the open the EDG's search for closer collaboration with the EPP. But the EPP, with Mrs Thatcher's Bruges speech and anti-European campaign pronouncements still ringing in its ears, gently made it known that the time was not yet right. On the other hand, there was promise of a review in two years' time and on 1 May 1992 the European Democratic Group formally dissolved itself and its individual members became 'allied members' of the Christian Democrats group, the European People's Party. A few Conservative MEPs were said to have objected to the move but, at the insistence of the EPP, each of the 32 signed a document listing common policy objectives. Sir Christopher Prout, who remained leader of the British Conservatives in the European Parliament, became a Vice President of the EPP, and Bill Newton Dunn became Chairman of 'the British Section of the EPP'.

It seemed that the move might parallel a genuine shift in the nature of British Conservatism. The new Conservative Party Chairman, Chris Patten, had been a long-time and enthusiastic supporter of the 'social market'. In a March 1991 speech to the Konrad Adenauer Foundation in Bonn, Mr Major declared 'Our philosophy in the Conservative Party has much in common with the basic tenets of Christian Democracy. Like you, we have stressed the encouragement of individualism and the obligations that flow from our responsibilities to others.' David Hunt, Secretary of State for Employment, told the Tory Reform Group in July 1993 that 'I have always, willingly, described myself as a Christian Democrat as well as a Conservative.'

The EPP group's acceptance of this potentially troublesome British contingent, much like the Socialist Group's acceptance of the British Labour anti-marketeers in the 1979–84 period, had much to do with the political realities of the evolving Parliament. Political and administrative power within it was increasingly being focussed on a two-group oligopoly of the Socialists and the Christian Democrats. In the first place, the Single European Act had granted Parliament legislative powers, but it had made them conditional on the mustering of absolute majorities. Neither the Socialists nor the Christian Democrats were sufficiently strong to muster absolute majorities on their own, and so they had no choice but to cooperate with one another. But the Socialist Group was the larger of the two, and the EPP has always been uncomfortable with its relatively weaker position. If only in purely numerical terms, the British Conservatives made that position less weak and could even, given the frequent lack of cohesion among the various socialist contingents, swing votes. Second, Vice-Presidencies, committee and delegation chairmanships, and important political rapporteurships within the Parliament are all distributed on the basis of the d'Hondt system of proportional representation; the larger the group, the greater the share it will get. Thus, the British Conservatives made the EPP numerically larger and helped it win a larger share of Parliament's hierarchical positions. The potential advantages for the British Conservatives in such an alliance were succinctly listed by Sir Christopher Prout when he successfully urged the Conservative MEPs elected in June 1994 to re-apply for allied membership (see Chapter 9).

Over the fifteen years since the first direct elections were held, British MEPs have gradually become more integrated into the British political system. This has been a two-way process, with a number of MEPs becoming MPs. Of the eight MEPs first elected to Westminster in 1983/4 and the five elected in 1987, every single one has since been promoted to positions in government or on the opposition front bench. Six have served on the Commons Select Committee on European legislation. Ann Clwyd (a Labour MEP from 1979 to 1984) played an important role in the Single European Act ratification debate, and Geoffrey Hoon (a Labour MEP from 1984 to 1994) played an important behind-the-scenes role in Labour's Commons strategy during the Maastricht Treaty ratification process. Joyce Quin, a Labour MEP from 1979 to 1989, became the Labour Party's European Affairs spokeswoman in November 1993.

MEPs have also become better integrated into their parties. Conservative MEPs have three seats out of twenty in the National Union of Conservative Associations, which runs the party and the party conference, and a seat on the Board of Management, which handles party finances. Conservative MEPs have a right to attend and speak at meetings of backbench committees of Conservative MPs, including the 1922 Committee and all sectoral committees. They are frequently invited to speak on certain subjects. On the drafting of the Euro-elections manifesto, Conservative MEPs played 'virtually no role in 1984, a better one in 1989, and better still in 1994' (a senior Conservative official, cited in Corbett, 1994). The gradual growth in the Conservative MEPs' role has been ad hoc and could be reversed, but it has enabled MEPs to counter prejudice and fight their own cause within the party.

For many years, Labour MEPs were kept at arm's length from their party. Like MPs, they could attend and speak at the party conference, and their leader could attend NEC meetings in an ex-officio capacity, but there was otherwise little interaction. The situation gradually changed in parallel with the Labour Party's policy review and changing attitude towards Europe (see Chapter 5). Finally, the 1991 Labour Party Conference adopted a wide-ranging package of changes to the party's constitution which greatly enhanced the role of MEPs. Labour MEPs were granted the same rights as Labour MPs to vote in the elections of the party leader and deputy leader (MPs and MEPs together form one of the three electoral colleges). The European Parliamentary Labour Party (EPLP), as the contingent of Labour MEPs is collectively known, was given five places on the party's policy forum and has input into its policy commissions. The manifesto for the European elections is drafted in consultation with the EPLP. An annual national conference for European constituency Labour parties, similar to the local government conference, was established in 1992, enabling the party to hold more detailed debates on European affairs. MEPs in each region can now elect one of their members to the regional executives, with voting rights.

Labour MEPs played a role in Labour's gradual conversion to Europe. In her memoirs, Barbara Castle, who was leader of the British Labour MEPs from 1979 to 1984, argued that her own conversion to Europe and the newly-emerging pro-European majority among the Labour MEPs helped to change the views of both Michael Foot and Neil Kinnock (Castle, 1993). The pro-European and increasingly pro-federalist majority within the EPLP after the 1989 European elections certainly helped build up Labour support for the Maastricht Treaty. Quite apart from formal structures, MEPs play an active part in the wider political debate within their parties. They write articles in party newspapers, speak at party meetings, socialise with party members, give interviews and take part in debates. The number of fringe meetings on European subjects at the Labour Party Conference increased from three in 1987 to 14 in 1993, and the number of MEPs listed as speakers at meetings increased from 13 to 32 in the same period (Corbett, 1994).

THE 1992 GENERAL ELECTION

If Mrs Thatcher had retired on the tenth anniversary of her premiership in May 1989, she would have kept an almost unalloyed record of triumph. But 1989 marked a turn of the tide for her and for her party. The largest recession since the war was beginning. The poll tax disaster was moving to a climax and senior ministers were growing restive at Mrs Thatcher's high-handed style of government. In October 1989 Nigel Lawson resigned in protest at her taking of economic advice. In October 1990 Sir Geoffrey Howe left in protest at her arbitrary anti-Europeanism and made a resignation speech which precipitated Michael Heseltine's challenge to her leadership, opening the door for John Major to take over at 10 Downing Street.

The Conservatives moved from a 4 per cent lead in the polls in April 1989 to a 16 per cent deficit in October 1990. Mr Major had a short honeymoon, lifting his party to a 5 per cent lead in January 1991, but by May it was again 6 per cent behind. By-election landslide losses in Mid Staffordshire (March 1990), in Eastbourne (October 1990), and in Ribble Valley (March 1991), as well as local council contests confirmed the government's profound unpopularity.

As the general election approached, it seemed that the Conservative era was coming to an end. Before the dissolution of Parliament in March 1992 the Conservative position had rallied slightly, but the opinion polls substantially agreed in putting Labour just ahead. Mr Major refused to admit defeat, choosing to campaign in his own style, taking his message to the people in the streets.

When the results were counted, the Conservatives had 64 seats more than Labour and a 21-seat overall majority. Mr Major's success was a great shock. The opinion polls had been wrong, and Mr Major drew high praise for his confident and dogged campaigning. The Conservatives had won on the theme of lower taxes and an assault on Labour's alleged fiscal irresponsibility. For the pundits, the overall message was that the British middle classes did not trust Labour on taxes.

Mr Major had come to power in the shadow of Mrs Thatcher and had been seen as her preferred successor. Now he had his own popular mandate, and the Euro-enthusiastic wing of the party expected him to be less cautious in realising his desire to put Britain 'at the heart of

Europe'. But Mr Major's majority of 21 left him with limited room for manoeuvre. The economic recession persisted. High German interest rates put increasing pressure on the economy and the currency, and the Euro-sceptical wing of the party was gathering strength. Indeed, 'Europe' as a theme had been strikingly absent from the 1992 election campaign, but it was to return with a vengeance.

THE MAASTRICHT TREATY

The process of intergovernmental negotiation that ultimately resulted in the Maastricht Treaty was an uncertain inheritance for John Major, but he was to make it his own. At the Hanover (June 1988) and Madrid (June 1989) European Councils, Mrs Thatcher had reluctantly acquiesced in the decisions which effectively set the intergovernmental conferences (IGCs) on EMU and on political union in motion, and her passionate opposition and isolation at the October 1989 Rome European Council was to lead directly to her downfall. At the second Rome European Council, just one month after he became Prime Minister, Mr Major took part in the decision to open the IGCs. From the outset, one of the areas where Mr Major was supposed to differentiate himself from his predecessor was on matters European. He developed a far less combative tone and, in the spring of 1991, he used two visits to Germany to mark out a new relationship with the German Chancellor (it being common knowledge that Helmut Kohl and Margaret Thatcher had disliked each other intensely) which, it was suggested, might even displace the traditional Franco-German alliance as the mainspring of European policy-making. Chancellor Kohl was said to have a photograph of the new British Prime Minister on his desk, and the two clearly got on well. The new relationship soon bore fruit. On EMU Britain remained outside the Continental consensus, and in the spring of 1991, in the run-up to the June Luxembourg European Council, the Euro-sceptical wing of the Conservative party, encouraged by Mrs Thatcher's US speeches and orchestrated by the Bruges Group, made this an issue of principle. To help out his new political friend, the German Chancellor agreed that no binding decisions should be taken at Luxembourg and, under Kohl's influence, Mitterrand later gave a similar undertaking. Despite his continued adherence to the concept of the hard ECU (and, later, to the concept of an opt-in clause), John Major's vision of the UK 'at the very heart of Europe' seemed genuine. In retrospect, the spring of 1991 probably marked the high point of such sentiments. Thereafter, pragmatism derived from the need to reconcile the pro- and anti- European wings of his party was to come increasingly to the fore.

The Maastricht Treaty was undeniably a personal triumph for the Prime Minister, both domestically and internationally, and one for which he had worked very hard. At home, he had to conduct a delicate balancing act between the Euro-sceptics and Euro-enthusiasts within his party. For the former, he could not be seen to have ceded sovereignty, particularly on their chosen battleground of EMU. For the latter, he had to put flesh on his 'heart of Europe' vision. He had to be seen as acting constructively, but not too constructively. To the heads of state and government meeting in Maastricht on 9 and 10 December 1991, Major was still largely an unknown quantity. He had attended various European Councils in his previous brief guises as Foreign Secretary and Chancellor, but had then been in Margaret Thatcher's shadow. He had attended two European Councils as Prime Minister (Rome and Luxembourg), but never an IGC. By contrast, eight of the other twelve heads of government, together with Jacques Delors, had participated in the last IGC in 1985 that had led to the Single European Act. Mr Major, they assumed, would not be the same difficult proposition as Margaret Thatcher had been.

In fact, John Major proved to be an expert negotiator and he was able to drive just as hard a bargain as his predecessor. The groundwork had been done by the UK's permanent representative to the EC, Sir John Kerr, and the Treasury officials who had participated in the EMU negotiations. But leaked reports show that one key to his success was his absolute mastery of detail; on several issues that were relatively minor but important to the UK, Mr Major easily got his way because no other head of state was as well informed. Another key was his patience, determination and refusal to be cowed or pressured into giving way. This tenacity won him his 'opt-in' on EMU and 'opt-out' on the Social Chapter against the opposition of the French and Germans, who saw these as dangerous precedents (the readiness of the Dutch Presidency-in-office, represented by Ruud Lubbers, to compromise on these matters was said to be one of the reasons why the Franco-German alliance decided not to back Lubbers' candidature for the Presidency of the Commission in 1994). These concessions, together with the intergovernmental 'pillar' structure for common foreign policy and justice and home affairs, enabled Mr Major to return home triumphantly with his first major personal political success as Prime Minister. It was, he declared, 'game, set and match for Britain.' He later told the Commons 'I set out the issues that would be argued over at Maastricht . . . I explicitly said that we would not change our position at the very end of the negotiations. We did not, but we did achieve our objectives.' And Douglas Hurd later told the House that 'Maastricht was an important step away from an increasingly centralized – and potentially arthritic – Community' (*Independent*, 22 May 1992). Above all, it was John Major's treaty.

The Maastricht Treaty was signed on 7 February 1992, and it was hoped that it could enter into force on 1 January 1993, on the same day as the single European market. On 11 March the government announced that the General Election would be held on 9 April, and both during the campaign and after John Major's unexpected triumph, divisions over Europe within the Conservative party were muted for a while. On 12 May, in a moment of great symbolic importance, Queen Elizabeth gave her first address to the European Parliament. The Queen was the last of the Community's heads of state to address the Strasbourg assembly. The Parliament had issued an invitation many years before (renewed during Lord Plumb's 1987–9 Presidency of the Parliament), but Mrs Thatcher had always blocked acceptance. The Queen's speech was widely interpreted as a conscious gesture on John Major's part. In it, she described the Treaty as striking the 'necessary balance' between the conflicting interests of the Member States. She declared herself to be 'conscious of the differences in national parliamentary traditions across the Community' but said that 'differences of style and opinion are insignificant against the background of the proven commitment of Europeans today to reconciliation and democracy'. Continental Europeans read this as part-explanation of and part-justification for the government's stance at Maastricht, but also as re-affirmation of Major's basic commitment to be 'at the heart of Europe'. In a speech in the Hague three days later, Mrs Thatcher warned that 'the problem of German power has again surfaced' and argued in favour of a looser confederation instead of a 'centralised superstate', and in a 21 May interview with the *European*, she criticised the Maastricht Treaty for passing 'colossal powers from parliamentary governments to a central bureaucracy'. But these pronouncements did not strike the same chord they might once have done, and on 21 May the House of Commons comfortably approved the Maastricht Bill in second reading by 336 votes to 92. The Labour Party, which was a low-key supporter of the Treaty but a critic of the opt-out on the Social Chapter, abstained. Twenty-two Conservatives and 59 Labour MPs defied their party line to vote against. Nevertheless, it seemed at that stage as though parliamentary ratification of the treaty would be almost as unproblematic and straightforward as that of the SEA had been.

Then, on 2 June, in a very close result, the Danish referendum unexpectedly went against the Treaty (50.7 per cent 'No'). The next day President Mitterrand announced a referendum in France and the British government decided to suspend consideration of the Maastricht Bill in the Commons. The Danish result sent shock-waves throughout the Community. The Foreign Ministers, in an ad hoc meeting in Oslo on 4 June, refused to countenance any renegotiation of the Treaty and agreed that the ratification procedures should be continued in the other Member States. A legal and political debate ensued about whether and how the other Member States could ratify under the circumstances. The UK was unwilling to proceed without Denmark, but the Prime Minister was firmly against any idea of renegotiation. He repeatedly pointed out that the Treaty was the best deal Britain could have hoped to get, and he was afraid that the concessions made to Britain would come under renewed attack. On 18 June the Irish people approved the Treaty in their referendum (69 per cent 'Yes'), and at the 26–7 June 1992 Lisbon European Council the Member States confirmed their position with regard to Denmark. This could be summed as patience, sympathy, adjustment if necessary, but no renegotiation. The idea of a second referendum was already gaining momentum in Danish political circles. John Major himself came under pressure at Lisbon to restart the ratification process in the UK. This he refused to do, but he did give an undertaking to complete ratification by the end of the year. On 1 July, the British government took over the Presidency of the European Community.

The Danish 'No' liberated the Thatcherite opposition to the treaty within the Conservative party. Over the summer, Mrs Thatcher herself and three of her former party chairmen (Norman Tebbit, Kenneth Baker and Cecil Parkinson) led a sustained attack, linking up with a campaign calling for a referendum led by Lord Blake. This obliged Mr Major to postpone renewed parliamentary consideration until the autumn, after the conference season. Opposition, led by Peter Shore and Bryan Gould, also coalesced within the Labour party, but on a much smaller scale. Neil Kinnock had effectively been a caretaker manager from the moment of his announcement after the General Election that he would be standing down. John Smith, a pro-European who as a junior minister had voted for continued membership of the Community, was subsequently elected on 18 July 1992 with a massive

91 per cent of the party's electoral college (Bryan Gould won just 9 per cent). The size of this majority, together with the traditional 'honeymoon period' extended to new leaders by their parties and the media, gave Mr Smith great authority, and this he used to dampen doubts and uneasiness about Labour's position. Bryan Gould's opposition focussed particularly on Labour's support for the EMU provisions in the treaty (in itself an indication of just how far the party had come since the early 1980s), but such was Mr Smith's popularity that he was not really troubled by Mr Gould's traditionalist arguments for retaining control over the exchange rate and the money supply. In any case, Labour support for the Maastricht Treaty expressly excluded the Social Protocol opt-out. By September, the Labour revolt had faded, and the annual party conference overwhelmingly endorsed Maastricht as 'the best agreement that can currently be achieved'. The Conservative conference was a far more unruly affair. As we shall see, much of this opposition was derived from the monetary turbulence of September and sterling's withdrawal from the ERM on 'Black Wednesday'.

Meanwhile, the British government, fulfilling the responsibilities of EC Presidency, was still actively searching for a solution to the Danish problem. This involved a conundrum. Constitutionally, the Danes could only hold a second referendum if something substantially different existed on which they could express an opinion, and yet the Member States had already decided, in Oslo and then in Lisbon, that the Treaty could not be renegotiated. A potential solution began to emerge at the 16 October Birmingham European Council, which adopted a series of statements of intent concerning such matters as transparency and openness in decision-making and the principle of subsidiarity. But it was clear that these statements were also addressed to potentially mutinous Conservative backbenchers.

On 4 November the government brought the Maastricht Bill back before the Commons. It sought to head off its own rebels by introducing a procedurally unnecessary 'paving motion' generally endorsing the government's position on Maastricht. Because of the Social Protocol, but also because the paving motion amounted to a vote of confidence, Labour decided to vote against it. Twenty-six Conservative rebels also voted against the motion but, with the support of the Liberal Democrats, it was carried by a three-vote majority (319 to 316). Labour reviled the Liberal Democrats for missing the opportunity to bring down the government. Paddy Ashdown replied that his party could not vote against a Treaty it approved. The vote was an extraordinarily fraught occasion, and the government had to bring all its powers of persuasion to bear. These included a number of concessions, both to its own backbenchers and to minority parties. In the moments before the division the Prime Minister himself was seen talking to some of the main rebels, and it later became clear that, in a last-minute concession, Mr Major had promised to defer consideration of the Bill until after the second Danish referendum, expected sometime in the new year. Since it was by no means certain that the Danes would vote 'Yes' the second time around, this gave the rebels something of what they wanted, and it relieved the immediate pressure on the government. But elsewhere this decision was greeted with consternation. It was not in keeping with the example-setting tradition of EC presidencies, and it went back on the undertaking the Prime Minister had given at the Lisbon European Council to ratify by the end of the year. It tied the UK into the Danish ratification timetable and, by default, the Danish result. Above all, the Prime Minister was now putting at risk the treaty he had so proudly carried back from Maastricht.

As the British presidency progressed, the bones of a solution for Denmark were traced and then, at the December Edinburgh European Council, fleshed out. The solution involved a decision and various 'declarations' specific to the Danish case, general guidelines on the implementation of the subsidiarity principle, and measures to increase transparency and openness in Community decision-making procedures. To some extent, Mr Major's able brokering of this and other deals redeemed his European reputation, although the suspicion remained that the non-Danish parts of the package were designed to please Conservative backbenchers as much as Danish voters.

The Commons' consideration of the Maastricht Bill recommenced in January 1993. What subsequently occurred is summarised in Chronology Table 2.5. In brief, the number of Tory 'rebels' opposed to the Maastricht Treaty outnumbered the government's majority, nor could the government rely on the support of Labour and the Liberal Democrats, since they were opposed to the opt-out arrangement on social policy. The result was extended consideration (163 hours on the floor of the house) through numerous amendments (mostly so-called 'probing amendments'), with the opposition using every opportunity to embarrass the government. The government made a number of substantial concessions, but would not be deflected from its social policy opt-out (as the Prime Minister privately admitted in a leaked interview, if the government had opted back into the Social Protocol

On the eve of the debate on the Maastricht Bill, the situation looked desperate for John Major
The Times (22 July 1993)

*Chronology Table 2.5   The long and winding road: negotiation and ratification
of the Maastricht Treaty*

27–8 Jun. 88	Hanover European Council decides to re-launch EMU process and establishes 'Delors Committee' to draft proposals
26–7 Jun. 89	Madrid European Council decides that: EMU stage I should begin on 1 July 1990; an IGC should be held on further EMU stages.
11 Nov. 89	Berlin Wall falls
28 Apr. 90	First Dublin European Council considers second IGC on political union
25–6 Jun. 90	Second Dublin European Council formally agrees on the principle of a second IGC running in parallel with EMU IGC
1 Jul. 90	EMU Stage I begins
3 Oct. 90	German unification
27–8 Oct. 90	First Rome European Council agrees some main features of EMU, but Mrs Thatcher opposes
30 Oct. 90	Mrs Thatcher reports back to the Commons
22 Nov. 90	Mrs Thatcher withdraws from second ballot in leadership competition
28 Nov. 90	John Major becomes Prime Minister
14–15 Dec. 90	Second Rome European Council formally launches two IGCs
1 Jan. 91	Luxembourg takes over EC Presidency
11 Mar. 91	John Major's 'heart of Europe' Bonn visit
15 Apr. 91	Luxembourg presidency publishes political union 'non-paper'
21 May 91	105 Conservative MPs sign resolution calling on Mr Major to reject moves towards EMU
6 Jun. 91	Luxembourg presidency publishes EMU 'non-paper'
9 Jun. 91	Kohl-Major summit results in agreement on no binding decisions at Luxembourg European Council
11 Jun. 91	Leaked 'Bruges Group' memorandum critical of PM
17–18 Jun. 91	Mrs Thatcher, in US speeches, attacks IGC process
28–29 Jun. 91	Luxembourg European Council takes no binding decisions, but takes redrafted 'non-papers' as basis for further discussion
1 Jul. 91	Netherlands take over EC Presidency
Aug. 91	Dutch Presidency circulates new drafts including concept of a 'two-speed' EMU
24 Sept. 91	Dutch presidency withdraws 'two-speed' proposal
1–3 Dec. 91	Finance ministers meet in 'conclave' in Scheveningen and Brussels
9–10 Dec. 91	Maastricht European Council reaches agreement on all outstanding points. Major wins 'opt-in' on EMU

	and 'opt-out' on social policy and returns to London triumphant
Jan. 92	Mini-IGCs to revise other treaties
7 Feb. 92	Maastricht Treaty signed
9 Apr. 92	General Election returns John Major as Prime Minister
21 May 92	House of Commons approves Maastricht Bill in second reading by 336 to 92
2 Jun. 92	Danish people reject Maastricht Treaty by 50.7 to 49.3 per cent
3 Jun. 92	President Mitterrand announces referendum. Mr Major suspends Commons consideration of Maastricht Bill
4 Jun. 92	Foreign ministers meeting in Oslo agree to continue ratification procedures
18 Jun. 92	Irish people approve Maastricht Treaty by 69 to 31 per cent
26–7 Jun. 92	Lisbon European Council. Mr Major agrees to complete ratification by the end of the year
1 Jul. 92	UK takes over EC Presidency
16 Sept. 92	ERM crisis – 'Black Wednesday'
16 Oct. 92	Birmingham European Council outlines potential solution for Denmark.
4 Nov. 92	Government brings Maastricht Bill back before House of Commons and wins 'paving motion' vote 319 to 316, but only after agreeing to postpone ratification until after second Danish referendum
11–12 Dec. 92	Edinburgh European Council agrees solution to Danish problem
13 Jan. 93	Danish Conservative-Liberal coalition falls
14 Jan. 93	Government brings Maastricht Bill back before the Commons. Committee stage begins
15 Feb. 93	After legal row the Attorney General controversially advises the government that the Social Protocol need not be incorporated into UK law
8 Mar. 93	Government concedes Labour amendment providing that UK members of the Committee of Regions should be elected local authority members
30 Mar. 92	Deputy speaker rules Labour amendment on Social Protocol out of order
5 May 93	Having been accepted by the Speaker, Labour amendment on Social Protocol is approved at report stage
20 May 93	Bill obtains third and final reading in the Commons (292 to 112) and passes to the Lords
20 Jul. 93	Lords approve the Bill by 141 to 29. Bill receives Royal Assent

22 Jul. 93	Commons debate on the Social Protocol (Geoffrey Hoon's 'ticking time-bomb amendment). Labour amendment (for adherence to the Protocol) defeated 318 to 317. But resolution 'taking note' of government's position also defeated, 324 to 316. Prime Minister announces confidence motion
23 Jul. 93	Government wins new vote on resolution and motion of confidence. 339 to 299
30 Jul. 93	High Court rejects Lord Rees-Mogg's claim that ratification process was flawed
2 Aug. 93	Lord Rees-Mogg rules out an appeal. Government deposits articles of ratification in Rome
12 Oct. 93	German constitutional court delivers ruling enabling German government to ratify the Treaty – the last to do so
1 Nov. 93	Maastricht Treaty enters into force

the three Euro-sceptical members of the cabinet, Peter Lilley, Michael Portillo and John Redwood, would have resigned). This gave Labour its best chance of embarrassing the government. A 'time-bomb' amendment, drafted by new MP and outgoing MEP Geoff Hoon, provided that the Act should only come into force once each House of the Parliament had come to a resolution on the question of adopting the Social Protocol. The full implications of the amendment were felt in July, bringing the government to the brink of collapse; the situation was only resolved when the government linked approval of its stance on the Social Protocol to a motion of confidence, which the government comfortably won (339 to 299). Meanwhile, on 18 May, by 56.8 per cent to 43.2 per cent, the Danish people voted to accept the Maastricht Treaty and the Edinburgh Agreement. Ultimately, the Maastricht Treaty entered into force on 1 November 1993.

The Maastricht Treaty ratification process had proved extremely costly to the government and to the Prime Minister, both domestically and internationally. Within his party, Mr Major's decision to postpone ratification had completely lost him the confidence of the pro-European wing (who were genuinely afraid that UK failure to ratify could result in exclusion from the European fast lane), while his readiness to make concessions had strengthened and encouraged the Euro-sceptics (and had also strengthened the bargaining position of Plaid Cymru and the Ulster Unionist MPs). Abroad, the Prime Minister was seen as being in thrall to a small group of maverick backbenchers, even to the extent of being prepared to sacrifice the treaty he had so skilfully negotiated. Above all, Mr Major's decision to postpone lost him the confidence, and hence the future support, of the German Chancellor.

ECONOMIC AND MONETARY UNION, THE EXCHANGE RATE MECHANISM AND 'BLACK WEDNESDAY'

Wednesday, 16 September 1992 – 'Black Wednesday' – is, as one Central Office worker put it, a date 'seared into the minds' of those on the pro-European wing of the Conservative party. For them sterling's hurried and undignified exit from the ERM represented the date after which the carefully-constructed consensus within the party on European matters – already under attack from the anti-Maastricht movement – began to crumble and the Euro-sceptical forces within the party began to surge forward. The crisis had its beginnings at the Madrid European Council in June 1989. Subsequent leaks and reports indicate that the then Prime Minister, Margaret Thatcher, was confronted over the principle of entry into the ERM by her Chancellor, Nigel Lawson, and her Foreign Secretary, Geoffrey Howe. Under pressure, she reluctantly conceded that sterling should enter the ERM 'when the time was right' (i.e. the British inflation rate should be falling and nearer to the average rate prevailing in the EC). Mr Lawson had previously 'shadowed' the EMS throughout 1987 and the first quarter of 1988, but his position had been undermined when the Prime Minister told the Commons in March 1988 that 'excessive intervention' was unwarranted and risked undermining the battle against inflation. The manner of this announcement created some ill feeling, and an ideological struggle ensued in the cabinet between those who had come to believe in the virtues of a managed exchange rate, including the Chancellor and the Foreign Secretary, and the Prime Minister, who instinctively believed that markets should be given free rein. It was also believed that Mrs Thatcher found the idea of asking permission to adjust the value of sterling unpalatable. But Mrs Thatcher's reluctance stemmed also at least in part from the knowledge that the ERM, perceived since its creation in 1978 as an enhanced means of averting currency fluctuations, was about to be subsumed into something far more ambitious.

The EC had first mooted the idea of economic and monetary union in 1969, leading ultimately to the 1970 Werner Report, which set out a parallel process towards convergence of economic policies and monetary integration by stages. In March 1971 the Council of Ministers even adopted a resolution establishing EMU by stages, with the first beginning on 1 June 1971, but the Werner plan was blown off course by monetary turbulence on the European markets and above all by the Nixon administration's August 1971 decision to suspend the gold convertibility of the dollar. Some form of monetary cooperation remained necessary, and in April 1972 the six established the 'snake in the tunnel' (narrow bands within a broad joint band). Sterling joined the snake in May 1972 but was forced out by speculative pressures in June. The snake carried on with an eclectic membership until 1978, when it was subsumed within the European Monetary System, which had been established by a Franco-German partnership on the basis of an initial proposal made by the then President of the Commission, Roy Jenkins. Swayed by the hostility of the 1978 Labour Party Conference, Prime Minister Callaghan decided that sterling should not join the EMS. Although Roy Jenkins, Helmut Schmidt and Valéry Giscard d'Estaing had conceived of the EMS as a way of re-launching the EMU process, it never progressed beyond the role of exchange rate management, and even on those grounds there was some academic debate as to its worth and efficiency.

However, as the legislative process for the establishment of the single market advanced, practical and political arguments in favour of an accompanying EMU increased until, at the June 1988 Hanover European Council, the heads of state decided to create a committee, headed by Jacques Delors, with the task of 'studying and proposing concrete stages' leading towards EMU. Mrs Thatcher acquiesced in this decision. The Delors Committee reported back to the June 1989 Madrid European Council. It proposed three stages of growing economic and monetary convergence, with the first stage building on and subsuming the existing EMS, which all Member State currencies were expected to join. The Madrid Council decided, again with Mrs Thatcher's acquiesence, that the first stage of the EMU process should begin on 1 July 1990, and decided to make preparations for an intergovernmental conference which would in turn prepare the further EMU stages.

Thus, less than a year after her September 1988 Bruges speech, the Madrid Council represented a Waterloo on European issues for Mrs Thatcher. And, in retrospect, the behind-the-scenes confrontation between Mrs Thatcher and her two deputies marked the beginning of the end both for their political careers and for her premiership. On 24 July 1989, Sir Geoffrey Howe was brutally reshuffled from the Foreign

Office to the Leadership of the House – a demotion in all but name, and widely interpreted as an act of revenge for his 'mutinous' behaviour at Madrid – and replaced by John Major. On 26 October 1989, Nigel Lawson unexpectedly resigned as Chancellor and was replaced by John Major, whose place at the Foreign Office was taken by Douglas Hurd. The new Hurd–Major tandem imposed a much less aggressive European policy stance on the now more emollient Margaret Thatcher, who could ill afford further departures from her Cabinet.

A significant example of the new emollience came on 5 October 1990, when the British government announced that sterling was entering the exchange rate mechanism. However, the move was badly botched. Normally, currencies wishing to enter the mechanism would do so through negotiation with the existing members and at a mutually-agreed rate. The UK's announcement was unilateral. This was widely seen as Mrs Thatcher's quid pro quo for her acceptance of the principle of entry – if it had to be done, it would be done on her terms. And many financial commentators believed that the announced rate was high – political braggadaccio rather than responsible economics. For these reasons the move was taken very badly in monetary circles, creating lasting resentments, and it was particularly dimly viewed by the German Bundesbank. Germany and its mighty mark was too fundamental to any EMU process, and although the German Chancellor was politically committed, the Bundesbank was sensitive about any encroachment on its constitutional prerogatives. The financial press frequently reported rumours about varying degrees of enthusiasm within the Bundesbank towards the EMU process and it was clear that, were EMU ever to happen, it would have to be on the Bundesbank's terms. British entry to the ERM at unilaterally decided rates were definitely not the Bundesbank's terms.

Impending German unification, and the concomitant political events in central and eastern Europe, had led the Community to accelerate and extend the process of constitutional reform. The 25–6 June 1990 Dublin European Council had fixed 14 December as the date for the opening of the intergovernmental conference on EMU (and decided that an intergovernmental conference on political union should run in parallel with it), and a further European Council, in Rome on 27–8 October 1990, sought to draft detailed instructions for the negotiators. The second stage (which would include the creation of an independent, if weak, monetary authority) was to begin on 1 January 1994. The third stage would begin within 'a reasonable amount of time' after that. It would include the irrevocable freezing of exchange rates and the creation of a single currency. All of the Rome Council's conclusions on EMU were anathema to Mrs Thatcher. She refused to put her name to them. Her opposition was noted, but the conclusions were nevertheless adopted by the other eleven Member States, as was their right.

The storm clouds were now banked high on the horizon. On 30 October Mrs Thatcher reported back to the Commons on the Rome Council. Her impassioned opposition provoked Sir Geoffrey Howe into dramatic resignation, and when Mrs Thatcher let it be known that she regarded his departure as being over style rather than substance, he was goaded into making a devastating resignation speech. It was now inevitable that Mrs Thatcher would face a leadership challenge, and Mr Heseltine duly entered the race. On the first ballot she led him by 204 votes to 152, two short of the required 15 per cent majority. A tearful Mrs Thatcher withdrew from the second ballot, in which John Major won 185 votes to Michael Heseltine's 131 and Douglas Hurd's 56. On November 28 Mr Major was sworn in as Prime Minister, and on 28 November Norman Lamont, a Euro-sceptic, was appointed as the new Chancellor of the Exchequer. On 15 December 1990 the second Rome European Council opened two intergovernmental conferences, one on political union, and one on EMU.

Norman Lamont enthusiastically took up Mr Major's former proposals on the 'hard ECU' (which Mr Major had in turn inherited from his predecessor, Nigel Lawson) within the IGC on EMU, publishing detailed proposals on 8 January 1991. But it was soon clear that the other eleven Member State governments were set on following the three-stage model towards a single currency initially set out in the Delors Committee's report, and thereafter the Chancellor and his team took to negotiating a flexible arrangement which neither excluded nor included the UK. The resulting 'opt-in' arrangement (based on an initial proposal made by Jacques Delors) was part of the Maastricht package that John Major brought home triumphantly in December 1991. It was an ideal solution for the Prime Minister, as it pleased both European 'camps' within his party. It pleased the Euro-sceptics because the government had signed up to nothing binding and left any decision to a future parliament. It pleased the pro-Europeans because it ruled nothing out and because, since the UK was already firmly ensconced in stage I of the EMU process (membership of the ERM), a future parliament would probably bow to the inevitable.

The unexpected result in the first Danish referendum and President Mitterrand's ensuing announcement of a referendum on the Maastricht Treaty in June 1992 created conditions of uncertainty about the EMU process which, in turn, created increasing pressures within the ERM, with the money markets and speculators playing off governments' determination to maintain parities through intervention against the fixed date (20 September) of the French referendum. By the beginning of September, sterling and the Italian lira stood near to their permitted floors against the deutschmark. On 3 September, the UK government announced large-scale borrowing on the currency markets in order to prop up sterling, and the following day the Bank of Italy raised its interest rates. The problem, from the Chancellor of the Exchequer's point of view, was that German interest rates were too high, but the Bundesbank had so far refused all pressure to reduce its interest rates. The problem, from the Bundesbank's point of view, was that German unification and the attendant process of reconstruction had led to large-scale domestic borrowing, and so to worrying inflationary pressures. Since the Bundesbank was constitutionally-bound to keep inflation low, it had no option but to keep its interest rates high. Moreover, there was some latent feeling within the Bundesbank that sterling would not have been under such pressure had it initially joined the ERM at a more realistic parity.

There was a third possibility, a realignment within the ERM, but this the government refused to countenance. Various deontological forces were at work. Although the ERM was specifically designed to permit occasional realignments, there had been none since January 1987 and, because the ERM was now to be an integral part of the EMU process, a general expectation had grown that realignments should be avoided. However, as monetary pressures grew, arguments against realignment declined in force, and indeed a first major realignment was to occur on 13 September (involving the lira). Fiscal orthodoxy also ordained that devaluations were to be avoided, arguing that any short-term gains in reduced interest rates and more competitive exports would soon be countered by inflationary pressures. But the government's chief concern was political; it had made currency stability into a totem, and any devaluation would be seen as an admission of weakness (compounded by the historical view that devaluation was a weakness for which Labour governments had been particularly partial).

Acting as President of the ECOFIN Council, Norman Lamont called an informal meeting of economics and finance ministers and central bank governors for 5 September in Bath. At the formal level, the Council confirmed that a change in the structure of central rates 'would not be an appropriate response to the current tensions in the EMS', declared that its members stood ready to intervene, and welcomed the

Bundesbank's announcement that it had no intention to increase interest rates for the present. But it soon became clear that Mr Lamont had used the occasion to try to browbeat the Bundesbank into lowering its interest rates, encouraging other Member States to add their pressure, while refusing the prospect of a realignment. The Council was described as a 'shocking' occasion, and the 'low point' of the British Presidency (Ludlow, 1993). Mr Lamont had been seen to use the Presidency in a partisan fashion and was said to have been so maladroit in his blandishments that the President of the Bundesbank had to be restrained from walking out. Worse, in the eyes of his continental counterparts, the Chancellor had briefed the British press in such a way as to present the occasion as a 'victory' for the UK. In reality, if the Bath Council had been intended to avert serious damage to the ERM, it had achieved nothing.

On 13 September, the same day that the lira was devalued, the Chancellor reiterated that the government would take whatever action was necessary to maintain the existing DM 2.95 central parity of sterling. On 14 September, the Bundesbank at last announced cuts but, although the move was accompanied by rate reductions in five other European countries, its small size provoked widespread disappointment in the UK, and on 15 September sterling again fell to just above its permitted floor.

On 16 September, pressure on the pound increased sharply despite massive official intervention, and the minimum lending rate was increased from 10 to 12 per cent. As the turbulence continued, it was announced that the base rate would rise further to 15 per cent the following day, while at the close of business in London the pound stood at DM 2.75. Later the same evening, Mr Lamont unilaterally announced that sterling's membership of the ERM was being suspended, and that the second interest rate increase was being rescinded. Once again, the UK had acted without respecting the rules on consultation. During the night of 16–17 September, an emergency meeting of the Monetary Committee decided to let the lira float and the Spanish peseta be devalued. It was widely reported that the UK had unsuccessfully argued for the suspension of the ERM and also that German interest rates be reduced.

The withdrawal of the pound and the lira from the ERM was followed by a 'war of words' between the UK and Germany, particularly over the role of the Bundesbank. In a radio interview on 18 September, Mr Lamont appeared to blame Germany for producing many of the tensions within the ERM. The German Chancellor said later the same day that such criticisms of Germany were 'inappropriate for a minister'. In a television interview on the same day, John Major referred to 'fault lines in the ERM revealed over the past few days', and said that there was no imminent prospect of the UK returning to the ERM, while on 21 September in Washington, the president of the Bundesbank, Helmut Schlesinger, said serious negotiations would be needed before sterling could be readmitted to the ERM.

Despite the Chancellor's brave and defiant statements, 'Black Wednesday' was an abject humiliation for the government. Sterling had come into the ERM under a cloud, and now it had left it under a cloud. Recriminations were to reverberate on the British and the German sides for several months – later to be rekindled by Norman Lamont's resignation statement – and it became clear it would take a long time to repair the wounded sensitivities of the Bundesbank. 'Black Wednesday' damaged the government's reputation at home and abroad. At home, the media were scandalised by the amounts of money the Bank of England had spent in trying to ward off the inevitable. More importantly, the episode badly damaged the government's record as a trustworthy manager of the economy. Together with the government's heel-dragging on the ratification of the Maastricht Treaty, the episode seemed to belie John Major's desire to be 'at the heart of Europe', and badly damaged Britain's newfound alliance with Germany. Perhaps the most insidious damage was done within the party itself. Its carefully-constructed consensus over the Maastricht Treaty had been based on a pragmatic argumentation which was, by and large, acceptable to both the pro-European and the Euro-sceptical wings of the party. Economic and monetary union, the argument went, seemed both inevitable and, particularly within the business community, desirable. Despite the huge pressures working against him, the Prime Minister had won an opt-in arrangement at Maastricht which would leave any decision with the UK Parliament. This, it was argued, was the best of both worlds; if EMU did look as though it would come about, Parliament could opt in at a time of its choosing. If it did not, the UK's economic and monetary sovereignty would have remained untrammelled. The Euro-sceptics were offered the further palliative of an opt-out on the Social Chapter. But everything else in the Treaty, from the extended legislative powers granted the European Parliament through to the common foreign and security policy arrangements, was predicated on the assumption of an inexorable evolution towards EMU, whether or not the UK participated. 'Black Wednesday' removed that assumption at one fell swoop. Not only did EMU no longer seem inevitable, but the timetable contained in the Maastricht Treaty, which foresaw all Member State currencies joining the ERM during Stage I (scheduled to end on 31 December 1993), now seemed most unlikely. A further nail in the coffin came on 2 August 1993, when the exchange rate mechanism effectively collapsed, and with it collapsed the consensus within the Conservative Party. Put crudely, if EMU was not going to come about, where was the need for all the political trappings of the Maastricht Treaty? From then on the Euro-sceptics were to become gradually bolder and more outspoken and the Prime Minister was rapidly to abandon all vestiges of his pro-European enthusiasm in favour of a more pragmatic stance.

THE 1992 UK PRESIDENCY

Member States tend to see their six-month Presidencies of the EC as a showcase for their organisational and political abilities. Looking ahead in April 1992, the British Prime Minister saw the forthcoming British Presidency as a chance to put flesh on his vision of the UK at the heart of Europe. After his personal general election triumph, John Major now had his own elective authority and an amicable relationship with the German Chancellor which would enable him to push ahead on his chosen priorities. The second six months of the year would, for example, see the completion of the single European market, a concept the British wholeheartedly supported and which was due to come into force on 1 January 1993. Confirmed supporters of the widening process, the British would also seek a decision enabling enlargement negotiations to go ahead. Any balance sheet of the six months would show that these and other priorities were met, and that the presidency finished on a high note at the December 1992 Edinburgh European Council. Yet despite this and all the enthusiastic pronouncements at the outset, the British Presidency was nevertheless widely regarded as a disappointment.

Luck, an important element in any presidency, was not on Mr Major's side. He inherited the Danish referendum problem, barely a month old, and could not be held responsible for the growing monetary pressures that were to follow President Mitterrand's snap decision to hold a referendum on the Maastricht Treaty. But two events, both dealt with separately in this chapter, disillusioned Britain's European partners and, most importantly, cooled Anglo-German relations, effectively putting a halt to John Major's friendship with Helmut

Kohl. The Chancellor of the Exchequer's partisan conduct at the informal ECOFIN meeting in Bath in September, compounded by the British press coverage, which represented the sorry episode as a victory for muscular British diplomacy, dismayed Mr Lamont's continental colleagues. But this paled in comparison with the shock waves that followed the revelation that, despite recent assurances, Mr Major had bought his 5 November majority of three on the Maastricht Bill by postponing final UK ratification until after the second Danish referendum. A week later, in a visit to London, Chancellor Kohl was understanding and supportive, but he later made it clear that his help was based on a cold rational calculation of the best way forward rather than the old friendship with a kindred spirit. John Major was able to redeem himself to some extent at the Edinburgh European Council, where he was praised for his adroit handling both of the Danish problem and of the tricky problem of future finance of the Community. But, as one commentator (Ludlow, 1993) has put it,

When every allowance is made for the UK's relative bad luck and its specific successes in terms of both personalities and policies, this must, one fears, be assessed as a presidency which singularly failed to provide the EC with the leadership that it needed in a period of considerable difficulty, which exposed the Community to quite unnecessary and unacceptable strains and which, as a result, left the EC weaker and the UK more vulnerable and isolated than either had been when the six-month period began.

Disillusionment abroad was matched by disillusionment at home, on the centre-left, pro-European wing of the Conservative party. Mrs. Thatcher's departure, Mr Major's arrival and his subsequent pro-European announcements had seemed like a new dawn. After more than a decade of Margaret Thatcher's combative stance in European Councils, culminating in her 1988 Bruges speech and her 1990 'no, no, no' to Jacques Delors, it seemed that John Major could play the more constructive role for which the pro-Europeans yearned, and they gave him their support on that basis. The Maastricht Treaty was recognised as a carefully-constructed balance and accepted as such. But as the Thatcherite and anti-Maastricht forces within the party gathered over the summer of 1992, the Prime Minister seemed unwilling to face them down but, rather, began to make concessions, and his language changed correspondingly. As was seen above, Black Wednesday removed the intellectual underpinnings of the Maastricht consensus within the party. As Mr Major's rhetoric became less pro-European, so disillusionment grew. Enthusiastic support was increasingly replaced by indifferent or even hostile tolerance and the search for a new standard bearer.

ENLARGEMENT AND THE BLOCKING MINORITY ROW

As post-Cold War Europe rearranged itself, it rapidly became clear that further enlargements of the European Community would be inevitable. In 1991 several of the EFTA countries (Austria, Finland, Norway and Sweden), who had together been negotiating the creation of a far-reaching European Economic Area with the European Community, tabled requests for accession to the Community. As prosperous and stable democracies, there could never be any doubt about their suitability for membership, and so the only question concerned the timing of these new accessions. The December 1991 Maastricht European Council made it clear that enlargement negotiations would have to take place on the basis of the yet-to-be-ratified Maastricht Treaty, and made the start of any negotiations conditional upon the resolution of connected negotiations about the future financing of the Community, the so-called 'Delors II' package. The June 1992 Lisbon European Council confirmed these decisions and further decided that, when they began, the enlargement negotiations should take place in parallel. Agreement on the 'Delors II' package was reached at the December 1992 Edinburgh European Council. Noting that this condition had been met, and that the ratification process of the Maastricht Treaty in the Member States was proceeding well, the heads of state and government decided that negotiations for accession to the Community could begin with Austria, Finland and Sweden at the beginning of 1993. Norway, which had tabled its request for accession later, was soon to join the negotiations.

From the outset the British Conservative government was an enthusiastic supporter of the prospect of further enlargement of the Community and saw the Edinburgh Council's decision as a *coup*. The government was convinced that the accession of four further Member States, and in particular the three traditionally more Euro-sceptical Scandinavian countries, would not only shift the Community's north–south balance in favour of the northern states but would brake centralising tendencies within the Community and encourage a more intergovernmental approach. It was for precisely the same reasons that the prospect of rapid enlargement had been initially greeted with some hesitation on the Continent. The 'deepeners' feared that a Community of sixteen Member States risked stagnation and even disintegration if it did not first adapt the political mechanisms it had inherited, largely unchanged, from the initial 1950s Community of just six Member States. The Maastricht European Council's decision represented a compromise between the 'wideners' and the 'deepeners'. A first round of enlargements could take place, but only after the 'deepening' of the Maastricht Treaty. Further enlargements would not take place until after the 1996 intergovernmental conference (provided for in the Maastricht Treaty), which was expected to deal with the substance of institutional reform.

Nevertheless, the first round of enlargements would necessarily require some institutional reform. In particular, decisions would have to be taken about the number of Commissioners, the number of MEPs, the order of future Presidencies and the size of the weighted votes in the Council of the four new Member States. The June 1993 Copenhagen European Council noted that the accession negotiations had accelerated and fixed 1 January 1995 as the date for accession. The October 1993 Brussels European Council fixed 1 March 1994 as the target date for the termination of the negotiations. This, it was calculated, would give the European Parliament three clear months in which to ratify the results before it dissolved for the European elections, leaving the rest of the year for the national ratification procedures in the Member States and the acceding countries. The October 1993 European Council further decided that the institutional aspects of enlargement should be concluded before the end of the year. The Foreign Affairs ministers had first considered the problem on 11 and 12 September, at their 'Gymnich' meeting in Alden Biesen. The Belgian Presidency had subsequently drafted and circulated a think-piece on what was termed a 'mechanical' transposition of the current arrangements. Divergencies were already clear in a 7 October ambassadors meeting which discussed the Belgian suggestions. The UK could not agree to a simple 'mechanical' transposition of the rules, but wanted reference to a demographic factor, particularly in regard to the weighting of Member States' votes. Its position was shared by the French and Spanish representatives. In one sense, it was a classic small-states-versus-large-states debate. (Tiny Luxembourg, with a population of just 380,000, enjoyed a fifth of the weight of mighty Germany, with almost 80 million citizens.) The attitude of the German government was crucial but, while some in the German diplomatic service said privately that they could see Britain's point, the German Chancellor, Helmut Kohl, was emphatic in his protection of the interests of the smaller states. In any case, it was argued, now was not the time to rock the boat. By late November France had withdrawn its opposition.

On 26 November 1993, the Belgian Presidency circulated a more considered set of proposals, but these were still largely based on a 'mechanical' transposition of existing arrangements. The paper, together with one British and two Spanish counter-proposals on weighted majority voting, was discussed at the 1 December 1994 meeting of the Member States' ambassadors to the EC Committee of Permanent Representatives (COREPER). The British proposal was that the existing 'blocking minority' of 23 votes should be maintained (see Chronology Table 2.6). The Belgian Presidency refused to discuss this or the Spanish proposals, claiming that its mandate only extended to a mechanical transposition. The problem was passed on to the 6 and 7 December General Affairs Council in Brussels, and from there to the December Brussels European Council. The Brussels Council decided on the votes of the acceding states (four for Austria and Sweden, three for Norway and Finland) but effectively sidestepped and postponed any decision on the blocking minority, leaving the matter to the General Affairs Council (i.e. the Foreign Ministers) to resolve 'in the context of the finalisation of the enlargement negotiations'.

The negotiations had been continuing apace, with the negotiators still aiming for 1 March 1994, and on 1 November 1993 the Maastricht Treaty had finally entered into force, removing the last remaining pre-condition originally set by the Maastricht European Council. On Friday, 25 February 1994, ministers and their negotiators entered into a final marathon round of negotiations. On the morning of Tuesday, 1 March, a political agreement with Sweden on all outstanding matters was announced. Similar agreements with Finland and Austria were announced on the Tuesday night, but problems subsisted in a number of important areas with Norway. Negotiations were renewed on 7 and 8 March and again on 15 and 16 March, when agreement was finally reached on the remaining issue of fisheries. One outstanding problem, the blocking minority, now came to the fore, and a new element, the European Parliament's assent, came into play.

According to newspaper reports, Douglas Hurd had been warning the cabinet 'for weeks' that the government might have to compromise, but paradoxically he found himself in an increasingly inflexible position. At the 25 February–1 March marathon, Britain reiterated its position and found itself isolated with Spain and Italy. When the

Chronology Table 2.6   *Council voting arrangements and the 'Ioannina compromise'*

Under the arrangements in force until the December 1993 Brussels European Council, Article 148 of the EEC Treaty provided that, where the Council was required to act by a qualified majority, 54 votes (out of a total of 76) would be needed. Germany, France, Italy and the United Kingdom each had 10 votes, and Spain 8. Belgium, Greece, the Netherlands and Portugal each had 5 votes, Denmark and Ireland 3, and Luxembourg 2. Thus, a 'blocking minority' consisted of 23 votes, or two large Member States and one smaller one. Under the Belgian Presidency's proposals, Austria and Sweden would have 4 votes, and Norway and Finland 3. By 'mechanical' transposition (i.e., by extrapolating the same proportion of 71 per cent for a qualified majority), a blocking minority would become 27. Both its proponents and its opponents thought this would make it more difficult for decisions to be blocked. The Ioannina compromise, and the subsequent 29 March 1994 Council decision, effectively took on board the Belgian Presidency's proposals, but added a form of institutionalised gentlemen's agreement. Under the agreement, if a group of Member States, whose votes together totalled between 23 and 26 votes, expressly opposed the holding of a vote by qualified majority, then the Council would do all in its power, within a 'reasonable time', to reach a 'satisfactory solution that could be adopted by at least 68 votes'. Its critics feared that this arrangement might lead to indefinite delay in sensitive areas. More sanguine observers point out that the Council rarely proceeded to an explicit vote on any matter, that the agreement was without prejudice to any deadlines laid down in the Treaties, and that it did little more than to enshrine existing arrangements in the Council. The agreement was to remain in force until the 1996 intergovernmental conference.

Reference: Council Decision of 29 March 1994 concerning the taking of Decision by qualified majority by the Council, Official Journal of the European Communities, N° C105, p1, 13.4.94.

Foreign Affairs ministers next met, on 7 March, Italy's support had faded, but a joint Greek Presidency/Commission compromise proposal, for a mechanical extension and a political declaration, was rejected by Britain and Spain. A similar proposal was again rejected on 15 March and on 22 March, and the issue was postponed to an informal General Affairs Council meeting on the Greek island of Ioannina on the weekend of 26 and 27 March.

For reasons that may never be entirely clear, John Major had chosen to make a political issue of the blocking minority problem – as one paper put it, to 'wrap himself in the flag'. The consequent increase in media attention stiffened his resolve, but it also painted him into a corner, ultimately leaving him no choice but an embarrassing climb-down. As one journalist pointed out, if Mr Hurd had settled for 27 votes earlier in the year 'few people would have noticed'; not only was the issue of voting rights typically arcane, but it was also relatively unimportant since the Council rarely moves to an explicit vote and prefers always to garner maximum consensus. In any case it would be up for reform in the 1996 intergovernmental conference.

At the beginning of the final round of negotiations, two of the government's more vociferous backbench critics, Tony Marlow and Bill Cash, raised the issue at the regular weekly meeting of the backbench 1922 committee, warning that if Britain gave in over the voting issue it would split the party in the run-up to the European elections. This set alarm bells ringing in the Whips' office, as did the re-election of Sir George Gardiner, in preference to a loyalist candidate, Sir Tony Durant, to the leadership of the 92 Group. Whatever the reason, John Major set his face firmly against any compromise solution, even telling the *Guardian* (25 March) that he was prepared to delay enlargement, supposedly a priority of the government, if necessary. The inflexibility of the government's position was reinforced from some unlikely directions. According to press reports, the Euro-sceptical members of the cabinet – in particular Peter Lilley, Michael Portillo, and John Redwood – were amenable to compromise. But at a 17 March cabinet meeting Douglas Hurd was urged to stick firm by the Chancellor of the Exchequer and the Home Secretary. Kenneth Clarke was reported to have been sympathetic to Mr Hurd's pro-QMV arguments in such areas as reform of the Common Agricultural Policy, but, despite his avowed Europeanism, was against overall compromise, a position he reaffirmed in Brussels on 21 March. Sceptics pointed out that he may have been motivated by the need to appear tough in the event of an early leadership contest. Mr Howard was said to have strong departmental reasons for opposing any weakening of the blocking minority.

With more pro-European elements in the cabinet proving inflexible, Mr Hurd had no choice but to stand firm, although he made it clear that compromise was more than likely. He had earlier told the Commons' European Affairs Committee that they could not expect the issue to be resolved by a straight 23-vote or 27-vote minority.

On Wednesday 24 March Conservative MEPs were reported to have held a 'stormy' meeting in Brussels at which fears were expressed that

Mr Hurd found himself isolated over the 'blocking minority'   *The Times* (16 March 1994)

the government was repeating the mistakes of 1989. The MEPs sent Mr Major a message reflecting deep unease at the Euro-sceptic tone of his remarks the previous day and urging a solution.

On Thursday 25 March, the eve of Ioannina, John Smith, who had previously seemed reluctant to enter into the fray, attacked the PM's position at question time. 'I believe we are right,' said Mr Major, 'to argue for principles that are important for Britain and Europe's future . . . We need a balanced decision which safeguards the rights of minorities.' Mr Smith asked why there was 'such confusion' over the government's policy. 'Is it not because the Prime Minister one day seeks to appease the anti-European faction in his party, and on the succeeding day seeks to reassure the pro-European faction? Why is he, as usual, seeking to face both ways?' Mr Major riposted that nobody knew where Mr Smith stood on the issue. But, Mr Smith said, enlargement was being put at risk by a 'wholly damaging dispute' which was, at most, about four votes out of 90. 'Is not the truth of this whole matter that the Prime Minister is more concerned to protect himself and his position from attacks from within his own party, than he is fighting for Britain's real and lasting interest in the EU?' Behind the political flak, pundits detected a hint of compromise in Mr Major's remarks.

But on Friday 26 March the *Guardian* published an interview with the Prime Minister in which he seemed to reaffirm his earlier position. 'It would be a great shame if enlargement were to be delayed,' he said. 'But that is what it is. It would be delayed.' In Brussels, meanwhile, the European Parliament had made it clear that it would only approve accession if the blocking minority figure was extended to 27, and the negotiators indicated that Britain and Spain would be made 'take-it-or-leave-it' offers at Ioannina. Before he left for Ioannina, a 'disgruntled' Foreign Secretary gave a gloomy and irritable speech to the Conservative Central Council meeting in Plymouth. He told the party, and particularly the Euro-sceptics within it, that a 'sour defensive attitude' to the EU harmed the country and would threaten its prospects in the European elections. It must not 'scratch away at old wounds' over Europe. 'Let us stop all this divisive nonsense about Europhiles and Eurosceptics. That is yesterday's game. Those are yesterday's battered toys. Let us put them back in the toy cupboard where they belong.' Mr Hurd seemed to be holding out an olive branch to the more pro-European wing of the party. As he left, he told ITN 'I have to see whether I can get a reasonable deal. I have got some flexibility from the Cabinet yesterday. There may well be a compromise, but it has to be a compromise that is acceptable to us'. The Plymouth Central Council meeting was perhaps not quite the distraction it should have been. Mr Major's speech on the Saturday was overshadowed by a 'barnstorming' speech by the President of the Board of Trade, and most of the Sunday papers ran with stories about how Mr Heseltine had rehabilitated his leadership chances. There was but one faint glimmer of sunlight. The *Mail on Sunday* published an NOP poll taken in a belt of 26 English Euro-constituencies south and east of the Wash and the Severn which showed the Labour vote holding up but the Conservatives still ahead. The poll figures would have delivered most of those seats outside London to the Conservatives. However, the poll must have been cold comfort for the beleaguered Prime Minister.

Ioannina coincided with the Plymouth meeting, and the Greek Presidency had the good grace to delay announcement of the compromise reached until after it had finished ('GREEK DELAY SPARES MAJOR KEBABBING', as a *Guardian* headline put it). The next day's headlines told the story: 'HURD GETS EU ULTIMATUM' (*Guardian*), 'CABINET GETS EU SURRENDER TERMS' (*Independent*). At the end of a weekend's haggling, Mr Hurd flew back to London with an agreement (see Chronology Table 2.6) which, however it was presented, seemed far from satisfying the British government's demands and was little different from the compromise proposals tabled several weeks before. Support for the Ioannina agreement had to be confirmed by the Spanish and British governments by the evening of Tuesday, 29 March. If that support was not forthcoming, the issue would have to be postponed to the Corfu European Council in June, and enlargement could have been postponed by anything up to one year.

To 'hoots of derision' from the opposition benches, the Foreign Secretary explained the proposed agreement to the Commons on Monday, 28 March, and to the cabinet on the Tuesday. The discussion in cabinet took up two hours. The four Euro-sceptics, the Home Secretary, the Social Security Secretary, the Treasury Chief Secretary and the Welsh Secretary, all expressed their reservations over conceding the principle of an increase from 23 to 27 votes, and Mr Redwood repeated his doubts at the end of the discussion, but they backed away from confrontation when it became clear that the powerful triumvirate of Douglas Hurd, Kenneth Clarke and Michael Heseltine were backing Mr Major. There were rumours – all denied –

and much press speculation that the Foreign Secretary had forced agreement by threatening to resign if the cabinet could not accept the deal. Some observers speculated on the sort of secret deals Mr Hurd might have managed to extract from his partners, particularly in regard to the avoidance of awkward votes and social legislation. Downing Street announced that the cabinet had agreed unanimously that Mr Hurd's package should be approved. Rumours of other ministerial resignations, particularly on the right of the party, proved unfounded.

Later the same day, his fifty-first birthday, Mr Major faced a difficult and uncomfortable hour in the Commons, as he attempted to explain the cabinet decision. To Labour jeers, he claimed that Britain had secured concessions 'that protect our most vulnerable flank on social affairs'. But even as he spoke, in Brussels Mr Delors was playing down the nature of the supposed concessions. Mr Smith said the agreement was a 'humiliating climbdown' and accused Mr Major of seeking to camouflage his 'retreat from vainglorious assertions of no surrender'. Mr Ashdown said that no amount of clever words or verbal gymnastics 'can hide the fact that the Government has made a fool of Britain in Europe, the Cabinet has made a fool of the Foreign Secretary and Mr Major has frankly made rather a fool of himself.' But the biggest shock came from a maverick rightwing Tory backbencher, Mr Tony Marlow who, to cheers from the Labour benches, told Mr Major that he now had 'no authority, credibility or identifiable policy' on Europe. He asked 'Why don't you stand aside and make way for somebody else who provides authority . . . and direction of leadership?' Although the whips and senior ministers brushed aside Mr Marlow's remarks as irresponsible eccentricity, the pundits pointed out that this was the first time for 30 years that a Tory MP had called in the Commons for a Conservative Prime Minister to stand down (the last had been Nigel Birch to Harold Macmillan in 1963). The next day's headlines told the story: 'MAJOR FACES CRISIS OVER LEADERSHIP' (*Daily Telegraph*), 'MAJOR FACING LEADER CRISIS' (*Daily Express*).

It seemed only a matter of time before a serious challenge to Mr Major's leadership would be launched, and there was much press speculation as to which of the probable contenders – Clarke, Heseltine, Howard, or Portillo – would be most likely to emerge as frontrunner. The *Times* (31 March) published a MORI poll showing Labour on 49 per cent, with 28 per cent for the Tories and 20 per cent for the Liberal Democrats. But succour came from an unexpected quarter. Mrs Thatcher let it be known 'privately' that another divisive leadership election would be a mistake, and this was seen as tacit recognition on the right that its preferred protegé, Michael Portillo, was still too young to beat either of the two main contenders, Kenneth Clarke and Michael Heseltine. With this unexpected help ('THATCHER WARNS OFF ANTI-MAJOR LOBBY' – *Guardian*), and Parliament going into its twelve-day Easter recess, the worst seemed over for the Prime Minister.

The spotlight now turned to Strasbourg. The British government's behaviour, which many MEPs saw as a form of blackmail, had infuriated the European Parliament, and sizeable elements of its membership were deeply unhappy about the precedent set by the Ioannina compromise. (Interestingly, the same level of opprobrium did not attach itself to the Spanish government, which had also accepted the Ioannina agreement. Although the Spanish foreign minister had agreed to stand firm with the British, the Spanish position had been softened by concessions reached in the earlier fisheries negotiations with Norway, in which Spain had also for strategic reasons adopted an uncompromising stance.) At a practical level, the Parliament insisted on receiving the full legal texts of the negotiated agreements with the candidate states, and although the Community's legal experts and translators worked flat out to get the texts to the Parliament as soon as possible, this still left it with little less than a month in which to carry out its work. Parliament resented the impression that it was being harrassed and harried into rubber-stamping the agreements. There was fear, too, that the Parliament would be unable to amass the requisite absolute majorities, since many of its members were retiring. In the event, on 4 May, after an extraordinarily atmospheric debate, all four enlargements were approved by 'yes' votes of well over 370 votes (out of a membership of 518). An important factor in the Parliament's calculations was a concession extracted at Ioannina: that there would be parliamentary participation in a working group being established to prepare for the 1996 intergovernmental conference. British MEPs had been in the thick of things. Gary Titley, Labour MEP for Greater Manchester West, was an enthusiastic rapporteur on Finnish accession, and Tom Spencer, Conservative MEP for Surrey West, was an equally enthusiastic draftsman on Swedish accession. During the debate, Edward McMillan-Scott proudly pointed out that every single one of the 32 Conservative MEPs, including a very ill Mr Simmonds (who stood down at the 1994 elections), was there for the vote. Labour MEPs were also out in force and, resisting any temptation to score political points, voted solidly for accession. Against the odds, therefore, accession remained on target for 1 January 1995.

The dispute and its resolution cost the government and the Prime Minister an enormous amount of political capital, both domestic and international. It may also, like Black Wednesday, have marked a sea change on European issues within the Conservative Party. Meanwhile Paddy Ashdown, who had visited Brussels on 25 March, reported that Jacques Delors had been 'utterly perplexed' by Mr Major's stance. There was bemusement in diplomatic and political circles as to why the Prime Minister had chosen an issue where he was so clearly outnumbered and why, if it was an issue of such importance, it had been left so late in the day. There was bemusement too as to why he should have decided to accept possible delay on an issue, enlargement, that was so dear to his government. There was irritation in some circles at what seemed to be blatant blackmail on such an important and politically sensitive issue. As the Greek Foreign Affairs minister put it, Britain had triggered a 'petty quarrel' for party political purposes. 'It is time for the majority in Europe not to let the blackmail of a tiny minority to win the day.' Other governments privately found Britain's actions cumulatively damning, following on as they did from the Maastricht Treaty ratification and ERM débâcles. The governments of the candidate states were also bemused, as the dispute risked undermining the results they had achieved in their negotiations and which they were delayed from selling to their already sceptical populations. But it was at home that the damage seemed greatest. As the *Guardian* put it, Britain had come 'unstuck on all demands'. The result was a personal humiliation for the Prime Minister, and talk of a stalking horse candidate in the autumn or even resignation after the European elections became rife. But it was also a humiliation for the Conservative government and for the country. Perhaps the experience was most deeply felt within the Conservative Party itself. One Central Office worker said there was an 'audible creaking' as the views of previously indifferent Conservative backbenchers shifted towards the Eurosceptical wing of the party. There were some attempts to pin the blame on the Foreign Office (creating some ill feeling) or on misleading political advice but, whatever the source of the misunderstanding, most commentators were agreed that the blocking minority row was a textbook example of a political mistake. As an editorial in the *Independent* put it, 'If John Major had been seeking to devise a sequence of events that would do maximum damage both to the Conservative Party and to Britain's not very good name in Europe, he could scarcely have improved on what has happened. This was an unnecessary and unwinnable battle.'

5 MAY LOCAL ELECTIONS

The three large political parties regarded the May 1994 local elections and the June 1994 European elections campaigns as part of the same continuum. One third of the seats on district councils in England and Wales, 12 Scottish councils and 32 London boroughs were to be contested on 5 May. Most of these seats had last been contested in 1990, at the height of the controversy over the 'poll tax' (community charge). Because of this, in the spring the Conservative party was relatively sanguine about its prospects, and the party chairman, Sir Norman Fowler, was even lulled into predicting on 10 April (*Frost on Sunday*) that the party would make gains. Gains in May, it was reasoned, could give the party a platform for an upbeat campaign for the following European elections and ward off European losses. For the Labour Party, the exercise was more one of preparing for damage limitation, it being reasoned that many of the seats it had won in 1990 would be lost. The *Independent* reported on 7 April that the party was 'braced to lose up to 200 seats'. The government's general unpopularity in the polls was not expected to translate proportionately to the local level. Damage limitation, particularly if it could see off the Liberal Democrat threat, would serve as a platform for the modest gains (given the 1989 outcome) which the party privately but realistically hoped for in the European elections. The local elections were crucial for the Liberal Democrats. The strong performance they expected could start a bandwagon rolling towards the European elections, via the Eastleigh by-election, which the Liberal Democrats were increasingly slated to win (and where, because of this, the government had not yet decided on the date of the by-election). The key was to establish a broader base which would enable the party to break out of the South-West pocket of the country in the European elections.

At the beginning of April, on the eve of the campaign launch for the local elections, the government's optimism was privately fast evaporating. The Easter recess had brought the Prime Minister little relief. A 3 April NOP poll in the *Independent on Sunday* gave Labour a 24-point lead (50–26) over the Conservatives, and 49 per cent of those polled thought John Major should stand down as Prime Minister. The Sunday papers were openly speculating about Mr Major's demise (For example, 'SIX WAYS TO GET RID OF A PRIME MINISTER', *Independent on Sunday*, 'NOT IF ... BUT WHEN', *Sunday Times*), and some, based on leaks from Conservative right-wingers, were slating a Heseltine–Portillo 'dream ticket'. It was becoming clear that the electorate were going to use the local elections as a referendum on the Prime Minister's unpopularity and the government's continued disarray. To counter this, Mr Major announced that he would be taking a 'leading role' in the local election campaign, hoping that he could repeat his 1992 success, but early visits to Essex (5 April) and Birmingham (11 April) revealed worryingly low levels of support and little enthusiasm for the Prime Minister, even among the party faithful. Worse, he was obliged to use the context of these visits to rebut his party critics, further compounding the impression of a government at odds with itself.

The government pulled out what stops it could. The *Sunday Telegraph* (10 April) reported that the government had quietly shelved some of its more controversial privatisation plans (such as disposing of the Forestry Commission). The *Observer* (24 April) reported on a leaked circular to all ministerial offices from Sir Robin Butler, Cabinet Secretary, which enjoined them to 'exercise particular care in issuing decisions with a local or European dimension'. As early as February, Michael Portillo, steadily emerging as the right-wing's standard-bearer, had been put in charge of the London local elections campaign in the hope – vain, as it transpired – that it would lessen open rivalry. But despite these measures and some good news on the economic front (on 16 April inflation was reported at its lowest since 1975, while on 21 April reports of a leap in high street sales strengthened hopes of full economic recovery), the Prime Minister seemed unable to throw off his problems, while others were to emerge.

On Thursday 14 April a Commons clash between Mr Major and Margaret Beckett during question time led the Speaker of the Commons to rebuke the Prime Minister. Thursday was the last day for moving the writ for the Eastleigh by-election for 5 May and when it became clear that the government had opted for 9 June, Sir David Steel was highly critical of Mr Major's departure from the three-month convention for the moving of writs (laid down by a 1973 Speaker's conference). In the 16–22 April period the government, and particularly the junior minister responsible, Iain Sproat, became enmeshed in a damaging dispute with Second World War veterans about the arrangements it had made to commemorate the fiftieth anniversary of the D-Day landings in Normandy. The row centred on differing emphases on 'commemoration' as opposed to 'celebration' and on the use of the controversial publicist, Sir Tim Bell, but the press had a field day in publicising inappropriate activities (the most notorious being a spam fritters contest in Scotland). The dispute culminated in an embarrassing 'ultimatum' from Dame Vera Lynn, and was only

defused when the Prime Minister took over the D-Day plans and conceded a consultative role to the D-Day veterans.
Above all, the leadership issue continued to fester. The *Independent on Sunday*'s 3 April poll had shown Michael Heseltine to be the voters' favourite, but both he and Kenneth Clarke kept low and basically loyal profiles, culminating in a joint protestation of loyalty to the Prime Minister at a 14 April press conference. That same day, the Major loyalist and former whip Tristan Garel-Jones gave an interview to the *Evening Standard* in which he said that the Prime Minister would 'fight like an alley cat to keep his job':

If push comes to shove, the overwhelming majority of us will fight with him and for him . . . There would be blood all over the floor. The Tory party would certainly go into opposition for a decade.

For the next seven days the media concentrated its fire on reshuffle stories (with Downing Street forced to deny rumours that a government reshuffle was planned before the local elections) and the D-Day dispute. But then, on 22 April in Fife, Michael Portillo gave a speech in which he spoke of the 'still, quiet majority' who wanted a government that stood up to pressure groups and passed laws. This was billed as a veiled attack on John Major's pragmatic style of leadership and interpreted as a play for the succession. It galvanised the Prime Minister into further reassertions of his authority, most notably in an interview with the German magazine *Der Spiegel*, in which he spoke of quitting when it was least expected. On 25 April, in a Radio 5 interview, Douglas Hurd described the Prime Minister as 'a man of steel'. He went on: 'This chat about leadership is unreal. Serious politicians are not talking about it inside the government or the party.'
Thereafter, a number of domestic and European rows came to the fore in rapid succession, compounding the PM's woes and, as it transpired, melding the government's poor performance in the local elections into its poor prospects in the European elections. On 27 April Chancellor Helmut Kohl visited the Prime Minister in London and Chequers. Although Mr Major was able to smooth out a row about whether Kohl would be invited to the D-Day celebrations and to reach agreement in principle with the German Chancellor on further enlargements of the Community, the summit was an indifferent affair and gave the Conservative party's right-wingers the chance for further sport.
On 9 March the *Guardian* had published an article (by the paper's

well-informed Brussels correspondent, John Palmer) claiming that the Germans and the French had struck a series of deals over the future development of the Community, particularly with a view to the 1996 intergovernmental conference foreseen by the Maastricht Treaty ('son of Maastricht', as the *Daily Telegraph*'s Christopher Lockwood dubbed it), and that Helmut Kohl and François Mitterrand had together agreed on the Belgian Prime Minister Jean-Luc Dehaene as their preferred candidate for the Presidency of the European Commission (Delors' term would end in December), in preference to the UK's preferred candidate and long-running favourite, Dutch Prime Minister Ruud Lubbers. Mr Dehaene was known in his own country as a supreme pragmatist and deal-maker (nicknamed 'the plumber'), who had managed to construct a working government coalition in very difficult circumstances and since then had overseen successive stages in the federalisation (i.e. devolution or decentralisation) of his country into Flemish and Wallonian communities. He had come to the attention of Kohl and Mitterrand during the successful Belgian Presidency in the last half of 1993, when a number of difficult decisions were ably brokered by Mr Dehaene at the October and December 1993 Brussels European Councils. But the British press and, through it, right-wing Conservatives, characterised Dehaene as an enthusiastic European federalist whose unilateral nomination by a Franco-German alliance represented yet another *fait accompli* illustrating Britain's, and the Prime Minister's, weakness. On 27 April, the day of the Anglo-German summit, the *Independent* reported that a row was brewing on the Tory right wing, and in effect one more future battle line had been drawn for the beleaguered Prime Minister.

As the Anglo-German summit was taking place, Lord Young, a former Thatcher minister, told the Institute of Directors that Britain was 'wasting its time in the EC', and 'fiddling while the Treaty of Rome burns'. The next day (Thursday, 28 April), the *Sun* published a story claiming that Mr Major was contemplating withdrawal from the EC, or a referendum on whether or not to withdraw, should the results of the 1996 intergovernmental conference be unacceptable to the British government. Downing Street aides immediately dismissed the story as 'total rubbish', and Mr Major sidestepped questions in the Commons from Teresa Gorman on the issue, but the damage had been done. Friday's *Daily Telegraph* carried a banner headline 'SCEPTICS RE-OPEN TORY WAR ON EC'. The report described how the 'fragile truce on Europe' within the party had been destroyed, as Tory Euro-sceptics began openly canvassing the option of an eventual British withdrawal and a referendum on a single currency. The Home Secretary, Michael Howard, told Saturday's BBC Radio 4 *Today* programme 'I don't think there is any question of us leaving the European Community. It doesn't work like that. That would never arise.' And Douglas Hurd was reported in the *Daily Telegraph* as having told Tory rebels that 'there is no alternative' to EC membership. But as Colin Brown wrote in the *Independent*, the net effect of the row was that 'the sceptics believe they are now in the centre of the party, so great has been the gravitational shift'.

The withdrawal/referendum row continued over the weekend of 30 April/1 May, and ended with a major split. The Sunday broadsheets concentrated on Mr Howard's implication that the UK might use its veto at the 1996 intergovernmental conference, and on the feasibility of ultimate withdrawal (e.g. *Sunday Telegraph* editorial: 'Should we get out?'). The *Observer* published an article by Tristan Garel-Jones entitled 'The folly of wanting to pull out of Europe'. The *Sunday Times* reported on a leaked briefing note prepared for ministers for the Euro-elections, in which they were instructed not to rule out a referendum, while stressing that this was a hypothetical question. But on the Sunday, Sir Leon Brittan stated in a BBC radio interview at lunchtime that a single currency by 1999 (as foreseen in the Maastricht Treaty) was 'not unrealistic', and that Europeans wanted a single currency for 'hard-headed business reasons'. And then, responding to these sentiments in a GMTV interview, Michael Portillo stepped out of line with agreed government policy by insisting that Britain should never sign up to a single currency. Mr Portillo's remarks sparked another major row within the party. Pro-Europeans were furious that Michael Portillo had, apparently wilfully, ignored the delicate truce within the party, and on Tuesday 3 May, just one day before the local elections, John Major was again obliged to re-assert his authority (and placate the pro-Europeans) by calling Mr Portillo to Downing Street and ordering him to 'toe the line'.

Another European row that surfaced in the last week of the local elections campaign concerned the Conservative party's manifesto (see Chapter 4). The story broke on 29 April, with the *Times* reporting that Sarah Hogg had been put in charge of a re-draft of Mr Hurd's initial draft, said to be too long and lacking punch. Next day's *Guardian* quoted Bill Cash, a noted backbench right-winger, as saying 'I should sincerely hope the manifesto is going through substantial firming up to ensure we can sell it to the country', and the Sunday papers (1 May) reported that John Major had demanded a new draft, putting more emphasis on political differences. As the account in Chapter 4 will show, much of this was editorial work or insubstantial window-dressing, designed to placate the right wing and assert the Prime Minister's authority. But its overall effect was to confirm the impression of the government as reactive rather than pro-active. To the many Conservative pro-Europeans not in on the secret, it provided further evidence that the Prime Minister was in the thrall of the Euro-sceptics and eager to placate them.

Despite Mr Major's upbeat *Der Spiegel* interview, the polls showed constant declines in his, and his government's, popularity. A 28 April MORI poll for the *Times* found that 75 per cent of respondents were dissatisfied with Mr Major and that the party's rating was, at 26 per cent, the lowest ever. (The *Times* went on to report that Lambeth's Tories had told Mr Major to stay out of their campaign.) On 30 April, the *Daily Telegraph* reported leaked internal polling figures showing the party 21 points behind Labour and only two points ahead of the Liberal Democrats, and a *Times* MORI poll published on the same day sparked the headline 'POLL POINTS TO TORIES SLIPPING INTO THIRD PLACE'. Gillian Shepherd committed a loyalist gaffe over the weekend of 30 April and 1 May by openly rebuking those campaigning within the party on behalf of the two Michaels, Heseltine and Portillo, thus confirming that such campaigning was going on. The 1 May *Sunday Times* published a damaging article on local party activists' reports that 'DOORSTEP CRITICS SEE MAJOR AS A WIMP'. On Monday 2 May David Evans, another maverick Tory backbencher, created more unwelcome headlines (on the fifteenth anniversary of the election of the first Thatcher government) by warning the Prime Minister that he would not survive as leader unless he sacked six members of his cabinet, and fired the party chairman, Sir Norman Fowler, and various personal advisers. Throughout the local elections campaign, the party was buffeted by depressing reports on lagging support in various parts of the country that would normally have been safe prospects.

Under these circumstances, Labour and the Liberal Democrats seemed happy at first to coast along on the back of the government's misfortunes and disarray. So 'laid back' was the Labour approach that it prompted Peter Riddell to ask rhetorically in the *Times* 'Could Smith coast to defeat?' But on 16 April the Labour leader was reported as having decided to 'turn up the heat' on John Major, in the belief that another change of Conservative leader (as seemed increasingly likely) would lead to irresistible calls for a general election. Mr Smith won a notable *coup* on 29 April, when he visited St Bartholemew's Hospital,

London, threatened with closure under the government's plans for the rationalisation of London hospitals. The government had sought to prevent 'electioneering' on NHS sites, but had had to let the visit go ahead. (Ironically, the dead Smith was brought to the same hospital just thirteen days later.) For its part, the Liberal Democrats' local elections campaign contained several hints towards their planned European elections campaign. On 16 April, in a speech at Stirling University, Paddy Ashdown affirmed that 'our people are our greatest resource', and he repeatedly returned to the theme of offering wider consultation. On 23 April the *Guardian* published a leaked internal strategy paper on how the party planned to 'unblock' Britain's potential. But the real battle in the local elections was between Labour and the Liberal Democrats, particularly in the cities (see Chapter 8). Hence such headlines as 'LIB DEMS AIM AT LABOUR STRONGHOLDS IN NORTH AND LONDON' (*Daily Telegraph*, 15 April) and 'LABOUR TARGETS THE LIB DEMS IN BATTLE FOR CITIES' (*Independent*, 16 April).

As polling day approached, and the Conservatives continued to 'squabble in the face of defeat' (*Independent*, 3 May), the government prepared for the worst. Norman Fowler was reported to be ready to shield the Prime Minister from 'poll liability', and some reports had hinted that he might stand down. Even a rallying speech by Kenneth Clarke on the eve of the poll was interpreted as a leadership bid. Two factors became increasingly plain. On 28 April, Downing Street had insisted that the EC would not be an issue in the local elections campaign, but it clearly was. And on Sunday, 1 May, Norman Fowler had insisted that 'The council poll is not a referendum on Major', but it certainly was.

When the results were out, the Conservatives learnt that they had polled just 27 per cent of the vote and lost nearly one-third of the seats which the party had won in the 1990 local elections, at the height of the poll tax controversy. In a performance dubbed as their 'worst ever', the Conservatives saw their representation in the contested seats fall by 429 seats to 888. As a result, the party lost its majority in 18 of the 33 councils where it had previously had control. Labour improved on its success in 1990, adding 88 seats net to give it 2,769 in all, and winning control of four councils, so that it now controlled 93. However, the main beneficiaries were the Liberal Democrats, who gained 388 seats net to lift their total to 1,098, bringing the number of district and metropolitan councils they controlled up to 19. In Scotland, both the SNP and the Liberal Democrats made gains, principally at Labour expense.

The disastrous results for the Conservatives triggered off a renewed bout of leadership speculation, but also fanned fears of 'meltdown' in the European elections. Mr Major, the *Independent* reported, would 'lurch from defeat to disaster'. The *Times* wrote of 'desperate hopes'. John Curtice predicted in the *Guardian* that Mr Major was 'facing disaster in Euro-vote'. The Labour Party was greatly cheered by the result; it had made gains where it had expected none, and its unanticipated success was a welcome fillip to the local party activists whom it would now be calling on to put their energies into the Euro-elections. But the clear victors were the Liberal Democrats. The results had exceeded the party's expectations and provided an excellent platform for the Euro-campaign. A *Channel 4 News* analysis on 7 May predicted that the Liberal Democrats would take nine Euro-seats and, although the party was wary of allowing the other parties to talk up its chances unrealistically, a breakthrough in the south of England now seemed a distinct probability.

John Major's humiliation was compounded by the sort of unfortunate timing all politicians must dread. On 6 May the Channel Tunnel was formally declared open. The Prime Minister was obliged to take part in a ceremony that began on a platform at Waterloo station and proceeded to, and through, the tunnel. Since she, together with President Mitterrand, had given the green light to the project, Lady Thatcher was much in evidence at the ceremony, and the next day's newspapers were full of photographs of a grim-faced John Major together with his predecessor.

LEADERSHIP CONTENTION AND THE MOOD ON THE EVE

From January 1994, until John Smith's untimely death on 12 May, the media was increasingly dominated by one issue; who would succeed John Major? The year began with the government's 'back to basics' campaign grievously undermined by a series of scandals involving junior ministers. The Prime Minister was dogged by the criticisms of ever more vociferous Conservative right-wingers and Euro-sceptics, and his personal opinion poll ratings continued to slump disastrously. Actions designed to reassert his authority did not have their desired effect, and visits to Russia in February and the United States in March did not enhance the Prime Minister's domestic stature as they might normally have been expected to do. The government's misfortunes were compounded by what journalists referred to as the 'sleaze factor', as a series of ministers and former ministers appeared before the Scott inquiry into the Matrix Churchill affair and the Commons select committee looking into the Pergau dam affair, and the press also ran stories about possibly corrupt practices in quangos. The humiliating climb-down that ended the blocking minority dispute (March) led to the first explicit call for Mr Major to go, and the calamitous local election results in May led to the first explicit stalking horse volunteer. Newspaper headlines shifted from 'not if but when', to 'not when but how', and as the polls' forecasts for the European elections grew increasingly dire it was broadly expected that the Prime Minister would either stand down in June or fall prey to a more traditional leadership contest in the autumn. The only person who persistently refused to countenance such scenarios was the Prime Minister himself.

Speculation focussed on three chief *dramatis personae*, and each was distinguishable primarily by his attitude to Europe. The pro-Europeans' darling was the Chancellor of the Exchequer, Kenneth Clarke. In his previous guise as Home Affairs Secretary he had been known as one of the more enthusiastic supporters of sterling's participation in the ERM, but by the time he came to replace the less enthusiastic Norman Lamont sterling had already been blasted out of the exchange rate mechanism into a loose float. It was, however, rumoured that Mr Clarke 'saved' the ERM at the Brussels emergency ECOFIN Council in August 1993 by suggesting a simple transformation of the narrow bands into wider bands. Relief from the discipline of high interest rates was a short-term advantage, but the new Chancellor had to be careful about sucking in inflationary pressures through higher-priced imports. More unpopular inheritances from his predecessor were Mr Lamont's spring 1993 budget commitment to introduce VAT on fuel oil, a measure which would particularly affect older and retired people, and the need to rein in the PSBR. For all of these reasons, Mr Clarke's popularity within the Conservative party suffered a decline in early 1994, said to have been reinforced by some uncertain performances in appearances before the Commons' Treasury Select Committee. The media continued to portray him as a heavyweight contender, although as one newspaper put it, Mr Clarke could have 'walked into the job' of Prime Minister in 1993, now he had to play a waiting game, whilst keeping his hand in. An early leadership election could not be in his interest. Thus, on 8 March, in an interview with the *Independent*, the Chancellor said 'I would like to be a contender, but at a time of John Major's choosing'. Thereafter he made repeated protestations of loyalty to the Prime Minister until he gave a speech to the City University Business School in London on the eve of the local elections, which was widely interpreted as a leadership bid ('CLARKE LAYS OUT HIS CENTRIST STALL', *Guardian*, 'MR CLARKE'S MANIFESTO', *Financial Times*), though it was probably intended to balance the previous weekend's coverage of Michael Portillo's single currency remarks. As John Major's pragmatism led him to make more and more concessions on Europe to the Tory Euro-sceptics, so the pro-European wing of the party became increasingly attracted to Mr Clarke's consistent stance. But they recognised that Mr Clarke could not win any early leadership election and that other, more Euro-sceptical candidates were better placed. Therefore, it was in the pro-Europeans' interests that Mr Major should remain Prime Minister in the shorter term, and thus in their interests that the party should avoid a disaster in the European elections, which it seemed increasingly likely would result in Mr Major's departure.

A second prime potential contender in the media's eyes was the Chief Secretary to the Treasury, Michael Portillo. As John Major was seen to depart further and further from the party's Thatcherite inheritance, so the mantle passed to the new Thatcherites in the cabinet. But, young, gifted, able and handsome, Mr Portillo was said to be more relaxed with the media than his senior fellow Thatcherite, Peter Lilley, who chose to play the role of loyalist throughout the local elections campaign. Mr Portillo's stock had been rising on the Euro-sceptical wing of the party ever since the Prime Minister had branded him, in a supposedly off the record interview immediately after the 23 July 1993 Commons vote on the Maastricht Bill, as a 'bastard' (together with Mr Lilley and John Redwood). Moreover, Mr Portillo's post in the Treasury enabled him to play the classic role of taking a Thatcherite knife to the spending departments. Throughout the January–May 1994 period, he made a series of carefully-scripted speeches which clearly mapped out his Thatcherite, anti-integration credentials and served to rally the growing ranks of right-wing and Euro-sceptical Tory MPs. Thus, on 14 January, Michael Portillo made a keynote speech to Young Conservatives in London in which he attacked the 'self-destructive sickness of national cynicism'. On 22 January, Mr Portillo made a speech to the Gloucestershire Conservative Political Centre in which he attacked 'creeping Euro-federalism'. The script of the speech was not released on instructions from Downing Street, following complaints from other ministers. On 4 February, in a speech to Conservative students at Southampton University, Mr Portillo argued that public standards in the UK far exceeded those to be found elsewhere, and went on to argue that academic qualifications and business contracts could be 'bought' in other countries. He apologised for his remarks within hours, but a national and international row nevertheless ensued. On 15 February, in a speech to the American Chamber of Commerce (and with John Major in Moscow), he criticised the European Union's protectionist instincts and uncompetitive industries. On 22 February in Fife, in what was widely interpreted as an attack on the Prime Minister's pragmatic approach, he spoke of the 'still, quiet majority' and their desire for strong government. Lastly, in a 1 May interview on GMTV, he stepped out of line by stating his belief that Britain should never sign up to a single currency, thus enraging the pro-European wing of the party. This resulted in his being 'called in' by Downing Street two days later and told to 'toe the line', but in the eyes of his supporters he had shown his independence. Mr Portillo's problem, as his supporters privately admitted, was his relative youth and inexperience (strangely, these were not to be a problem for Tony Blair). Though John Major had been relatively young when elected party leader, he had already served in two of the three great offices of state (Foreign Secretary and the Chancellorship). Thus, for similar reasons to those adduced by Mr Clarke's supporters, it was in Mr Portillo's interest that Mr Major should remain Prime Minister in the short term, and hence that the party should avoid disaster in the European elections, unless a viable alternative could be found.

The man who had begun to stake out a claim as that viable alternative was the President of the Board of Trade, Michael Heseltine. Guilty in the eyes of all Thatcherites of the heinous crime of regicide, Mr Heseltine had sought to redeem himself through loyal service to the new Prime Minister. Nobody doubted that he still ardently desired to be Prime Minister one day, and so as Mr Major's difficulties multiplied the media and the pundits inevitably turned to him as an obvious potential contender. Mr Heseltine's recent political career had suffered two major reverses. The first was his maladroit handling of the announcements of large-scale coal pit closures in October 1992. The second was the heart attack he had suffered on 21 June 1993 whilst on holiday in Venice. The first incident had thrown his political abilities into doubt; the second, his physical abilities to continue with the heavy workload of a minister. But Mr Heseltine had returned to work and, to the pundits' surprise, had soon rehabilitated his political reputation. This was in some large part due to the evidence he gave before the Scott inquiry on 27 February 1994, it becoming clear that, unlike other ministers involved in the case, Mr Heseltine had expressed strong doubts about signing a gagging order, and had only ultimately signed after the Attorney General had told him he had a duty so to do. But others saw Mr Heseltine's robust self-defence as a deliberate attempt to differentiate himself as a potential leadership contender. On 3 March, Mr Heseltine set out his views in the Stockton lecture to the London Business School. Four days later when, on the *Jimmy Young Show*, it was suggested that Michael Heseltine or others might oust him, the Prime Minister said:

> It isn't real. I was elected at the last election with the largest vote any party or any leader has ever had and I was elected to remain Prime Minister of this country at least until the next election and beyond it if I win the next election. I have never run away from a challenge in my life, and I am surely not doing it now.

Later in the month, Mr Heseltine was rumoured to have played a Machiavellian role in the blocking minority row (see above), urging Mr Major further out along the plank against ten other Member States in the expectation that he might fall, but in his public declarations he was still loyal to the Prime Minister, stating that a delay in enlargement would 'not be a bad thing'. On Saturday 27 March, at the Conservative Central Council meeting in Plymouth, Mr Heseltine delivered a 'barnstorming' speech, far outshining the Prime Minister's more low-key attempt to rally the troops. In it, he wooed the party's right wing by attacking those (the Party Chairman, Sir Norman Fowler, among others) who had urged caution over further rounds of privatisation, enthusiastically endorsing a more radical agenda. Mr Heseltine, the *Mail on Sunday* subsequently reported, was 'back in the running', and the next day's *Guardian* reported him as making an 'early run' for the leadership. That same day (31 March), on BBC Radio 4's *Today* programme, Kenneth Clarke stated his intention 'to succeed John Major when he, of his own volition, goes, which I think will be a long way ahead'. But he later insisted that there was no leadership dispute. Mr Heseltine, as the political correspondents put it, had 'spotted an opening on Clarke's right and gone for it'. This was an all the more extraordinary achievement given that Mr Heseltine had until recently been known for his pro-European credentials, and had even written a book setting them out. Three days later, the *Independent on Sunday* published an NOP poll which revealed Michael Heseltine to be the favourite to lead the Conservatives. The *Observer* reported that a

Heseltine–Portillo 'dream ticket' threatened to topple Mr Major, and the *Sunday Times* ran a front page headline declaring 'MANY TORY MPS EXPECT MAJOR TO GO. HESELTINE EMERGES AS FRONTRUNNER'. Mr Heseltine's stock was thereafter to remain high until the beginning of the European elections campaign. On 13 April, the *Guardian* reported that 'Mr Heseltine has clearly pulled away from the pack and emerged as the favourite with the public', and on 23 April an NOP poll published in the *Independent* put John Smith on 26 per cent, Michael Heseltine on 16 per cent, John Major on 11 per cent, Kenneth Clarke on 5 per cent, and Michael Portillo on 3 per cent as the person people would most like to see as Prime Minister.

In the face of this speculation, the Prime Minister remained defiant. Loyal deputies tried to steady and calm the troops. The Foreign Secretary, his eye already firmly on the European elections, played a particularly important role in this regard, and the former Tory whip Tristan Garel-Jones also played a part in heading off arguments about EC withdrawal. On the day of the local elections, the *Independent* ran an extraordinary story in which, it claimed, two-thirds of the Whips' office were prepared to break with convention and campaign openly for Mr Major in the event of a 'stalking horse' campaign. The next day, Mr Major pledged to 'fight to the end', and told his critics 'I'll be waiting', but it really did seem only a matter of time before a challenge to his leadership came. The Prime Minister's dilemma was succinctly revealed in a 29 April interview with the *Independent*. 'I'm not going to get into the "Euro-sceptic" or "Euro-enthusiast" argument,' he said. 'I am a Euro-realist. I think that is the position of most people in this country.' In seeking to alienate neither the pro-Europeans nor the Euro-sceptics, Mr Major had alienated both and, in the eyes of his critics, his pragmatic search for support had laid him open to charges of vacillation, opportunism and lack of leadership.

Thus, the eve of the European elections campaign found a beleaguered Prime Minister at the head of a government in open disarray, with the forthcoming European elections expected to deal a further crushing blow to the Conservative party's political standing and encourage the Prime Minister's opponents to mount a challenge to his leadership. John Major's only hope – clear signs of an across-the-board upswing in the economy – obstinately refused to appear. His attempts to assert authority in Europe had come badly unstuck with the blocking minority climb-down, and a further row over the nomination of Jean-Luc Dehaene was in the offing (see Chronology Table 2.7). The party badly needed to show unity if it was to stave off

THE SHOW'S NOT OVER
'TIL THE FAT LADY SINGS...

EURO-ELECTIONS

♪ I'M GOING TO
WASH THOSE MEN
RIGHT OUT OF
MY HAIR ♪

RIDDELL

A comment on the aftermath of the local elections

disastrous losses, and yet the leadership contenders continued to manoeuvre semi-publicly, sending coded messages to their supporters through speeches and interviews, and the battle between Euro-sceptics and pro-Europeans increasingly surfaced in the media. The mood on the eve of the European elections campaign was that the Prime Minister's future was on the line.

Chronology Table 2.7   1990–4: John Major's shifting European policy

28 Nov. 90	John Major becomes Prime Minister
11 Feb. 91	Prime Minister describes a Bonn working visit as marking 'the start of a new era'
11 Mar. 91	During second Bonn visit John Major describes his vision of Britain 'at the very heart of Europe'
21 May 91	105 Conservative MPs sign resolution calling on the Prime Minister to reject moves towards EMU
9 Jun. 91	Kohl–Major summit results in agreement that there should be no bindings decisions on EMU at forthcoming Luxembourg Council
24 Jun. 91	Mitterrand–Major summit results in similar agreement
9–10 Dec. 91	Prime Minister wins Social Chapter opt-out and EMU opt-in at Maastricht European Council
7 Feb. 92	Maastricht Treaty signed
7 Apr. 92	British Conservative MEPs dissolve their group and become allied members of the EPP group
9 Apr. 92	General Election returns John Major as Prime Minister
12 May 92	Queen Elizabeth addresses the European Parliament in Strasbourg
21 May 92	House of Commons approves Maastricht Bill in second reading by 336 to 92
2 Jun. 92	Danish referendum rejects Maastricht Treaty
3 Jun. 92	John Major suspends Commons consideration of Maastricht Bill
26–7 Jun. 92	At Lisbon European Council the Prime Minister agrees to complete ratification by the end of the year
1 Jul. 92	UK Presidency begins
16 Sep. 92	'Black Wednesday' – sterling is unilaterally withdrawn from the ERM
9 Oct. 92	The Prime Minister tells the Conservative Party Conference non-ratification of the Maastricht Treaty would mean 'breaking Britain's future in Europe' but that he would never allow Britain's distinctive identity to be lost in a federal Europe

Chronology Table 2.7 continued

4 Nov. 92	Government wins 'paving motion' vote by 319 to 316 but only after agreeing to postpone ratification until after the second Danish referendum
3 Jan. 93	Prime Minister states that there is no imminent prospect of sterling's return to the ERM
3 Feb. 93	European Christian Democratic parties sign common manifesto in Brussels, with British Conservative MEPs disassociating themselves
18 May 93	Second Danish referendum approves Maastricht Treaty
23 Jul. 93	Government wins final vote of confidence over Maastricht Bill ratification by 339 to 229 votes
2 Aug. 93	ERM effectively collapses. John Major says the EMU timetable in the Maastricht Treaty is now 'totally unrealistic'
25 Sep. 93	In *Economist* article the Prime Minister states 'It is for nations to build Europe, not for Europe to attempt to supersede nations.'
5–8 Oct. 93	John Major makes Euro-sceptical speech to the Conservative Party Conference at Blackpool
27 Mar. 94	Blocking minority row. British government forced to climb down
27 Apr. 94	Unproductive Kohl–Major summit
23 May 94	John Major's Bristol 'veto' speech
27 May 94	Prime Minister tells the *Daily Express* that EMU is unlikely, whilst Chancellor Kohl tells German television it is definite
31 May 94	John Major's Ellesmere Port speech envisages a 'multi-track, multi-speed, multi-layered' Europe
1 Jun. 94	Lord Tebbit endorses the Prime Minister's Ellesmere Port speech
7 Jun. 94	John Major's 'seven deadly sins of Europe' speech
24–5 Jun. 94	John Major vetoes Jean-Luc Dehaene's nomination

3 Framework

THE ELECTORAL SYSTEM

One of the many innovations of the 1957 Treaty of Rome was an article that states that 'The Assembly shall draw up proposals for elections by direct universal suffrage in accordance with a uniform procedure in all Member States. The Council shall, acting unanimously, lay down the appropriate provisions, which it shall recommend to Member States for adoption in accordance with their respective constitutional requirements' (Article 138,3). The nature of appointment of delegates to the earlier Common Assembly of the European Coal and Steel Community (founded in 1952) had been left up to the governments of the Member States, with direct election a possibility. The principle of a directly-elected assembly was conceded just one year later, in the ill-fated European Defence Community treaty. By the time of the negotiation of the Treaty of Rome, therefore, a directly-elected assembly was an accepted concept. Indeed, the 'founding fathers' expected direct elections to take place soon after the Treaty entered into force, believing that a European assembly directly elected through universal suffrage would act as an integrative force. However, almost forty years on, the full provisions of Article 138(3) had yet to be met.

The EEC's parliamentary assembly, 'provisionally' composed of delegated national parliamentarians, set up a working party to draft proposals for a uniform electoral system in October 1958, and adopted a full-blown draft convention on 10 May 1960 (see Chronology Table 3.1). However, the publication of these proposals came when Charles de Gaulle's views on the pre-eminence of intergovernmental cooperation were in the ascendant. The parliamentary assembly forwarded its draft convention to the Council four days after French Prime Minister Michel Debré had told the French national assembly 'I do not see what direct elections by universal suffrage . . . can accomplish'. De Gaulle put forward his own proposals for an intergovernmental community, and these were subsumed into the negotiations leading up to the first (November 1961) and second (January 1962) Fouchet Plans for a more intergovernmental Europe. With all attention focussed on these negotiations, the parliamentary

Chronology Table 3.1   Chronology of direct and uniform elections

15 Mar. 57	Treaty of Rome signed – EEC comes into being
29 May 58	President De Gaulle comes to power
Oct. 58	EEC parliamentary assembly establishes working party to draft convention – Article 138(3)
10 May 60	Parliamentary assembly adopts draft convention (Dehousse report)
20 Jun. 60	Convention forwarded to the European Council
Nov. 61	First Fouchet Plan
Jan. 62	Second Fouchet Plan
30 May 62	European Assembly decides to call itself 'European Parliament'
Mar. 69	Parliament 'reminds' Council of its duties
28 Apr. 69	President De Gaulle stands down
2 Dec. 69	Hague summit decides to give 'further consideration' to the question of direct elections
Jun. 1973	Parliament decides to redraft its convention
10 Dec. 74	Paris summit announces wish that Council should act in 1976, with a view to holding of direct elections 'in or after 1976'
14 Jan. 75	Parliament adopts Patijn report, which distinguishes between uniformity and directness and sets target date of May 1978
5 Jun. 75	UK referendum votes 67 per cent Yes for continued membership
17 Feb. 76	UK government publishes Green Paper
13 Jul. 76	Brussels European Council reaches agreement on number and distribution of seats
20 Sep. 76	European Assembly Elections act signed, and sets May–June 1978 as date for first direct elections
Aug. 76	Commons select committee favours first-past-the-post
23 Mar. 77	Lib Lab pact
1 Apr. 77	Government publishes White Paper – cabinet favours regional list
13 Dec. 77	Commons votes in favour of first-past-the-post (with STV for NI)
8 Apr. 78	Copenhagen European Council recognises delay and sets 7–10 June 1979 as period for first direct elections
5 May 78	UK Direct Elections Bill receives royal assent
9–12 Jun. 79	First direct elections
10 Mar. 82	Parliament adopts Seitlinger report, which calls for PR in multimember constituencies. Council fails to act
14–17 Jun. 84	Second direct elections
28 Feb. 85	Bocklet report on a uniform system adopted in committee, but Parliament ultimately unable to adopt new convention
15–18 Jun. 89	Third direct elections
10 Oct. 91	First de Gucht report adopted (rules out identicality)
10 Jun. 92	Second de Gucht report adopted (recommendations on number and distribution of members)

assembly's draft convention was at first sidelined and then became outdated. It was clear that little progress could be made whilst de Gaulle remained in power.

In 1969, with de Gaulle gone, the European Parliament (so called since May 1962) began to show impatience, and the Hague summit in December 1969 decided to give further consideration to direct elections. In 1973, it being clear that the convention of May 1960 was hopelessly out of date, Parliament began drafting another, culminating in the January 1975 adoption of the Patijn report. This embodied a revolutionary approach, separating off the problem of uniformity from the problem of directness. The 1960 draft convention had proposed a transitional period during which only part of the Parliament's membership would be directly elected. Patijn borrowed the concept of a provisional period, proposing that, since it was uniformity rather than directness that was more problematic, the Parliament could be directly elected during a transitional period, leaving a uniform system to be negotiated later. The Patijn report led directly to the breakthrough that enabled the first direct elections to go ahead, some twenty years later than originally envisaged

Agreement on the number and distribution of seats was reached at the July 1976 Brussels European Council, and in September 1976 the 'Act Concerning the Election of the Representatives of the European Parliament by Direct Universal Suffrage' was signed. The Member States reaffirmed their desire to see the first direct elections take place in the May–June period in 1978. The Act built on the Parliament's detailed preparatory work. The Parliament was to be elected for a five-year term. Dual mandates were permitted, but the Act listed a number of offices, such as ministerial posts or membership of the Commission, that would be incompatible with parliamentary membership. The Member States would each fix the date for their European elections, but would agree on a common Thursday-to-Sunday period within which all would have to take place. Votes would not be counted until after the close of polling in all Member States. Article 7(1) of the Act provides that 'the European Parliament shall draw up a proposal for a uniform electoral procedure', and Article 7(2) provides that, 'Pending the entry into force of a uniform electoral procedure and subject to the other provisions of this Act, the electoral procedure shall be governed in each Member State by its national provisions.'

In February 1976 the UK government published a Green Paper on direct elections which avoided making any detailed proposals on possible systems. In May 1976 a select committee was established, and in its first report (August 1976) it opted firmly for the traditional first-past-the-post system. On 22 March 1977 the Labour government entered into a 'pact', a weak arrangement falling short of a governing coalition, with the Liberal Party. One of the conditions imposed by the Liberal Party was that legislation for direct elections should be put to the House during the summer, with a free vote on proportional representation. On 1 April 1977, the government published a White Paper on direct elections which left open the choice between a regional list approach, the single transferable vote, and first-past-the-post. However, two weeks earlier the cabinet had opted for a regional list system. Thereafter, the bill to establish direct elections fell prey to various political forces and parliamentary filibustering. It contained two proposals, one for a regional list system, and the other for first-past-the-post. On 13 December 1977 the House voted by 319 to 222 in favour of the first-past-the-post system. On 5 May 1978 the bill received the Royal Assent.

The April 1978 Copenhagen European Council recognised that the initially-envisaged 1978 date for direct elections had become unrealistic (the Netherlands was also badly behind schedule), and set a precise period, 7–10 June 1979, for the first direct elections. These duly went ahead, with each Member State adopting its own particular system. However all, with the exception of mainland Britain, used some form of proportional representation (because of its particular circumstances, STV was used in Northern Ireland). The June 1979 UK European elections provided immediate proof of the potentially distorting effects of first-past-the-post; the Conservatives won 60 of the 78 mainland seats to Labour's 17. Although they secured 12.6 per cent of the vote, the Liberals won no seats, and their absence from Strasbourg after the elections was all the more remarked since an appointed delegation of Liberal MPs and peers had sat in the European Parliament from 1973 until 1979. However, the main perceived distortion was the size of the Conservative contingent. The British Conservatives alone (with three token Danish conservatives) displaced the Liberal Group (with representatives from eight of the nine Member States) as the third largest Group within the Parliament, and gave the centre-right (with 216 MEPs) a majority over the left (with 156 MEPs).

Soon after the first direct elections, the Parliament began work on the drafting of a convention on uniform elections, culminating in the March 1982 adoption of the Seitlinger report, which called for proportional representation in multi-member constituencies of varying sizes. The Council set up a working party, but had not reached any substantial conclusions by the time of the second direct elections in June 1984. A major sticking-point was the British first-past-the-post system, the British government having made it clear that it would not countenance the introduction of PR. The chief reason given was the British political tradition and the legitimacy that resulted from it, but an underlying reason was the fear that the introduction of PR for European elections might act as the 'thin end of the wedge' for the introduction of PR for national elections. After the 1984 European elections, the Parliament decided to make a fresh attempt at drafting a convention, but the Bocklet report ran into political controversy, and although the report was adopted in committee (28 February 1985), the Parliament was unable to adopt a draft before the third direct elections, in June 1989. Thereafter Parliament opted for a new approach, illuminated by the debate over the subsidiarity principle. The rapporteur on this occasion was a Belgian Flemish Liberal, Karel de Gucht. With great ingenuity (reminiscent of Patijn's approach), de Gucht distinguished between the problem of the single-member constituency link on the one hand, and the principle of proportionality on the other. de Gucht proposed that two-thirds of the seats assigned to 'a Member State' (i.e. the UK) could be distributed in single-member constituencies, but that the remaining third should be distributed among the political parties in such a way as to 'top up' their representation to proportionality. The de Gucht report also provided for 'limited special arrangements in order to take account of regional features', thus allowing for the traditional over-representation of Scotland and Wales. As de Gucht put it, he had tried to make it 'as difficult as possible for Britain to say no'.

The de Gucht report was forwarded to the Danish presidency during the first half of 1993. Given its own problems with the Maastricht Treaty at that time, the Danish government did not react to the report. The succeeding Belgian presidency (July–December 1993) preferred to pursue the related matters of European citizenship and voting rights, both of which arose directly out of provisions in the Maastricht Treaty, which had finally entered into force on 1 November 1993. The Belgian government may have been discouraged by legal advice questioning whether the de Gucht report actually amounted to a proposal for uniform elections within the meaning of Treaty of Rome Article 138(3) and Article 7 of the 1976 Act. Time had effectively run out, and the 1994 European elections were therefore held under the same diverse conditions as the 1979, 1984, and 1989 elections. There was just one significant difference: the number of members.

The pre-1979 appointed Parliament had been composed of just 198 members, a number set out in the 1957 Rome Treaty. The 1976 Brussels European Council decided to more than double the directly-elected Parliament's size, to 410 members. The complicated negotiations behind this number had involved two conditions. The first was that Luxembourg's initial 1957 attribution of six seats could not be reduced. (This condemned the Community to a system of regressive proportionality, as the 1975 Patijn report had recognised.) The second was that German and French representation should be equal. This condition arose out of an April 1951 undertaking agreed between Konrad Adenauer and Jean Monnet. With the accessions of Greece, Spain and Portugal, the overall number of MEPs increased, but the initial 1976 distribution remained the same for the existing Member States.

German unification in October 1990 brought the old distribution into question, particularly in the eyes of the European Parliament. It was inconceivable that the five new *Länder* should not be represented. At the same time, it was inconceivable that the representation of the old eleven Western *Länder* should be reduced in any way. The Parliament immediately decided to create 18 'observer' posts for representatives from the new *Länder*, and Karel de Gucht was charged with the drafting of a report on the number and distribution of seats with a view to further enlargements of the Community. (The Parliament chose the number 18 primarily because it would give the Federal Republic enough new members to cover the representation of the five new *Länder* without going beyond the threshold of 100 MEPs.) Agreement on this enlarged representation was almost reached at the December 1991 Maastricht European Council. In May 1992, the European Parliament adopted the de Gucht report. It used a regressive proportional method based on population similar to Patijn's 1975 calculations again taking Luxembourg's six seats as the point of departure. The quid pro quo for increased German representation was an increase, though lesser, in French representation (and hence by extrapolation that of seven other Member States). Finally, at the December 1992 Edinburgh European Council, the Member States reached a political agreement based strictly on the European Parliament's recommendations (and the December 1993 Brussels European Council was later to follow the Parliament's recommendations in deciding on the number of MEPs for the four applicant countries). The overall number of MEPs was raised from 518 to 567. German representation was raised from 81 to 99. French, British, and

Italian representation was raised from 81 to 87 (six new seats). The Netherlands also got six extra seats; Spain received four; Belgium, Greece and Portugal each received one. For most countries with nationwide or even regional PR systems, these increases presented no serious problems. But for Britain, with its 78 single-member seats, the increase involved a wholescale redrawing of the map. The first challenge was to decide how the six extra seats should be allocated as between England, Scotland and Wales. The problem could have been sidestepped. The Liberal Democrats suggested that the six extra seats could be used to 'top up' parties' representation on a PR basis, leaving the 78 British single member Euro-constituencies intact. But after a brief flirtation with the idea by Douglas Hurd, John Major insisted on first-past-the-post for all of the British seats.

For the drawing of boundaries a quota is established by the simple expedient of dividing the electorate by the number of seats. Table 3.2 shows the 1993 quotas for England, Wales and Scotland and what would have been the case under the three possible distributions of the six extra seats. Scotland had no numerical claim to an extra seat. With eight MEPs, it was already 16,000 below the UK quota of 507,000. With nine seats it would be 81,000 below. Were Wales to remain with four seats, its quota would be 54,000 larger than the English quota, but with five seats its quota would be 69,000 smaller than the English quota. The mathematical case for giving all the extra seats to England, or for allotting one extra to Wales, was evenly balanced.

The government took a long time to decide, with the Home Secretary, Kenneth Clarke, hesitating between the alternative solutions. Ian Lang, the Scottish Secretary, got some Cabinet support when he argued for an extra Scottish seat. Michael Howard, when he took over from Kenneth Clarke in May 1993, initially favoured allocating

Table 3.2 *Alternative consequences of the six extra seats*

	1993		6–0–0		4–1–1		5–1–0	
	78 seats	Average electorate	84 seats	Average electorate	84 seats	Average electorate	84 seats	Average electorate
England	66	552,000	72	501,000	70	521,000	71	513,000
Wales	4	555,000	4	555,000	5	444,000	5	444,000
Scotland	8	491,000	8	491,000	9	436,000	8	491,000

all six seats to England. The Scottish case, as set out in later parliamentary debates, depended partly on the physical size of the country and partly on the fact that Scottish representation (eight MEPs, and a population of 5.1 million) compared unfavourably with that of countries such as Ireland (15 MEPs, population of 3.6 million) and Denmark (16 MEPs, population of 5.2 million). But the Welsh case was statistically much stronger, and it ultimately prevailed with the Prime Minister who, in effect, was left to decide the matter on which the cabinet remained divided. Since the Conservatives had no serious hope of electoral gains anywhere in Wales, the decision effectively gave Labour an extra European seat. It has been suggested that the extra seat was part of a deal to ensure the support of the four Plaid Cymru MPs during the Maastricht Treaty ratification process, but this is firmly denied on both sides. Plaid Cymru did win concessions from the government in return for their cooperation, even though they were in favour of the Treaty, but a fifth Welsh seat was not part of the deal. In fact, Plaid Cymru was ambivalent about the advantages of a fifth seat, since they calculated that they would have had a better chance of winning in the old Wales North seat (where Plaid had come a good third in 1989) than in any of the five likely new seats. On the other hand, there was said to be a possibility that some form of PR might be introduced for the 1999 European elections, and under those circumstances Plaid Cymru would have stood a much better chance of gaining representation, but this was to offset a probability against a possibility.

Because of the fraught Maastricht Treaty ratification process (see Chapter 2), which ran on through the 1992–3 session of Parliament, the government decided to postpone legislating to bring the new boundaries into effect, fearing that Conservative Euro-sceptics might use the Bill as a further weapon to wreck the parliamentary timetable, delaying or even frustrating the ratification of the treaty. There was also a real fear among Home Office ministers that the Bill might be lost through an unholy alliance between Labour and the Euro-sceptics, but the government Whips were proved right in believing that the Euro-sceptics would do no more than abstain (the only Conservative MP to vote against was Rupert Allason, who had already lost the Conservative whip because of his absence during the critical Maastricht Bill confidence motion). The European Parliamentary Elections Bill did not receive its second reading until 30 June 1993, and only completed its passage through the House of Lords in time for the Royal Assent on 5 November 1993, at the very end of the session.

Another problem came to the fore. The Boundary Commissions for England and Wales were already busily involved in a wholesale redrawing of the Westminster boundaries. The Bill therefore provided for the new Euro-boundaries to be drawn by two special, ad hoc, committees which would not be bound by the procedures laid down in the European Parliamentary Elections Acts of 1978, 1981 and 1986. The ad hoc committees would be serviced by the Boundary Commissions' staff and would be largely composed of Boundary Commissioners but, because of the shortage of time and pressure on resources, there would be no public enquiries, as would normally have been the case. Introducing the Bill, Michael Howard, the Home Secretary, announced that the committees were being set up at once under Executive Order. They would produce draft reports by August. Representations against the committees' proposals and against any counter-proposals would be carefully considered, but the final reports would be ready before the end of the year.

This parallel working of the Boundary Commissions and the ad hoc boundary committees was to have one grievous consequence from the point of view of UK MEPs. The 1993 Bill provided that the ad hoc committees should use Westminster constituencies as their basic building blocks, grouping them together to create constituencies as near to the ideal quota as possible. Thus, the ad hoc committees were obliged to base their work on the existing Westminster constituencies, even though they knew that new constituencies were in the process of being drawn. This meant that the new European constituency boundaries would be out of date as soon as the new Westminster boundaries came into force. This, in turn, meant that the European constituency boundaries would have to be redrawn for the 1999 European elections which, in turn, could mean a new round of reselection procedures.

Tony Blair, then shadow Home Secretary, moved the rejection of the European Parliamentary Elections Bill because it would not allow for public enquiries and also because it did not propose an extra seat for Scotland but, after a fractious and undistinguished debate, a Labour wrecking amendment was defeated by 300 votes to 254. Labour was unable to get the Euro-sceptic Conservative backbenchers to do anything more than abstain. At the committee stage a week later the government survived various opposition amendments by similar margins. Labour's opposition was less than full-blooded, and the House almost got counted out when it came to the Liberal Democrats' inevitable pro-PR amendment.

Once established, the boundary committees worked fast. The English proposals were published on 9 August. Objections to the proposals were received until 22 September, and comments on the objections until 22 October (13 September and 19 November respectively for the Welsh proposals). A final report was submitted to the Home Secretary on 20 December. As a consequence of the observations and comments received, the original proposals were modified for 13 of the 71 English constituencies, and for three of the five Welsh constituencies. The main changes were in the Merseyside to South Yorkshire area (Brian Simpson, the sitting Labour MEP for Cheshire East, launched a particularly effective local campaign against the committees' initial proposals), and in a stretch west of London. In Wales, a proposal for a peculiar seat stretching from Milford Haven in the south to Holyhead in the north was abandoned, even though it would have concentrated the Welsh-speaking areas into one constituency. The committees' reports (Cm 2440 and 2441) explained in detail why the changes had been made, and there was not much complaint about the final outcome, which both the major parties considered to be fairly neutral. It was calculated that, if everyone were to vote as they had in 1989, the seats would divide 49 Labour to 34 Conservative, a gain of four for Labour and two for the Conservatives. In itself, the provision of extra seats lessened the blow of redistribution.

The announcement of the final proposals, and their 15 February 1994 endorsement by Parliament, allowed the parties to get on with candidate selection or reselection, but one further uncertainty remained; would all Member States be able to ratify the December 1992 Edinburgh agreement in time for it to enter into force for the 1994 elections? Two Member States in particular were responsible for delay. In the case of Italy, a continuing government crisis and the search for a new coalition meant that the country was formally unable to ratify the agreement, although it was clear that ratification would occur just as soon as a new government took office. But in the case of France, the uncertainty was more substantial.

Since 1957, the European Parliament and its secretariat had been provisionally seated in, variously, Luxembourg, Strasbourg and Brussels. But in December 1992, the Edinburgh European Council definitively decided, in fulfilment of the various treaty requirements, that 'the European Parliament shall have its seat in Strasbourg where the twelve periods of monthly plenary sessions . . . shall be held'. However, the European Council also decided that 'The periods of additional plenary sessions shall be held in Brussels.' Although it contested the legality of this decision, the Parliament soon began to hold additional plenary sessions in Brussels, where a far-sighted private consortium had built a complex that was not only large enough to house the 567-member 1994 Parliament, but also the 639-member Parliament that would be created if all four applicant states were to join the European Union. This presented the French government and the Strasbourg local authorities with a quandary. The old hemicycle in the Strasbourg Palais de l'Europe had been stretched thrice to deal with the Greek, Spanish and Portuguese enlargements and the arrival of the 18 German observers. It could be (and was) stretched once more to house the 567-member Parliament, but it would then have reached its uppermost limit. The arrival of further representatives from new Member States would require the construction of a new, much larger, hemicycle. But before work began the Strasbourg authorities and the French government sought guarantees from the European Parliament (which was still formally contesting the Council's decision and seemed to be happy with its Brussels hemicycle) that it would occupy the new building. In order to exert pressure on the Parliament, the French *assemblée* made its ratification of the Edinburgh agreement conditional, demanding that the government should not deposit its instruments of ratification until such guarantees were forthcoming. Ultimately, on 31 March 1994, Parliament's outgoing President, Egon Klepsch, signed a contract with the Mayor of Strasbourg, committing the Parliament to renting the new hemicycle for twenty years. The French government's instruments were duly deposited on 5 April. The Italian government deposited its instruments on 11 April.

Had Klepsch refused to sign the contract, or had the Italian government crisis continued, the 1994 European elections would have had to have been fought on the basis of the pre-Edinburgh agreement provisions. In the case of the UK, this would have meant contesting the election on the old boundaries, with only 79 constituencies (78 on the mainland and the Northern Irish three-member constituency). In theory, this possibility should have obliged the parties to select two sets of candidates. In practice, selection only on the new boundaries went ahead, with the parties hoping (on pretty risky grounds) that the French government would not see through its ultimatum. In the event, it was the Parliament and not the French *assemblée* that conceded, much to the chagrin of British MEPs. (The Labour Party had made its opposition to the construction of a new hemicycle in Strasbourg part of its manifesto, and the issue was forcibly raised by John Tomlinson, MEP, in a national press conference, but the media did not rise to the story.)

VOTING RIGHTS AND CANDIDATES

As long as Member States continue to decide the basis on which European elections are held, it is *national* legislation in the separate states that governs who may vote and and stand in European elections, and under what circumstances. Conditions in the United Kingdom are primarily regulated by the 5 May 1978 European Assembly Elections Act. British and Irish citizens resident in the United Kingdom and aged eighteen years or over are entitled to vote. Contrary to the practice in national elections, members of the House of Lords may vote, as may the Queen. British citizens resident outside the country may vote if they are government officials or members of the armed forces or if their names appeared on an electoral register in the United Kingdom in the twenty years preceding the election. Candidates must be at least twenty-one years of age. Members of the House of Lords and clergymen may also stand for election.

However, the Maastricht Treaty (and a subsequent December 1993 Directive adopted by the Council) introduced a quiet revolution in these conditions. In its first (1960) draft Convention for a uniform electoral system, the European Parliament had proposed that Member State nationals resident in another Member State should be allowed to vote in elections to the European Parliament. This call was repeated at various intervals and was ultimately heeded by the draftsmen of the Maastricht Treaty. In 1994, for the first time, resident Union citizens could vote and stand in European elections in their Member State of residence if they so wished. The December 1993 Directive was based on the principle of mutual recognition; if a Union citizen satisfies the criteria that would apply in the Member State of Residence, then he/she may vote or stand as a candidate in the Member State of residence under exactly the same conditions. The directive's other provisions were concerned principally with the avoidance of double-voting and double candidatures. (In the United Kingdom, one originally French Conservative (Christine Adamson) and one originally German Labour (Gisela Gscheider) candidate stood, though both were married to British citizens and had been resident in the UK for a long time.)

Disappointingly few Member State nationals resident in the UK availed themselves of their right to vote. The Home Office estimated that some 400,000 Member State nationals were resident in the UK at the time of the European elections. Only 7,800 registered to vote in the UK, the highest number being in London Central (1,678), London South Inner (383), and Cambridge (381), and the lowest in South

Wales East (5) and Merseyside East (only one). Critics of the government pointed to the very early deadline for registration (29 March 1994, and 22 April for appeals) and the lack of any publicity about the deadline, in addition to the lack of any general publicity about the new provision. The German embassy took out newspaper advertisements to alert its citizens, estimated to be about 230,000, telling them how to register. Some local authorities (Lewisham, for example) also did their best to publicize the new arrangements. The Association of Metropolitan Authorities was sharply critical of the government because of its refusal to pay the extra expenses of local authorities for registering foreign voters, despite the tight budgetary constraints under which most were working. (The London borough of Richmond estimated that about 2.7 per cent of its electorate were foreign EU citizens and put the cost of trying to get them to register at £15,200.) A spokesman for the Electoral Reform Society said 'It's bizarre not to let people know they have the right to vote'. Others pointed to the millions of pounds spent futilely a few years earlier on publicising the right to vote of Britons living overseas. Some critics believed the government deliberately played down the new arrangement because of its problems with right-wing backbenchers. (One prominent Euro-sceptic, Sir Teddy Taylor, feared that letting the newly enfranchised foreigners know of their rights 'could have a distorting effect' on the outcome, because of the likely low turnout in the UK.) But the Home Office denied that the government had played the matter down. A spokesman said 'appropriate steps' had been taken. It had distributed information sheets (in English only) to embassies of the Twelve, and a press release had been issued ((28 February). A further brief press statement was issued on 10 March, and the Home Office minister, Peter Lloyd, authored an article on 'Your right to vote on June 9' and had it sent to over 100 local newspapers. Whatever the reason, the number of registrations was disappointingly low throughout most of the twelve Member States of the European Union, and it seems likely that the short time span plus the low levels of publicity were primary culprits.

FINANCE

Through an unspoken gentlemen's agreement with the Council, the European Parliament is the master of its own internal budget, but in 1986 it found that there were limits nonetheless to its budgetary autonomy. The 1979–84 Parliament had created a special budgetary 'line', ostensibly designed for the dissemination of information about the Parliament and its political groupings. In practice, the money was destined for the existing political groups within the Parliament, distributed to them on a proportional basis and in part used as a form of reimbursement for election expenses. In 1983 the French Green Party, which had no seats in the European Parliament at that time, brought an action against the European Parliament before the European Court of Justice, arguing that the financing arrangement penalised political parties which did not already enjoy representation within the Parliament. But in its 1986 ruling (*Les Verts v. European Parliament* (1986) ECR 1339 Case 294/83), the Court went further, ruling that payments for the reimbursement of election expenses per se are within the sole competence of the Member States. Parliament could not justify, through its power of internal organisation, such a reimbursement scheme. The Parliament acted on the Court's ruling, but did not do away altogether with its budgetary line on information. In election years, Parliament imposes a cut-off date upon itself; four months before the elections all disbursement of information fund money must stop. Nevertheless, the amounts of money involved are cumulatively important and are typically put to use in raising awareness before the elections campaign proper starts.

In the United Kingdom detailed regulations for the conduct of the European elections, published by the Home Office, do not differ much from the regulations governing general elections. The candidate's deposit has been set at £1,000; the number of nominators at fifty. The expense limit is based on the number of electors in each constituency. In 1994 the average limit was about £42,000. As in general elections, candidates are entitled to one free postal communication for each elector.

4 The Conservatives

The Conservatives once regarded themselves as the party of Europe. In 1961, after much soul-searching, Harold Macmillan made a first application for membership of the EEC. Although Harold Wilson made the second in 1967, it was Edward Heath's crowning achievement to negotiate entry (1972) and secure admission (1973). Thereafter, the Labour Party's increasing ambivalence over membership, culminating in its 1983 manifesto commitment to wholesale withdrawal from the EEC, served to consolidate the Conservatives' pro-European image.

Nevertheless, even at the height of the party's pro-Europeanism, true enthusiasm for matters European was restricted to a relatively small proportion of the party's leadership and rank and file, with the bulk of the party remaining agnostic. A much smaller group of front and backbenchers had been strongly opposed to membership. This opposition had reached its cathartic finale in Enoch Powell's call to Conservative voters to vote Labour in the February 1974 General Election and his subsequent departure from mainstream British politics. After the 1975 referendum, outright opposition to membership largely disappeared from view, leaving a residual scepticism about the European Community among a small sector on the right wing of the party.

The election to the Conservative leadership of Margaret Thatcher, who had played an indifferent role in the 1975 referendum debates provided a first fillip to this small band of what were later to become known as 'Euro-sceptics'. In the first place, Mrs Thatcher was instinctively antithetical to her predecessor and therefore to his policies and achievements. Secondly, Mrs Thatcher was spiritually on the right of her party and therefore predisposed to be sympathetic to the right's concerns. Lastly, Mrs Thatcher chose to make correction of the unbalanced British budgetary contribution one of her early European policy priorities. This meant that, throughout the 1979–84 period (the contribution problem was finally solved at the June 1984 Fontaine-bleau European Council), Mrs Thatcher was most commonly portrayed as a champion of British interests, doing battle in Brussels. This stance struck a popular chord with the bulk of the Conservative

Party's membership, thus leaving the small number of Euro-enthusiasts within the party (who disliked Mrs Thatcher's strident tone and adversarial position) as a largely silent dissenting minority.

The resolution of the budgetary rebate problem, together with the growth of a new deregulatory spirit in Europe, gave rise to a shift in Mrs Thatcher's stance, culminating in her 1986 signature of the Single Act. The Single European Act was the legislative embodiment of the internal market, which had been largely drafted by a British Commissioner and former Thatcher minister, Lord Cockfield. As a keen deregulator in her own country, Mrs Thatcher was an instinctive enthusiast for similar deregulatory moves at the European level, which she saw as Thatcherism writ large in Europe and so made permanent, and her new approach was encouraged by the City (which stood to gain from any liberalisation of capital movements) and by the Confederation of British Industry, representing influential sectors of British business, such as the insurance sector.

Mrs Thatcher recognised that the single market could never be achieved by the EC's decision-making machinery, crippled as it was by the need for unanimity, without substantial reform, and she consciously signed up to a series of institutional innovations, the most important of these being the extension of qualified majority decision-making in the Council of Ministers. To her, this was a limited step, to be confined to the achievement of the single market. But, to her continental counterparts, the Single European Act was but the beginning of a renewed integration process. As the extent of that process gradually became clear, Mrs Thatcher's doubts hardened, and she was increasingly to cultivate a British version of Gaullism, emphasising the role of sovereign states and their governments and playing down the alleged benefits of 'supranationalism', as embodied in the so-called 'Community method'.

The new, dynamic President of the European Commission, Jacques Delors, whom she herself had been instrumental in appointing in 1984, was determined to forge ahead with a far-ranging raft of policy initiatives. He envisaged the creation of a European 'social space' to counterbalance the employment consequences of the liberalisation of the four factors of production, and increasingly urged Economic and Monetary Union as a logical parallel to the single market. Social policy and EMU, and the centralisation in Brussels that Mr Delors argued that both implied, were anathema to Mrs Thatcher. She felt aggrieved that the institutional reforms she had signed up to were not to be limited to the realisation of the internal market alone, and she felt particularly provoked by President Delors' claim before the European Parliament on 6 July 1988 that up to 80 per cent of economic and social legislation could originate at the Brussels level within ten years and by a speech he gave to the TUC's annual conference in which he urged support for his proposed Social Charter. The result was a renewal of Mrs Thatcher's neo-Gaullism, its spirit famously set out in her 20 September 1988 Bruges speech: 'We have not successfully rolled back the frontiers of the state in Britain only to see them reimposed at a European level with a European super-state exercising a new dominance from Brussels.'

The Euro-enthusiasts within the Conservative party had been cheered by Mrs Thatcher's acceptance of the Single European Act which, through the coincidence of economic argument and political interest, put them back in a relatively frictionless mainstream position. Correspondingly, the rise of her renewed Euro-scepticism caused the Euro-enthusiasts increasing discomforture. In their eyes, for example, the party's disastrous performance in the 1989 European elections was largely due to Mrs Thatcher's indifference and hostility (see Chapter 2). The difference between the 1979–84 and 1988–90 periods was that, while 'Euro-scepticism' undoubtedly remained a more easily populist position to adopt within the party, Mrs Thatcher and her style of politics no longer enjoyed widespread and unconditional support. On the contrary, a series of ministerial resignations and policy clashes had raised doubts about her political future. With the internal market clearly a success, and with German unification fuelling fresh integrationist initiatives, the Euro-enthusiasts feared that Mrs Thatcher's renewed adversarial stance would steadily marginalise the United Kingdom's position within the European Community.

Matters came to a head over the EMU process, as documented in Chapter 2. At the 1989 Madrid European Council Mrs Thatcher was pressured by her Chancellor and Foreign Secretary into conditional acceptance of the principle of ERM membership. Mrs Thatcher's primary concern was bound up in the political symbolism of monetary sovereignty, but Sir Geoffrey Howe and Nigel Lawson were primarily motivated by pragmatism. Both felt that ERM membership, with its exchange rate discipline and stability, was in itself a good thing, but they were also strongly aware that the EMU process was once again a very real prospect. Put simply, sterling's membership of the ERM, or at least the real prospect of it, would buy the UK a place at the negotiating table. When, in October 1990, Britain's continental partners sought to define the EMU process, Mrs Thatcher stridently opposed the exercise, saying that she would veto any EMU treaty, and it was this impassioned opposition that caused Sir Geoffrey Howe to resign as her deputy and led soon after to the election of John Major as the new leader of the Conservative party.

John Major was Margaret Thatcher's choice to replace her and was perceived as a loyal Thatcherite and yet, with his election, the pendulum seemed to have swung once more back towards the more Euro-enthusiastic section of the party. (Mrs Thatcher's fall was brought about by many factors, but her supporters primarily blamed those who opposed her views on Europe, and anti-European resentment lingered thereafter on the Thatcherite wing of the party.) To the growing disappointment of right wing and Euro-sceptical Conservatives, Mr Major sought to distinguish himself from his predecessor, notably by seeking a new, more enthusiastically pro-European consensus within the party. In the second of two visits to Germany early on in his leadership (spring 1991), Mr Major spoke of his wish for the UK to be 'at the heart of Europe' and spoiling operations such as the 'hard ECU' proposals were presented as positive contributions to the European policy debate. The Euro-enthusiasts, encouraged by Mrs Thatcher's departure and John Major's more positive approach, felt that their view was once more in the ascendant within the party.

But the intergovernmental process which John Major had helped to sign into being in December 1990 was soon to divert his new found enthusiasm. In particular, as the EMU IGC progressed under the Luxembourg Presidency (in the first half of 1991), Conservative backbench MPs became alarmed by rumours that the UK would be subject to a *fait accompli* over the transition from Stages 1 and 2 (preparatory phases) to Stage 3 (irrevocably fixed exchange rates). These fears culminated in the signing of a resolution by 105 Conservative backbench MPs on 21 May 1991, urging Mr Major to reject outright moves towards EMU. These pressures led to the Kohl–Major agreement on 9 June 1991, consolidated by a similar agreement with François Mitterrand on 24 June, whereby no concrete decisions would be taken at the 28–29 June Luxembourg European Council. However, the agreement did little to relieve the pressure and throughout the summer and autumn of 1991 an alliance of right-wing and Euro-sceptic backbenchers, encouraged by several speeches which Mrs Thatcher gave on a June tour of the US, constantly sniped at the government's apparent openess to a more pro-European approach.

As Chapter 2 described, the deal Mr Major brought home from Maastricht in December 1991 was presented as a personal negotiating triumph. It was a carefully-wrought balancing act between the Euro-enthusiastic wing of the Conservative party (which had welcomed Mr Major's pro-European stance) and the resurgent Euro-sceptical wing (which was vociferously opposed to further integration). Both were able to live with the 'opt-in' arrangement on EMU, which effectively left any decision on UK participation in monetary union to a future parliament. But the narrow Danish 'No' of 2 June 1992 swept away the party's consensus and encouraged the Euro-sceptics into more open rebellion. As he sensed the large agnostic mass of the party swinging towards a more Euro-sceptic view, Mr Major altered his vocabulary, toning down his Euro-enthusiasm in an attempt to regain consensus. But the effect was to disillusion and alienate the Euro-enthusiasts and to encourage the Euro-sceptics to impose further conditions on the Prime Minister's European policy. The departure of sterling from the ERM on 'Black Wednesday' (16 September 1992), which seemed to make EMU a distant prospect at best, undermined the Euro-enthusiasts' pragmatic arguments in favour of the Maastricht Treaty's political union provisions. Thereafter, and with increasing resentment, the Euro-enthusiasts found themselves once again on the defensive within the party and those frontbenchers with a pro-European past, such as Douglas Hurd and John Gummer, were more inhibited than the Euro-sceptics' chief spokesmen, Michael Portillo and Peter Lilley, in signalling their views. Was Europe to be a rock on which the Conservatives might split asunder? The 1994 European election constituted a new hazard to a party that was already in deep trouble.

The Conservatives had unexpectedly won in the April 1992 General Election by raising the spectre of tax increases under Labour and promising tax cuts if the government was re-elected. The euphoria soon evaporated as the recession persisted, and tax increases became necessary to meet the soaring PSBR. Black Wednesday heavily, and perhaps irrevocably, damaged the Conservative Party's reputation as the party best qualified to manage the economy. In the event, although the recession had reached its trough before Black Wednesday, the near 20 per cent devaluation of sterling helped to turn the economy around, and soon ministers were able to claim that Britain was leading Europe out of the recession. But there was no early reward in the opinion poll figures, and in the summer of 1993 two safe Conservative seats, Newbury and Christchurch, fell to the Liberal Democrats on record swings which, if replicated at a general election, would have been sufficient to defeat every sitting Conservative MP. Conservatives became fearful of a two-pronged offensive, with tactical voting for the

Liberal Democrats in the south and Labour resurgent in the midlands and north.

The 1992–3 saga of the ratification of the Maastricht Treaty was followed in March 1994 by the government's humiliating climbdown over the blocking minority row. The government's disarray led to increasing speculation about the future of the Prime Minister as Chapter 2 described, and about possible successors. But there were many other shadows overhanging the Conservatives as the spring of 1994 advanced. Mr Major's moralistic 'back to basics' theme at the October 1993 Conservative Conference was mocked, as a succession of personal scandals led to the resignation of three ministers and two PPS and generated rumours about others. The Scott inquiry into the Matrix Churchill prosecution over arms for Iraq had shown in a questionable light the judgement of many leading figures from Mrs Thatcher downwards. The Select Committee investigation into overseas aid (and in particular the financing of the Pergau dam in Malaysia) was also casting doubt on governmental ethics and administration in the late 1980s. Current policies too were attracting adverse publicity. The proposals for privatising the railways and the post office were criticised by Conservatives as much as by the opposition. The imposition of VAT on domestic fuel, higher National Insurance contributions and lower income-tax thresholds, which began to bite in April 1994, caused widespread discontent. Even the recovery of the economy, evident since late 1993, with low inflation and steady reductions in unemployment, was unable to resuscitate the 'feel-good' factor, the optimism on which the Conservatives relied for a return to favour. The outcome of the 5 May local elections was the worst ever for the Conservatives in a nationwide test, and it was against this background of disarray, dissension, open revolt, government failures and leadership speculation that the 1994 European election campaign was set to open. At the back of many Conservative minds was the fate of the Canadian Conservative Party which, in September 1993, lost office in a most spectacular way, falling from a clear majority to a mere two seats. Government was not at stake in the Euro-elections, but some pundits were seriously predicting that the Conservatives could fall back to third place in terms of votes, behind the resurgent Liberal Democrats, and face a 'wipe-out' or a 'melt-down' in terms of seats.

In organisational terms, the upper reaches of the Conservative Party were well prepared for the European elections. Sir Norman Fowler had taken over from Chris Patten as Party Chairman in May 1992. He had inherited, among other problems, a massive financial deficit that went back to the days of Kenneth Baker. Costs were cut, and there was a limited reduction in the bank overdraft, which had at its peak approached £20 million. The parlous state of the party's finances imposed severe restraints on the its capacity to fight a national campaign. Central Office parsimony also gave the Conservative MEPs rather more influence than might otherwise have been the case, since they had access to their own funding, in the form of the European Parliament's information fund, until February 1994 (when the European Parliament's cut-off date applied). Total expenditure from the information fund on documents, conferences, etc. amounted to some £440,000 in the year running to February 1994. The new Party Chairman also instituted a substantial reform of Central Office. An independently wealthy businessman, Paul Judge, was brought in as director general to oversee general administrative reform. Andrew Lansley, former private secretary to Norman Tebbit, continued to head the Research Department, while Tony Garrett took over as Director of Campaigning, with Stephen Gilbert as his number two. John Guthrie, former chairman of the Tory Reform Group, was appointed from business as head of the party's International Office, with specific responsibility for preparing the European campaign.

In March 1993 Anthony Teasdale, who had had long experience in Brussels and Strasbourg and had been Sir Geoffrey Howe's political adviser during the 1989 European elections and at the time of the 1990 leadership crisis, was appointed head of the London office of the Conservative MEPs. Although technically part of the EPP Group secretariat, Anthony Teasdale became a key Central Office player and he had less and less to do with the EPP as the campaign approached. Mr Teasdale worked in tandem with Mr Guthrie throughout the preparatory period and the campaign itself. A confirmed pro-European, Mr Teasdale was a close ally of Sir Christopher Prout. His office was physically located just above the Party Chairman's in Central Office, and he acted as the administrative bridge between Central Office and the European wing of the party. The result of these changes and appointments was a relatively well-organised and balanced Central Office team which to some degree offset the organisational weakness of the Conservative party in the country at large.

Norman Fowler's strength as Party Chairman lay in his closeness to John Major (he had acted as his chief-of-staff during the 1992 election) and in the fact that no one suspected him of using his office to manoeuvre for position. He received important backing from Gerry

Malone, an MP who had been brought in as Deputy Chairman and who was to play a particularly important part in the later stages of the European election campaign.

Electoral campaigns require strategic plans. The disastrous 1989 European election and the successful 1992 General Election had left their marks on party thinking. The unexpected 1992 victory was seen, in part, as the reward for careful planning and skilful publicity. Thus, for the 1994 European election the Conservatives decided to work, as in 1989, through a strategy committee and manifesto committee, both set up a year in advance, but with one important difference. In 1989 there had been a lack of coordination between the two committees, and dismayed Conservative MEPs and Euro-enthusiastic MPs had seen the campaign diverted from the balanced approach of the manifesto into a more hostile and negative attack on 'Brussels'. The Euro-enthusiasts, together with the party's pragmatists, who were well aware of the dangers of the open splits of 1989, were determined not to repeat this mistake; they therefore exerted great effort to keep the manifesto and strategy in line.

The strategy committee, which first met on 14 June 1993, was composed of six representatives of the Conservative MEPs (five members plus one staffer), seven representatives from Central Office, one from Downing Street, two from the Foreign Office, plus one from the National Union of the Conservative Party (see Table 4.1). There were some later changes of personnel, but the principle was maintained of keeping the four key elements – MEPs, Central Office, Downing Street, and the Foreign Office – represented and, as far as possible, in harmony. The strategy committee met monthly from July to December 1993, fortnightly from January to March 1994, and then weekly until May, when it turned to daily meetings once the campaign proper had begun.

On 15 July 1993, following a 1 July meeting between the Prime Minister and Conservative MEPs, Sir Christopher Prout submitted a paper to the strategy committee entitled *A Winning Strategy*. This paper, which formed the basis for the strategy committee's early deliberations, was largely drafted by Anthony Teasdale and was based on the earlier work of an internal 'strategy' group of MEPs under Peter Price. The paper's key themes were that:

1. The Conservatives should campaign primarily on European issues;
2. They should point to a clear left–right choice, stressing the evils of the left-of-centre majority that had existed in the European

Table 4.1   The Conservative Party's strategy committee for the 1994 European election

Conservatives in the European Parliament: Sir Christopher Prout (Leader of the British Conservatives in the European Parliament), Bill Newton Dunn (Chairman of the British Section of the EPP Group), Edward McMillan-Scott, Peter Price, Michael Welsh (MEPs), Anthony Teasdale (Head of the London Office of the EPP Group)

Conservative Central Office: Sir Norman Fowler MP (Party Chairman), Sir Geoffrey Pattie MP, Paul Judge (director-general), Andrew Lansley, Tony Garrett, Tim Collins (directors), John Guthrie (European election campaign organiser)

Downing Street: Jonathan Hill (political secretary to the PM)

Foreign and Commonwealth Office: Maurice Fraser, Michael Maclay (special advisers to Douglas Hurd)

Party National Union: Sir Basil Feldman (Chairman of the National Union)

Parliament in the 1989–94 period, compared to the benefits of the centre-right majority of the preceding 1979–89 period;

3. They should argue that the European Parliament now had real power and that who held a majority would make a significant difference;

4. They should concentrate on economic rather than institutional issues;

5. They should draw the moral that it was a real election, with real consequences that mattered.

The Conservative MEPs still bore the scars of the 1989 campaign, and the paper clearly reflected this. Above all, negativism had to be avoided. Central Office and Downing Street were initially opposed to the proposed emphasis on European issues, but here the MEPs were able to persuade them; after all, the polls indicated that it was not a good moment to fight on domestic ground. The left-right distinction was one which all in the party could happily unite around and fight on. However, the various elements in the committee found it harder to reach consensus on whether an emphasis on economics should be at the expense of institutions. The Euro-enthusiasts had been harrowed by the Maastricht Treaty ratification process, as they were to be later by the blocking minority row. For them, institutional issues were dangerous ground, liable to crack open the party and perhaps push in a Euro-sceptic direction and were therefore to be avoided. In the end, the committee came to an undefined agreement based on a mixture of both themes, concentrating uncertainly on the preservation of the veto on the one hand, and on the consequences of the Social Chapter on the other. This mixture created some uneasiness among the MEPs, but they felt that at least they had prevented the party from indulging in a more general onslaught on Brussels and all its ways, thus preventing a repeat of the crude 'diet of Brussels' approach of five years before.

Electoral campaigns traditionally require manifestos. Whether for European or national elections, these documents are in fact little read by the electorate but, apart from containing commitments which may come to haunt the authors in future years, they do provide ammunition for commentators and for political opponents; therefore they are pored over by journalists and opposition politicians in search of a chink in a party's armour. The 1994 European elections presented the Conservatives with a challenge, since the European People's Party was intent on adopting a pan-European manifesto for the elections, as it had done in 1989 and, among other things, its draft manifesto gave wholehearted support to the Social Chapter. The Conservative Party could never have signed up to such a document, and yet an open split between the British MEPs and their Christian Democrat allies would have badly undermined their coalition strategy in Strasbourg. Long aware of the potential risk involved, Sir Christopher Prout successfully waged a backstage diplomatic campaign that enabled the British Conservative MEPs to disassociate themselves from the EPP manifesto. Technical grounds – the Conservatives' allied status within the EPP Group in the European Parliament and their non-membership of the EPP transnational party (which was strictly speaking the source of the manifesto) – were carefully elaborated for this disassociation. The manifesto was duly adopted by the bureau of the EPP on 3 February 1994 in Brussels and, in answer to journalists' questions, the then President of the EPP, Wilfried Martens, confirmed that the allied British Conservative MEPs were not bound by it. The issue was further defused as a potential hazard in early March, when the *Guardian* ran a story claiming that some British Conservative MEPs had been present at the meeting where the EPP manifesto was adopted. The report resulted from the fact that five Conservative MEPs, including Sir Christopher Prout, had signed the attendance register for the meeting, but Sir Christopher was able to point out that they had only been present, entirely legitimately, for an earlier part of the meeting, and then only as observers. In a letter to the *Guardian*, he definitively asserted that 'Neither the Conservative Party nor Conservative MEPs are entitled to play, or have played, any part in debating or drafting the EPP manifesto or in voting for it.' A journalist raised the matter of the EPP manifesto at the launch of the party's election campaign on 23 May. The Prime Minister and Sir Christopher were able to refute both any obligation to the EPP manifesto and any idea of a major split from the EPP, and thereafter, although it remained in the air, the issue was effectively dead.

For 1994, as for all previous European elections, the Conservative Party drafted its own, national manifesto. In 1989 the Conservatives' drafting operation had run smoothly under the chairmanship of Sir Geoffrey Howe, but once the document was completed the committee had disbanded and the pro-European emphasis had subsequently been lost, as Central Office, with its Thatcher-inspired attacks on 'Brussels', took over the day-to-day campaign. In 1993–4, the drafting exercise was very different. The manifesto committee, chaired by Douglas Hurd and serviced by Maurice Fraser, his political adviser, met only six times, mainly from October 1993 to February 1994. It was a much more symbolic body than Geoffrey Howe's 1989 drafting committee. Much of the real business was done behind the scenes by staffers. It took advice from many sources, but care was taken to exclude Euro-sceptics from membership (see Table 4.1) and, despite press reports to the contrary, from influence. As one insider put it, 'there was a firm determination that nobody who had voted against the Maastricht Treaty in the House of Commons should be rewarded for their disloyalty.' (This determination, it should be noted, was shared by all four elements in the strategy committee.) However, the later stages of the manifesto-drafting exercise took place in an atmosphere of increasing Euro-sceptic militancy, following the blocking minority climb-down and stories of Franco-German *faits accomplis*. The Euro-secptics became increasingly unsettled by their exclusion from the manifesto exercise. In summer 1993 Douglas Hurd made a placatory gesture towards them by writing to a selection of Conservative MPs representing the various wings of the party, asking for their suggestions. This was pragmatically intended as a way of keeping the Euro-sceptics off the committee, but one of the Maastricht rebels, Bill Cash, brandishing this letter in a *Newsnight* interview, had misleadingly implied that he had been invited to participate in the manifesto-drafting exercise. The Euro-sceptics became increasingly restless as they realised during the Spring that they had been completely excluded from manifesto process. Douglas Hurd could take credit for his decision to keep the drafting committee's membership absolutely secret (see Table 4.2).

Early in the drafting committee's life, each government minister was asked to submit a memorandum detailing his or her department's past achievements and its future plans in the European sphere. The Conservative MEPs were invited collectively to make a similar input. In their submission, the MEPs went a long way beyond government policy in suggesting positive new pro-European commitments while, in theirs, government departments fought shy of offering anything new. There was a vacuum between the two approaches. Douglas Hurd wanted a unifying document and not an agenda. The MEPs wanted a unifying text which was also a specific legislative agenda in Europe for the next five years, focussed directly on the European Parliament. This, they believed, would show that how people voted in the Euro-election would make a real difference to policies pursued in Europe. In the end the manifesto was long on generalities and short on specifics. As an insider put it, 'it was a frustrating exercise because it had to be so cautious'. The first draft chapter, circulated in October, was gradually built up into a full text by Maurice Fraser, with assistance from

Table 4.2   The Conservative Party's manifesto committee for the 1994 European election

---

Foreign and Commonwealth Office: Douglas Hurd MP (Foreign Secretary and Chairman of the Committee), David Heathcoat-Amory MP, Maurice Fraser, Michael Maclay (special advisers to Douglas Hurd)

Treasury: Stephen Dorrell, MP

The Conservatives in the European Parliament: Sir Christopher Prout (leader of the British Conservatives in the European Parliament), Bill Newton Dunn (Chairman of the British Section of the EPP Group), Edward McMillan-Scott, Christopher Beazley, Caroline Jackson (MEPs), Anthony Teasdale (Head of the London Office of the EPP Group)

Conservative Central Office: Sir Norman Fowler MP (Party Chairman), Sir Geoffrey Pattie MP, Andrew Lansley, Tim Collins, Tony Garrett, John Guthrie, Laura Adshead

10 Downing Street: Sarah Hogg, Jonathan Hill

MPs: Sir Peter Hordern MP (Chairman of the backbench Europe Committee), David Martin MP (PPS to Douglas Hurd)

National Union: Bill Stuttaford

Andrew Lansley and Anthony Teasdale. An 18,000 word draft was submitted to the Prime Minister at Easter. It was regarded as too long by Downing Street and, when it was vetted in early April by an inner core of senior ministers, together with Sir Christopher Prout, it was decided to charge the Policy Unit at 10 Downing Street with the task of shortening the draft and giving it more of a campaigning edge. By the second half of April, Sarah Hogg had reduced it to 13,000 words. In the meantime, however, stories of more substantial re-editing had leaked out to the media and were coupled with the Euro-sceptics' claims that they had finally succeeded in gaining influence over the drafting exercise. Although Sir Norman Fowler disdainfully dismissed such stories, they were given apparent credence by Douglas Hurd's public admission that the initial version was indeed being re-drafted by the Policy Unit, further compounding Euro-enthusiasts' fears that the Prime Minister might be veering towards a more Euro-sceptical approach to the campaign. In fact, most of those involved in the exercise described Sarah Hogg's task as being primarily editorial, as by any standards the initial draft was too long. 'There was nothing of any substance in the final text which didn't appear in the original draft' said one insider. 'Sarah Hogg's role was essentially that of a wordsmith and she was good at that'.

The shorter and reworked manifesto was approved with few amendments at a political Cabinet meeting, which included Sir Christopher Prout, on 5 May. *A Strong Britain in a Strong Europe* was divided into seven sections, each concentrating on a separate theme. The first, 'A Conservative Europe', displayed signs of the compromise reached in the strategy committee. It stressed the Conservatives' strong economic management record at home, and the government's positive influence, particularly on deregulation, in Brussels. It argued that Labour would 'put Britain last', and that the Liberal Democrats would 'put Brussels first'. It accused the two parties of a 'Lib/Lab Euro-pact', with virtually indistinguishable policies on Europe, including readiness to cede 'Britain's veto' in various policy areas and to sign up to the Social Chapter. The following sections dwelt on the economy (tax, trade, the single market, bureaucracy), agriculture (reform, the environment, animal welfare), 'a people's Europe' (decentralisation, subsidiarity, greater transparency), law and order (immigration, asylum, fraud), a wider Europe (stressing early enlargements), and security and defence. The manifesto sported a foreword from the Prime Minister and an end piece by Sir Christopher Prout. Throughout, it mixed examples of the policy successes of the

Conservative government with examples of the 'risks' posed by Labour and the Liberal Democrats. It was very thin on policy proposals. Particular mention was made of the Manifesto of the Party of European Socialists (PES), which was described as 'a lethal concoction of high taxation, high borrowing, bureaucratic meddling and extra burdens on business'. However, this reference was to lead to a major embarrassment when John Smith died on 12 May, as the original version, which had to be hastily rewritten, had included a reference to him signing up to the PES Manifesto in Brussels the previous November.

In preparing for the 1992 General Election, Chris Patten and Andrew Lansley had recognised that a manifesto normally provides just a one-day news story. If the content is to be noticed and absorbed, parts of it must be leaked, item by item, over a period of time. The 'near-term campaign' of January to March 1992 was just such an exercise in maximising publicity. But the absence of any substantial new policy proposals or of anything else that could be considered newsworthy in the 1994 Euro-manifesto meant that such an exercise could not be repeated. The government did have one major policy initiative up its sleeve, its White Paper on industrial competitiveness, but this was to be launched separately during the campaign and therefore could not be 'pre-leaked' in the manifesto. It was rumoured that the government's plans in other, more controversial areas, such as its Post Office privatisation plans, had been quietly postponed to avoid controversy. Other parts of the manifesto were effectively pre-empted by events. Nowhere was this more the case than with the emphasis on the 'national veto', a subject which had received a considerable airing during the blocking minority row in March.

Campaigns require leadership. In 1989, although Mrs Thatcher was very much at the helm in Downing Street, she had appeared at only two press conferences in London and had gone out campaigning on only two days. Her indifference and lack of involvement were cited as major factors in the party's poor performance, and there was a general determination that this mistake should be avoided. John Major had always liked campaigning, and was proud of his personal achievement in the 1992 General Election. He was much more active than his predecessor had ever been in a European election, involving himself in detailed decisions and in the manifesto drafting exercise, putting his name to two direct-mail letters, attending three national press conferences (it would have been four if the campaign had run its full length) and altogether spending six days actively campaigning in the field, including several major policy speeches.

The Conservative party still owed a substantial amount of money to Saatchi and Saatchi (allegedly nearly £2 million) for their massive advertising efforts in the 1992 General Election campaign. In 1994, the party had neither the resources nor the will to engage in large-scale advertising and there could be no question of changing agencies. Maurice Saatchi, Steve Hilton and David Kershaw worked on a programme which included the presentation of press conferences, and more importantly the preparation of two broadcasts and of poster advertising. For the Euro-enthusiasts, the advertisements chosen (by Mrs Thatcher) for the 1989 European election had been nightmarishly negative. One of their primary goals was to prevent the 1994 campaign veering towards explicit Euro-scepticism and in this they were broadly successful. Initially Saatchi and Saatchi supported an approach which backed a left-wing economic appeal which avoided any institutional issues; then they changed sides, backing Central Office's instinctive preference for more of an anti-Brussels approach. MEPs and Foreign Office representatives on the strategy committee forced Central Office to abandon its preferred slogan 'Putting Britain First in Europe' and to use the more unifying themes 'A Strong Britain in a Strong Europe' and 'Backing Britain in Europe'. For them, the monitoring and supervision of campaign material was an important means of preventing any 1989–style diversion of the campaign into a nationalist cul-de-sac.

The party had initially only allocated £1.25 million (later raised to £1.4 million) to spend on the local elections and the Euro-elections combined. The central expenses on administration, tours and broadcasts, as well as on security and press conferences, left no money for newspaper advertising (and, after the excesses of the 1987 general election campaign, the party had anyway lost enthusiasm for pouring money into this bottomless pit – one single-page advertisement in all national newspapers for just one day could cost £0.3m). But as the 1992 General Election had demonstrated, a considerable splash could be made with a quite limited nationwide poster display. As Chapter Seven shows, Saatchi and Saatchi's posters, though criticised by some, were among the more visible aspects of a largely invisible campaign.

Although the party was not able to avoid the complications caused by redistribution (see Chapter 3), it was able to minimise them. Initially, Central Office drew up advice arguing that any candidate whose new seat included less than 80 per cent of the old seat would have to submit to a full renomination process. This figure was later decreased to 70 per cent, and the calculation only applied to sitting members. Then Sir Christopher Prout pointed out that the National Union's rules of procedure were clear that an association did not in fact need to reselect where the new seat contained more than 50 per cent of the old one (since it was not reconstituted), although this interpretation only applied to sitting members. This view prevailed, and was accepted by the party, thus saving a number of incumbent MEPs from reselection processes. Where reselection was necessary, most associations ran accelerated processes, going straight to five-people shortlists.

In the event there were few problems. Having already switched from Midlands West, where he was first elected in 1979, to Wight and Hampshire South, where he had sat since 1984, Richard Simmonds gave up his seat to contest the nomination for South Downs West, but then had to abandon the quest when his health suddenly failed. Caroline Jackson had a difficult decision when her Wiltshire seat was reconstituted, at first with seats from Thames Valley and later with seats from Avon. She was in potential rivalry with her neighbour, Edward Kellett-Bowman, in Hampshire Central. But the clash was avoided when, thanks to careful timing of selection conferences by Central Office, she successfully moved west to the new Wiltshire North and Bath seat and he, after failing to win nomination in Hampshire North and Oxfordshire West, successfully moved south to the new Itchen, Test and Avon seat. All the other reselections passed off tranquilly, although there was a minor row in the unwinnable Cheshire North seat.

All but seven of the 32 incumbent Conservative MEPs stood again. Of those who stood down, two did so for reasons of health and five for reasons of age (including some reluctant retirees whose constituency activists had made it plain that they were regarded as being too old) – the average age of the five was 72, and one was 76. Fourteen of the 25 veterans seeking re-election had sat continuously since 1979, six since 1984 and four since 1989. The candidates included four other 1979 veterans. Edward Kellett-Bowman was first elected to Lancashire East in 1979, lost the seat in 1984, was selected for and won the seat of Hampshire Central in a 1988 by-election (following the death of Basil de Ferranti), and was successfully returned in 1989, only to have the seat redistributed out of existence. As was seen above, he was then selected (and successfully returned) to the new seat of Itchen, Test and Avon. Tom Spencer was first elected to Derbyshire in 1979, lost the seat in 1984, and then in 1989 was selected and returned to the seat of Surrey, first of the two safest Conservative seats in the country. Two former Scottish MEPs were also among the candidates. James Provan, who had been MEP for North East Scotland from 1979 to 1984, was selected for the new seat of South Downs West, second of the two safest Conservative seats. Alasdair Hutton, who had been MEP for South of Scotland from 1979 to 1989, stood again (unsuccessfully) for the same seat. Of the new candidates, only three had previously stood before for the European Parliament, but 27 had fought Westminster seats (altogether, 39 of the 85 candidates had previously contested a Westminster seat). One former MP (John Corrie) had previously been a member of the pre-1979 appointed European Parliament. One MP and former minister (Edwina Currie) and one peer (Earl of Stockton) joined the challengers. A number of former MPs and MEPs were rejected by selection committees. In all, the candidates included one MP, two former MPs, four peers, eleven former assistants to MPs, one former member of the Prime Minister's staff, and one minister's wife. Four candidates were former European Commission civil servants, four were former European Parliament officials, and one was previously an adviser to the leader of the British Conservatives in the EP. As to former professions, the vast majority of the candidates were concentrated in banking, consultancy, communications, management and publishing. The law represented the only other significant concentration, with three barristers, five solicitors, and two QCs (and four JPs). For the rest, there were eight farmers, five academics, three teachers, two civil servants, one army officer, one diplomat, one doctor, and one trade unionist. Only twelve of the 85 candidates were women. Over half of the candidates were in their late thirties or forties, and over two-thirds were married, with children. Fifty-seven of the candidates were university-educated, 25 of them at Oxbridge, and another 13 had had further education of some sort. The Conservative candidate for the Yorkshire South West seat, Christine Adamson, was French by origin, though she had long since married and worked in the United Kingdom.

Conservative MEPs have naturally tended to be on the pro-European wing of the party. Among the incumbent MEPs, only Bryan Cassidy claimed to be less Euro-inclined, although his election material, like that of most incumbents, stressed his achievements in the European Parliament. Among new candidates, Giles Chichester, the candidate for Devon and East Plymouth, and Andrew Turner, the candidate for Birmingham East, came nearest to the Euro-sceptical line although, at least before the election, there were no true Euro-sceptics. In a well-publicised initiative, Sir Teddy Taylor, one of the most prominent of anti-Maastricht MPs, sought nomination for the Essex South seat but, with the active connivance of the party organisation, he failed even to make the shortlist. As one of the most senior Conservatives said, 'Of course we could not have him. How could a Euro-sceptic run convincingly for Europe?'

At the beginning of the European elections campaign, the Conservative party was down to just 220 full-time constituency agents, its lowest level in post-war years (although still far more than the other parties could boast). Membership was seriously depleted and morale low. The party's Euro-constituency organisations depended on the gatherings of a few officers from the Westminster seats and an agent drawn from one of these who had to coordinate the seven or eight diverse associations. In seats with sitting MEPs, there existed a staff and hence a potential focus for organisation, but elsewhere there could be an almost complete void. Even where there were sitting MEPs, coordination could be very poor. In its routine activities, the Conservative organisation, nationally and in the regions, managed a considerable number of one day schools and conferences for candidates, for agents and for activists. Candidates were given the opportunity to do media training. The candidates met collectively on two occasions, once at a hotel outside Coventry (25–26 June 1993) and once at Central Office (14 February 1994). On both occasions the candidates were addressed by the Foreign Secretary, the Party Chairman, and Sir Christopher Prout. The February meeting was preceded by drinks with the Prime Minister at 10 Downing Street. In addition, the sitting MEPs met with the Prime Minister on three occasions.

Like their rivals, the Conservatives naturally targeted their efforts. But their chosen focus was almost entirely defensive. Even assuming that there would be no swing from the 1992 General Election, redistribution had only put two Labour seats, London North and Leicester, on the margin and there was no serious expectation of victory in either of these. However, London North West, Cumbria and Lancashire North, Lancashire Central, and several Midlands and Eastern seats were clearly under serious threat from Labour, and there was a chance of a Liberal Democrat breakthrough in almost every southern shire seat. The Conservatives recognised openly that they were engaged in a damage limitation exercise. They initially designated some twelve, eventually almost twenty, of their existing seats as 'critical', and made available to them special Central Office assistance of various kinds, including direct mailing. Preparations made at the centre were typical of a national election. Systematic media monitoring was arranged, so that opposition remarks in national and regional broadcasts and newspapers could be collated (and, on one occasion at least, during the 'beggars' controversy–see Chapter 8, this was to provide valuable evidence of Labour confusion). Arrangements made for the daily campaign routine consisted of an overnight news digest and field report, an early meeting with preparations for the press conference, a 10.30 gathering to wrap up arrangements after the press conference, and an evening meeting to prepare for the next day. Each national press conference was to be chaired by the party chairman, Sir Norman Fowler (though his place was taken occasionally by Gerry Malone), who would share the platform with one or more ministers and normally two MEPs (including one or both of Sir Christopher Prout or Bill Newton Dunn plus a spokesman). With the exceptions of the three addressed by the Prime Minister, which were held at Church House, the daily national press conferences were held at Central Office in Smith Square. By tacit agreement with the Labour Party, these generally began at 9.30 a.m., and the chairman was at pains to ensure that they ended in good time for journalists to be able to cross Smith Square to Transport House for the Labour Party conferences at 10.30. Like the Labour Party and the Liberal Democrats, the Conservatives had a 'spy' present in most of their rivals' press conferences.

As in general elections, a Questions of Policy committee was established under the chairmanship of Tony Newton. Its ministerial members included Baroness Chalker, Ann Widdecombe and Sir John Cope. Other members included Ben Patterson, a sitting MEP, Adam Fergusson, who had been an MEP from 1979 to 1984 and Damian Green from the policy unit at 10 Downing Street. The committee met from April to mid-campaign. Its role was to monitor election issues and to ensure consistency between the campaign and government policy.

The party, and particularly its Euro-enthusiasts, was presented with a particular problem in the form of its internal dissenters. The traumas of 1989 were at the back of many people's minds. Prominent backbench Euro-sceptical MPs, such as Sir Teddy Taylor and Bill Cash, refused to be silent, voicing their disenchantment from the sidelines throughout the spring, and the Whips seemed unable to draw the dissidents back into line. Backbench dissidence was one matter, but the 1989 campaign had involved disastrous slanging matches between the party's senior politicians. Here there were also grounds for worry. The cabinet's three acknowledged Euro-sceptics, Michael Portillo, Peter Lilley and John Redwood, had been making their private doubts indirectly known, but they were not expected to rock the boat. As described in Chapter 2, the Euro-sceptics were playing a longer game, and the early departure of John Major, which disaster in the European elections might well have provoked, whether in July or November, would not serve their purposes. They did not want the blame for disaster, and they did not have a sufficiently credible candidate in place to profit from the ensuing turmoil. The Euro-sceptics also had their eyes on another, potentially more divisive date: 1996. As one whip remarked, 'They are keeping their powder dry for the fight over the IGC.' More worrying for the party was the potential role of its grandees in the Lords, over whom the Prime Minister was known to have little influence. Would Norman Tebbit or Cecil Parkinson rock the boat? Worse still, what would Margaret Thatcher do? So poor were relations between the government and these still influential former ministers that there was little contact between them and little attempt was made to persuade them to play a constructive role or, at the least, to lie low. As late as the day of the campaign launch it was not known what role, if any, Baroness Thatcher intended to play, although an ambiguous statement made on 30 March suggested that, in the logic of the Euro-sceptics' long game, she would not actively undermine the Prime Minister.

Despite such uncertainties, the Euro-enthusiasts within the party were quietly satisfied, having largely warded off what they saw as the twin dangers of a repeat of 1989 and an overly Euro-sceptical campaign. The question arises as to how this was achieved, given the apparent strength of the Euro-sceptics. Part of the answer lies in the lack of overall organisation among the Euro-sceptical camp. Whereas Conservative backbench opposition to the Maastricht Treaty had been centrally funded and organised, a more Euro-sceptical approach to the Euro-elections was more a matter of attitude than anything else. Second, although Mr Major was prepared to shift his political language towards a more Euro-sceptical tone, this did not mean that he was personally close to the Euro-sceptics; on the contrary, he saw the Euro-sceptics within his cabinet as a thorn in the flesh. Third, the Conservative Euro-sceptics did not all gravitate around the same figures within the party, and none of the major figures were prepared to act as disloyal standard-bearers during the Euro-elections campaign. Thus, what seemed like a united front was more a loose and

uncoordinated coalition of like-minded forces. Under these circumstances, it was relatively easy to keep the Euro-sceptics out of the
strategy committee and the manifesto committee, and outbreaks of
disgruntlement among backbench Euro-sceptics were effectively
'bought off' through such devices as statements from the Prime
Minister or the consultative exercise initiated by Douglas Hurd.

5 Labour

Until the late 1980s the Labour Party was far more divided over Europe than any other British political party, but, as Conservative divisions grew through the late 1980s and the early 1990s, so Labour seemed to find a new, positive and enduring consensus. The 1964 Labour government was opposed to Britain's entry to the EEC but, after re-election in 1966, the party's approach softened, and in April 1967 the cabinet agreed to apply to join the Community. Because of de Gaulle's opposition and the November 1967 devaluation this 'second try' was aborted. However in 1968 the Hague Summit decided that negotiations should start in June 1970. Labour unexpectedly lost the 1970 General Election, so that it was the new Conservative government of Edward Heath that reopened entry negotiations on 30 June 1970, and, on 22 June 1972, signed the Treaty of Rome. Back in opposition, the majority in the Labour Party had meanwhile swung back to its former anti-Market stance. In the 1972 House of Commons vote on EC membership, the Labour leadership imposed a three-line whip against membership. Sixty-nine Labour MPs, among them John Smith, defied the Whips, and a further 20 Labour MPs abstained. Britain joined the EEC on 1 January 1973, and thereafter the Labour Party's outright opposition softened into a commitment, repeated in the February and October 1974 manifestos, to renegotiate the terms of entry and to put the result to a General Election or a referendum, the referendum commitment springing from Harold Wilson's determination to avoid an irrevocable split within his party. In 1975, following the Wilson government's much-trumpeted renegotiation, seven cabinet members still voted 'no' in the referendum and the Special Labour Party Conference on 26 April 1975 supported a 'no' recommendation by 3.7 million to 1.4 million votes. The referendum produced a 67 per cent to 33 per cent victory for the 'yes' camp, with Labour supporters being evenly divided. The episode caused deep wounds. Recognising the depths of feeling within his party, Harold Wilson had allowed members of the government to take opposing sides in the referendum campaign. This led to the sight of Labour pro-Marketeers, chief among them Roy Jenkins, campaigning on the same platform alongside prominent Conservative and Liberal politicians. Although the anti-Market camp, mostly to be found on the left wing of the party, was demoralised by the 'yes' vote in the referendum, it was not disarmed. In particular, lingering anti-Market sentiments decided Mr Callaghan against joining the European Monetary System. Labour continued to back membership, accompanied by reform, at the 1979 General Election, but following the Callaghan government's defeat, the left wing of the party became resurgent. Michael Foot was elected party leader, and at the 1980 Labour Party Conference delegates backed a motion calling for withdrawal. The irrevocable split in the party that Harold Wilson had feared finally occurred on 26 March 1981, when the Social Democratic Party was launched by four prominent former Labour politicians, Roy Jenkins among them. In July 1981 Labour's National Executive Committee issued a policy statement explaining that 'Labour will have no choice but to carry through a radical, socialist economic strategy . . . which would inevitably bring us into direct conflict with the EEC. . . . (O)ur policies are in conflict with either the letter or the practice of the Treaty of Rome.' Labour subsequently fought, and badly lost, the 1983 General Election on a manifesto that, among its promises, contained an express commitment to take Britain out of the Community without a further referendum. Following Labour's heavy electoral defeat, Michael Foot stood down as party leader and was replaced by Neil Kinnock. Thereafter, the party begun a slow shift away from its former extremism, culminating in the 1987–9 policy review. In the 1984 European elections Labour promised only to 'retain the option of withdrawal' while working for further reform. In the 1987 General Election manifesto, withdrawal was spurned in favour of continued membership, but Labour would continue to 'reject EEC interference with our policy for national recovery and renewal'. Labour's 1987 defeat led Neil Kinnock to launch a fundamental policy review, and this was to include a shift towards a more positive attitude to Europe. Some of the intellectual ground for this change was prepared in a Fabian pamphlet written by David Martin MEP, then leader of the Labour MEPs, and published in February 1988, which argued that Labour should work with other socialist parties in Europe to 'bring common sense to the Common Market'. Neil Kinnock wrote the preface to the pamphlet. In September 1988, Jacques Delors addressed the TUC Congress and spoke at length of the social dimension to the EC. In October, at the Labour Party Conference, Neil Kinnock took up the theme, calling for Britain to 'take a lead in building a social Europe'. The changing attitude of the trades unions was important in facilitating this policy shift, and so was Mrs Thatcher's increasingly strident position; as the Conservatives vacated a moderate European policy stance Labour was increasingly encouraged to take it over. The start of the 1989 European Election campaign saw the publication of Labour's policy review document, *Meet the Challenge, Make the Change*, which took a decisively pro-European stance. The accompanying 1989 manifesto, *Meeting the Challenge in Europe*, stated 'It is in Europe in the 1990s that our most important challenges and valuable opportunities will arise.' The 1989 European Election was a success for the Labour Party. Labour rallied around its new policy and, as Chapter 2 showed, was able to profit from the Conservative's disarray and their confused and misjudged campaign. For the first time since 1974, Labour won more votes in a national election than the Conservatives. It was Mrs Thatcher's first national electoral defeat. Labour gained 13 seats from the Conservatives and took 40.1 per cent of the vote. The election consolidated Labour's pro-European stance. After articles and statements by Neil Kinnock in the autumn of 1986, the idea of proposing a conditional possibility of joining the ERM developed, although it took until 1989 for the leadership generally to back UK entry. In 1991 the party's economic sub-committee adopted a recommendation in favour of economic and monetary union. The 1991 Labour Party Conference overwhelmingly passed a resolution supporting the right of legislative initiative and codecision powers for the European Parliament, the creation of a democratically accountable single European central bank, and further moves towards 'eventual economic and monetary union on terms acceptable to the British Parliament'. There were no critical motions or speakers in the 1991 Conference debates. Some eminent Labour politicians, particularly Bryan Gould, Tony Benn and Peter Shore, still maintained a less enthusiastic stance and opposed moves to economic integration, but they were increasingly marginalised as a diminishing minority within the party.

Labour's MEPs had an important part in encouraging the party towards a more pro-European stance. They played a growing role within the party's structures with, for example, ex officio representation on the NEC. The 1991 party conference created a new and increasingly important role for them as part of the electoral college for leadership positions, and this was to give them more influence over the policy stance of leadership candidates. Because of their increased numbers and greater coherence, Labour MEPs also carried more political clout within the European Parliament.

The party's manifesto for the 1992 General Election pledged that Labour would 'play an active part' in EMU negotiations and end the Conservative opt-out from the Social Chapter. Following the trauma of the party's unexpected defeat, Neil Kinnock decided to stand down at once. The pro-European John Smith's decisive 91 per cent majority in the ensuing leadership election consolidated the party's new European policy, and Bryan Gould's 9 per cent vote further undermined the influence of the Euro-sceptics within the party. However, the Gould–Shore–Benn view was to surface once more during the protracted debates accompanying the ratification of the Maastricht Treaty in 1992–3. The Labour leadership was fully in favour of the treaty. However, the party chose to abstain at the second and third reading stages of the Maastricht Bill because of the government's opt-out on the Social Chapter, which Labour's Shadow Foreign Secretary, Jack Cunningham, described as being 'fundamentally unacceptable to us'. Behind these official positions, the party found it difficult to resist the temptation provided by the Conservative Party's disarray, and the ratification process was accompanied by a large number of Opposition-inspired filibustering and spoiling amendments (which carefully avoided wrecking the Treaty itself), one of which only narrowly missed bringing down the government. The media's interest was focussed chiefly on the government's difficulties, but leading Labour Euro-sceptics, including Diane Abbott, Tony Benn, Denzil Davies, Bryan Gould, Peter Hain, Austin Mitchell and Peter Shore unsuccessfully tried to re-launch a fundamental debate about the Labour Party's basically pro-Maastricht stance. Nevertheless, a powerful indication of how far the party had come was provided by the simple fact that Labour MPs had never before all voted the same way on Europe. The ascendancy of the party's Euro-enthusiasm was confirmed on 27 September 1992, when a disgruntled Bryan Gould finally resigned from the shadow cabinet, citing among other reasons the party's support for the ERM and the EMU process, and on 9 February 1994, when he announced his forthcoming resignation from Parliament.

Before the 1992 General Election a proposal was made to hold annual European Conferences of the party. The first took place in Brighton in 1993. On 4–6 February 1994 the party held a combined European and Local Government Conference in Glasgow. The conference was effectively the pre-launch of the two campaigns, with the elections being described as 'rungs on a ladder leading towards the next General Election'. Keynote speakers included John Smith, Pauline Green as EPLP leader, and the leader of the German SPD, Rudolf

Scharping. The conference showed strong support for the party leadership and for the line on Europe. Recurring themes included Labour unity, contrasted with Conservative disunity, unemployment, and the use of both elections as referendums on the government's economic policies, with particular emphasis on tax. In her speech, Pauline Green was applauded when she said that 'Labour leads for Britain', and 'Europe is now part and parcel of our domestic policy in Britain . . . . This is a message that Labour has understood.' Labour's European policy stance was further underlined by a 1 March 1994 visit to Brussels by Gordon Brown. The Shadow Chancellor met with the Commission President, Jacques Delors, and the British Labour Commissioner, Bruce Millan, and addressed a meeting of the EPLP.

Thus, the Labour Party approached the 1994 European Elections united around a popular leader and a positive policy stance and media image. Morale was high. The disappointment of April 1992 had largely died away and had been replaced by fresh enthusiasm. Ever since the government's 16 September 1992 'Black Wednesday' débâcle, the Labour Party had consistently enjoyed high scores in the polls. Under John Smith's leadership the party had continued to flourish, although its active membership and its finances left much to be desired. Even during its procedural manouevres and at times ambiguous positioning in the Maastricht Treaty ratification process, Labour continued to draw sympathetic publicity. Most of the big and bitter policy battles had been fought, and won, under Neil Kinnock's leadership and, with the all-important 1993 OMOV reform under its belt, the Smith leadership team had opted for quiet and patient consolidation of these achievements. There was little factional fighting. Two traditional scourges of the centre-right of the party, Dennis Skinner and Tony Benn, had been voted off the NEC in 1992 and 1993 respectively. It seemed that Euro-sceptic MPs like Peter Shore and Austin Mitchell were unlikely to rock the boat. Having fought and lost his policy battles, Bryan Gould was preparing to step down. Thus, the party would go into the elections safe in the knowledge that there would be no contradictory policy rows and no eminent personalities to champion them.

After the April 1992 General Election and John Smith's election to the leadership there had been substantial reorganisation at party headquarters in Walworth Road. Larry Whitty, a noted pro-European, continued as General Secretary. David Hill's role as Director of Publicity was extended to being chief spokesman for John Smith. The new Policy Director, Roland Wales, brought a different approach to the job from the long-serving Geoff Bish. Under Sally Morgan the job of National Agent was transformed to campaigns and elections, whilst Peter Coleman looked after structure and organisation; a new division in the organisation was introduced between Sally Morgan's campaign and elections department on the one hand, and David Hill's press and presentations department on the other.

As Deputy Leader of the party, Margaret Beckett took general charge of campaign planning, but the Shadow Foreign Secretary, Jack Cunningham, naturally had a special interest in the preparations for the European elections. In October 1990, following the recommendations of a consultancy firm on the rationalisation of the EPLP's organisation, Dianne Hayter, who had long experience of national and European politics, was appointed Chief Executive of the European Parliamentary Labour Party's secretariat. London-based, Hayter had particular responsibility for relations between the EPLP and the party's front bench and Walworth Road, and was to play a leading role in coordinating preparations for the European elections. A campaign strategy group was set up in May 1992 (and, at staff level, a 'task force' was set up after the 1993 party conference) and it met monthly until May 1994, when it was transformed into the Campaign Management Team (CMT). The CMT met daily during the local election campaign and, in slightly different form, the European election campaign (see Table 5.1).

The hurried redistribution of Euro-constituencies produced its organisational problems for Labour, as it did for the other parties,

Table 5.1   *The Labour Party's strategy committee for the 1994 European election*

The European Parliamentary Labour Party: Pauline Green, MEP (Leader), Dianne Hayter (Chief Executive)

The Labour Party Front Bench: Dr Jack Cunningham, MP (Shadow Foreign Secretary), George Robertson, MP (European Affairs spokesman until October 1993), Joyce Quin, MP (from November 1993), Jack Straw, MP (only from 12 May 1994)

Walworth Road: Larry Whitty (General Secretary), Sally Morgan (National Agent), David Hill (Director of Publicity), Jo Moore (Chief Press Officer), Roland Wales (Policy Director), Karen Buck (Campaign Strategy Officer)

The leadership: Margaret Beckett (Deputy Leader – Chair), Nick Peccorelli (Margaret Beckett's office)

but there were few upsets. The party's redistribution expert, David Gardner, had had great success in arranging convincing submissions to the Boundary Commissions during the contemporaneous redistribution of Westminster seats. He had some similar success in affecting the modification of the initial proposals made by the European Constituency Committees in August 1993. Notable changes included the dropping of the proposed Wales coastal seat, which would have favoured Plaid Cymru, and of a proposed North Cheshire and South Manchester seat, which would have been Conservative. An adverse rearrangement of Central Lancashire was avoided, and the English European Constituency Committee accepted Labour's proposal in South and West Yorkshire, though these were Labour seats in any case. Labour almost 'won' a seat by insisting on keeping the Thames Valley constituency intact and not moving Reading, but failed to get the changes it wanted in the East Midlands, Hereford and Derby.

As in the Conservative Party, there were some jitters over whether the French government would continue to hold up the increase in the number of Euro-seats, but the new boundaries themselves led to surprisingly little trouble over candidates. The rules for reselection had been set out in the 1993 NEC report and a code of conduct had been drafted. There was a briefing for all candidates at the October 1993 party conference. By December, letters had been sent asking everyone for their preferences as to which seat they wished to fight. The NEC rules were clear about reselection procedures in changed Euro-constituencies where only one sitting MEP wished to stand. They were more ambiguous in cases where more than one sitting MEP was involved. In the event, all forty incumbent Labour MEPs who had decided to stand again found seats. There was some awkwardness for Mel Read, first elected in 1989 to the old seat of Leicester, and Christine Oddy, first elected in 1989 to the old seat of Midlands Central. The redrawn seat of Leicester was a Conservative marginal which, it was calculated, the Conservatives would have won in 1989 and which, on the basis of the April 1992 vote, they would easily take, but which they were likely to lose on current polling figures. Nevertheless, a discouraged Read tried unsuccessfully for Oddy's redrawn seat of Coventry and North Warwickshire (which had gained the Westminster constituencies of Nuneaton and North Warwickshire from the old Leicester Euro-constituency), before finally settling for the new Euro-constituency of Nottingham and North West Leicestershire, which had been 'freed' by incumbent MEP Ken Coates' move to the safe Labour seat of North Nottingham and Chesterfield. Sue

Waddington was later selected for the new Leicester seat and, in the event, all three candidates, Read, Oddy and Waddington, were successfully returned. The only other problem was a close-fought battle between two local women candidates for the new and winnable European seat of Sussex South and Crawley. Joyce Edmond Smith secured the nomination although she was narrowly to lose the election (by 1,746 votes).

The selections to the European constituencies provided the Labour Party with a first test for its 'One Member One Vote' (OMOV) procedures, which the new leader had fought so hard to get through the October 1993 party conference. The consensus was that all had gone well. Numbers voting ranged from around 500 to 1,500 – with turnout in the range of between 50 and 60 per cent, although well over 2,000 votes were cast in Wales South East. The OMOV procedure was only triggered in the case of three sitting MEPs, Stan Newens (London Central), Richard Balfe (London South Inner), and Michael McGowan (Leeds), and all three won reselection easily. Indeed, it was noted that the procedure gave a considerable advantage to well-known local (or national) personalities (including incumbent MEPs) and tended to minimise the traditional selection criteria of performance on the hustings and trades union influence. Despite the special shortlist provision whereby one of the five shortlisted candidates had to be a woman, it was also argued that the procedure tended to favour male over female candidates, although in the end there were more female Labour candidates (22) than Conservative (12). In general, candidate selection passed off smoothly. Forty of the 45 Labour MEPs stood again. The long-serving MEP for Glasgow, Janey Buchan, retired, and ill health obliged John Bird, MEP for Midlands West, to stand down. Three MEPs, Geoffrey Hoon (Derbyshire), Llewellyn Smith (South East Wales) and George Stevenson (Staffordshire East), had been elected to Westminster in the April 1992 General Election and now relinquished the Strasbourg part of their dual mandates. Of the 17 Labour MEPs first elected in 1979, six still held their seats. Three of these, Alf Lomas, Tom Megahy and Dr Barry Seal, retained some of their original Euro-scepticism, but almost all the new candidates were enthusiastically pro-European, and one or two of them were described at party headquarters as being 'too enthusiastic', and at least one as an 'ultra-federalist' who needed to be 'kept in line'. However, there was a complete absence from the selection processes of the old distinction, which had so beset the party in the early 1980s, between pro- and anti-marketeers.

Labour candidates were slightly more likely to have been university educated than their Conservative counterparts (60 as opposed to 57; another eight Labour candidates went on to further education after school), but less likely to have been at Oxbridge (seven as opposed to 25). Fewer candidates had previously stood for a Westminster seat (15, as opposed to 39) but more had had local government experience (47, as opposed to 29). A further twelve had been active in local politics. Altogether, four candidates had previously been MPs (including one former minister, John Tomlinson), and two had been MPs' assistants. Six candidates had former EC or European Parliament experience, including a translator, an interpreter, a former *stagiaire* in the Commission, a former Socialist Group *stagiaire*, an 'experienced lobbyist of the European Parliament', an MEP's assistant, and a former assistant to the Socialist Group in the European Parliament. Three candidates had previously contested a Strasbourg seat. Gisela Gscheider, the Labour candidate for Worcestershire and South Warwickshire, was of German origin though, like her French counterpart among the Conservative candidates, Christine Adamson, she had studied, married, and settled in England. Half of the Labour candidates were in their late thirties or forties. Ten were over sixty, and five in their twenties. Labour's oldest candidate, Ken Stewart, the sitting MEP for Merseyside West, was sixty-eight years old. Labour's youngest candidate, Eluned Morgan, twenty-seven years old. She went on to become Britain's youngest MEP. The bulk (61) of Labour candidates were married and had children.

Only fourteen candidates came from a traditional trade or manual background. These included three miners, two engineers, a foundry-worker, a steel works apprentice, a shipyard worker, a railwayman, a railway signalman, a bus driver, a postal worker, and a gardener. Ten candidates had previously been full-time trades unionists or party activists and one had been a full-time party agent. Six candidates considered themselves to be authors, two were preachers, two were former policemen, and one was a magistrate. Two candidates expressly pointed out that they were practising Roman Catholics. A strikingly high proportion – over a third – of candidates were, or had been, involved in school or higher education. Five were school governors. A similar proportion were in communications (publishing and journalism), the law, management, consultancy work and public services.

Among the fresh contenders, Glenys Kinnock undoubtedly enjoyed the highest profile, and the media ran several joint profiles of her (frequently together with Pauline Green) and Edwina Currie, the highest profile Conservative candidate. Phillip Whitehead, MP for Derby North from 1970 to 1983 and a former television producer, and Tony Gardner, MP for Rushcliffe, 1966–1970, also stood out, and several candidates enjoyed high local prominence from their positions in local government.

Where sitting MEPs had managed to build up their own local networks, there was some semblance of a structure of Euro-constituency organisation, but otherwise everything tended to be administered through the component Westminster constituencies. In some cases, Euro-structures were reluctantly established, even though, with further redistributions ahead, they could only be very temporary.

Party headquarters arranged two national meetings for candidates, one at the October 1993 Party Conference, and another in January 1994. Brief schools for Euro-agents, one national and two regional, were also organised by Walworth Road and, for the EPLP, Dianne Hayter (who, together with the rest of the London EPLP secretariat, was based at the European Parliament's offices in Queen Anne's Gate until the beginning of the campaign). The Labour Party has traditionally fought shy of direct involvement with advertising firms, but it has developed the concept of a 'shadow agency', with Labour-sympathetic professionals lending their skills in the preparation of advertising and broadcasts. A polling committee was established. Poll presentations were done by Nick Moon and NOP. The committee included Sally Morgan, Karen Buck, Rex Osborn, as well as one well-known journalist and polls specialist, and Roger Jowell, together with the shadow agency and NOP. Walworth Road sent out letters to activists and supporters in key seats. Practical preparations were made for the campaign proper. A media monitoring meeting would be held every day at 7.00 a.m. to prepare the ground for the a 9.30 a.m. meeting, held at Transport House, of the participants in the morning's press conference. Basing itself on the model of the Clinton presidental campaign organisation, Walworth Road set up a 'rapid rebuttal' team of some five party officials. Jo Moore and David Hill produced most of the scripts for the press conferences themselves. These were to be held at Transport House and, by tacit agreement, most would begin at 10.30 a.m. The EPLP leader was to attend every press conference, and it was hoped to have another MEP, preferably an appropriate EPLP spokesperson, on the platform beside her. The role envisaged for the party leader was, as we shall see, vital.

If party morale was unusually high in the run up to the Euro-elections, expectations were nevertheless modest. In large part, this was based on the knowledge that the Conservative Party had fought a poor and divided campaign in 1989. Uncharacteristically, Conservative voters had tended to stay at home, and this had allowed the Labour Party to win thirteen seats from the Conservatives on an 8.5 per cent national swing. As party activists knew only too well, it was the Labour Party that traditionally had trouble in motivating its voters to go to the Euro-polls, a problem always exacerbated by the proximity of the May local elections. Even assuming Labour voters wanted to 'kick the government while it's down', would they want to kick it twice within one month? Moreover, the party had concluded that losses were inevitable in the local elections, and was afraid the expected Liberal Democrat advances would dampen enthusiasm. The party was particularly wary about the apparently encouraging opinion polls. The polls had spectacularly failed in 1992, and a *Guardian*/ICM poll published on 13 April seemed to show that a sizeable Tory vote was hidden among the 'don't knows'. For all of these reasons, Labour expectations were low, and some even feared the loss of three or four Euro-seats. On the other hand, the worst consequences of redistribution had been avoided, and some of the six additional seats were expected to go to Labour. But if the party was on a roll, this was felt more likely to lead to a consolidation of the 1989 result than any significant advances.

Thus, like the other parties, Walworth Road targetted its efforts. Ten possible gains were focussed on, together with the marginal seats of two incumbent MEPs, London North and North East Scotland. Pauline Green's London North seat had been an unexpected gain in 1989. The seat mainly consisted of solid Tory suburbia between the Green Belt and the M25 in the north, and the North Circular to the south. It included Baroness Thatcher's old Finchley constituency. The Boundary Commission had left the seat untouched, and a projection based on the April 1992 General Election results gave the Conservatives a 12 per cent majority. It figured high on the Conservatives' 'hit list'. Pauline Green was a prestige candidate for the party. Not only was she currently leader of the EPLP, and a valued member of the NEC, but she had been confirmed by John Smith at the party's 4–6 February 1994 Glasgow conference (where she had delivered a rousing speech) as its candidate for the presidency of the socialist grouping within the Parliament, and the party was therefore eager to ensure that the seat was held. Henry McCubbin's 1989 win in North East Scotland was the result of one of those rare phenomena, a genuine three-way split, complicated still further by a strong fourth party showing. He had unseated the Tory incumbent, James Provan, with 30.6 per cent of the vote. The SNP had won 29.4 per cent, and the Conservatives 26.6 per cent. However, projections based on the April 1992 General Election gave the Conservatives a clear majority, with the SNP second, Labour only third, and the Liberal Democrats in a strong fourth place. This was the SNP's top target, especially given the government's unpopularity, and Labour were particularly eager to keep the seat to demonstrate the limits of the SNP's appeal. Party organisers were sent to all the target seats. Direct subsidies were made avaliable to a few seats, but the bulk went to North East Scotland. In the event, the SNP's momentum in North East Scotland proved as irresistible as Labour's advances in the south east of England but, with the exception of Mr McCubbin's defeat, the Labour Party's targets were not only won, but in several cases far exceeded.

Because of their proximity, the local elections and the Euro-elections had always been seen as parts of a continuum. The Euro-campaign was frequently described as a 'ten-week campaign' and several strategy papers referred to the two as a 'double referendum' on the government's record. Given this perspective, the local elections provided Labour with a good send off and, it should perhaps be stressed, an unexpected one. Because the party had fared so well in the anti-poll tax atmosphere of 1990, a net loss of seats was feared (on 31 March the *Guardian* reported that Labour was privately admitting it could lose up to 200 seats), but the Conservative slump was such that Labour made a net gain of 88 seats nationally and won 45 per cent of the vote to the Liberal Democrats' 27.5 per cent and the Conservatives' 27 per cent. In total, Labour had control of 17 of London's 32 boroughs (having gained control of four and lost control of one). This triumph was only marred by some disturbing losses to the Liberal Democrats in provincial city centres. In retrospect, several high-ranking party officials were privately prepared to admit that the party had been too pessimistic in its expectations, but they also pointed out that, because the campaigns had been planned together, it had been difficult to change the overall campaign strategy, predicated as it was on local government losses in May. (John Smith's untimely death was to complicate matters even further.)

Because they were to be held on the same day, the five by-election campaigns became an integral part of the overall campaign effort. Four of the by-elections were expected to return Labour candidates with comfortable majorities, but a feature of Labour's strategy that was much criticised at times was its determined challenge in the Eastleigh by-election, a seat where it had come third in 1992. A year earlier the party's vote had been more than halved in the two nearby seats of Newbury and Christchurch, although both were classic Liberal Democrat versus Conservative battlegrounds. Nevertheless, as early as February there were press reports that Labour was planning a 'fight to win' campaign, and two senior shadow Cabinet members, Frank Dobson and Jack Straw, were dispatched to study the lay of the land. In a campaign rally on 22 March John Smith said, 'There are risks in running such a high-profile campaign . . . but there is a risk in not trying . . . we can win.' Eastleigh was a strange constituency, combining coast, countryside and urban communities, but Eastleigh itself had once been a major railway town and still contained pockets of traditional working-class Labour voters. The decision was taken in order to demonstrate the limits of the Liberal Democrat 'surge' and to show that Labour remained an electoral force in the south. A strong showing would make Labour seem a serious challenger in areas that had previously been assigned to a simple Conservative–Liberal Democrat struggle. In the event, the government's decision to choose the same date for the by-election as the Euro-elections risked swamping this strategy, but Labour's determined challenge also had the more prosaic advantage of pinning down Liberal Democrat activists and resources.

The three major European political groupings, the European People's Party (EPP), the Party of European Socialists (PES) and the European Liberal Democrat and Reformist Party (ELDR), all adopted pan-European manifestos for the 1994 European elections. The British Conservatives disassociated themselves from the EPP manifesto, but the PES manifesto was enthusiastically and very publicly signed by John Smith in Brussels at a special 5–6 November 1993 PES Congress. However, despite John Smith's enthusiasm, the Labour Party was obliged to provide its own interpretation of some of the manifesto's commitments, which were to provide the Conservative 'spin doctors' with a rare piece of ammunition.

The Euro-manifesto exercise was in many respects a repeat of the successful 1989 experience in drafting the manifesto of the Confederation of Socialist Parties of the EC (as the predecessor of the PES was known). In 1988–9, Neil Kinnock had opted for a constructive and enthusiastic role in the drafting process. It was a way for the new, post-policy review Labour Party to confirm its European credentials and to erode the anti-European image of it that many of its continental partners still retained. Positive participation also gave the party a chance to control the content. The overall experience was judged to have been advantageous, and there was no question of not participating in the 1994 exercise. On 9 December 1992 the PES Bureau agreed its procedure for adopting what would be the first PES manifesto. Gerd Walter, the German SPD Minister for European Affairs in the Land of Schleswig-Holstein was given overall responsibility for drafting the manifesto. Early in 1993, the PES established a series of drafting sub-committees, each concentrating on a particular major policy theme. Jack Cunningham, together with a Spanish Socialist MP, Elena Flores, co-chaired the drafting sub-committee on international relations, but the Labour Party's European Affairs spokesman, George Robertson, also had overall responsibility for the Labour Party's input. A first draft of the manifesto was presented to the PES Bureau (comprised of the leaders of the component national parties) at the beginning of March 1993, where a timetable for the rest of the process was agreed. The end of April was set as the deadline for amendments from the national parties, to be considered by the Bureau in May, with final adoption scheduled for November.

The final draft, signed in Brussels on 5–6 November 1993, was an action programme divided into seven areas; jobs, sexual equality, the environment and the consumer, peace and security, immigration and racism, fighting organised crime, and democracy. The first and the last of these categories were to prove problematic for Labour. Employment-creation had long been identified as a major concern of all the European socialist parties, a concern further emphasised in the adoption of a 9 December 1993 declaration, *Put Europe to Work*, by the leaders of the Party of European Socialists (also referred to as the Larsson Report, after the former Swedish Finance Minister who drafted it). The PES manifesto spoke about the need 'to create and maintain more jobs by reorganising work . . . with measures agreed between the social partners'. It went on; 'These include a substantial cut in working time to ensure a better division of the available work. Several approaches are possible, including a working week of 35 hours or four days, leave for training and voluntary part-time work.' The Conservatives were quick to pick up on this clause and were able to make much political capital from it; was it a solid policy commitment and, if so, did the Labour Party subscribe to it?' Asked specifically about a 35-hour week, Mr Smith said 'No, we are not in favour of that' (*Sunday Times*, 7 November 1993), but contradictory statements from other Labour politicians obliged the party to distance itself from the PES manifesto. On *Newsnight* on 2 February 1994, Jack Cunningham said that whilst 'we don't opt out of any' of the manifesto's provisions, they were only 'broad statements of the kind of Europe we want to see'. A second provision, in the 'democracy' section, was to prove similarly problematic. 'We want the European Parliament,' said the manifesto, 'to have a right of initiative, and for co-decision between the European Parliament and the Council of Ministers and majority voting to be the rule.' The ambiguity about the proposed scope of majority voting was skillfully turned by the Conservatives into an apparent Labour commitment to do away with the British veto. The charge was to be a major theme of the Conservatives' campaign and was the basis of Mr Major's March jibe in the House of Commons that Mr Smith was 'Monsieur Oui, the poodle of Brussels'. Once again, the charges obliged the Labour leadership to distance itself from the PES manifesto and to downgrade its importance from a commonly-agreed policy platform to a 'shared vision' existing 'alongside' the Labour Party's national manifesto. The PES manifesto pointed out that 'for the first time, we are fighting the European elections as the Party of European Socialists', but it went on to acknowledge that 'we all have different traditions and our own responsibilities'. In the case of the Labour Party, those differences were to enjoy a far higher profile than the broad raft of policy provisions where there was complete agreement.

Accounts vary as to how the veto and 35-hour week provisions became potentially damaging issues. In the opinion of one senior Labour politician, 'It wasn't a policy cock-up. It was political mismanagement. It could easily have been smoothed over.' A high-ranking party official pointed out that 'the annoying thing about the whole episode was that there was no substantial problem'. Labour's increasingly enthusiastic participation in the International Socialist Confederation and the PES meant that, by now, a number of leading Labour politicians were seasoned hands at the European drafting process, where often translation inadvertently changed words and meanings and long battles could be fought over nuances. Vigilance was the key, and both references had been spotted as being potentially dangerous. George Robertson had ringed them as 'issues to fight on' but in the November 1993 reshuffle of the shadow cabinet, following the annual elections in the parliamentary Labour Party, he had been made Shadow Secretary of State for Scotland and had thereafter taken his 'eye off the ball'. Neil Kinnock, who was involved in the parallel exercise in drafting the national manifesto, had spotted both as being potentially awkward, but had assumed they would be dealt with by the leader's office. The qualified majority voting reference was a straightforward translation error. The original English language version had used the word 'norm' rather than 'rule'. But there was no firm commitment in the PES manifesto's reference to a 35-hour working week. The most likely explanation here was that the Conservatives, and through them the press, had managed to obtain an earlier draft of the manifesto, where the commitment to a 35-hour working week had indeed been more substantial. Early Conservative electoral material appeared to refer to this draft, rather than to the final PES manifesto version. Several senior figures within the party felt that both charges could have been rebutted. In the event they weren't, and as a result the PES manifesto was slightly discredited and played a lesser part in the campaign. This was a disappointment to the party's Euro-enthusiasts, who had seen the PES manifesto as part of a genuinely European campaign, but it was not entirely unexpected (see Table 5.2).

The PES manifesto was attractively presented as a large, glossy brochure, with its contents concentrated into small, readable paragraphs and simply-presented key sentences. The text was illustrated with many photographs and the PES's official symbol of a red rose was much in evidence. In 'advertising-speak', it was 'anchored around a

Table 5.2   A 'non-problem': the Labour Party's manifesto commitments and the 35-hour week

PES Group European manifesto	Labour's European manifesto	Conservative manifesto
to create and maintain more jobs by reorganising work . . . with measures agreed between the social partners . . . These include a substantial cut in working time to ensure a better division of the available work. Several approaches are possible, including a working week of 35 hours or four days, leave for training and voluntary part-time work.	This might involve reductions in working time to ensure a better division of the available work. There are many possible approaches to this. But we will not introduce legislation to enforce a 35-hour week. It is a matter primarily for agreement between employers and employees . . .	Labour MEPs supported plans for a vast job-destruction package – including a Europe-wide minimum wage and a 35-hour or a 4-day week . . .

strong and consistent strategic core, a consistent typographic style, and recurring visual images'. Because the costs of its publication were borne by the PES Group within the European Parliament, and because it had been adopted so early, the PES manifesto was abundantly available in all of the Member States from early on in the year. It was very popular with Labour Party candidates, who found it an attractive campaign aid, and its early publication assured it a broader readership than the national manifesto, which (because of John Smith's death) was not finally released until 23 May, just two weeks before the elections. Nevertheless, a striking feature of the manifesto drafting exercise was the lack of any broad consultation within member parties' memberships, and at the February 1994 Glasgow European Conference concern had been voiced about how little democratic debate there had been within the Labour Party, and also about how little input all but the top leadership of the party had had into the process.

Preparations for the wider European campaign had begun in early 1994. A PES working party on the election campaign was established, and in February 1994 a Luxembourg Socialist MEP and leader of the Luxembourg Socialist Party, Ben Fayot, presented a report, setting out proposed procedures for the coordination of national campaigns and the exchange of speakers. However, the report was not enthusiastically received for the simple reason that in five of the Member States, including the 'big four' (France, Germany, Italy and the United Kingdom), the socialist parties were at the time in opposition and much preferred to fight the elections on the performance of governing parties rather than on broader European issues. The PES campaign working party's role was largely reduced to the provision of complementary materials for the various national campaigns. Nevertheless, the broader campaign issues in the report were again raised at an April 1994 PES Bureau meeting, which was to prepare the agenda of an Extraordinary Leaders' Summit on the European elections, to be held on 19 May. On this occasion Jack Cunningham expressed concern about the report's repetition of the PES manifesto's commitment to a reduction in working hours and was also concerned that, with over fifty people in attendance, the leaders' summits were no longer capable of making proper decisions about detailed policy commitments. In the event, John Smith's death led to the cancellation of the Extraordinary Leaders' Summit, and although almost all the PES leaders informally met together in Edinburgh after having attended the funeral service, policy debate on the European elections was inevitably overshadowed and subdued. In any event, it could be no substitute for the originally planned high profile Extraordinary Leaders' Summit.

The PES Group had commissioned large-scale opinion poll surveys in the spring and autumn of 1993 and smaller-scale 'focus group' research in ten Member States, including Britain. These underlined a number of issues of common concern to the electorate throughout the European Union. The prime concern was unemployment, but the survey also revealed growing scepticism about Europe and low awareness about the EU's structure and institutions. A number of policy papers circulated within the PES Group stressing the need to keep a common front on unemployment and to strike a reasoned balance about the supposed iniquities of 'Brussels'.

There was one other way in which a broader European campaign might have been encouraged. The Maastricht Treaty, which had finally entered into force in November 1993, had given the European Parliament consultation powers over the European Council's nominee for the post of Commission president. Some speculated that the European parties would adopt their own candidates for the Commission presidency, or that one of the component national parties might make them *tête de liste*, and thus make them an integral part of the European election campaign. The reasoning was that the European Council would find it difficult to reject the electoral choice of a clear majority of European voters. The EPP could never have contemplated such a gesture in 1994 because there were far too many potential candidates amongst its ranks, but the PES had a popular potential candidate in Felipe Gonzalez. The Spanish Prime Minister was rumoured to be tired of domestic politics and ready for a change. His many advantages included the fact that he was a long-serving and highly experienced politician. Above all, he would have been acceptable to the German Christian Democrat Chancellor, Helmut Kohl, with whom he got on very well. But Gonzalez was never an enthusiastic fan of this scenario (he was said to detest the Belgian weather), and in the end his hands were tied by a deteriorating domestic political situation.

Notwithstanding these disappointments, the PES could legitimately claim to have laid the basis for a truly European campaign. The policy content of the PES manifesto and the national party manifestos was broadly in agreement, and all were produced in matching styles. The distinctive PES logo, a red rose in a circle of twelve blue stars, was used extensively by all the component parties. A great deal of literature was produced, particularly about the activities of the PES Group in the European Parliament. Much of the impetus for the modernisation and harmonisation of the PES campaign material had come from Philip Gould, a publicity consultant who had been appointed to a part-time advisory post within the PES secretariat in 1993. In this context, one of the most successful PES initiatives was a common campaign video. Made by the PES group press office, with some involvement from Jacques Seguela, who had been involved in the media campaign that led to François Mitterrand's famous 1981 victory, the video consisted of over 200 images, each a fraction of a second long, thought best to encapsulate the image of modern European socialism. The images were accompanied by a linguistically neutral soundtrack, and space was left on the tapes for national parties to add their own messages and slogans. However, despite its professional excellence, the video was little used and, indeed, hardly seen in Britain.

The PES was to play a role in the British Euro-elections in one other way. Unlike the British Conservative MEPs, who had had to distance themselves from the EPP (for the duration of the campaign, at least), the Labour Party was able to draw fully on the resources of its parent group. A rapid response unit, composed of two British members of the PES secretariat, was set up in Brussels. With direct access to the PES Group's, and the Parliament's, archives, the unit was able rapidly to provide information, by fax or by phone, to party headquarters, Transport House, the leader's office, candidates or party organisations at the local level. It was specifically conceived of as a way of rebutting 'scare stories' before they could gain momentum. In addition, several British members of the PES secretariat went to London for the later stages of the campaign. (Several MEPs' assistants were also seconded to London and other parts of the country to assist in the campaign.)

In the summer of 1993 the Labour Party NEC set up a national manifesto drafting sub-committee (see Table 5.3). The sub-committee was formally chaired by the Chairman of the NEC International Committee, Neil Kinnock. In practice, the former party leader preferred to keep a low profile and to avoid becoming, as he put it, 'a back seat driver', and so many of the drafting sessions were chaired by the Shadow Foreign Secretary, Jack Cunningham, or by the party's national chairman, Tony Clarke (Union of Communications Workers). Membership of the drafting sub-committee was to change during the drafting process. The sole EPLP input came from its leader, Pauline Green, who sat on the sub-committee in an ex-officio and non-voting capacity. At the pre-drafting stage, Pauline Green had contacted all

Table 5.3   *The Labour Party's manifesto drafting committee for the 1994 European Elections*

NEC: Neil Kinnock , MP (Chairman of the International Committee and of the NEC manifesto drafting sub-committee), Nick Sigler (International Secretary), Tom Sawyer (NUPE), Roland Wales (Policy Director), Gordon Collin (Chairman of the Organisation Committee)

Shadow Foreign Secretary: Dr Jack Cunningham, MP

European Affairs Spokesman: George Robertson, MP (European Affairs Spokesman until October 1993), Joyce Quin, MP (European Spokeswoman from November 1993)

European Parliamentary Labour Party: Pauline Green, MEP (ex-officio, EPLP leader), Dianne Hayter (EPLP Chief Executive)

Labour MEPs and asked them to list priority policy ideas. These were collated and fed into the sub-committee by her. When a first rough draft had been established, she had sent out relevant passages on the different subject areas to the appropriate EPLP spokespersons for their comments. Again, these had been collated and fed back into the process by her. Most Labour MEPs were broadly happy with the final text, but many remained unhappy with the marginal and distant role they had been assigned. A senior party politician agreed that MEPs should perhaps have been involved more, but pointed out that there had been constraints of time and place.

The manifesto had been based on two elements. The first was the PES manifesto. The second was a statement put to the October 1993 Labour Party Conference (Composite 50), itself the result of resolutions put to Conference in 1992. This statement had established the manifesto's central theme of growth through a prosperous Europe. The broad outlines of the manifesto had been agreed at a 16 February meeting of the NEC. The party's experts had submitted drafts on particular areas. Lord Eatwell, Neil Kinnock's economics adviser, had been responsible for the part on ERM policy, for example. On 3 March 1994 the sub-committee considered an initial draft, prepared by the party's International Secretary, Nick Sigler. Jack Cunningham insisted on strengthening the draft in such areas as the veto, the Social Chapter and the 1996 IGC. And because the drafting process took place in early 1994, there were essentially reactive passages and qualifications to the Conservative attacks on the PES manifesto. A reference to Northern Ireland was inspired by Roger Stott, one of the party's frontbench team, who put it to Kevin MacNamara and then Neil Kinnock, who quickly received endorsement from John Smith. A reference to the threatened privatisation of the Post Office was introduced in late April, when the NEC conducted a last trawl through the penultimate draft. A notable omission was any reference to the party's policy on proportional representation (for European elections), but only one journalist (Patrick Wintour, in the *Guardian*) made any reference to this. In the words of one NEC member, it was 'the dog that didn't bark'. A last-minute inclusion was the reference to the construction of a new building for the European Parliament in Strasbourg, a project which Labour MEPs, led by John Tomlinson, fiercely opposed. All in all, the drafting process went remarkably smoothly, with only one minor spat with the party's shadow spokesman on health, David Blunkett, over references to the NHS, though even this was about length rather than content.

Finally adopted by the NEC on 27 April 1994, Labour's national Euro-manifesto was a curious affair. It was there, said one senior party member, because it was there. One participant described it as a 'non-event'. 'Frankly, not the most interesting of experiences', said another. 'All our long meetings on the manifesto were pretty futile', said a third. And yet, said another, its absence would have been 'cataclysmic'. The manifesto had four broad themes: the new Europe; working for prosperity; 'more than a market'; and 'Europe as a Community'. The third theme was divided up into several policy priorities; signing up to the Social Chapter, the promotion of equal rights (sexual and racial equality), reforming the CAP, attacking waste and fraud, the environment and health. Conservative charges on the veto ('we have always insisted . . . on maintaining the principle of unanimity for decision-making in areas such as fiscal and budgetary policy, foreign and security issues, changes to the Treaty of Rome, and other areas of key national interest') and the 35-hour working week ('we will not introduce legislation to enforce a 35-hour week') were specifically rebutted. Like the PES manifesto, it was attractively presented, not too lengthy and easy to read. Labour was the only one of the three big parties to produce its manifesto in Welsh.

6 Liberal Democrats and Others

Despite the £1,000 deposit and the need to find 50 seconders, there were many more candidates and parties in 1994 than in any previous Euro-contest. The number of candidates rose to 552 (6.3 per seat), far more than the 387 (4.6 per seat) of 1989. The Conservatives, Labour, the Liberal Democrats and the Greens were joined by the Natural Law Party in fighting all of the seats. The breakaway Liberal Party fielded 27 candidates, and the UK Independence Party fielded 24. There was a diversity of more or less eccentric and anti-European candidates. Although the UK Independence Party and, to a lesser extent, the Greens, played important spoiling roles, the Welsh and Scottish Nationalists and the Liberal Democrats provided the main challenge to the two dominant parties.

THE LIBERAL DEMOCRATS

The Liberal Democrats had a grand, long-term strategy for gradually expanding their bridgeheads in local government, at Westminster and at Strasbourg. The Euro-elections were seen in this perspective and played down as only one step on a long road. The past record in Euro-elections of the Liberal tradition parties (Liberal in 1979, Liberal and SDP in Alliance in 1984, Social and Liberal Democrats, and Social Democrats separately in 1989) in European elections had been disappointing, and the 1989 contest had been a disaster. Some within the party argued that the poor performance in Euro-elections was structurally caused by tensions between the traditionally Euro-enthusiastic views of the party's leadership and the more Euro-sceptical attitudes to be found at grass roots level. Polls showed that those who voted Liberal Democrat included almost as high a proportion of Euro-sceptics as the rest of the population. Whatever the underlying reasons, the Liberal Democrats set more store on increasing their local government representation and on doing well in by-elections. Here, they had cause for optimism. The party's traditional role as the repository of the protest vote – a role its predecessors had

135

squandered to the Greens' advantage in 1989 – had netted spectacular by-election victories in 1993 at Newbury and at Christchurch, and a third, at Eastleigh, seemed in the offing. The party was also set to make significant new gains in the May local elections. Nevertheless, the Liberal Democrat party, the party most unequivocally in favour of a federal Europe and increased powers for the European Parliament, saw its continued exclusion from Strasbourg as an aberration that badly needed to be corrected. Moreover, the party was well aware of the publicity opportunities Euro-elections presented and of the resources that even a few MEPs could bring to the party.

In their 1992 General Election manifesto, the Liberal Democrats stated plainly that 'Our vision of the new Europe is of a federal community.' The party was firmly behind the Maastricht Treaty and, like Labour, opposed to the opt-out on the Social Chapter and the opt-in on EMU, though Nick Harvey, Liberal Democrat MP for North Devon, was conspicuous as a mild Euro-sceptic. The parliamentary party's support for the government in the crucial paving motion division in November 1992 saved the Maastricht Bill. However, the party's strategists were aware that, particularly in the new, more Euro-sceptical post-Maastricht atmosphere, an unconditionally federalist stance could leave them vulnerable, and early Conservative attacks seemed to confirm this. As Roger Liddle, the party's manifesto coordinator, put it in December 1993, 'dreamy talk of an abstract Europe will play into the hands of the party's opponents . . . The overwhelming evidence reveals that most people think a federal Europe means a centralised Europe.' Thus, great efforts were made to emphasise that the party's vision was not of a European superstate, but of a decentralised system where, as Paddy Ashdown put it, decisions are 'taken at the lowest possible level but where we join together when it helps us all.' This 'change of presentation', as Mr Ashdown described it, was the subject of much debate within the party and, as the Euro-election campaign was to reveal, the matter was not entirely resolved.

The Liberal Democrats were full members of the European Liberal Democrat and Reformist Party (ELDR). Founded on principles of 'freedom, individual responsibility and tolerance', the pan-European ELDR traced its roots back to the Liberal International, founded in 1947. All member parties were required to sign the 'Stuttgart Declaration', which called, *inter alia*, for a common foreign and security policy in the European Union. The ELDR was composed of 18 member parties, including the UK Liberal Democrats, and Paddy

Ashdown was one of the party's three vice-presidents. During the 1992 General Election campaign, in a much-publicised event, Paddy Ashdown crossed the English Channel to Calais to attend and speak at the Congress of European Liberal Parties. In 1993 the ELDR Congress was held in Torquay. Within the European Parliament, ELDR parties sat together in the ELDR Group, which was composed of representatives from all of the Member States except Greece and the United Kingdom, and it was clear that, were any to be returned, Liberal Democrat MEPs would sit in this group. (A senior Liberal Democrat official, Richard Moore, had worked in the group secretariat since 1979). The Liberal Democrats, together with their continental sister parties, were committed to fighting the Euro-election on a common ELDR manifesto. The ELDR manifesto was unabashed in its Euro-enthusiasm and was to become a hostage to fortune for the Liberal Democrats. It demanded that the Council of Ministers should 'evolve into a full democratic legislative body . . . [including] the extension of majority voting . . . to other main policy areas'; that 'co-decision between Parliament and Council, which is the key to the development of European Union, must be made to apply to all legislation'; that the ECU should become 'a truly European currency'; and that ultimately there should be a 'European Constitution, including a Charter of European Citizenship'.

As with the Labour Party, the existence of a pan-European manifesto did not prevent the Liberal Democrats from drafting their own, UK-specific, national manifesto. Under the chairmanship of Roger Liddle, and with Ben Rich, the party's Deputy Research Director, as coordinator, work on the national manifesto began in early 1993. The first product was a policy document, *Making Europe Work for Us*, launched on 8 February 1994 which, though it reiterated the party's commitment to qualified majority voting in the Council of Ministers, placed much emphasis on the devolution of powers and decision-making. (Ironically, one of its suggested titles in draft had been *A Strong Britain in a Strong Europe*, which, by chance, was the title later chosen by the Conservatives for their manifesto, and which Margaret Thatcher had herself devised for the 1989 contest.) By the time of the publication of the national manifesto, 'Making Europe Work for Us' had become a sub-title, and the main label of the manifesto was *Unlocking Britain's Potential*. The manifesto was a detailed and densely written 28-page policy statement. The party's yellow and black colours were much in evidence, but the print was fine and faint. Many journalists found it inaccessible, but few had trouble in finding the party's renewed assertion that 'the use of qualified majority voting on the Council should be extended'. In fact, the party's views on European constitutional reform were more sophisticated. The extension of QMV should, the party felt, be accompanied by a reform of the system 'perhaps to require a "double majority" (e.g. three-quarters of the states, plus the votes of states representing three-quarters of the EU's population) for particularly important issues.' The idea of a double majority had been circulating in Brussels and Strasbourg for some time and would represent a considerable restraint on QMV. (The suggested proportions were similar to those set out in Article V of the United States Constitution). It was repeatedly stressed by the party's spokesmen during the campaign but, perhaps because it seemed esoteric, went largely undiscussed.

Tim Clement-Jones, the party's Chairman and European Campaign Director, insisted that the campaign should concentrate heavily on domestic issues and place less emphasis on European matters. Many of the party's elder statesmen, such as Sir David Steel and Sir Russell Johnston, felt uneasy with this strategy, as did many of the party's candidates, and these tensions were to give rise to public policy differences at the beginning of the campaign. Despite the change of image and emphasis, the party had left one other hostage to fortune; the pronouncements of its leader and other politicians. These were to be used to devastating effect by both the Conservatives and the Labour Party, who were able to establish the impression that the Liberal Democrats were eager to divest the country of its veto rights and sovereignty. Paddy Ashdown's statement, 'I don't believe in the sovereignty of parliament but in the sovereignty of the people', was intended as an epigrammatic pointer to the party's new policy on popular assent to constitutional reform, but the media concentrated on the first part of the phrase and neglected the second part.

Despite these potential problems, the Liberal Democrats went into the Euro-election with a great boost from the 5 May local elections, in which they gained 388 seats and pushed the Conservatives into third place in national share of the vote (see Table 6.1). To some extent, the party was saved from over-optimism by past experience. As one Cowley Street activist put it, 'We know more about electoral disappointment than anyone else.' They were strongly conscious that the party had always fared worse in Euro-contests than in general elections.

They also knew that, after the great efforts of the local elections, and with the alternative temptations of summer approaching, there was no

Table 6.1   *Liberal/Liberal Democrat vote shares in General Elections and European elections*

General Election	% vote	% vote	European Election
May 1979	14	11	June 1979
June 1983	25	19	June 1984
June 1987	23	6	June 1989
April 1992	18	16	June 1994

great enthusiasm for the June Euro-elections among activists. Another reason for pessimism lay in the obvious diffusion of one of the Liberal Democrats' normal resources, the protest vote. In this contest, the Greens, who had been so triumphant in 1989, the breakaway Liberals, and the various species of eccentric and anti-marketeer, not to mention the Welsh and Scottish nationalists, were well set to siphon off the votes of many of those who were not prepared to vote Conservative or Labour. However, notwithstanding these reasons for cautious forecasting, the tempting prospect of a Liberal Democrat whitewash in the South-West was held out to the party by the media, egged on perhaps by Conservative spin-doctors, and some activists found it difficult to resist what seemed like an increasingly plausible scenario.

The Liberal Democrats had selected roughly half of their candidates for the old Euro-constituencies before the new boundaries came into force. Most of the candidates were allowed to continue, with three-person tribunals sorting out disputed cases. Only one former candidate was stranded by the reshuffle. As in 1989, candidates were selected on a 'one member one (postal) vote' system after local hustings meetings. They were drawn from a centrally-approved list of some 200 names, and were generally judged to be of a higher quality than in previous such exercises. Seventeen of the candidates were under 40 years of age, the youngest being 24-year-old John Ault (Lancashire South). Thirty-six candidates were in their forties and 20 in their fifties. The oldest candidate was 63-year-old John MacDonald (Kent East). Twenty-one of the 84 candidates were women. Sixty of the candidates were married, 54 of them with children. Liberal Democrat candidates were a learned group; only ten had received Oxbridge educations (more than Labour, less than the Conservatives) but, altogether, 54 candidates had received university educations, including 22 MAs and five doctorates. Surprisingly, only eight candidates claimed to have been active in local politics, but 15 had previously stood for Strasbourg, and no less than 51 had previously stood for Westminster. These veterans included the indefatigable James Walsh (South Downs West), who had stood in all three previous Euro-elections and in five Westminster elections. Other perennial candidates included Michael Pitts (North Yorkshire, six elections), Philip Goldenberg (Dorset and East Devon, five elections), and John MacDonald and Stuart Mole (Essex North and Suffolk South, four elections). Two candidates expressly pointed out that they were practising Quakers.

Liberal Democrat candidates came from a far more disparate array of professions and activities than their Conservative or Labour counterparts, though virtually all were white collar. The candidates included a diplomat, an airline pilot, a graphic designer, four teachers and a senior lecturer, seven school governors, a nursery director, a biomedical scientist, a caterer, a crime prevention consultant, two doctors, a medical translator, three solicitors and three barristers, a caterer, two senior managers, four company directors, three people working in the financial services, two accountants, a quantity surveyor, two local government officers, four journalists or writers, five consultants/lobbyists, two EC/EP officials, a sporting goods distributor, a Sports Council official, a director of the Commonwealth secretariat, one person describing himself as 'self-employed', and one person describing himself as unemployed. Virtually all of the candidates had European connections or qualifications, primarily through business, EC law, consultancy and lobbying, and academic contacts, and many were members of the European Movement. With the exception of two former MPs, David Belotti (Sussex East and Kent South, MP for Eastbourne, 1990-92) and Mike Hancock (Wight and Hampshire South, MP for Portsmouth South, 1984-7), both of whom were current members of the newly-established Committee of the Regions, there were no high-profile national figures. Lembit Opik (Northumbria), who had Estonian parents and strong links with the Estonian Liberal Democrats, provided an exotic link to the new Europe.

The party did some limited work in the training of candidates and agents. About a dozen constituencies had full-time professional agents in the months preceding the elections.

Opinion polling was taken very seriously. Caroline White, a full-time Cowley Street activist, worked on commissioning and analysing the polls. A new and sophisticated polling model was being developed but was unavailable for the Euro-elections. Nevertheless, the party had done a considerable amount of private polling, particularly in its key seats. Polls had been carried out before the 1992 general election and the 1993 by-elections, and for two-and-a-half years the party had been conducting regular polling in Cornwall and Somerset, extending the polling further east as the election approached. Such polls had been used to 'fine tune' the Liberal Democrat message in the regions. The party's pollsters saw the Euro-elections in the perspective of their longer-term strategy, which looked already to the local elections of 1995 and the general election of 1996.

From the outset, Paddy Ashdown had insisted that the party could only advance by targetting its relatively scarce resources. Cornwall and West Plymouth and Somerset and North Devon stood out as the most winnable of Euro-seats, and for two years money and effort had been concentrated on them and, to a lesser extent, on neighbouring seats in the south west and south. There was some resentment at this regional focus among activists in the rest of the country, since the Liberal Democrats had established a presence in local government almost everywhere. Their prospective candidates had been in place for Somerset and North Devon since the autumn of 1989, and for Cornwall and West Plymouth since the summer of 1992. The Cornish prospective candidate had additionally been a Westminster prospective candidate in the region from 1990 to 1992.

A minor distraction to the Euro-campaign was provided by the by-elections in Bradford and East London, and a major distraction by the by-election in Eastleigh. The party had thriven on by-elections and had developed great skill in their conduct. It had been hoped that the government would move the writ for the Eastleigh by-election before the Euro-elections. If this, an eminently winnable seat, had been fought a few weeks earlier, it could have given a great boost to Liberal Democrat fortunes and created further momentum in the run-up to the Euro-election. It would also have freed-up the many party officials and volunteers who flocked to the Hampshire battle, and given them a chance to direct their skills and energies elsewhere. Some Conservatives have since argued that the Liberal Democrats missed a trick in not forcing an earlier call of the Eastleigh by-election writ. But the procedural rules on these matters are obscure and the Liberal Democrats, who protested strongly at the government's delay and apparent contempt for the ruling of a 1973 Speaker's Conference, deny that anything more could have been done.

Mr Clement-Jones, an executive with Kingfisher PLC, took charge of the Euro-campaign. Graham Elson, General Secretary of the party, was responsible for the management of the Cowley Street head-quarters, and Chris Rennard, the party's overall director of campaigns and elections, was appointed field director, which meant that he spent most of his time away at the Eastleigh by-election or in the critical West country seats. Olly Grender, the party's parliamentary director of communications, was in overall charge of the press conferences. The Liberal Democrats were squeezed out of the best time slots. Their conferences had to be alternated between 8.30 a.m. and 11.30 a.m. and were generally ill-attended, partly because of the timing, and partly because the party's few 'big guns' were rarely in London to take the conferences. Paddy Ashdown could fill a hall, and the party had other crowd-pullers in such senior politicians as Sir David Steel, Charles Kennedy and Baroness Williams, but their help was directed chiefly to the regions. Mr Ashdown was subjected to an exhausting routine of travel.

As with the other parties, there were morning and evening organisational meetings at the Cowley Street headquarters throughout the campaign. Tim Clement-Jones assembled his team at 8.00 or 8.30 a.m. to consider the media reports and tie up the press conference arrangements. At 7.00 p.m. there was a planning meeting for the next day. The number of people attending these meetings grew to up to 20 people and they were acknowledged in retrospect to have been over-large for effective decision-making. Although the party did not use an agency, the party political broadcasts, one on 11 May and a specific electoral broadcast on 6 June, were largely written on a voluntary basis by Jeremy Bullmore, a former chairman of J. Walter Thompson. Unlike the Conservative and Labour parties, the Liberal Democrats were on a sound financial footing, with no serious overdraft, although they were not rich. They allocated a global sum of £260,000 to the Euro-campaign and managed to keep within this budget.

Much psephological expertise was devoted to the party's electoral strategy. On the basis of the results of the 1992 General Election, it was calculated that the party would have come second in 15 of the 84 Euro-constituencies, all in the south of England. If they could educate Labour voters about the benefits of tactical voting – the best way of ousting Conservative incumbents, then a rich harvest could be reaped. But, despite their by-election skills, the party lacked the resources to reach out to constituencies of half a million voters through such methods as intensive canvassing, carefully-phrased direct mail or repeated leaflet drops. Labour voters, who might be convinced by the solid evidence of a result in a Westminster constituency, would naturally be less impressed by hypothetical figures about anonymous and newly-drawn Euro-seats. Moreover, with soaring support for Labour in the opinion polls, why should they abandon their party on the basis of some unproven psephological statistics? A further difficulty for the Liberal Democrats lay in the reverse logic of the tactical voting argument. How should Liberal Democrat voters behave in the Euro-constituencies where Labour would come second? A nationwide appeal to vote tactically would, over most of the country, imply that Liberal Democrat supporters should desert their own candidates and vote Labour, if the Conservatives were indeed the prime enemy. For all of these reasons, the Liberal Democrats were themselves dubious about the possibilities of tactical voting in the Euro-election and revised their expectations down accordingly. They were privately confident about their prospects in Cornwall and Somerset. Anything more would come as a bonus. As one party official put it, 'We know we will have an advanced base, whether or not we win seats. We see the election primarily in terms of consolidating support in winnable Westminster seats. We are not expecting the massive gains the press are touting.'

THE GREENS

In the 1989 Euro-elections, the English Green Party secured almost 15 per cent of the national vote, driving the Social and Liberal Democrats (as they then were) into fourth place in every seat in England (except Cornwall). However, they were unable to sustain the momentum this unexpected success had brought them. They were dogged by poor organisation, by a system of dispersed decision-making, by bad publicity generated by the eccentric behaviour of some of their big names (particularly a former party spokesman, David Icke, who had declared himself to be the 'Son of the Godhead'), by public rows and the desertion of some of their leading politicians, by the way in which all the parties had taken on board the green agenda, and by the economic recession, which shifted ecological issues down the scale of public concern. In the 1992 General Election, the Greens contested only 256 of the 651 seats, securing an average of just 1.3 per cent of the vote in the seats they did contest. Of the 5,071 council seats to be filled in the 5 May 1994 local elections, the Greens were able to contest just 597. They defended five seats and lost two.

The party undertook a fundamental restructuring of its organisation at the beginning of 1994. The Scottish Green Party had already become independent of the English one. An executive, consisting of nine voting members and two 'principal speakers' (all elected annually by postal ballot of all members) was responsible for the day to day running of the party, and a regional council, consisting of two representatives from each of the 14 area parties (elected on a two-year basis) was responsible for policy and strategic direction. The party's best known politician was the Chair of the Executive, Jean Lambert.

The 1989 Euro-elections saw a strong Green performance throughout the European Community; eight Green MEPs were returned in France and Germany, seven in Italy, three in Belgium, two in the Netherlands, and one each in Portugal and Spain. The Green Group in the European Parliament was the fourth largest and was able to exert considerable political influence, particularly because the Socialist Group, which was easily the largest and most influential, looked benignly on the Greens, who sat on the left of the parliamentary chamber and frequently entered into loose coalitions with the Socialists. There was much sympathy for the UK Greens who, despite winning a far higher percentage of the vote than the French, German and Italian Green parties, fell foul of the British electoral system and failed to return a single MEP (a system based on proportional representation would have given them up to 12 seats). Jean Lambert was given 'honorary status as an MEP' by the Green Group in the European Parliament, and close links were developed between the sister parties.

The various Green Parties in the EU contested the 1994 Euro-elections on a 'common platform', a distinctive 40-page manifesto which was launched in Brussels on 24 March. The common platform, with which the UK Greens fully agreed, called *inter alia* for a European eco-development project, with a radical reorientation of the EU's policies, including eco-taxes, fundamental reform of the CAP, a re-evaluation of road transport, ecological and social clauses in world trade, the phasing out of nuclear power, waste management schemes, and a shift to 'clean' productive processes. But, as with Labour and the Liberal Democrats, the existence of a European manifesto did not prevent the English Green Party from drafting its own, national, manifesto. This demanded close cooperation between countries and regions, but was wholly opposed to a single currency and the centralisation of power and functions in Brussels. The Greens opposed the single market which, they argued, discriminated against local production and generated too much traffic and pollution. They opposed further trade liberalisation. They wanted to see tax and subsidy policies redirected to discourage pollution, cut back carbon emissions, and favour local economic production.

On 10 May the UK Green Parties announced that they would be running a full slate of candidates in England, Scotland and Wales (the Greens supported the Peace Coalition candidate in Northern Ireland). This was a considerable financial undertaking – £84,000 in deposits alone although, in line with the party's decentralised structure, most constituency organisations had been self-financing with regard to deposits and leaflets. A little European information fund money had been made available by the Green Group in the European Parliament in the months preceding the election, but subscriptions and donations had to cover the day-to-day running of the campaign. Large expenses included mail shots to identified supporters, based to some extent on the 1989 campaign exercise. Slightly more effort was directed to areas where the Greens had existing councillors (Stroud, the Cotswolds, Hampshire), but the party was intent on giving a general spread of support.

Although the Greens resented the 'arrogant' assumption of the Liberal Democrats, who assumed that the bulk of the protest vote would return to them, their expectations were low, and they were not particularly perturbed by this prospect. As their elections coordinator, Darren Johnson, put it, 'Whatever the result, we will have established our message. There are much higher levels of awareness about green issues today than there were in the 1980s and a much sharper focus. Our primary object has always been to change the agenda, and in that we are succeeding.'

THE SCOTTISH NATIONAL PARTY

Until 1975, the SNP was opposed to membership of the European Community. The party was prominent in the 1975 referendum campaign, urging its supporters to vote 'no'. Thereafter, its views gradually changed in acknowledgement of the clear verdict of the Scottish people in the referendum. The party's President, Winifred Ewing, played a significant role in this transformation. Between 1974 and 1979 she was an SNP MP for Moray and Nairn (she had been MP for Hamilton, 1967–70). After the referendum, she was delegated to the European Parliament as the SNP's representative on the British delegation of MPs. She was at that time a Vice-President of the SNP and, principally through her, the party began to reconsider its position on Europe. An indefatigable constituency MP and a fiery orator, she was effective in defending Scottish interests, such as fisheries and agriculture, in Strasbourg (earning herself the French soubriquet, 'Madame Ecosse'). At first she sat as an Independent, but, recognising that more could be achieved in a group, she joined the European Democratic Alliance (EDA) largely composed of Fianna Fail and Gaullist MEPs. In the 1980s the party strengthened its representation in Brussels, and it has now adopted an enthusiastic pro-European stance. As the party's sole MEP, Winifred Ewing had chosen to sit with the broadly inclusive Rainbow Group, of which she was a Vice-President. Membership brought its own rewards, in terms both of information fund money and other resources such as political backing and committee appointments. The party envisages a confederal Europe in which Scotland would regain its independence. As the party's leader, Alex Salmond, told the House of Commons (21 May 1992), 'It is time to stop Scotland being misgoverned and misrepresented in Europe. We need real government and real representation in the European Community. The Prime Minister suggests that up to 20 states could be members of the Community by the end of the century. The ancient nation of Scotland will be a full part of that process as an independent state.' The Euro-election, he later asserted, offered the Scottish people 'a choice to go forward into the mainstream of Europe or be stuck in a backwater of Britain'.

The SNP had been disappointed by the 1992 General Election. Although it raised its overall vote from 14 to 21.5 per cent, its representation fell from five to three MPs. But in 1994 the party was on a roll. It had made significant advances at Labour's expense in the 5 May local elections. Labour's vote fell back in contrast to its English performance. The result showed that the SNP, as much as the other two parties, could profit from the government's unpopularity and act as the repository of the protest vote. Above all, the result was an ominous signal to Labour. In the 1989 Euro-elections, the SNP had comfortably retained Highlands and Islands and come second to Labour in every other seat except Lothians and Scotland South. Their nearest miss was Scotland North East, where Allan Macartney (29.4 per cent) had run Henry McCubbin (30.7 per cent) a very close second. The SNP used the local elections as an effective platform to the Euro-elections, targetting their efforts very carefully. The Highlands and Islands seat, where once the Liberal Democrats had been able to give the SNP a close race (in 1979 Sir Russell Johnston won 30.7 per cent of the vote to the SNP's 34 per cent), was now effectively a personal fiefdom of the high profile Winnie Ewing (34.8 per cent majority in 1989); she treated the huge geographical expanse as if it were a Westminster constituency. The SNP were not complacent, but they knew the seat was theirs. This left them to concentrate their efforts on Scotland North East, a mixture of urban (Aberdeen, Dundee) and rural constituencies with sizeable fisheries interests.

The 1992 General Election saw Labour lose Aberdeen South to the Conservatives and, although Labour's majority improved slightly in Dundee East, there was a general decline in the Labour vote in the two cities. In 1993, the joint Labour/Liberal Democrat coalition in Grampian broke up, and the SNP then joined forces with Labour. This was a highly significant breakthrough for the SNP, enabling it to shrug off Labour's 'Tartan Tories' jibe. In the May 1994 local elections, the unpredictable consequences of the expected collapse in the Conservative vote saw advances for the SNP in rural Tayside, where they formed a minority administration, and for the Liberal Democrats in Grampian, where they entered into a coalition with the SNP. The SNP took its first regional seat in Aberdeen. These events were widely publicised, further consolidating the SNP's credibility. The SNP's psephological advisers had noted a swing from the Conservatives to the Liberal Democrats and the SNP between the 1992 General Election and the 1994 local elections. In the Euro-elections, they expected further Conservative voters to defect, but they also hoped to squeeze votes out of the Liberal Democrat support. In the end, Labour's national strategy of attacking the government's record may have handed the SNP an additional bonus which could have helped clinch the seat for them, as Conservative voters deserting their party were as likely to vote SNP as Labour.

PLAID CYMRU

Like the SNP, Plaid Cymru originally opposed membership of the EC but has warmed to Europe as it has increasingly seen the EC as a way of enhancing the stature and influence of Wales. The party's manifesto for the 1992 General Election argued 'In the 1990s, full self-government is no longer a distant but an urgent necessity. As we rejoice in the renewed nationhood of long-oppressed and submerged nations in Europe, we feel a growing impatience that Wales is falling behind.' At the launch of its Euro-manifesto, the party's President, Dafydd Wigley, said 'Our objective is full self-government for Wales within the EC. That gives us in a Welsh parliament elected in Wales the full control over all those policy areas that can be run efficiently and effectively at the all-Wales level.'

Plaid Cymru had a strategic goal of establishing itself as the second party in Wales. It wanted to expand from its Welsh-speaking heartland in the West to the populous Anglophone areas of South Wales, but the only seats where it had any real chance were North Wales and Mid and West Wales. The party's subsidiary aim was to try to take over the role of principle anti-Labour party (a role shared by the Conservatives and the Greens in 1989). It was successful in presenting itself as a sensible receptacle for the protest vote, and the results were to show that Greens and other fringe candidates made less impact in Wales than elsewhere. Part of the reason for this was that Plaid Cymru had enjoyed good relations with the Welsh Greens for several years; Cynog Dafis was elected for Ceredigion and Pembroke North in 1992 with Green endorsement, and Jonathan Porrit was to be expelled from the Green Party for endorsing Plaid Cymru candidates during the Euro-elections (see Chapter 8).

Dafydd Wigley was himself a candidate in the North Wales seat. Because he was a candidate, coverage of his remarks was subject to the perverse consequences of the Representation of the People Act, which tended to lower media coverage to the lowest common denominator. The party was also to be surprised by the lack of media attention in its Cardiff press conferences. Dafydd Wigley suffered from one other handicap. His intentions over the holding of a dual mandate were not clear, and there were even rumoured to have been Welsh nationalists in Gwynedd who abstained in order to make sure that he stayed at Westminster.

THE UK INDEPENDENCE PARTY AND OTHER ANTI-EUROPEAN PARTIES AND CANDIDATES

A new departure for several Member States in the 1994 Euro-elections was the intervention of anti-European parties and a number of independent anti-European candidates. The Anglo-French business-man, Sir James Goldsmith, attracted some British media attention by standing (successfully) as a candidate for Philippe de Villiers *Majorité pour l'autre Europe* (anti-Maastricht) list in France. Denmark, which had always had anti-European parties, saw four anti-EU MEPs elected on two different lists. In Germany former Free Democrat Manfred Brunner headed a ten-member anti-Maastricht list. In the case of the United Kingdom, there were two small anti-European parties, the UK Independence Party, and a much looser group of candidates under the title 'New Britain Against New European Union'. There were a large number of independent anti-European candidates, some of them linked, running under such titles as 'British Home Rule', 'For British Independence and Free Trade', 'Conservative Non-Federal Party', 'Independent Anti-European Superstate', 'Britain', 'Third Way Independence Party', 'Independent out of Europe', 'National Independence Party', 'Independent Euro-Sceptic', and 'Independent Britain in Europe'. The best known of the independent candidates was the former Conservative MP for Winchester, John Browne.

In November 1991 Dr Alan Sked, a lecturer in international history at the London School of Economics, set up an Anti-Federalist League to oppose the Maastricht Treaty. This attracted some interest, but little concrete support. Dr Sked, who had once been a Liberal candidate in a Westminster seat, stood as an Anti-Federalist candidate in the 1993 Newbury and Christchurch by-elections, again attracting some interest and enough support to convince him to set up something akin to a proper political party, with a view to fighting the Euro-elections. The UK Independence Party was founded in August 1993. An embryonic national structure was established, with a national executive committee, initial appointments to it being made by Alan Sked, and some functioning branches. The party's membership was vaguely put at 'a good few thousand', but Dr Sked relied heavily on the offices of a few energetic volunteers, particularly the party's European election organiser, Gerard Batten, to get the organisation up and running. At Easter an article in the *Daily Mail* about the party suddenly aroused considerable interest. More followed the feature articles which Dr Sked wrote for the *Times* and the *Sunday Telegraph* in the month before the Euro-election. The party attracted some support from public figures. Professor Norman Stone and Lord Dacre signed the nomination papers of a candidate. Two, Lords, Neidpath and Deramore, together with another peer who preferred to remain anonymous, joined the party.

The party raised some £15,000 through subscriptions and donations in the run-up to the election campaign. The largest individual donation was said to be £1,000, but most income came from £10 subscriptions and modest donations. A benefactor made a small office above a clothes shop in Regent Street available to the party for the duration of the campaign. Some candidates put up their own deposits. Others were funded centrally.

The party fielded 24 candidates in the Euro-elections and also fought four of the five by-elections: Eastleigh, Barking, Dagenham and Newham North-East. The Euro-constituencies fought had 'largely selected themselves', based on membership figures and the availability of candidates. Dr Sked chose to contest the Bedfordshire and Milton Keynes Euro-constituency in the hope he would benefit from some of the publicity brought to the contest by Edwina Currie, but he later regretted the travelling involved to and from his Islington flat, which jointly served as the party's headquarters. The party claimed to get support from all sections of the community, citing the fact that it was contesting one SNP, 11 Labour and 12 Conservative Euro-constituencies as proof of this, but the party was strongly hostile to the Conservative government's pro-Maastricht Treaty policy, and was rumoured to be attracting primarily disenchanted Conservative voters. The party's candidates were pledged not to take up their seats in Strasbourg if elected, and this quixotic stance was said to have caused occasional problems on the campaign trail. Dr Sked was at pains to avoid extremism and eccentricity. All candidates were asked if they had a criminal record, a history of mental illness, or if they had previously belonged to an extreme party.

The party did not produce a full-scale manifesto. A glossy broadsheet set out its policy. The principle theme was opposition to the UK's membership of the EU, and support for a 'free Britain in a free Europe'. The party argued that EU membership was damaging British political and economic interests, and that British influence in the world would be enhanced by quitting the Union. The party was the only one to campaign on a call for outright withdrawal.

The party's early campaign was badly affected by the emergency hospitalisation of Dr Sked with a perforated appendix. But the campaign later received a huge boost from its election broadcast, which went out on 31 May. To save money, the broadcast was recorded in Dr Sked's flat, and consisted simply of him expounding the party's views to the camera. Ironically, the party was one of the few to enlist European support; Manfred Brunner made a flying visit to London and held a conference at the LSE in support of the UKIP. The party's ultimate aim was to contest the next General Election on the anti-Maastricht theme.

Although, as will be seen, the party did have some electoral effect, it would be easy to dismiss it as a temporary phenomenon. However, its minimal effect was to have acted as an extreme Euro-sceptical ginger group, and there is no doubt that it did tap in to a real vein of protest.

THE LIBERAL PARTY

When the Liberals merged with the Social Democrats in 1988, a small hard core of traditionalist Liberals, led by the former MP, Michael Meadowcroft, broke away and formed their own, 'true' Liberal Party. They found enough support to run candidates in by-elections and to fight 73 Westminster seats in the 1992 General Election. They attracted very little support, although Michael Meadowcroft managed to save his deposit in Leeds. The Liberal Party was firmly opposed to the Maastricht Treaty, which it believed would lead to a 'centralised and undemocratic super-state'. The party argued for a wider Europe of 49 European nations, 'cooperating together to achieve mutually agreed aims' within a European Confederation. The party fielded 20 candidates in the Euro-election, entitling them to an election broadcast, which was transmitted on 2 June. With the exception of Devon and East Plymouth, the Liberal Party made little impact.

THE ULSTER UNIONIST PARTY

The Ulster Unionists were long opposed to the UK's membership of the EC. However, in the 1980s the party dropped its outright opposition in favour of a more nuanced stance, working within the Community for a looser federal Europe. The party opposed the Maastricht Treaty and called for a referendum before it was ratified. John Taylor, a former Ulster Unionist MEP, set out his party's approach in the Maastricht Bill paving debate (4 November 1992); 'Ulster Unionists strongly support greater cooperation in Europe on the basis of sovereign states. We reject federalism, common security and defence forces, common European citizenship and a European central bank, which would have adverse implications for our national economic policies.' The UUP, like the DUP, had an ambivalent attitude towards the Community. It had regularly returned one Euro-MP, and welcomed the financial aid that came to the local community from Brussels.

THE DEMOCRATIC UNIONIST PARTY

The DUP's leader, the Reverend Ian Paisley, an MEP since 1979, was a long time opponent of the Treaty of Rome. He set out his approach during the paving debate of 4 November 1992: 'I am a consistent anti-marketeer . . . I raise my voice – I shall continue to do so – against something which I believe is detrimental to the United Kingdom.' Again, whilst philosophically opposed to EU membership, the DUP recognised the worth of the EU's regional aid to Northern Ireland.

THE SOCIAL DEMOCRATIC AND LABOUR PARTY

The SDLP was always an enthusiastic supporter of the European Community and the integration process. The party's leader, John Hume, an MEP since 1979 and a colleague of Labour MEPs in the PES Group, speaking in the debate on the Social Chapter on 22 July 1993, told MPs, 'I am a strong supporter of the steady evolution towards European Union.' The party was firmly opposed to the opt-out on the Social Chapter and the opt-in mechanism on EMU. Mr Hume, who served on the executive bureau of the PES, was an active and widely admired member of the European Parliament. Like Ian Paisley, he was also adept at defending and furthering the interests of his constituency.

THE NATURAL LAW PARTY

Despite the esoteric nature of its views, the Natural Law Party could genuinely claim to the status of a European party, as it fielded candidates in all 12 Member States of the European Union. In the United Kingdom it fielded candidates in all 84 Euro-constituencies. The party claimed that its philosophy was based on eternal laws taught by Maharishi Mahesh Yogi; it campaigned for a Europe of 'truly independent, sovereign nations'. The UK party, led by Dr Geoffrey Clements, made much of its 'scientific evidence' that the concerted efforts of its yogic flyers had reduced Merseyside crime rates. Its party political broadcast provoked a host of cartoons on the yogic flying theme, and the party was mostly regarded as a distraction, though its candidates were to take over 2,000 votes in four constituencies.

OTHERS

The sheer size of Euro-constituencies and the £1,000 deposit is but a limited deterrent to determined protestors and eccentric independents. There was a Protestant Reformation Party and a European People's Party Judaeo/Christian Alliance candidate, a 21st Century Party fielded several candidates and there was a Humanist Party candidate. At the other end of the scale, there was a Restoration of Capital Punishment candidate, and a 'Make Criminals Concerned About Our Response to Hostility and Yobbishness (MCCARTHY)' candidate. The North East Ethnic Party (The Neeps) fielded a candidate, and there was a Wessex Regionalist. The Network against the Child Support Agency fielded a candidate. Among more eccentric candidatures were the Boston Tea Party (a *Guardian* journalist), the Corrective Party, and a certain 'Eurobean from the Planet Beanus'.

The National Front fielded five candidates. Eleven candidates used a socialist or communist label of some kind. Voters in Glasgow had a choice of four. The Monster Raving Loony Party fielded five candidates, including a Mr John Major.

7 The National Campaign

Although most parties had fixed an official campaign launch date for the middle of May, unofficial campaigning began immediately after the local elections on 5 May (see Chronology Table 7.1). Indeed, all accepted that there would inevitably be some overlapping between the two campaigns and, as was seen in Chapters 5 and 6, both Labour and the Liberal Democrats saw the two as part of a wider continuum. Seen from this perspective, the Conservatives got off to a disastrous start, and the next six days seemed to make calamitous defeat in the Euro-elections inevitable.

On Friday 6 May, the day of the local election results, John Carlisle, MP, a rebellious backbench Euro-sceptic, offered to act as a stalking-horse candidate, and the weekend media devoted much coverage to the defiant Prime Minister's prospects of remaining at the head of his party. On Saturday 7 May, the *Independent* reported a *Channel Four News* analysis based on the local election results that would give the Conservatives 21 Euro-seats, Labour 52, the Liberal Democrats 9, and the SNP 2. The *Guardian* declared that John Major was 'facing disaster in Euro-vote' and Paddy Ashdown told the *Independent* that the Liberal Democrats expected victory in the Eastleigh by-election, a claim supported by several recent opinion polls. Matters got worse as the weekend progressed.

On Sunday, 8 May the ill-fated 'Back to Basics' theme was mocked when it was announced that Michael Brown, a junior Government Whip, was resigning from the Government following newspaper allegations about his private life. The former Conservative minister, David Mellor, attacked John Carlisle during a *Frost on Sunday* interview, describing him as a 'stalking hearse'. The former Conservative Prime Minister, Sir Edward Heath, told Radio 4 that John Major ought to reshuffle his Cabinet, and the statement raised private fears that Sir Edward might once more be tempted into a public battle with the Euro-sceptics, as had occurred during the disastrous 1989 campaign. Policy differences within the Cabinet were again on display. On Radio 4, the Chancellor of the Exchequer declared himself 'not at all attracted by the idea' of a referendum, whilst another Cabinet

Chronology Table 7.1   European election campaign and beyond

6 May 94	John Major warns potential leadership rivals that he will be 'standing there waiting' for them. Rightwing backbencher John Carlisle announces that he will reluctantly stand against Major in the autumn. Channel tunnel opens
7 May 94	Junior government whip Michael Brown resigns after allegations about his private life
8 May 94	Kenneth Clarke against referendum on single currency. John Redwood prevaricates
9 May 94	Norman Lamont for a referendum. David Hunt says 'it is irrelevant'. Paddy Ashdown calls for 'public assent'. Downing Street strategy meeting announces PM against a referendum
10 May 94	N. Scott, Social Security Minister, admits having misled the Commons over Disabled Persons Bill
12 May 94	John Smith dies. Margaret Beckett assumes interim Labour leadership. Tony Blair rapidly emerges as favourite. European elections campaigning suspended until after Smith funeral. Scottish Conservative Party's Inverness conference (Major speech). Nominations close
15 May 94	UK and French governments agree on UK operators' access to Orly
16 May 94	EU Council of Ministers formally approves the four accession treaties. Bryan Gould resigns his Westminster seat. Lib Dems start campaigning in Eastleigh
17 May 94	Writs for Newham, Barking, Bradford, Dagenham and Eastleigh by-elections are moved for 9 Jun.
18 May 94	Shadow cabinet appoints Jack Straw campaign manager. Royal Mail sell-off story breaks
20 May 94	John Smith's funeral service Scott controversy reignites after the Minister talks out the bill
21 May 94	John Smith's burial on Iona. Conservatives launch campaign. Gardiner article
22 May 94	Paddy Ashdown 'pre-launches' Lib. Dem. manifesto. Gordon Brown Welsh Labour Party speech
23 May 94	Conservative, Labour, Lib. Dem., SNP and Plaid manifestos launched. Major's Bristol 'veto' speech. *Express* ICM poll: Lab. 46, Con. 27, Lib. Dem. 23
24 May 94	BBC strike. Government launches competitiveness White Paper. Press full of 'rampant killer virus' stories
25 May 94	Labour NEC fixes 21 Jul. as date for leadership election. Margaret Beckett resigns deputy leadership

156## 156   *British Politics and European Elections 1994*

26 May 94	Michael Howard immigration remarks. MORI poll: Lab. 46, Con. 27, Lib. Dem. 23. House of Commons rises for Whitsun recess
27 May 94	John Major's Bristol *Evening Post* 'beggars' interview. Major tells *Daily Express* EMU is unlikely, Helmut Kohl tells German television it's definite
30 May 94	Straw-Brown-Beckett contradictions on assistance to young
31 May 94	Alan Sked election broadcast
30–31 May 94	Mulhouse summit between Helmut Kohl and François Mitterrand. The two agree, *inter alia*, on joint EC presidency plans for the next year, and on their preference for Jean Luc Dehaene. Lamassoure *Le Monde* article
31 May 94	John Major's Ellesmere Port 'multi-track, multi-speed, multi-layered' speech
1 Jun. 94	Gordon Brown announces withdrawal from leadership stakes and backing for Tony Blair. Tebbit endorses Major's Ellesmere Port speech.
2 Jun. 94	Tony Blair speech in Eastleigh. Major's Nottingham anti-Social Chapter speech. Commons rises for Whitsun recess
3 Jun. 94	Chinook helicopter crash. Labour's 'tax bombshell' press conference. John Major's 'you should go' appearance on *Election Call*. 'Lilley in France' story. Clinton in London and Cambridge. Gallup poll: Lab. 54, Lib. Dems 21.5, Cons. 21
5 Jun. 94	D-Day minus 1 ceremonies. President Clinton on Brittania. John Major VAT interview on *Frost on Sunday*. Major urged to veto Dehaene
6 Jun. 94	D-Day commemorations in Normandy. Gummer two-speed gaffe
7 Jun. 94	OECD report. Major's 'Europe's deadly sins' final speech (Hammersmith)
8 Jun. 94	Final press conferences. European Court of Justice ruling on acquired rights directive. John Prescott taxi crash. President Clinton in Oxford. Liberal Demcrat candidate in Newham by-election defects to Labour
9 Jun. 94	Polling day.
10 Jun. 94	Lib. Dems take Eastleigh, with Labour second. Margaret Beckett, John Prescott and Denzil Davies announce candidatures
11 Jun. 94	Tony Blair declares candidature at Sedgefield. Bobby Charlton knighted.
12 Jun. 94	Ken Livingstone announces candidature
13 Jun. 94	European election results (results in the UK: Lab. 62, Con. 18, Lib Dem 2, SNP 2, others 3). Major gives Number Ten garden 'reshuffle' press conference

14 Jun. 94	Commons returns
15 Jun. 94	Railway signalmen strike. Livingstone withdraws
16 Jun. 94	Labour leadership nominations close. Gordon Brown backs Blair/Beckett ticket. Sir Norman Fowler announces resignation. Sir Leon Brittan still UK's official candidate, but *Financial Times* reports Britain still open to Dehaene
17 Jun. 94	Lib Dem reshuffle. 18 Conservative MEPs vote to rejoin the EPP. Michael Heseltine pre-emptively refuses party chairmanship
24–5 Jun. 94	Corfu European Council. Sir Leon Brittan withdraws candidature. PM vetoes Dehaene's appointment
4 Jul. 94	Lord Plumb elected leader of British Conservatives in the EP. Tom Spencer elected Chairman of the British section of the EPP
5 Jul. 94	Wilfried Martens elected President of EPP in the EP
6 Jul. 94	Pauline Green elected leader of the PES Group in the EP. Wayne David elected leader of the EPLP
15 Jul. 94	Brussels European Council nominates Jacques Santer
21 Jul. 94	Tony Blair elected Labour leader. John Prescott elected deputy leader. Government reshuffle. Michael Portillo becomes Employment minister. Jacques Santer's nomination approved by 22 vote majority in EP (Conservatives vote for, Labour against)
28 Jul. 94	Commons rises for the summer recess
29 Jul. 94	Neil Kinnock nominated as Britain's second Commissioner. Sir Leon Brittan reconfirmed
1–5 Aug. 94	Three of the 'gang of four' urge closer Lib Dem ties with Labour
5 Aug. 94	Gallup poll puts Labour a record 33.5 per cent ahead of the Conservatives

member and prominent Euro-sceptic, John Redwood, told the BBC's *On the Record* that 'you have to wait and see whether you get a big enough issue'. The same programme reported a Gallup poll finding that a majority of voters wanted the Prime Minister to go and would prefer Michael Heseltine in his place.

On Monday 9 May senior Conservative Party managers and ministers were reported to be meeting in Downing Street for a 'combined post mortem and planning session'. But as they met the referendum row continued to rage. Norman Lamont and Lord Young told Radio 4 there should be a referendum, while David Hunt told the same programme that a referendum was 'irrelevant'. This open disagreement led an anxious Sir Christopher Prout, the leader of the British Conservatives in the European Parliament, to declare that the row was bad for morale and should be held in private. Under the headline 'Tories admit Euro-poll may sink Major', the *Guardian* ran a report, based on 'a straw poll of MPs', that the Prime Minister's aides feared open revolt and that some backbenchers were floating the idea of a special party conference after the Euro-elections. The *Times* similarly reported that 60 Conservative MPs wanted a leadership contest. On Tuesday, all of the broadsheets carried banner headlines on the referendum issue, and the *Times* carried pro-referendum articles by Normant Lamont and Lord Tebbit. Yet another junior minister seemed on the brink of resignation when a hapless Nicholas Scott, Minister at the Social Security Department, came under pressure after admitting to the Commons that he had given a misleading reply about the origin of filibustering amendments designed to block the passage of a Bill for the Disabled.

On Wednesday 11 May an ICM poll in the *Guardian* put Labour on 44 per cent, the Conservatives on 27 per cent and the Liberal Democrats on 24 per cent, but there seemed to have been a temporary lull in the onslaught on the government, as the media's expectations turned to the Scottish Conservative Party's Inverness Conference. Douglas Hurd was to be the main speaker on the Wednesday afternoon, but most expectations were focussed on the Prime Minister's keynote address, to be delivered on the Friday, with many commentators seeing it as a make-or-break occasion for Mr Major. The *Times* believed he would 'rally the troops' for the Euro-election, but other papers were less sanguine about his prospects of success. What all commentators seemed agreed on, however, was that the Prime Minister's political future would depend on his party's performance in the Euro-election. And then, early on the morning of Thursday 12 May, the day nominations for the European election closed, John Smith died of a heart attack, and thereafter the political world changed with extraordinary rapidity.

Two aspects of the brief pre-campaign period between the local elections results and the Labour leader's death are worthy of comment. The first was the low-key role played by John Smith himself, which caused much apprehension among those outside the immediate circle of the leader. In particular, the leader's late and *sotto voce* intervention in the referendum debate gave his opponents an opportunity to claim that Labour was ducking or fudging the issue and later indirectly

John Smith and Paddy Ashdown both   *The Times* (11 May 1994)
made play with Conservative ambivalence
over Europe

fuelled the Conservative's campaign strategy on the veto. Euro-enthusiasts within the party and not privy to John Smith's intention of heading a strongly pro-European campaign additionally feared that the leader's reticence might indicate a change in attitude designed to reflect the new, more Euro-sceptical atmosphere abroad in the population at large. These apprehensions were only partly calmed when John Smith joined in attacks on Nicholas Scott with his customary wit and effectiveness.

A second aspect of the pre-campaign was the relatively high profile enjoyed by the Liberal Democrats. In part this was due to their strong regional showing in the local polls, particularly in Eastleigh, and in part it was due to the pronouncements of the party's leader. Although the writ for the Eastleigh by-election had yet to be moved, it was widely assumed that it would be held on the same day as the Euro-elections. However, at this stage the two campaigns remained distinct. For the Liberal Democrats, Eastleigh was seen in the same perspective as the party's landslide wins in the Newbury and Christchurch by-elections the previous year. Normally a safe Conservative seat, it seemed increasingly likely to fall to the Liberal Democrats. There was some media interest in Labour's decision to fight to win, with most at least initially seeing it as a symbolic gesture. But the chief interest among commentators was the size of the Liberal Democrat vote as, first, a gauge of the Government's unpopularity and, second, a gauge of the degree of threat to Conservative MPs throughout the south of the country (and hence to the Prime Minister's position).

On Sunday 8 May at the height of the Conservative row over the referendum issue, a 'leaked' letter from Paddy Ashdown to Tim Clement-Jones, the party's European campaign manager, called for 'public assent' for any further major constitutional change within the European Union. The 'leak' was a perfect example of the tactic used by Christopher Patten and Andrew Lansley in the Conservatives' April 1992 general election campaign, enhancing the impact of a manifesto by gradually leaking its contents. Moreover, coming, as it did, at the height of the referendum row, it enabled Paddy Ashdown to 'piggy-back' into public prominence with a clear policy position. Nevertheless, some saw the move as counterproductive. Although the proposal was in fact drawn from the party's Euro-election manifesto, many journalists took it out of context and presented it as policy made 'on the hoof' by the party leader in response to the specific circumstances of the referendum debate. In the second place, the provision was one of the more contentious in the manifesto, and came with a series of conditions attached; for example, 'public assent' could come through a general election, if one happened to be taking place after an intergovernmental conference. Media reportage largely neglected these conditions, and Mr Ashdown's apparent departure from them led to the public disgruntlement of a number of the party's elder statesmen, including Lord Jenkins of Hillhead and Sir David Steel, who were not enthusiastic about the referendum idea.

Although increasingly obscured by the media's growing interest in the Government's disarray, many of the policy themes of the Euro-election campaign had been apparent since the early spring. The Conservatives' campaign themes had been largely set out in a widely reported speech made to the Conservative candidates by Douglas Hurd on 14 February. The Foreign Secretary spoke of a 'Lib/Lab Euro-pact' which would pursue interventionist economic policies and centralise power in Brussels. Labour's economic policies and the Liberal Democrats' constitutional commitments would create a European superstate. Their European sister parties wanted Europe to be fully federal. 'Labour and the Liberal Democrats', he said, 'are fully signed up to the Euro-Socialist and Euro-Liberal manifestos which are binding on all party members.' He claimed that Britain's job strategy, with its stress on low social costs, was becoming 'orthodoxy' across the European Union. Early enlargement would assist the process. A strong NATO and a common foreign policy without an EU 'straitjacket' would deliver peace, while similar intergovernmental cooperation would deliver 'practical benefits' on crime and other issues. Only the Conservatives could be trusted to defend Britain's prerogatives unconditionally. These themes were echoed in a note circulated to Cabinet colleagues after the Qualified Majority Voting crisis and then, in an amended form, distributed to all Conservative MPs, MEPs and Euro candidates. Most remarkably, the 'multi-speed Europe' concept, which was to become such an issue during the campaign proper, had been set out in detail by Douglas Hurd on two occasions without occasioning much comment. The first was in a keynote speech delivered in Warsaw on 6 May. On that occasion, the vision of a 'multi-track, multi-speed and multi-faceted Europe' was aimed primarily at an attentive audience of central and East European countries eager to join the European Union as soon as possible. The second was on 11 May at the Scottish Conservative Party's Inverness Conference, but it went largely unreported as it occurred on the eve of John Smith's death. A short series of pre-manifesto press conferences after Easter stressed how Conservative policies were designed to deregulate business and improve competition. By early May the basic messages of the Tory campaign were already clear: the left-wing majority in the European Parliament was building a socialist super-state; such a process was economically destructive and politically misguided; only Conservative policies would put competitiveness first, safeguard Britain's national interest and decentralise power.

Labour's twin-track approach, of fighting on domestic and European issues, was also apparent in the early spring. The chief domestic issue was to be the Government's record in managing the economy, and particularly the Conservatives' traditional home territory of tax. The Labour Party tried to capitalise on public resentment about the way in which the Conservatives had seemed to renege on their April 1992 manifesto commitments. Many people within the Labour Party and beyond argued that the general election had been won under false pretences. A claim by the Conservatives that Labour would increase a family's tax bill by £1,250 was widely credited with winning them the general election, with a high-profile poster campaign drawing attention to 'Labour's tax bombshell'. Throughout early 1994, the shadow Chancellor, Gordon Brown, and the shadow Chief Secretary, Harriet Harman, conducted a sustained offensive against their opposite numbers, and on 17 February this strategy paid off when, in a written answer to a parliamentary question, the Financial Secretary, Stephen Dorrell, admitted that the tax bill of an average family would increase by £22 a week by April 1995. Gordon Brown said the 'two-year tax ratchet reveals the truth of a bigger demand from the Tories than ever they were able to claim with lies at the last election about Labour'. The divide, he continued, was now between 'fair taxes under Labour and unfair taxes under the Tories'. With the Chancellor obliged to implement the increases on VAT on domestic fuel introduced by his predecessor, Labour was presented with a broad and continuous target. The party's campaigns coordinator, Margaret Beckett, told a 23 March meeting of the Parliamentary Labour Party that the European elections in particular would be a referendum on the Government. 'We will denounce tax increases day by day', she said.

The European approach was spelt out by Pauline Green, leader of the EPLP, in her 6 February speech to the party's European Conference in Glasgow. Labour's unity on Europe was to be contrasted with the Conservatives' disarray. Labour was committed to economic recovery and social justice and these could best be achieved through enthusiastic cooperation in Europe. A number of policy issues could only effectively be dealt with through Europe; sexual equality, the environment, consumer protection, racism and xenophobia, and organised crime. The Conservatives' negative approach, particularly the Social Chapter opt-out, disqualified them from exploiting the full benefits of Europe. Only Labour could do this. A 1 March internal strategy paper enumerated three themes; the Conservatives had failed in Britain and in Europe, they had not provided a strong voice in Europe but, rather, a weak voice, and only Labour, with its 'coherent, united European vision', could be strong and effective in Europe.

The Liberal Democrats had also set out most of their campaign themes early in the year. On 8 February Paddy Ashdown launched the policy document, *Making Europe Work for Us*, which was to form the core of the Euro-manifesto. The document backed majority voting in the Council of Ministers and equal legislative rights for the European Parliament. It reiterated party backing for devolution of powers to national governments and local and regional authorities. 'Our task,' said Mr Ashdown, 'is to show that Britain needs to take a lead in making Europe work for people.' But, in a reflection of events to come, it was clear that the leader was not altogether at ease with a concentration on constitutional affairs. It was important to 'make sure that the people of all our countries understand that Europe is important to them in their everyday lives', he said. At the same time, 'Anyone who has just been through the last year of Maastricht . . . would be foolish if they didn't feel their fingers [had] been burned.'

JOHN SMITH'S DEATH (12 MAY) AND ITS CONSEQUENCES

John Smith's death had a dramatic effect on the British political scene. He was a genuinely popular figure within the Commons, liked and admired in equal measure. His sudden disappearance shocked and saddened his colleagues on both sides of the House and all appetite for the political fight was suddenly dissipated in a general numbness which was to persist for over a week. Upon hearing of the death, the Scottish Conservative Party's Inverness Conference unanimously decided to suspend the day's sitting, and the news virtually obliged the next day's keynote speakers, the Prime Minister and Michael Heseltine, to re-draft their speeches in more reflective and conciliatory terms.

Labour politicians were desolate. In addition to suffering personal grief at the loss of a friend, most of the front bench felt that the loss of an inspirational leader on the eve of an election campaign could only have a deleterious effect. Under the Labour Party's constitution, the deputy leader, Margaret Beckett, automatically became leader until a leadership election could be held, thus becoming the first woman ever to lead the party. Although most Labour politicians refused to respond to questions about the leadership succession, they knew the subject could not long be avoided. In the afternoon, the Commons held a special session devoted entirely to the memory of the dead Labour leader during which the Prime Minister paid warm and generous tribute to his erstwhile political adversary. The mood of shock and sadness was caught up by the country at large and was reflected by a subdued and respectful media.

The next day, the three main political parties announced that, out of respect for the dead John Smith, they had agreed to suspend all political campaigning until after the funeral. All of the day's newspapers devoted many pages to coverage of the Labour leader's death, but also to its consequences, with most commentators concentrating on three; respite for the Prime Minister, the entry into force of the Labour Party's new electoral mechanism, and potential candidates for the leadership contest.

All were agreed that, as one Labour frontbencher put it, John Major was 'let off the hook', and this in more ways than one. In the first place, there was a general suspension of political hostilities, both by the political parties and, perhaps more importantly, by the media. The steadily mounting pressure on John Major and his beleaguered Government was suddenly relieved, and most Labour politicians were later to acknowledge that, because of the truce, the Labour campaign had lost virtually all of its momentum. In addition, the Government's latest difficulty – the pressure on Nicholas Scott to resign (which had been led by John Smith) – evaporated. Second, the chief threat to Mr Major's leadership, in the form of Michael Heseltine, suddenly receded. Like John Smith, Mr Heseltine himself had already suffered a heart attack (in Venice the previous August), and, despite his protestations, doubts were inevitably raised about his physical ability to cope with the pressures of leadership. Since the only other potential contenders, Kenneth Clarke and Michael Portillo, were playing a long game (see Chapter 2), the immediate threat to Mr Major was gone. In the third place, John Smith's death led to a sudden change in the political atmosphere, and Mr Major was able to respond to this in his conciliatory speech at the Scottish Conservative Party's Conference. 'There is friendship in politics,' he said. 'There is decency, there are private relationships across all parties, there is principle and there is respect and understanding for the beliefs and convictions of others.' There was a growing tiredness with the 'sleaze' theme, and this in turn helped the Government by temporarily diverting attention away from the ongoing Scott inquiry.

Fourth, the Prime Minister's clearly sincere reactions to the sad circumstances of Mr Smith's death, and particularly his tribute in the Commons, gently redeemed him in the eyes of the general public. By the following weekend, most talk of an early departure had been replaced by speculation about when, and how, Mr Major would re-shuffle his Cabinet. 'What explains the new unity?' asked the *Economist*: 'Most Tory MPs now believe that the party leadership is John Major's for the keeping, no matter what happens in the Euro-elections. They may change their mind yet again but for the time being they no longer have an appetite for damaging the man who is likely to lead them into the next election.'

Labour's new mechanism for electing the party leader had been introduced at the 1993 Party Conference, its general aim being to reduce the preponderance of the trades unions and to create a more balanced electoral college. Media covereage concentrated on two aspects of the mechanism: its potential cost, and the date of the contest. The problems of cost were bound up in the probability that the trades unions would have to hold more than one ballot. As to the date, there was much speculation as to when the leadership contest could be held. The debate was reminiscent of that which took place when Neil Kinnock decided to stand down immediately after the 1992 general election. Some party activists feared that, if the contest took place before the summer break, there was a possibility that, as in the case of Mr Smith's candidature, an early frontrunner would snowball support and prevent a more detailed consideration of the merits of the other candidates on offer. On the other hand, if the party waited until after the summer break an awkward power vacuum could develop, with the new leader lacking direct legitimacy and other potential leadership candidates engaging in protracted shadow boxing. Such internal rivalry could sap the party's strength, undermine its morale, and allow the Conservative Government a further period of respite.

Linked to the problem of choosing a date for the leadership contest was the matter of the likely candidates. There were two immediate frontrunners, both of them John Smith protégés: Gordon Brown, the Shadow Chancellor of the Exchequer, and Tony Blair, the Shadow Home Secretary. Other potential candidates identified by the media included the new interim leader, Margaret Beckett; the shadow spokesman on employment, John Prescott; the shadow spokesman on trade and industry, Robin Cook; and, as an outside choice for the left, the maverick former leader of the GLC, Ken Livingstone. John Smith's death affected the Labour Party's campaign organisation far more than was admitted at the time. During the spring of 1994, as the Prime Minister became increasingly embroiled in backbench dissension, ministerial imbroglios and leadership intrigue, the leader of the Opposition had been urged to capitalise on his rival's problems, but John Smith clearly preferred to leave the Conservatives to squabble among themselves. This led to criticism that his approach was too laid back. One Labour critic yearned for 'the spirit of Thatcher' (*Independent*, 19 April) and Peter Riddell speculated in the *Times* that Labour might 'coast to defeat'. On European matters, the Opposition leader seemed also to prefer late entries into the debates, much to the disappointment of the party's Euro-enthusiasts. He did not attack the Prime Minister over the blocking minority row until late in the day and then seemed to prevaricate. Similarly, he bided his time before coming out against a referendum on EMU in May. Kinder observers suspected that John Smith was keeping his powder dry.

It had early been decided that the party leader should play an up-front, key role in the European elections. The offensive was to have begun on Sunday 15 May, on the eve of the party's manifesto launch, with a major, set-piece 'vision of Europe' speech from the party leader. Instead, John Smith died on Thursday 12 May. The previous evening he had been attending a party supper designed to raise funds for the Euro-elections, at which the leader of the French Socialist Party, Michel Rocard, had made a rousing speech about his belief in the resurgence of European socialism. The party's European policy was to have been emphasised by an extraordinary summit of European socialist leaders on 19 May, where the Opposition leader had planned to play a prominent and enthusiastic part. On 21 May he was to have been the key speaker in the party's planned National Policy Forum. Indeed, the party's overall campaign was to focus on its leader, whose European credentials were incontestable. John Smith was to have attended most of the party's press conferences, and so his sudden disappearance left a huge organisational gap – 'massive dislocation', as one senior Labour politician described it – and an unfillable public void. According to the original plans, Margaret Beckett was to have chaired the press conferences, whilst the Shadow Foreign Secretary concentrated his energies on Labour's key seats. After the leader's death, Margaret Beckett became leader. Jack Straw, who had managed the party's local election campaign, was brought in as campaign manager, and either he or Jack Cunningham chaired the press conferences. Joyce Quin took over the Shadow Foreign Secretary's duties in the target seats. In the event, this new organisation more than sufficed, but everybody involved in it agreed that it was not the same.

After the election, *sotto voce* criticisms of the late party leader's leadership style were to extend to his choice of electoral strategy, but such criticisms were based on an inaccuracy. The basic campaign strategy was elaborated in the Campaign Management Team, where the Shadow Foreign Secretary and the Deputy Leader had early decided that the best policy was a twin-track approach, with an assault on the government's domestic record on the one hand, and emphasis on Labour's positive European policy on the other. The twin-track approach was later confirmed in a series of policy papers throughout the early spring. However, much of the emphasis on the European policy was to have come from John Smith, and could not come from Margaret Beckett, who was much cooler in her attitudes towards the EC. Jack Straw was also suspected of Euro-scepticism, and so it was perhaps inevitable that the national press conferences tended to focus more on criticism of the government's domestic political record. On the other hand, as Pauline Green has pointed out, if the campaign did not focus on a positive European theme, it was not for lack of trying; two Labour MEPs were always present at the national press conferences, and at least one always spoke. But the Lobby was interested in other things, principally the shadow boxing for the Labour leadership elections.

John Smith's death deprived Labour of its leader, but it also deprived the Conservatives of their prime target. It was already clear that Margaret Beckett would be no more than an interim leader, so that attacks on her would be largely ineffective. And, although front-runners for the Labour leadership contest rapidly emerged, it would have been a strategic error for the Conservatives to have concentrated their fire on the favourites. As Chapter 4 showed, an important element of the Conservatives' planned campaign was to lambast the Labour leader for having signed up to the Socialist Euro-manifesto, and the party was obliged hastily to rewrite parts of its own manifesto to expunge any reference to John Smith. Labour continued to run on its pro-European platform, but the simple fact was that Margaret Beckett had not herself signed the Euro-manifesto and, although she said nothing, was known to be cooler towards Europe than her predecessor.

'Monsieur Oui, the poodle of Brussels', was no more, and the Conservatives had to turn their offensive into a more generalised attack on the party rather than its personalities. All of the parties suffered in practical terms. Campaigns were truncated and dislocated, and planned activities had to be compressed into an eighteen-day period. The momentum of the local elections campaign was lost, as activists and campaign teams had to be stood down. Much electoral material had to be redrafted or even reprinted. Perhaps most importantly, the media became distracted by the Labour leadership contest.

THE CEASEFIRE PERIOD (13–21 MAY)

By Saturday 14 May, Tony Blair had emerged as the clear favourite and the media's darling, and a broad consensus had simultaneously begun to emerge within the Labour Party that there should be an early leadership election. A Shadow Cabinet meeting was scheduled for the evening of Wednesday 18 May, to discuss the leadership issue. The two chief rivals, Tony Blair and Gordon Brown, were reported to have been sounding out their colleagues, but the *Guardian* was predicting a 'swift duel' between Tony Blair and John Prescott. The *Sunday Times* of 15 May reported that there was a 'secret pact' between Mr Blair and Mr Brown, with both agreeing that, to avoid a bloody fight and split vote, only one of them would stand. According to the Sunday broadsheets, a clear majority within the NEC favoured an early contest, and the party chairman, David Blunkett, gave a series of interviews throughout the day in which he spoke of his personal preference for a rapid succession. A Gallup poll in the *Sunday Telegraph* sparked the headline 'Voters back Blair'. At the Wednesday shadow cabinet meeting, it was agreed that the leadership campaign should only begin after the European elections. All of the potential candidates on the NEC (Tony Blair, Gordon Brown, John Prescott, and Robin Cook) gave their strong support to this decision. It was agreed that the NEC should meet a week later to decide the leadership contest timetable. Notwithstanding these decisions, the media continued to take a strong interest in the potential candidates and the electoral mechanism, and there was much expectation that Gordon Brown would set out the themes of his covert leadership bid in a speech to the Welsh Labour Party's Conference on the following Sunday.

The 'ceasefire' period was marked by a number of events. Having previously announced his intention to retire, Bryan Gould resigned as an MP on Monday 16 May. It was reported that he had come under pressure to resign so that his seat could be filled in an early by-election and the next day the writs were duly moved for by-elections in the five Westminster seats of Barking, Bradford, Dagenham, Eastleigh and Newham North East. All were to be held on the same day as the Euro-elections, encouraging several journalists to borrow from American primary election parlance and dub Thursday 9 June as a 'super Thursday'. The departure of Mr Gould added to a general impression that the Labour Party's 'modernisation' process was inexorable.

The Conservatives had a mixed week. On the Monday, Sir Edward Heath was heckled in the House of Commons by backbench Conservative Euro-sceptics, and his characteristically spirited ripostes renewed fears that an open row would take place between the party's Euro-enthusiasts and Euro-sceptics during the campaign proper. On Wednesday, 18 May, the *Guardian* published a leaked story that the Government was planning to privatise the Royal Mail in the near future. The story triggered a mini-row, with the President of the Board of Trade doughtily arguing the need for international competitiveness. The controversy was effectively quelled the next day, when the Government published its 'comments' in response to Sinn Fein's requests for clarification of the Downing Street declaration. By the end of the week the Government was once more embroiled in political controversy, when the unfortunate Nicholas Scott was obliged personally to filibuster out the draft Bill for the Disabled.

For the Liberal Democrat leadership, the week began with a propaganda slip-up. Despite the moratorium on campaigning, eager Liberal Democrat activists in Eastleigh began their activities on Monday 16 May. Faced with a *fait accompli* in a strategically vital seat, the grim-faced leadership's explanation was that the moratorium concerned national campaigning only and did not extend to local campaigns, but Cowley Street was privately prepared to admit that the news was a public relations gaffe.

On Friday 20 May, a funeral service was held for John Smith in Edinburgh. The service dominated the media and was carried live by BBC television and radio. It was attended by the Prime Minister and a large number of Mr Smith's British Labour and European socialist colleagues. It brought to an end an extraordinary and unprecedented week during which the normal cut and thrust of partisan politics was virtually absent.

THE CAMPAIGN OPENS (21 MAY)

The major political parties had agreed on a moratorium on campaigning until John Smith's funeral had taken place, but Conservative Central Office came under increasing pressure from frustrated candidates in endangered seats, afraid that the hiatus was robbing them of valuable campaign time. And so the Conservatives launched their campaign (although not their manifesto) at Smith Square on Saturday 21 May, on the same day that John Smith was finally laid to rest on the island of Iona. Nobody protested. The Labour front bench team was still subdued but it seemed that most other politicians were glad to fling themselves back into the fray.

The press conference was chaired by Sir Norman Fowler, with short speeches from the Foreign Secretary, the Home Secretary and Sir Christopher Prout. Each hammered away at the left/right theme, with the Lib/Labs bracketed together as centralisers, in contrast to the Conservatives' vision of a more flexible intergovernmental Europe which, asserted Douglas Hurd, 'the overwhelming majority of the British people' wanted. The party's first campaign poster was unveiled afterwards in Smith Square. It consisted of a simple legend in white lettering on a blue background; 'Backing Britain in Europe. The Conservatives on 9th June.' As one party official told a journalist, 'You would not believe how much blood was spilt and how many hours were spent agreeing on that.' There was one ill omen. The party's intention of launching its campaign on the Saturday had been leaked several days before in the *Daily Telegraph*, and on the day of the campaign launch, in what was clearly a spoiling operation, the Euro-sceptical Conservative 'Way Forward' group published an edition of its journal, *Forward*, with a critical article penned by one of the party's arch Euro-sceptics, Sir George Gardiner. The next day's headlines raised the spectre of the split campaign in 1989: 'TORY RIGHT CLAIMS SUPPORTERS ARE ON STRIKE AGAINST MAJOR' (*Sunday Times*); 'LEAD FROM THE FRONT OR PAY THE PRICE, MAJOR IS WARNED' (*Sunday Telegraph*); 'TORY SPLIT HITS EURO CAMPAIGN' (*Daily Mail*).

The Liberal Democrats were eager not to give the Conservatives a head start. On the Saturday they published a document entitled 'ten broken promises', which set out ten areas where the government had allegedly reneged on policy commitments. Taxation, one of the Labour Party's chosen themes, figured prominently, and the Liberal Democrat chairman, Charles Kennedy, gave a series of interviews throughout the day repeating the theme. The next day, Paddy Ashdown 'pre-launched'

1 (*above*) John Major and Jacques Delors, 27 April (*Financial Times*).

2 (*below*) John Major and Chancellor Helmut Kohl of Germany (*Ashley Ashwood, Financial Times*).

3 (*above*) Conservative manifesto launch, 23 May (*Simon Kreitem, Reuter/Popperfoto*).

4 (*below*) Sir Christopher Prout in the European Parliament, Strasbourg, France (*Tony Andrews; Financial Times*).

15 (*above*) Labour press conference, 23 May; John Cunningham, Margaret Beckett, Gordon Brown, John Prescott (*The Times*).

16 (*below*) Tony Blair in Eastleigh, 2 June (*The Times*).

12 (*left*) Diana Maddock, vice-chair, European election campaign, with Paddy Ashdown, leader of the Liberal Democrats (*Trevor Humphries, Financial Times*).

13 (*below*) Paddy Ashdown with victorious Liberal Democrats: Graham Watson, David Chidgey, Paddy Ashdown, Robin Treverson (*Trevor Humphries, Financial Times*).

14   Conservative poster, Smith Square, 7 June (*The Times*).

15   Labour poster, Smith Square, 7 June: Pauline Green, John Cunningham.

16 (*left*) Alan Sked broadcast, 31 May (*The Times*).

17 (*centre*) Margaret Beckett (acting Labour leader) and Jack Cunningham (Shadow Foreign Secretary) greet the party's new MEPs in London (*Press Association*).

18 (*bottom*) Peter Snow and the BBC election results, 12 June (*The Times*).

the Liberal Democrat party's manifesto. 'We want a Europe which provides practical opportunities for people, not grand theories for politicians,' he said. 'We don't want Europe for Europe's sake. We want Europe for Britain's sake.'

The Labour Party's hands were initially tied; to have begun campaigning on the day of the former leader's funeral would have seemed indecent if, indeed, the front bench had had the stomach for it. On the Sunday, Margaret Beckett, the new leader, gave a 'flawless' performance on the BBC's *On the Record*, concentrating on the government's failures and refusing to be drawn on the leadership issue. However, it was clear that, whatever tacit agreement the potential candidates had made between themselves, the media were determined to concentrate on the matter. The broadsheets were full of biographical pieces on the favourite, Tony Blair, and speculative articles about whether Gordon Brown would stand against his friend. In the afternoon, the Shadow Chancellor delivered his long-awaited speech to the Welsh Labour Party's Conference. It was the first set-piece speech by one of the potential leadership contenders and was interpreted almost exclusively in that context, dominating Monday's (23 May) headlines: 'BROWN STAKES HIS CLAIM TO THE LEADERSHIP', trumpeted the *Daily Express*; 'BROWN FIRES OPENING SHOT FOR LEADERSHIP', declared the *Times*; 'BROWN MAKES PITCH TO LEFT', asserted the *Guardian*. An important consideration in the contest would be the attitude of the trades unions, and the Shadow Chancellor's call for 'full employment and fulfilling employment' and references to a minimum wage were seen as attempts to woo union leaders.

On Monday 23 May, the three major parties launched their manifestos. In what was to become an established pattern, Gordon Brown's speech of the previous day dominated the morning's headlines, the national press conferences dominated the midday news, and a speech given by the Prime Minister on the campaign trail was the major evening news story. Throughout the rest of the campaign, these three elements – the Labour leadership, the party's national campaigns, the Prime Minister's personal interventions – jostled beside one another in the news coverage. The morning's *Daily Express* reported an ICM poll that put Labour on 46 per cent, the Conservatives on 27 per cent, and the Liberal Democrats on 23 per cent. The paper predicted that the Conservatives would lose 13 of their 32 Euro-seats. The poll found that a new Prime Minister could cut Labour's 22–point lead to 14 per cent; 79 per cent of respondents said the political situation in Britain would be the most important influence on how they

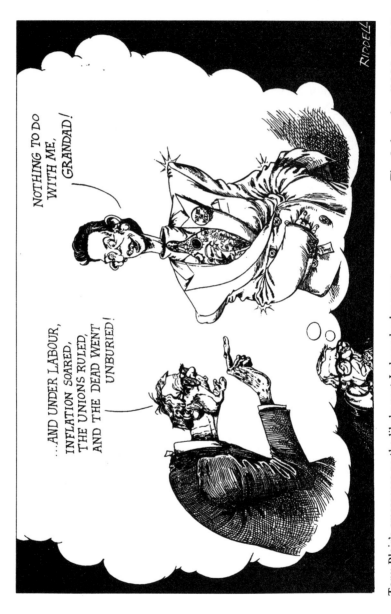

The *Independent* (16 May 1994)

Tony Blair's emergence as the likely next Labour leader upset
Conservative strategy

voted 40 per cent saw Europe as a threat, and 71 per cent were against granting any further powers to the European Parliament.

Against this sombre background, the Conservative manifesto launch took place at Church House. A cheery and upbeat Prime Minister was accompanied on the podium by the Foreign Secretary, the Chancellor of the Exchequer, the Party Chairman, Michael Heseltine, Michael Howard, Gillian Shepherd, David Hunt and Sir Christopher Prout. The Prime Minister emphasised the Conservatives' deregulatory record, the internal market, subsidiarity, and enlargement. Labour's 'corporatist concept of Europe' needed to be 'consigned to the slagheap of history'. The election was not 'a trivial opinion poll'. The European Parliament would have a real role and its powers would grow; it was important to elect candidates of quality. Sir Christopher Prout reinforced this message; the European Parliament had real powers. There had been a socialist majority in Europe, hence Europe's intrusiveness over the past decade. The Conservatives favoured an open, free-trading, decentralised Europe. The British Conservatives held the swing of votes within the Parliament, so the elections were important. In part recalling the government's recent problems, journalists' questions focussed on Cabinet unity, the referendum issue, particularly in relation to a single currency, the veto and qualified majority voting, and the possibility of ERM re-entry. There were also questions about the Conservative MEPs' alliance with the Christian Democrats, and about further increases in the European Parliament's powers. The Prime Minister took most of the questions himself, but passed some on to Sir Christopher Prout. The Chancellor of the Exchequer dismissed the possibility of early re-entry into the ERM. Mr Major took Labour to task for its concentration on the Government's domestic record: 'What do they have to hide about Europe?', he asked, waving a copy of the PES manifesto. The general atmosphere was perhaps surprisingly cheerful, with none of the gloom at the party's poor poll performance showing through.

The Labour Party's manifesto was launched in the more intimate atmosphere of the press room at Transport House. Despite the scrum of television cameramen at the back of the room, the atmosphere was sober, although not sombre. On the platform were Margaret Beckett, Jack Cunningham, Jack Straw, Joyce Quin and Pauline Green. With the exception of Mr Straw, all four read out prepared speeches. Mrs Beckett promised that the campaign would be fought on the 'whole picture – the Tory record in Britain and in Europe'. The election would inevitably be a referendum on John Major and his government:

recession, taxation, crime, the Conservative Party's divisions over Europe, the dangers of the government's negativism in Europe, the social cost of the opt out from the Social Chapter, and failure to reform the CAP. 'This Tory government', she said, 'has failed Britain and failed Britain in Europe . . . And because their record is one of failure their campaign will be based not on their own positive message, but on lies about the Labour Party.' She dismissed the Liberal Democrats as offering 'unconditional, unquestioning support to whatever comes out of Europe'. Labour, she claimed, was a 'party committed to Europe and to Britain's place at the centre of Europe. But equally determined to use that strength and authority in the interests of Britain and its people'. The other speakers reinforced certain themes. Jack Cunningham highlighted the government's confusion over Europe, the weakness of its position, and the dangers of its policy: 'The Tory vision of Europe is of a low-wage, low-skill Britain in the Union. It's a dismal prospect, offering only insecurity and low standards.' Joyce Quin concentrated on the Conservatives' 'lies about Labour', particularly on the veto and the Social Chapter. Pauline Green detailed the work of the Labour MEPs before concluding that 'The British people want . . . a Britain strong in Europe and strong in the world, with Labour MEPs and a Labour government fighting effectively for Britain's interests.' Many of the questions raised by journalists were similar to those that had been addressed to the Conservatives: the veto, and qualified majority voting, the party's attitude to a single currency and the ERM, and whether the EP should have greater powers. Mrs Beckett was asked about the possibility of a referendum over the results of the 1996 IGC, a theme dear to Mr Ashdown, and said that 'we certainly don't rule it out'. Mr Cunningham, quizzed over the PES manifesto, spoke of a 'shared vision'. A hapless BBC journalist asked about the leadership contest. Mr Straw upbraided him. All such questions were banned. 'This election', he went on, 'is about the leadership of Britain'. At the end of the conference, Jack Cunningham gave a neat summary of the party's views: 'We believe in a Community of nation states and of devolution within the nation states. Union can be greater than the sum of its parts.'

The Liberal Democrats launched their manifesto in the Assembly Room of the old Methodist Central Hall. Diana Maddock (deputy leader of the Euro-campaign) chaired the meeting, flanked by Paddy Ashdown and the party's Euro-campaign manager, Tim Clement-Jones. There were noticeably fewer journalists present. A prepared speech had been distributed, but Mr Ashdown ignored it, restricting himself to claiming that the manifesto contained 'the policies Britons need and should get'. Mr Clement-Jones gave a psephological interpretation of the party's chances and strong points. His overall message was the need for caution and realism, and he concluded with a 'little ditty': 'One's a breakthrough, two's a joy, three's fantastic, four, oh boy!' Journalists' questions were directed only at the party leader. The second question concerned the veto; would the Liberal Democrats give it up, as Mr Major had claimed? This, Mr Ashdown retorted, belied the Tory attitude; they wanted to stop Europe doing things. 'The best veto of all would be to put it in the hands of the people'. He went on to speak about the advantages of QMV in such areas as CAP reform, but concluded by saying that the Liberal Democrats would sustain the veto in the European Council. He was then asked to clarify the referendum issue. Mr Ashdown explained how he would favour a referendum on any further substantial constitutional reform unless it coincided with a General Election and there was a sufficient choice between the parties. A puzzled *Sky News* journalist then said, 'It seems like a fudge on the veto business.' Mr Ashdown denied it; the veto would be maintained for executive decisions of the Council, but there would be more QMV for legislative decisions. He was asked to elaborate and gave the example of Bosnia. Twice more he was asked to explain exactly what he meant about the veto and the referendum. By now, even journalists well-versed in Euro-jargon through their coverage of the Maastricht Treaty and the blocking minority row were lost. Few were sufficiently aware of the distinction between the European Council (of Heads of Government) and the Council (of Ministers), and the press conference seemed to have become irretrievably bogged down in technical discussion. It was not the best of starts, particularly since the Prime Minister had decided to make the veto a prime issue of his campaign.

THE PRIME MINISTER'S CAMPAIGN

John Smith's death had the disadvantage of removing the traditional electoral element of the duelling between the party leaders, but it also meant that the media concentrated more attention on the Prime Minister alone. This attention was enhanced by the feeling that Mr Major's future would depend on the result for, although an immediate leadership challenge after the Euro-elections was now considered

Tweedledum, Tweedledee and Tweedledo

unlikely, the more traditional period of the party conference season loomed in the autumn, and the media continued to run stories about backbench plots throughout the Euro-campaign. The April 1992 General Election result had been interpreted as a personal victory for the Prime Minister. He had chosen a highly active, high-profile role and had taken his campaign out onto the streets and to the people. In May/June 1994, the Prime Minister again opted for a highly active, high profile personal campaign, but on this occasion his tactics were very different. Although Mr Major toured the regions energetically and conducted a number of 'walkabouts', these were not the main aspect of his campaign, as they had been in 1992. Instead, the Prime Minister opted for a carefully targeted offensive on core voters. This consisted of two elements: selected audiences, and keynote speeches. As Colin Brown wrote in the *Independent* (26.5.94),

> Central Office appears to have decided that the big street meetings with the Prime Minister which were the turning point in 1992 would be counterproductive. At the general election, Mr Major had to win over the country to win seats at Westminster, and he was massively successful. The Tories have adopted a different strategy to win seats to the European Parliament. The Tory campaign is concentrating on the bedrock supporters who can swing seats on a low turn-out. The aim is to maximise the effect of personal contact with Mr Major. They are playing to his personal strengths in small meetings, influencing a few core supporters to spread the message in their own communities. It is a small, low-key campaign hitting the erogeneous zones which get the party faithful excited: national identity, fear of over-bearing foreigners, Euro-socialism and immigration.

These tactics were clear from the first day of the campaign. Mr Major toured the West country, culminating in the evening in a set-piece speech in Bristol, in which he concentrated his fire heavily on the veto theme, arguing that Labour and the Liberal Democrats could not be trusted to defend Britain's prerogatives. His message was reinforced when the Conservatives' first party political broadcast went out later on the same evening. The broadcast began with deliberately nostalgic images of green fields, a castle, typical English countryside, a steam engine – all overlaid by the Purcell music which had served as their campaign theme in 1992. The broadcast switched to the Prime Minister. Historical references were much commented upon by the media: 'This British nation has a monarchy founded by the kings of Wessex over 1,100 years ago,' he said. 'A parliament and universities formed over 700 years ago, a language with its roots in the mist of time, and the richest vocabulary in the world. This is no recent historical invention. It is the cherished creation of generations . . . ' His core message was that 'In their hearts people fear a loss of identity. We won't let it happen.' Mr Major's speech dominated the next day's headlines, and the veto theme continued to run for several days.

Perhaps inadvertently, the Prime Minister's speeches and interviews began to supplant the traditional agenda-setting function of the daily national press conferences. Indeed, the Bristol veto speech set the trend. In the Conservatives' 24 May press conference, the Party Chairman and the Chancellor of the Exchequer hammered away on the veto theme. Despite initial intentions, the Labour Party's conference was inevitably reactive. The speakers (Jack Cunningham, Jack Straw, Gavin Strang and John Tomlinson, MEP) concentrated on the themes of 'waste, fraud and lies', with Mr Strang arguing for fundamental reform of the CAP; but the journalists were far more interested in the veto theme. Jack Cunningham hit back hard; 'This election has become a referendum on the honesty and integrity of the Prime Minister. Judging by his statements over the past twenty-four hours, he has none. . . . True patriots', he said, 'do not go around breast beating'. The need for a clearly-established leader was cruelly revealed for, despite the authoritative statements of the party's frontbenchers, the party could not entirely shake off the veto story.

The Liberal Democrat press conference was similarly reactive. Charles Kennedy took the podium with the party's agriculture spokesman, Paul Tyler. By coincidence, the party had also chosen the theme of CAP reform but, once again, the journalists were far more interested in the veto issue, and Mr Kennedy was called upon to clarify the position set out by Mr Ashdown the previous day. 'The national veto', Mr Kennedy declared, 'is the last refuge of the scoundrel for the Tories. They were responsible for the extension of qualified majority voting under the Single European Act and the Maastricht Treaty. . . . We want more consensual decision-making, but the intergovernmental pillars would be retained.' Once again, the technical nuances of the party's position proved difficult to get over, for a television journalist immediately riposted 'So you *are* going to sacrifice the national veto!'

This pattern, of the Prime Minister establishing a theme, and of the other parties being obliged to react, was to be repeated on three further occasions. On Friday 27 May, the *Bristol Evening News* published an interview with Mr Major that had taken place on the previous Monday. In it Mr Major said that 'The problem about begging is as old as the hills. It is very offensive to many people . . . It is damaging to everybody . . . We should not shrink from using the (available penalties)' (*Times*, 28 May). The weekend newspapers were dominated by the 'beggars' theme: 'SWEEP BEGGARS OFF THE STREETS, PM DEMANDS' (*Independent*); 'PM ATTACKS "OFFENSIVE" BEGGARS' (*Guardian*); 'MAJOR CALLS FOR TOUGH LINE ON BEGGARS' (*Daily Telegraph*); 'MAJOR WINS STREET CRED. IN FIGHT AGAINST BEGGARS' (*Sunday Times*); 'MAJOR'S BEGGARS ATTACK "PANDERS TO RIGHT"' (*Sunday Telegraph*). To his critics, the Prime Minister's interview was further evidence of his pragmatic search for support from the right wing of the party. The views it contained aroused little enthusiasm to centre-left Conservatives. So much attention did it receive that some political commentators thought the 'beggars' interview had 'derailed' the Conservatives' campaign, but most agreed that Mr Major was deliberately – or inadvertently – mobilising the core Tory vote in the shires, where low differential turnout could spell disaster. Certainly, at the constituency level, a large number of Conservative candidates were heartened by the effects of the Prime Minister's interview. 'It certainly touched a popular chord,' said one; 'It got a very positive reaction,' said another. But what was appealing in the south west could be unhelpful in the London area. The 'beggars' story ran on into the next week. Once more, Labour and Liberal Democrat politicians found themselves reacting to an established theme, attacking the Prime Minister and the government for their hard line. As we shall see, an apparent front bench contradiction in views led the Labour Party into making a gaffe.

On the evening of Tuesday 31 May, the Prime Minister made a speech in Ellesmere Port, Cheshire, in which he set out his vision of a 'multi-track, multi-speed, multi-layered Europe'. As was recorded above, the Foreign Secretary had already developed this theme as a response to the prospect of a steadily-enlarging European Union but the media now discovered it in a very different context. A summit was taking place on the same day in the Alsatian town of Mulhouse between Chancellor Helmut Kohl and President François Mitterrand, and this was interpreted as an example of Franco-German dominance, since the two heads of state were said to be discussing a common approach to the 1996 IGC. Moreover, the French Minister for European Affairs, Alain Lamassoure, had published an article in *Le Monde* on the same day, explicitly calling for the 1996 IGC to reconstitute Europe into a hard core of Member States and a slower track. Seen in this context, Mr Major's speech seemed to be a direct response to the Franco-German two-speed model. It also restated the

Beggars

established Douglas Hurd position – that the EU was more flexible and multi-speed than people realised – in a much more prescriptive way. Europe had to become more flexible and countries should not be forced to do everything at the same speed: 'that was a socialist way of acting'. Crucially, although perhaps inadvertently, the Prime Minister had transformed Mr Hurd's description of the way Europe *was* developing into a far more prescriptive vision of how he thought it *should* develop. The speech also included a sweeping denunciation of centralisation which, to Conservative Euro-enthusiasts, seemed worryingly close to a denunciation of all that the Community had so far achieved. Again, the next day's election coverage was dominated by the 'multi-track' theme, with the broadsheets interpreting the speech as a Euro-sceptical device, and the *Financial Times* reporting that 'MAJOR SIGNALS UK WILL GO SLOW ON EUROPE'. Whatever his intention, the Prime Minister's speech certainly cheered the Euro-sceptical wing of the Conservative Party, and on Wednesday Lord Tebbit publicly endorsed Mr Major's views. Like the 'beggars' interview, the 'multi-track' view elicited different responses from the right and left wings of his party, but, again, many Conservative candidates spoke in positive terms about the speech with its convenient ambiguity. Lastly, the Labour and Liberal Democrat parties once more found themselves reacting to an established theme which inevitably became tangled up with the more general issue of the veto. In the morning press conference, Margaret Beckett said Mr Major's stand would keep Britain in the 'bicycle lane'. He was not keeping the right to say no, she argued, but 'forfeiting the right to say anything'. But Mr Major riposted that Labour's policy was 'the most craven foreign policy I have ever heard from a British political party'. The Liberal Democrats were troubled even more by the veto theme. They had begun their campaign in some confusion and with the public exposure of an apparent policy difference between the leader and other party grandees such as the former leader, Sir David Steel, and the Chairman, Charles Kennedy, as Mr Ashdown sailed closer to the Euro-sceptical line. Every return to the veto or related issues highlighted these differences still further.

On Tuesday 7 June, Mr Major gave his final campaign speech at a Hammersmith hotel, again striking a more Euro-sceptical note, warning against 'the deadly sins of Europe'. Since it came two days before the Euro-elections themselves, there was insufficient time for the speech to develop into a running story, even if it had sufficient actual content. Nevertheless, several broadsheets, including the *Times*, led with his remarks on the eve of the election.

Daily Telegraph (2 June 1994)

Running with the hounds

Several aspects of the Prime Minister's personal role in the campaign are of note. A first is that, although Mr Major exercised an agenda-setting function, he exercised only imperfect control over how this worked. For instance, not all of the Prime Minister's speeches and interviews provoked such media reactions, and at times it seemed almost as though the media were picking through the Prime Minister's contributions for those parts which could be fitted into the Euro-sceptical/Euro-enthusiast theme. The 'multi-speed' speech was a good example of this phenomenon, leading Douglas Hurd to express bemusement at a press conference that a theme he had already aired on several occasions should have suddenly taken off as it did. The 'multi-speed' speech is also a good example of a second point, which is that it is unclear how far the Prime Minister intended or expected his interventions to have the effect they did. The Ellesmere Port speech was a major campaign speech but was not considered potentially controversial, and even senior Central Office figures were surprised to see the splash it had made on the later evening news programmes. The 'beggars' interview raised similar comment since by the time it was published Mr Major had long since moved on from Bristol. Some of the Prime Minister's speeches were rumoured to have been written fast and late, and not necessarily in accordance with some overall game plan; it seems that the Ellesmere Port speech reached the Foreign Office too late for effective comment. At the other extreme, Mr Major had set much store by the Government's White Paper on competitiveness, which was launched on 24 May, and intended as a major policy plank in the Government's attempt to reap maximum benefit from the economic recovery, but the White Paper story obstinately refused to fly. A last aspect of Mr Major's campaign is that his speeches and interviews were only one part of his chosen strategy. Much of his time on the campaign trail was spent in small meetings of Conservative activists and voters. Their exclusivity sometimes upset the local press, with some journalists refusing to pay the Central Office-imposed fee of £25 for late applications for press cards. The Prime Minister was reputed to be at his most effective in smaller meetings, but it was difficult to quantify the effect of the many small meetings he attended over the three-week period. The views of those at the coal face – Conservative candidates – were mixed, but most felt that the overall effect of the Prime Minister's interventions was positive and helpful. As one said, 'He gave us some meat.'

The Prime Minister made a highly effective contribution to the campaign in one other way. Personalised letters from Mr Major were sent out to over a million selected Conservative voters at two stages in the campaign. Party activists and candidates spoke highly of the impact of the letters, which were designed above all to mobilise core support. In conclusion, John Smith's death removed a sparring partner, but it also cleared the stage. Margaret Beckett proved an able interim leader, and engaged in a fiery exchange with the Prime Minister during question time at the outset of the campaign, but she could not enjoy the legitimacy nor the authority of a popularly-elected leader, and had to 'share' Labour's publicity with the other potential leadership candidates, particularly Tony Blair. As a result, Mr Major's activities were subject to more intense attention than might otherwise have been the case. And, as in 1992, Mr Major's decision to play an active and high-profile role in the campaign meant that he would inevitably be associated with the outcome of the election, whether good, or bad – or, as was to be the case, good because it was less bad than expected.

THE LABOUR LEADERSHIP

The 18 May shadow cabinet meeting had agreed unanimously that the leadership elections should only begin after the Euro-elections but, in reality, the Labour leadership was a constant, and at times dominant, theme throughout the Euro-campaign. On the day after the manifesto launches, Tony Blair made his first speech since John Smith's death, in which he called for a concerted drive to reverse Britain's social and industrial decline: 'The task is one of national renewal,' he said, 'rebuilding a strong civic society and basing it on a modern notion of citizenship where rights and duties go hand in hand' (*Guardian*, 25 May). There was much comparison with Gordon Brown's speech in Wales on the previous Sunday about 'full and fulfilling employment'. Later, a minor row erupted when John Patten revealed the contents of a train conversation he had had with Mo Mowlam, who was close to the Blair camp. According to the story, Tony Blair was said to be worried that there was insufficient room for his family at Number 10, Downing Street. But press reaction to Tony Blair's pretensions – if such they were – was not entirely hostile. Rather, there seemed to be agreement among the political pundits that the image of Tony Blair at Number 10 was a not an implausible one.

The next day the NEC established a timetable for the leadership elections, with nominations for the leadership opening on 10 June.

Margaret Beckett unexpectedly resigned her position as deputy leader, a post she would have been entitled to continue to hold once the party had elected a new leader, so that there would be two sets of elections. The results would be announced on 21 July, probably the last day of the parliamentary session. To avoid the ruinously expensive possibility of holding more than one round of elections, as the party's rules seemed to suggest, the NEC confirmed that the ballot would be undertaken by a system of preference voting on a single ballot paper. (The NEC decided that the Labour MEPs who would form part of the electoral college would be those elected on 9 June, even though, technically, the outgoing MEPs remained in place until 18 July. This meant that, after the gain of 17 seats in June, Labour MEPs became a more numerous part of the electoral college.) Mrs Beckett's resignation was the subject of much speculation. Did this mean she would run for the post of leader? But most commentaries recognised that she had 'done the right thing' by resigning the deputy leadership, thus opening up the way for the election of a 'ticket' in July. Some confusion arose when, by not explicitly ruling himself out of the leadership contest, Jack Cunningham seemed to be implying that he would like to be ruled in. But behind the speculation Tony Blair remained odds-on favourite, with an ICM poll for the *Guardian* establishing him as the across-the-board favourite within the Labour movement, with John Prescott as his main challenger.

On Thursday 26 May, John Prescott delivered a speech in which he evoked the memory of the Labour values of 1945. Like the Brown and Blair speeches that had preceded it, the media saw Mr Prescott's speech as a bid to establish his leadership credentials, and the next day's headlines reflected this: 'PRESCOTT CALLS ON LABOUR TO RENATIONALISE INDUSTRIES' (*Daily Telegraph*); 'PRESCOTT STAKES CLAIM BY EVOKING THE MEMORIES OF 1945' (*Guardian*); 'PRESCOTT CHAMPIONS LABOUR PARTY'S SOCIALIST VALUES' (*Times*). Throughout the weekend of the 'beggars' speech controversy, which so dominated the headlines, the second story remained the Labour leadership contest. On Sunday 29 May, a poll conducted for the BBC's *On the Record* showed Tony Blair with a clear 48 per cent support within the party and made it clear that, were Gordon Brown to withdraw, Mr Blair would be an easy winner. On Tuesday 31 May, the *Daily Telegraph* detected the 'strongest hint yet' that the Shadow Chancellor would give way. And then, on 1 June, Gordon Brown announced that he would not be standing for the leadership, and that he would be supporting Mr Blair's candidature. The next day, in what was clearly a carefully timed intervention, Mr

Dream ticket

The Times (10 June 1994)

Blair made a 'landmark' speech at Eastleigh, and his ascendancy seemed assured, as the headlines affirmed: 'BLAIR GIVEN A CLEAR RUN' (*Daily Telegraph*); 'WAY CLEAR FOR BLAIR' (*Times*); 'BROWN GIVES LABOUR CROWN TO BLAIR' (*Independent*). Indeed, Mr Brown's withdrawal and Mr Blair's emergence as clear favourite received blanket media coverage until the Chinook helicopter crash on Friday 3 June, and the D-Day anniversary celebrations of that weekend. Nevertheless, media speculation about the most likely leadership candidates and their probable fortunes continued right up to the eve of the elections.

Thus the death of John Smith and the Shadow cabinet's decision to opt for an early leadership contest had three effects. The first was a generally high level of publicity for the party and its front bench. Moreover, as it soon became clear that Tony Blair and/or Gordon Brown and the 'modernisers' within the party were in the ascendant, most of the media coverage was positive or, at the least, not negative. The second effect, soon to be dubbed the 'Blair effect', came into force immediately after Gordon Brown's withdrawal from the race, and was seemingly reinforced by the opinion polls. A Gallup poll published in the *Daily Telegraph* the day after Mr Brown's withdrawal put Labour on 54 per cent and the Conservatives on 21 per cent. Since the fieldwork was done weeks before, Labour's highest rating for 23 years could have had nothing to do with Mr Brown's announcement, yet the poll news seemed to consolidate and reinforce the momentum of the modernisers. The speed of the 'Blair effect' took the other parties by surprise. Liberal Democrat activists felt it had taken some of the wind from their sails for, as one candidate put it, what was Tony Blair if not a younger Paddy Ashdown? Labour's sudden appearance of electability also caught the Conservatives by surprise. As one senior politician put it, 'We didn't spot the Blair effect until too late.' The leadership contest had a third, unquantifiable, effect. At the November 1993 PES Congress in Brussels, the Labour Party had agreed, together with its continental confrères, that a major theme of the Euro-elections should be unemployment, and there were plans to launch a policy paper on 'jobs and social justice' during the Euro-campaign. Many candidates complained that by not in the end running hard on this issue, the Labour Party had deprived itself of a major positive campaign plank, and several suspected that the absence of any major policy initiatives during the campaign was somehow bound up with the leadership issue.

THE PRESS CONFERENCES

The decision of the major parties to hold daily national press conferences (except on Sundays) throughout the campaign was an indication of the importance they attached to the Euro-elections. The conferences provided the focal point for national party organisation but they also represented a considerable drain on resources, and so it is of interest to examine what role they played and how effective they were. Presentation, location and timing were early considerations. Most of the Conservatives' conferences were held in Central Office. Party spokesmen sat at a blue-fronted desk on a blue podium against a blue background, with the party's torch symbol outlined in red above the slogan 'A Strong Britain in a Strong Europe'. The emphasis was on familiarity. Labour held all of its conferences in Transport House, 50 yards from Conservative headquarters at 32 Smith Square. Smith Square was far more accessible for the media, but the location did exacerbate Labour's traditionally fragmented organisation, which was thus split up between Transport House, Walworth Road, and the leader's office at Westminster. Party spokesmen sat at a white and off-grey podium, with a grey background. The party's red rose symbol, which was also the symbol of the PES, was much in evidence. The background sported a slogan, 'Make Britain work for you', to the left and, to the right, a large Union flag, with a circle of the EU Member States' flags beneath it. Several newspapers commented on the size of the Union flag, with Labour clearly intending subliminally to shrug off Conservative accusations about the veto. (The slogan changed in the last week to 'Britain's turning to Labour' and 'Tell the Tories you've had enough.') The Liberal Democrats held some of their conferences in Cowley Street and some in the assembly room of the old Methodist Central Hall. The podium was grey, as was the background, though with two yellow stripes. The party's bird motif and title were repeated several times in yellow lettering and in the centre of the background was the party's main manifesto slogan, 'Unlocking Britain's Potential'. At the party's first press conference, Paddy Ashdown destroyed whatever respectability the arrangement might have had by apologising to journalists for the presentation, which with each election, he said, 'looks more and more like the Soviet politburo'. The timing of the conferences was tacitly agreed among the parties, with the Conservatives usually going first at 9.30 a.m., followed by Labour at 10.30 a.m., and the Liberal Democrats at 11.30 a.m. The conference chairmen stuck strictly to this timetable which, as will be seen, put the

Conservatives at a considerable advantage and the Liberal Democrats at a considerable disadvantage, and the latter switched some conferences to the earlier time of 8.30 a.m.

Halfway through the Euro-campaign a *Sunday Times* journalist remarked that the Conservatives had won the campaign, but lost the election. This was certainly true of the press conferences. The Conservatives effectively set the agenda, choosing the issues on which they wished to run: the veto, the Social Chapter, immigration, crime. In contrast, Labour's main campaign tactic – of attacking the Government's record – was dissipated as the campaign team found itself repeatedly forced to respond to the Conservatives' charges, relayed on by the journalists. Labour was frequently on the back foot and to a considerable extent this was a matter of timing.

As was seen above, the Conservatives had stolen a march by holding a press conference on the day of John Smith's funeral, where they immediately launched their opening and underlying theme, the veto, and used a 'big gun', in the form of the Foreign Secretary, to do the job. As intended, this set the scene for the Sunday newspapers so that, by the Monday of the official manifesto launches (23 May), the veto was at the centre of the political agenda, and the Prime Minister was able to build upon it. Conservative tactics were inadvertently assisted by Paddy Ashdown's 'pre-launching' of selected parts of the Liberal Democrat manifesto, and above all by his playing of the referendum card. This reinforced the Conservatives' claim that important constitutional changes might be in the offing and that the electorate would be better off with experienced hands at the helm.

By contrast, Labour got off to a faltering start. Although they wanted to talk about the government's record, the journalists wanted to talk about the veto and, covertly, about the Labour leadership (the party had banned them from doing this – BBC journalists tried twice and Jack Straw upbraided them); in addition Margaret Beckett seemed in danger of losing her voice. In the evening, the Prime Minister made his Bristol 'veto' speech, putting Labour onto the back foot the next day. Labour's faltering start was compounded by the BBC's strike on the Tuesday, and by the cancellation of the Wednesday press conference because of the meeting of the NEC. Indeed, the Labour Party, as opposed to potential leadership contenders, did not capture the initiative until the VAT story broke on Friday 3 June.

Gordon Brown and Harriet Harman had been repeatedly stressing the Government's alleged untrustworthiness on tax issues, but although these attacks were reported they were not seen as a major story. However, on the Friday morning (3 June), during an interview on the Radio 4 *Today* programme, Gordon Brown asked whether the Government was prepared to rule out further extensions of the VAT base. The question was relayed, via John Humphrys, to the Chancellor of the Exchequer, who refused categorically to rule out such an extension. The Prime Minister, questioned on *Election Call*, similarly declined to rule out the possibility. At that morning's conference, the Shadow Chancellor, backed up by Harriet Harman and a large amount of well-researched documentation, launched a strong offensive, raising the possibility that the government might impose VAT on currently zero-rated items such as books, food and children's clothing. Labour returned to the theme the next day, making use of a shopping basket of vulnerable children's clothing and food. On 5 June, the Prime Minister gave a major interview on the *Frost on Sunday* programme, and was obliged to spend a large part of it denying the Labour accusations, which he described as 'scare tactics', but his denials led to renewed media coverage on the Monday. The 'tax bombshell' press conference was clearly the most effective that Labour organised, enabling them to capture the initiative, but events seemed to conspire against them. On the same day, an army Chinook helicopter carrying 30 high-level security officers from Northern Ireland to a conference in Scotland crashed on the Mull of Kintyre, killing all on board. Inevitably, the crash story and its security implications pushed the VAT story off the front pages.

When their major players – Mr Ashdown, Mr Kennedy, Sir Russell Johnston – were absent, the Liberal Democrats' press conferences suffered very low profiles. Again, timing was involved. The 11.30 a.m. slot seemed a long way from the morning news programmes and perhaps uncomfortably close to the midday news deadlines. The party's problems were compounded by its initial confusion over QMV and the referendum. Paddy Ashdown, sensing a Euro-sceptical shift in the electorate's views, played down QMV and played up the referendum, but more Euro-enthusiastic party elders insisted on doing the reverse. As this debate was being fought out elsewhere, interest in the press conferences declined. The Liberal Democrats also suffered from a simple lack of resources, most of which were focussed in Eastleigh and the south west. The party had no MEPs and could not afford to have MPs on the podium every day, obliging it to hold several conferences where only party officials were present.

The consensus among most journalists was that the Conservatives won on presentation, both in terms of organisation and chairing.

Journalists arriving at Central Office received a press pack containing the scripts of the day's speeches, researched background documents and outlines of the day's campaigning. This information was almost always available in its entirety before the conferences began. By and large, the speakers, always including one minister, kept to their scripts. There were never more than three speeches. These were short and on linked themes. The net effect was that journalists had time to read up and absorb the morning's theme or themes and prepare their questions accordingly. In a subtle way, this enabled the Conservatives to determine the agenda for the day, and it was fairly common for journalists to table questions to the Labour conference that stemmed from earlier exchanges in Central Office. Labour's presentation was comparatively poor. The scripts of most speeches were available at the door, but were frequently distributed during or after the conferences. Labour also produced research documents, but there were no press packs. Whereas the Conservatives were asked a proportionately high number of questions based on the documentation they had circulated, it was rare for a journalist to ask the Labour team anything directly flowing out of the day's documentation. Labour speeches were also brief, but there tended to be more of them, and they did not always relate to the same theme; for example, Labour's VAT offensive, described above, was followed by a speech about the absence of Peter Lilley, on holiday in France. Labour's determination to rebut Conservative claims as soon as they were made also led to a more fragmented message.

Sir Norman Fowler, who had been much criticised for his handling of the local election campaign, steered questions and his panel firmly and made few mistakes. The Conservatives seemed more media conscious, particularly through the use of the soundbite. Lengthy explanations from panel members would be recapitulated and summarised in simple themes, and these would be hammered home through frequent repetition. Difficult questions were brazenly deflected or simply ignored. Journalists' high spirits were met with wry and not unfriendly ripostes. Sir Norman Fowler's deputy, Gerry Malone, handled one press conference with great aplomb and greatly enhanced his reputation within the party during the campaign.

Jack Straw and Jack Cunningham had a different and more difficult job, primarily because Labour had chosen to run on an essentially negative theme, but also because they were frequently forced onto the back foot by the Conservatives' agenda-setting. The Labour front bench had a far more uneasy relationship with the press, often treating them with suspicion, and the awkwardness was exacerbated by the fact that most of the party's heavyweight performers – Blair, Brown, Beckett, Prescott, Cook, Cunningham – were also potential candidates for the leadership. Perhaps some of this uneasiness was derived from a generalised suspicion of the press, after the role the tabloid newspapers played during the 1992 general election, although the tabloids were not much in evidence at the 1994 conferences.

Did any of this matter? The national press conferences were in fact strikingly limited in their impact. For the most part, the morning newspapers ran with the previous evening's speeches. Here, the Prime Minister's speeches and those of the Labour leadership candidates were much to the fore. The morning radio and television bulletins also used the previous evening's speeches, or generated their own news through interviews (the VAT story being a good example). The Radio 4 *Today* programme and BBC television's *Election Call* were important generators of morning news. The press conferences tended to get reasonable coverage in the midday news bulletins but they had already to do battle with the lunchtime news programmes. Again, Radio 4's *The World at One* was an important news generator. By the early evening news the national press conferences had been overtaken by the campaigning activities in the regions (much of which was used to advance the national campaigns, rather than concentrating on local or regional issues), and by 'leaks' of the evening's speeches. By the late evening news, the evening's speeches were being given heavy coverage. From any objective point of view, the organisation of daily national press conferences involved an extraordinary amount of effort for very little return.

Most incumbent Euro-MPs and most candidates felt that the national press conferences had been an irrelevancy. Both the Conservatives and Labour had at least one MEP on the platform every morning. In the case of the Conservatives, this was mainly Sir Christopher Prout, who would typically be accompanied by another Euro-MP to speak on a particular topic. Sir Christopher was helicoptered 150 miles back to his geographically huge constituency (Herefordshire and Shropshire) after each press conference, and was driven back to London late at night, after a full day's campaigning. In addition to the physical strain involved, Sir Christopher's London duties deprived him of valuable campaigning time in a seat that he narrowly lost. Pauline Green was present at almost all of the Labour press conferences. Again, although her task was physically easier, her London constituency was also considered to be highly vulnerable. Like

Sir Christopher, she would sometimes give speeches herself, and was occasionally accompanied by other MEPs. Despite this constant presence and active part in the proceedings, MEPs were asked few questions and the journalists treated them very much as mute accessories. Some Conservative MEPs were baited about the exact nature of their relationship with the EPP Group, but there were few questions about policy. This indifference was to some extent due to a lack of familiarity. For example, when Labour Euro-MP John Tomlinson attended a conference with MPs Gavin Strang and Jack Straw, he was the most ministerially experienced person on the platform (he had been a junior minister in the Foreign Office during the 1974–9 Labour Government), yet journalists preferred to direct questions at the Westminster politicians because they knew them. Pauline Green, soon to be one of the more powerful women in Europe, wryly recounted that despite her constant attendance, she only once appeared on national television, and then mutely holding up a pair of boy's trousers (to illustrate the Conservatives' threat to put VAT on children's clothing).

In conclusion, the daily morning press conferences were neither decisive nor determining, and were frequently reduced to little more than background footage. On occasion they could be disadvantageous, as the media sought 'gaffe' stories (see below). They were not completely irrelevant, but the bulk of the campaign was fought elsewhere, in the national media, where rival soundbites and images joined battle. The only way such conferences could have recaptured the agenda-setting initiative would have been by holding them earlier, but this would have meant absurdly early starts to the day. The tacit agreement between the parties to hold their conferences at staggered intervals during the morning did little to enhance the policy debate which, to the extent that it existed, took place on *Newsnight*, or *On the Record*, or *Election Call*, or *Question Time*, or *Frost on Sunday*, or the *Brian Walden Show*, or on Radio 4's *Today*, *The World at One*, and *The Six o'Clock News* on television. It seemed that, like national manifestos, the conferences were there largely because they were there.

'EUROPE'

Much to many candidates' chagrin, and as had been the case in the previous three rounds of Euro-elections, 'Europe' remained a mostly tangential issue in the 1994 campaign. Sticking to their game-plan, the

Conservatives went to some lengths to underline their claim that Europe, and the European Parliament, had been dominated by socialists for the past five years, but the media did not follow this lead, instead preferring to concentrate its attention chiefly on the national consequences of the European elections. When European issues did arise, they were largely interpreted in their domestic context. Thus, the 'veto', 'referendum', 'single currency' and 'multi-track' issues were primarily of interest to the media because of the known divisions within the government and the Liberal Democrat party respectively; this explains the relatively high profile given to the Ashdown/Kennedy/Steel, Heathcoat Amory and Gummer 'gaffes' (see below). The 'multi-track' speech in particular was seen as the Prime Minister's response to Conservative Euro-sceptics, rather than a response to the broader issue of enlargement. When Michael Howard spoke at a press conference (26 May) of the benefits of intergovernmental cooperation (which the Government had championed over the 'Community' method) in the fields of immigration, drugs and crime, this was rapidly transformed into a 'race row'; ' "RACE CARD" CHARGE IN EUROPEAN ELECTION' (*Daily Telegraph*); 'EURO-CAMPAIGN HEATS UP AS TORIES PLAY RACE CARD' (*Guardian*); 'HOWARD SPARKS RACE ROW WITH IMMIGRATION CLAIMS' (*Times*). The row about the possible extension of the VAT base and the imposition of VAT on domestic fuel was taken purely in its domestic context of the government's policy commitments, with no reference to the larger theme of gradual European fiscal harmonisation which lay behind it.

When it did arise, 'Europe' tended to be portrayed in a critical light. The two exceptions to this trend were the ruling of the European Court of Human Rights on the SAS shooting of IRA terrorists in Gibraltar (which ruled in the SAS's favour) and the OECD report on economic policy (which the Government successfully spin-doctored to its own advantage). On the other hand, coverage of the 8 May ruling of the European Court of Justice in the case of the acquired rights directive (which, although it arrived too late for Labour to use it in the campaign, found against the Government) was generally critical: 'BRUSSELS LAYS DOWN THE LAW YET AGAIN' (*Daily Mail*).

Euro-MPs received occasional coverage, but there were few serious examinations of their role and activities. Two significant exceptions were a 24 May *Independent* report on the attendance record of British MEPs (which found that, bar a few cases, British MEPs were 'good value for money'), and a 1 June *Guardian* story on MEPs' alleged 'scams' on airfares and allowances. There was some irreverence: the

Guardian published a fold-out 'game', allegedly based on the ways of Brussels and Strasbourg, and one of its journalists, Richard Boston, ran as a maverick candidate for the 'Boston Tea Party' in the Hampshire North and Oxford Euro-seat. On the other hand, there was considerable in-depth coverage of 'celebrity' candidates, particularly Glenys Kinnock and Edwina Currie, and of other important candidates (Pauline Green and Sir Christopher Prout, for example) and marginal constituencies. The views of Conservative MEPs, particularly the more Euro-enthusiastic among them, came in for some sustained press attention on 29 May, when the *Sunday Telegraph* published a poll of Conservative candidates which showed clear divisions over the single currency issue, and the *Sunday Times* ran a piece on 'federalist' Conservative MEPs. These stories were derived in part from Labour and Liberal Democrat documentation on the voting records and policy pronouncements of Conservative MEPs.

An important factor behind the way in which European issues were perceived and treated was a generalised impression, sensed by Euro-candidates, Westminster politicians and journalists alike, that there had been a general shift in public opinion towards a more sceptical and suspicious stance. A *Daily Express*/ICM poll published on manifesto launch day found that 40 per cent of respondents saw 'Europe' as a threat (as opposed to 26 per cent in 1991). As one candidate put it, 'The blocking minority row didn't only damage the government's reputation; it wounded national pride.' In addition to the more traditional suspicion of 'Brussels', several candidates detected popular apprehension about Franco-German dominance. A number of events may have encouraged such apprehension. On 27 May the *Daily Express* published an interview with the Prime Minister in which he said that Economic and Monetary Union was very unlikely. But on the same day the German Chancellor, Helmut Kohl, gave a television interview in which he said that EMU was a definite prospect. The British press were not slow to report the contradiction: 'KOHL CURRENCY HOPE ALARMS TORIES' (*Independent*); 'KOHL STIRS UNEASE ON SINGLE CURRENCY' (*Guardian*); 'KOHL TESTS TORY LINE ON SINGLE CURRENCY' (*Daily Telegraph*). The 31 May – 1 June Franco-German summit in Mulhouse was widely reported, particularly the 'pacts' over the coordination of the forthcoming French and German EU Presidencies, and the candidature of the Belgian Prime Minister, Jean Luc Dehaene, to replace Jacques Delors as President of the European Commission. Two days later, under the title 'Franco-German steamroller', a *Daily Telegraph* editorial urged Mr Major to veto Mr Dehaene's nomination. On 6 June the

Financial Times published an interview with the Bundesbank President, Hans Tietmeyer, in which he enthusiastically supported the idea of an 'inner core' of Member States, and on 7 June the *Guardian* ran a story ('BRITISH FACE TEST ON MAASTRICHT OPT-OUT') about the forthcoming German EU Presidency's rumoured plans to face down the British government.

'ANTI-EUROPE'

For the first time, a UK Euro-election saw anti-European candidates and parties fielded, although only one of these, Dr Alan Sked's UK Independence Party, made any national impact. Because the UKIP fielded over seven candidates, it was entitled to an electoral political broadcast on prime time television and radio. Earlier press coverage had aroused some interest, but the broadcast, which went out on 31 May, was undoubtedly the key to the party's impact. The party claimed that initial interest was so high that seven telephone lines had to be installed and manned around the clock (the UKIP claimed to have signed up 50 new members between 4 and 5 a.m. alone on the day after the broadcast). The party's electoral impact is examined in Chapter 9 below. Although handicapped by a tiny and inexperienced organisation and a thin spread of candidates, the UKIP had clearly touched a chord.

GAFFES

The truncated Euro-campaign was just 17 days long, and the steadily-rising expectations about the Prime Minister's fate had to a considerable extent been dissipated. The result was a certain sense of anti-climax among the media, which was consequently on the look out for 'big' stories. As was seen above, the speeches of and interviews with the Prime Minister and the potential Labour leadership candidates provided the media with much fuel, but journalists remained eager to discover contradictions between politicians within the parties. Indeed, a characteristic of the Euro-campaign was a number of 'gaffe' stories. The basic model was similar, with apparent contradictions among party spokesmen worked into broader stories about policy disarray.

The first such story was based on the differences between Paddy Ashdown and other Liberal Democrat politicians over the possibility of a referendum and the extension of qualified majority voting.

(*Independent*, 27 May: 'TORY ATTACK OVER EU VETO FLUSTERS LIB DEM LEADERS'; *Daily Telegraph*, 31 May, 'TORIES HIGHLIGHT THE LIB DEM SPLIT OVER THE VETO'). The second campaign 'gaffe' took place at a 27 May Conservative press conference. Treasury minister and noted Euro-sceptic David Heathcoat-Amory was questioned by a *Financial Times* journalist over the government's position on a single currency. Mr Heathcoat-Amory replied that 'it would be extremely damaging to have a single currency imposed on us. That is why the Prime Minister negotiated the opt-out from the compulsory aspects of Stage Three of European Monetary Union.' The chairman at the press conference, Gerry Malone, tried to finesse his colleague's comments, but it was clear that the minister had gone beyond the established party line.

A third campaign 'gaffe' arose out of the continuing row over the Prime Minister's 'beggars' speech, and effectively allowed the Conservatives to turn the tables on the Labour Party on the issue. The Labour Party's Social Justice Commission, established under John Smith, was due to publish a report on 31 May. One of its recommendations, enthusiastically embraced by the party's Chairman, David Blunkett, was that unemployed 16- to 18-year-olds should be encouraged to take part in volunteer activities, a 'Citizens' Service', in return for a weekly allowance. However, a split was reported to have emerged within the shadow Cabinet as to whether the party would spend extra money on welfare payments to young people forced onto the streets. Donald Dewar, the party's social security spokesman, thought Labour should be prepared to spend more money if necessary. But at the party's 30 May press conference, the shadow Chief Secretary to the Treasury, Harriet Harman, refused to confirm that Labour would introduce any further spending measures. Gordon Brown, the Shadow Chancellor, would not go beyond saying that 'something has got to be done', but would not countenance further spending, while Mr Dewar stuck to his comments. With the party thrown on to the defensive, Mrs Beckett tried to clarify the issue by saying that help would have to be found if the young homeless could not get work or training. Later, Mr Prescott, the party's shadow employment spokesman, told the BBC that 'Whatever the arguments about money we must finance it for the youngsters.' These Labour differences were exploited by the Conservatives. Mr Portillo, Chief Secretary to the Treasury, said that 'after twenty-four hours of chaos' Labour had been forced to admit that 'their policy on welfare payments for 16- to 17-year-olds is no different from the Government's. . . . Once again

Labour has been caught trying to have it both ways, promising to increase spending and not to increase burdens on the taxpayer.' The result was a series of media stories about Labour 'splits' and 'divisions': 'Labour differences over begging' (*Financial Times*); 'TORIES EXPLOIT LABOUR CONFUSION OVER BENEFITS FOR YOUNG' (*Guardian*); 'PARTY SPLITS OVER YOUNG JOBLESS' (*Daily Telegraph*).

A fourth 'gaffe' came at a Conservative press conference on 6 June. A BBC journalist had asked the Environment Minister, John Gummer, how the Government could square talk of European unity with the Prime Minister's views on a multi-speed Europe. In the midst of a prolix reply, Mr Gummer argued that what was clear was 'that Britain is not going to be at a slower speed than the rest of Europe. That will be quite unacceptable. We are at the heart of Europe; we have no intention of being at a slower speed than that.' Sir Norman Fowler tried unsuccessfully to slip away from the subject, but journalists were swift to latch on to the contradiction between the minister's views and those of the Prime Minister, which had been enthusiastically endorsed by Lord Tebbit. Most of the next day's broadsheet newspapers reported on 'Tory disunity'. The *Guardian*, for example, ran a banner headline, 'Cabinet in Euro-chaos', whilst the *Independent* reported that 'Gummer spikes PM's attempt to unite party.'

SPIN-DOCTORING

There were several examples of what has come to be known as 'spin-doctoring' during the campaign. One of the most successful was the Conservative allegation about the PES manifesto, which committed socialist parties to working for majority voting as the norm in the Council of Ministers, and Labour's apparent commitment to an erosion of the national veto. During campaign press conferences, the Labour leader and frontbenchers repeatedly stressed their insistence on maintaining the veto in the areas of fiscal and budgetary policy, foreign and security issues, constitutional reform, and 'other areas of key national interest'. Labour's national manifesto made the commitment similarly clear, but the party was never quite able to shake off the charge made against it. A similar, long-term Conservative strategy was their 'talking up' of the Liberal Democrat threat, expectations being as important to the Liberal Democrats as objective results. (The Liberal Democrats tried with mixed success to counter unrealistically high predictions of the number of seats they would win.) A linked example

Conservative elation at the OECD remarks on the British economy reminded some people of the Natural Law Party's broadcast advocating yogic flying as a solution to national ills

The Times (8 June 1994)

of spin-doctoring was the 'talking down' of the Conservatives', and the Prime Minister's, prospects. On the weekend before the Euro-election the *Sunday Telegraph* and the *Sunday Times* both carried reports, ostensibly based on soundings with Conservative backbenchers, indicating that Mr Major would 'have to go' if the party got less than 10 (the *Sunday Times* said 12) Euro-seats. These were extraordinarily low figures, given that the Conservatives had 32 Euro-seats in the previous Parliament, that the 1989 campaign had been disastrous (down from 45), and that six more seats were to be contested this time.

Another Conservative success came with the publication of an OECD report two days before polling day. Selected leaks to some Sunday papers created the impression that the report would be supportive of the Government's economic policies, and on the day of publication the earlier BBC radio news bulletins led with a story, based on a Government briefing, that the OECD report supported the Government's views on such issues as the Social Chapter. The Labour Party had prepared its own briefing for the BBC and was alarmed to hear the Conservative 'spin' on the news. Walworth Road brought great pressure to bear on the BBC to alter the approach of its bulletins, and this was gradually done, although probably too late to alter the impression created by the earlier bulletins.

The Labour Party was proud to have been able to reverse the 'spin' on the OECD report but, perhaps distracted and self-absorbed because of the forthcoming leadership contest, it engaged in little 'spin-doctoring' itself. The VAT story was the party's greatest success, with the Government's orthodox Treasury reply that it had 'no plans' to extend the VAT base transformed into an implication that the Government might have such plans for the future. Like the Conservatives, Labour tried to play down electoral expectations. A private NOP poll done for the party (and deliberately leaked), showing that the Conservatives would probably win more seats than was generally expected, was published on the eve of the elections.

THE POLLS

The polls played three roles in the campaign. There were the usual election polls about voting intentions, both in the Euro-elections and in the Eastleigh by-election, but there were also opinion polls about the attractiveness of the various potential candidates for the Labour leadership, and the latter clearly had some effect on the former, particularly once the 'Blair effect' was under way. Lastly, there were more general polls on public attitudes to European issues, such as the prospect of a single currency (see Table 7.2).

The polling organisations had been badly caught out in the 1992 General Election, having failed to predict the Conservative victory. The Market Research Society launched a major internal inquiry to discover what had gone wrong, and the results of this were published on 6 July (the role of the polls was also re-considered in *Labour's Last Chance?* by Heath and others, which was published on 26 May, in the middle of the Euro-elections campaign). The report concluded that there had been a late shift towards the Conservatives which, since it occurred after most interviewing had been completed, few polls had been able to detect, but that the main reasons for the polls' failure were related to sampling inadequacies and a greater tendency among Conservative voters to refuse to say how they would vote. With the partial exception of the local elections, the 1994 Euro-election represented the first nationwide contest since April 1992, and the polling organisations were eager to re-establish their former reputation. The organisations themselves treated their findings with much more prudence (for example, an 11 May ICM poll for the *Guardian* reduced Labour's apparent poll lead by 10 percentage points by introducing the 'realism' of probable Conservative voters among the 'don't know' category). However, there was surprisingly little distrust among the public and politicians, perhaps because Labour's lead was much larger. Perhaps, with no government at stake, it was also more plausible. The polling data on voting intentions was occasionally backed up by more sophisticated analysis. Peter Spencer and John Curtice had constructed an econometric model for Kleinwort and Benson, and this showed clearly that the ERM crisis had initiated the Conservatives' poll slump.

CAMPAIGN ADVERTISING

The 1994 Euro-election campaign was a relatively poor one. The Conservatives, who might otherwise have wished to spend most, were hampered by their heavy indebtedness, spending in the end some £0.3 million on national campaign posters. The Labour Party spent £380,000. The Liberal Democrats forewent national campaign posters altogether, preferring to concentrate their resources on their regional campaign. The two parties' posters were of varying quality.

Table 7.2 Opinion polls, their subjects and dates of release during the European election campaign, 14 May – 9 June 1994

Voting intentions	Labour leadership	European issues
14 May: *Daily Telegraph*/Gallup	15 May: *Sunday Telegraph*/Gallup	15 May: *Observer*/ICM (single currency)
23 May: *Daily Express*/ICM	25 May: *Guardian*/ICM	23 May: *Daily Express*/ICM
24 May: *Southern Daily Echo*/Southampton University (Eastleigh)	26 May: *Independent* and *Newsnight*/NOP (of levy-paying trades unionists)	1 June: *Financial Times*/Harris (single currency)
26 May: *Times*/MORI and *Guardian*/ICM	27 May: *Times*/MORI	2 June: *European*/MORI, and *Daily Telegraph*/Gallup (attitude of business to the Social Chapter)
3 June: *Daily Telegraph*/Gallup	29 May: *Observer*/MORI (of GMB members) and *On the Record*	
4 June: *Glasgow Herald*/System 3		
5 June: *Sunday Times*/Plymouth University (Rallings and Thrasher)		
7 June: *Daily Telegraph*/Gallup, and Labour Party/NOP ('leak')		
8 June: *Daily Express*/ICM		
9 June: *Times*/MORI		

The Conservatives had four. The first was the indifferent and neutral 'Backing Britain in Europe – Vote Conservative on 9th June' – a simple white legend on a blue background which was prone to attract graffiti. The second was a more witty attempt to ram home the alleged similarity of the Labour and Liberal Democrat policies on Europe. It showed red, yellow and blue ballot boxes, with the Liberal Democrat and Labour votes leading to the same prospect of a 'socialist Europe'.

The third poster was considered a failure. Later mirrored in the Conservatives' election broadcast, it showed a doormat in the shape of the United Kingdom. A senior minister was rumoured to have commented that it looked like a 'pool of sick'. It was much criticised by candidates for its obscurity. The Conservatives' fourth campaign poster was adjudged to have been their most effective. It showed a broad axe, with the legend 'British jobs cut' on the blade, and 'Labour's hatchet job' printed beneath. The theme was given a new lease of life when the OECD report story broke on 7 June, and the poster was relaunched in Smith Square with a red ribbon across it bearing the legend 'It's official – socialist policies cost jobs'. Altogether, the Conservative posters occupied 1,000 sites for the first week and some 500 sites for the second week; too little to have any concerted effect on the campaign. Each of the Conservatives' posters was launched in Smith Square after a press conference, and it was clearly hoped that the message of each poster might thus be relayed through the media.

Labour published three posters. The first concentrated on Labour's chosen strategy of a tax offensive. The simple legend in white lettering on a red background stated 'Tory taxes up by £500. It's time you saw red.' A second poster was considered a flop. The basic message, repeated many times, was 'Help the Joneses keep up with the Schulzes. Vote Labour on 9th June.' The point of the message was obscure. On the other hand, Labour's third poster was considered a great success. It showed a photograph of an apparently dejected Mr Major with his head in his hands. The poster bore the legend 'Come in Number 10 your time is up. Tell the Tories you've had enough. Vote Labour in Europe on 9th June.' Altogether, the Labour posters occupied 1,418 sites for two weeks. Again, there were too few posters for them to have any profound effect on the campaign.

The Conservatives' habit of unveiling each poster in Smith Square provided one of the lighter moments of the campaign. The posters were carried on mobile 'ad vans'. On the morning of the OECD report (7 June), the Conservative ad van was 'hijacked' by a Labour ad van, which drove into Smith Square and parked in front of Central Office, bearing a 'Come in your time is up' poster. The two vans then chased one another several times around Smith Square before disappearing off into the London traffic.

Overall, the posters can have had very little effect on the campaign, and their chief value probably lay in the photo opportunities their unveiling provided.

THE MEDIA

The media's expectations were transformed overnight from a climactic campaign which was seriously expected to end in the Prime Minister's downfall, to a truncated campaign which was in large part regarded as an interlude before the Labour leadership contest began. The Euro-elections had been invested with expectations going far beyond their intrinsic interest, and it was difficult for the media to cover them in the same way that they would have done if John Major had still been battling John Smith for his political survival. With John Smith gone, and John Major let off the hook and deliberately playing to a selective audience, the result was patchy, but informed, coverage.

In fact, because of their coverage of the Maastricht Treaty ratification process and the blocking minority row, the Westminster lobby correspondents had become surprisingly knowledgeable about the institutions and procedures of the European Union and this knowledge resulted in far more sophisticated policy analyses than had been the case in previous Euro-elections. For example, in a new departure, most of the broadsheet newspapers and several of the tabloids carried double-page spreads comparing the party manifestos on such issues as the veto, a single currency, constitutional reform, and a common foreign and security policy.

Coverage was patchy, because the media found it difficult to sustain attention in what had become a fairly low-key campaign, but also because of a large number of distractions. Chief among these was the forthcoming Labour leadership contest, but coverage of the Euro-elections was also interspersed with a series of completely unconnected and sometimes outlandish stories. The first week of the campaign, for example, was dominated by news about a 'killer virus', after a cluster of seven cases of necrotising fasciitis occurred in Gloucester. The award of the contract for the national lottery was the main story on 25 and 26 May, and developments in the Northern Ireland peace process on 27 May. The exploits of a former Conservative minister, Alan Clark, attracted much interest in the penultimate week of the campaign, and the Chinook helicopter crash and the D-Day commemorations dominated the last weekend. It was suspected that the Prime Minister and the government would turn the D-Day anniversary events, which included a visit by President Clinton, to their own advantage, but apart from a *Frost on Sunday* interview delivered from Plymouth, Mr Major did not exploit his position unduly. Moreover, Mrs Beckett and Mr Ashdown participated in the commemorative ceremonies on the

Normandy beaches with the Prime Minister and the Queen, so that all three major political parties were associated equally with what was a solemn national occasion. There was an identifiable cyclical rhythm to all 'stories' during the campaign, with most midweek stories being revived by the Sunday newspapers and television programmes before ultimately fading out.

On the whole, the media scrupulously observed the requirement of balanced coverage imposed upon it by the Representation of the People Act. Indeed, many candidates with good reason to have expected more coverage (party spokesmen, party officers) complained that, to their detriment, the Act was too scrupulously observed. Others complained that, particularly where television and radio coverage was concerned, the absence of a spokesman for one party or candidate frequently encouraged local journalists to downgrade their coverage of all candidates and parties. (One incumbent MEP recounted how, a television interviewer having failed to recognise him, he was granted several minutes of illicit coverage, being portrayed as a knowledgeable voter!) There were two important exceptions to the general balance.

The Labour Party's decision to open nominations for the leadership competitition immediately after the Euro-elections inevitably created a climactic 'phoney war' atmosphere, with the speeches of front bench politicians interpreted as coded leadership manifestos. As a result the party received a huge amount of neutral publicity that it could not otherwise possibly have hoped to generate. This publicity worked to Labour's advantage over all the other political parties, but the Liberal Democrats felt particularly aggrieved, especially with the BBC. The Chairman of their Euro-campaign, Matthew Taylor, wrote a letter of protest to the BBC's Director General, John Birt, on 25 May. When this received no response, a second was fired off on 3 June. 'Your coverage of the Labour Party', Mr Taylor wrote, 'has been out of all proportion to the coverage of anybody else.' The party calculated that Labour had enjoyed 52 per cent of BBC coverage since the three main parties launched their manifestos on 23 May, compared with 34 per cent for the Conservatives and 14 per cent for themselves. Another, more muted, set of complaints concerned relative neglect. The Green Party felt particularly aggrieved, arguing that its coverage should at least in part have been based on the 15 per cent of the national vote that it polled in the 1989 Euro-elections. No formal complaint was lodged, but faxes were 'flooded', and the party was particularly upset that it was not given a slot on the BBC's *Election Call*. Complaints also came from the anti-Maastricht UK Independence Party. They calculated that the BBC had altogether given them less than one minute's coverage, and that the other television channels had concentrated exclusively on pro-Maastricht parties. The BBC played an important role in the coverage of the campaign. Its television and radio programmes were important generators of news and provided forums for policy debate. But the BBC management was embroiled in an industrial dispute which led to strikes on 24 May, the day after the manifestos were launched, and 9 June, polling day. These disrupted more general news coverage, although a skeleton staff ensured that news bulletins continued. (A few listeners complained about Radio 4's choice of repeat programme on the morning of 24 May: an *On the Ropes* interview with an embittered Norman Lamont.) Fortunately, a strike planned for 12 June, the day when the results were to be announced, was called off. This would have had a grievous effect on coverage, as the BBC was the only television channel to provide non-stop coverage of the results. BBC television's decision to revive *Election Call* was lauded. All of the party leaders appeared on the programme, but its most effective moment came when a disgruntled caller told the Prime Minister 'You should go'.

The European television channel MTV, increasingly popular among young people, broadcast several programmes devoted to the European elections, including interviews with European politicians such as Jacques Delors.

A curiosity of the Euro-elections was that the voices of Sinn Fein politicians could be heard again, since the original ban laid down that access should be provided to candidates during elections.

In conclusion, although media interest was not as high as it would have been during a General Election, the media could not be accused of indifference, and some coverage, particularly in the broadsheet newspapers and the 'magazine' television programmes was sophisticated and well-informed.

PARTY POLITICAL BROADCASTS

The number of party political broadcasts allotted to political parties is governed by ad hoc rules agreed between the broadcasters, in consultation with the Whips of the political parties at Westminster. Thus, the Conservatives, Labour and the Liberal Democrats are normally entitled to five, five and four broadcasts respectively in a year (each of ten minutes' duration), with the parties deciding when they wish their broadcasts to go out. In addition, the industry decided that political parties contesting at least 12.5 per cent of all UK Euro-constituencies (i.e. at least twelve seats) would be entitled to one broadcast (of ten minutes' duration for the larger parties and five minutes for the rest) during the Euro-campaign, with lower thresholds for Wales and Scotland. Minor parties have no entitlement to party political broadcasts. The Conservative, Labour and Liberal Democrat parties each 'saved up' one of their entitlement of annual broadcasts, so that these three parties had two party political broadcasts during the Euro-campaign. The first Conservative broadcast went out on the day of the manifesto launch (23 May). It was followed by a Labour broadcast on 25 May. The Liberal Democrat broadcast had gone out on 11 May.

Where European election broadcasts are concerned, the two largest parties automatically share the last two evenings before polling between themselves, with the order alternating in successive elections. Labour went last in 1994, and hence the Conservatives will go last in 1999. The Liberal Democrats get third choice. The minor parties were allotted slots on an arbitrary basis, but there were no complaints.

The UK Independence Party's election broadcast went out on 31 May. That of the (Meadowcroft) Liberal Party's went out on 2 June. The Natural Law Party's election broadcast went out on 1 June; and that of the Greens on 3 June. The Liberal Democrats' election broadcast went out on 6 June, the fortieth anniversary of the D-Day landings. The party had been apprehensive that this date would work against them, but in the end made a virtue of a necessity, using images of the landings and Elgar's Enigma Variations as background music. The broadcast concentrated on its leader, who stressed the advances the party had made in the local elections. 'Europe' came late in the broadcast, with emphasis on the 1996 IGC and the party's promise of a referendum. 'We have the greatest resource,' Mr Ashdown concluded. 'To liberate, to equip, to encourage and empower. For everybody to be a somebody. Your vote is your democratic right – please use it.'

The Conservatives' broadcast went out the next evening. There was much emphasis on the need to turn out, and the broadcast began with a printed message about the date of the election and the opening hours of the polling booths. A voice-over countered Labour's claims on growth and employment. Sir Christopher Prout developed the argument of the 'socialist majority' in Europe over the previous five years. The image of the United Kingdom as a trampled doormat was used to underline the Liberal Democrats' European policy. The broadcast ended with the

Prime Minister emphasising the strengths of the Government's economic record, the merits of the opt-out on the Social Chapter, and the need to defend the veto. Labour's election broadcast went out on the eve of polling day. It was adjudged to have been a great success. The party had opted to use a well-known actor and Labour sympathiser, Neil Pearson, which raised taunts about 'luvvies', but was clearly effective in getting the message over. Mr Pearson walked up Whitehall to Downing Street, reciting a litany of the government's failures: the long recession, tax increases, VAT on domestic fuel, the NHS, unemployment, and crime. Mrs Beckett then further developed the argument against the Government's economic record. 'The Government has let you down,' she said, 'and is letting you down in Europe,' but European matters were scarcely mentioned. The broadcast concluded with Mr Pearson urging 'vote for a party that believes in investing in people. Now the good news. You can vote tomorrow.'

Both the Greens and the UK Independence Party claimed that their broadcasts had been highly successful in mobilising support, and both said that they were 'inundated' with inquiries about membership in the days after their broadcasts. The Natural Law Party's broadcast, with the strange claims of the urbane, moustachioed Dr Geoffrey Clements and its images of yogic flyers, was the source of considerable amusement. A tongue-in-cheek *Daily Telegraph* reported that Screaming Lord Sutch was 'raving mad' that his Monster Raving Loony Party had missed out on the opportunity of an election broadcast by fielding too few candidates, but these experiences raised a serious point. For the extremely low price of just £12,000 (twelve deposits), any party or group would be entitled to five minutes of prime time national television and radio (see Table 7.3).

THE EVE OF POLL

The last day of campaigning was characterised by three fast-breaking stories. The first was an unexpected ruling of the European Court of Justice which found against the British government over its implementation of the acquired rights directive. Both the Prime Minister and the Labour leader were questioned about this during their morning press conferences. Both had been hurriedly briefed but were unable to make much political capital, although the media tended to portray the ruling as a further example of interference from Brussels. The second

Table 7.3 *Major stories in the broadsheet newspapers during the 1994 European election campaign, 23 May – 8 June 1994*

23 May (manifesto launch date)	– Gordon Brown's speech to the Welsh Labour Party Conference
24 May	– Conservative offensive on the veto – the 'killer virus'
25 May	– Tony Blair and Number Ten (Mo Mowlam and John Patten 'leaks') – Tony Blair's first speech since John Smith's death – Government White Paper on competitiveness – millionaire immigrants
26 May	– national lottery – Labour NEC meeting and Margaret Beckett's resignation – Norman Lamont speech
27 May	– Northern Ireland/Downing Street Declaration (John Major message to Sinn Fein) – John Prescott speech – Michael Howard's immigration remarks
28 May	– Prime Minister's 'beggars' interview – Helmut Kohl's comments on EMU
29 May	– Beggars interview
30 May	– Beggars interview
31 May	– Beggars and Labour confusion – Alan Clark 'coven'
1 June	– Prime Minister's 'multi-track' speech – Alan Clark 'coven'
2 June	– Gordon Brown's withdrawal from Labour leadership race – 'Multi-track' speech and Lord Tebbit's endorsement of it
3 June	– Labour leadership – Robin Cook's policy paper on industry and finance
4 June	– Chinook helicopter crash – President Clinton in Rome – VAT
5 June	– D-Day anniversary commemorations – Tony Blair – Conservatives' electoral prospects
6 June	– D-Day anniversary commemorations – European Court of Human Rights Ruling (on SAS in Gibraltar) – VAT and John Major interview – Post Office privatisation
7 June	– D-Day anniversary commemorations – John Gummer 'gaffe'
8 June	– OECD report – John Major's 'deadly sins of Europe' speech

was news that John Prescott, one of the potential Labour leadership contenders, had been injured in a taxi crash though, as the morning wore on, it became clear that Mr Prescott had not been seriously hurt. The third came in the evening when, in what was clearly a carefully timed announcement, the Liberal Democrat candidate in the Newham by-election, Alec Kellaway, announced that he was defecting to Labour. Although Paddy Ashdown shrugged off the defection, it was a severe embarrassment to the party at a crucial moment.

A striking aspect of the Euro-campaign was that none of the three major parties had stored up a good issue on which to make a strong finish to the campaign (and see Table 7.3). The spin-doctored OECD report was a welcome surprise to the Conservatives, just as the European Court of Justice's ruling was a welcome surprise to Labour. If Alec Kellaway had not defected, and if these two stories had not broken, then the end of the Euro-campaign would have been very low key.

President Clinton was in Oxford to receive an honorary degree from the university. In the evening, Labour's election broadcast went out. An ICM poll for the *Daily Express* put Labour on 45 per cent, the Conservatives on 27 per cent, and the Liberal Democrats on 22 per cent, inspiring the headline 'NEW EUROPOLL BOOSTS TORIES'. Despite this, there was a generalised expectation that the Conservatives were about to face another Waterloo at the hands of the electorate.

Table 7.4 Comparison of selected provisions of the three major parties' European election manifestos, 1994

Subject	Conservatives	Labour	Liberal Democrats
CAP	The CAP needs to be simplified, made more responsive to the market and less bureaucratic. Its costs must be kept under firm control, and fraud pursued rigorously. It needs to be reformed in ways which help farmers to care for the countryside.	Labour is committed to replacing the CAP with a new strategy, aimed at reinvigorating the countryside; producing healthy food; improving animal welfare; safeguarding the environment and satisfying the customer.	Liberal Democrats want the CAP replaced by a much more broadly-based Common Rural Policy, in which support for agriculture would play the core but not the only role.
Social Chapter	. . . at Maastricht, we steered clear of the Social Chapter trap . . . we will not allow Europe to damage our labour markets by re-imposing handicaps we have abolished in Britain.	The next Labour government will immediately sign the Social Chapter.	Liberal Democrats would . . . reject Britain's Social Chapter 'opt-out'. Britain should be seeking to shape European legislation on matters such as works councils, not standing ineffectively on the sidelines.
Unemployment	Our flexible markets give us the best jobs prospects of any European economy.	(reiterates) the need for investment in people and their skills, and for the kind of practical jobs strategy which Labour has long advocated. (The Delors White Paper's) approach is a policy for promoting employment. . . . Labour will . . . further these proposals and help get people back to work. Labour will press for: coordinated monetary and fiscal policies. . . more and better use of the European Investment Bank and the new Investment Fund . . . creation of a European Recovery Fund . . . the development of trans-European networks . . .	We support the conclusions of the White Paper . . . which is fully in line with our strategy. Liberal Democrats would work with our EU partners to develop a European recovery plan including coordinated lower interest rates across Europe, cross-border public and private investment programmes, trans-European networks and aid for Central and Eastern Europe.

cont. overleaf

Subject	Conservatives	Labour	Liberal Democrats
EMU and a single currency	Our criticisms of the faults in the way the European Exchange Rate Mechanism worked are now widely shared. We will not re-enter such a mechanism in the foreseeable future. Nor could we consider doing so until it was clear that such faults no longer existed. As for the question of a single currency, events since Maastricht have shown how important it was to secure for Britain the freedom to make a proper judgement of events. We will retain the right to make our own decision on whether or not to be involved in any single currency for Europe. If and when such a choice ever has to be made, it will be for our own national Parliament to decide.	We continue to support the principles of a managed exchange rate system of fixed but adjustable exchange rates. Labour supports progress towards economic and monetary union . . . but we strongly believe that convergence of the real economic performance of member states has to take place before any such moves. Convergence must be based on improving levels of growth and employment, and not just on monetary objectives alone. That is why we have long argued that the convergence criteria must be applied flexibly, and that real economic convergence is of primary importance.	We would move in step with Britain's European partners towards the Maastricht goal of a single currency . . . we would give the Bank of England responsibility for setting interest rates and keeping inflation low, prior to the establishment of an independent European Central Bank.
Defence and security	NATO must remain the cornerstone of Europe's defence and our collective security . . . The continued presence of American forces on the mainland of Europe has underpinned NATO . . . We welcome President Clinton's . . . commitment. NATO's first task in the new Europe must be to extend peace and stability eastwards . . . Europe's defence can only be built on NATO . . . The Western European	We support moves to make the WEU the European pillar within NATO and we remain firmly committed to the Alliance as our principal bulwark of peace and security. Within this framework we support greater efforts to encourage military cooperation with east European nations, and welcome initiatives in this direction, including 'Partnerships for Peace'.	We support the common European policy for arms procurement, and gradual moves towards the integration of EU armed forces . . . We call for the evolution of burden-sharing agreements . . . The principle that member states should retain the ultimate right not to have their forces committed to combat must be maintained. We support greater cooperation between NATO and the

Common foreign and security policy	Union is an important bridge between NATO and the European Union . . . Our aim is a European defence effort fully compatible with NATO – not an alternative to it. Conservatives have always been leading supporters of European co-operation in foreign policy . . . Britain will preserve its position where it needs to – on the Falklands, Gibraltar and Hong Kong, for example . . . our objective is to build the CFSP brick by brick, identifying areas where it makes good, practical sense to work together.	We look forward to the European Union developing common foreign and security policies based on agreed principles and objectives.	Western European Union . . . and welcome links between NATO and Central and Eastern European nations . . . the 'Partnership for Peace' initiative is a welcome first step. The peace and stability of Europe depends upon an effective common European foreign and security policy . . . EU nations must work together more effectively . . .
1996 IGC	Any successor treaty will need to build on (the Maastricht Treaty's) decentralised model for Europe, respecting national diversity . . . Our aim in 1996 will be to ensure that future arrangements (on the structure and weighting of voting decisions in the European Council) properly reflect our national interests.	We believe that the European Union must consider further steps to promote . . . convergence (of growth and employment) at the next Intergovernmental Conference in 1996 . . . Labour believes that the ending of the present Common Agricultural Policy should be a priority for the next round of Treaty reforms in 1996 . . . all the Union's procedures should be simplified to make them understandable and open to review.	. . . the Inter-Governmental Conference will seek to bring the nations of the European Union still closer together. Liberal Democrats are in no doubt that closer ties with Europe will be to the benefit of Britain.

cont. overleaf

Subject	Conservatives	Labour	Liberal Democrats
A referendum?	—	—	. . . if the 1996 Intergovernmental Conference proposes fundamental changes amounting to a new constitutional settlement between Europe and the nations, then Liberal Democrats believe it would be appropriate to seek popular assent for them.
Council voting and the 'veto'	Conservatives will retain Britain's veto on issues of vital national interest.	Whenever they make laws, Council meetings must be open, with all votes recorded and published. In recent years, qualified majority voting has been significantly extended to become the norm for the bulk of Community legislation. The Labour Party has long argued for qualified majority voting in important areas such as the environment and social affairs. But we have always insisted, too, on maintaining the principle of unanimity for decision-making in areas such as fiscal and budgetary policy, foreign and security issues, changes to the Treaty of Rome, and other areas of key national interest.	The Council of Ministers must take its decisions in public. The use of qualified majority voting on the Council should be extended and the system reformed, perhaps to require a 'double majority' (e.g. three-quarters of the states, plus the votes of states representing three-quarters of the EU's population) for particularly important issues

8 The Campaign in the Regions

CANDIDATES' VIEWS AND ACTIVITIES

In Britain, European campaigns offer an odd caricature of Westminster campaigns. Nationally and in the constituencies the level of interest and activity is far lower and so is the extent of media coverage. Leaders, candidates and party workers go through the familiar motions of campaigning – but mostly with less enthusiasm or conviction.

In particular, constituency organisation is very different. Most Westminster seats have about 70,000 electors and there is usually a local party with a real and continuing existence. The candidate and the agent know their area in a way that is almost impossible in a Euro-seat eight times larger. In the 15 years since the first European elections in 1979 nothing has happened to make Euro-constituencies have a life of their own; they can seldom be more than a loose committee of Westminster constituency officials.

Euro-constituencies may have a largely notional existence, but British MEPs have a very real sense of identity. The 1987 doubling of the European structural funds after the restructuring of the Community's finances and the implementation of the Single European Act has probably been the most important factor in consolidating the British Euro-MPs' sense of constituency representation. Virtually all incumbent MEPs made mention in their campaign literature about the ways in which they had been able to help their constituencies, with Community funding much to the fore. This almost universal sense of achievement explains a similarly universal sense of frustration about the campaign's virtually exclusive concentration on the domestic policy agenda and the lack of local media interest, with many candidates mentioning the Representation of the People Act as the chief villain of the piece. At the local level, as at the national level, 'Europe' was largely tangential to the campaign. Many Labour candidates tried to make the Social Chapter and unemployment into campaign issues. Environmental concerns were also favoured. Conservative candidates were more reactive, building on the issues raised by the national campaign and the Prime Minister, such as the veto, sovereignty, 'multi-

215

speed' Europe, and a single currency. Conservative candidates seeking out Conservative voters seemed far more likely to encounter the anti-federalist phenomenon. Some candidates were thankful for the Euro-sceptical tone the Prime Minister had struck. Others found the situation awkward.

Some Labour candidates noticed an appreciable reaction of sympathy to the death of John Smith among the electorate, but others sensed bemusement. Some Labour candidates felt the leader's death had reinforced the party activists' resolve, but others complained that the suspension of campaigning had caused practical problems, such as unfocussing and dislocating the campaign, stopping postal vote work, or causing leaflets to be destroyed or stickered. A sizeable group of Conservative candidates felt that John Smith's death had helped to consolidate the Labour vote, with this a plus or a minus, depending on the local circumstances. One Conservative candidate was not sorry to have lost a week from the campaign. Many mentioned the practical problems which the postponement of the campaign had caused, but a sizeable minority were convinced that another week of campaigning could have made a substantial difference to the Conservatives' fortunes. Among the Liberal Democrat candidates, several felt Mr Smith's death and its consequences had helped Labour at Liberal Democrat expense, but others were struck by the solemnity of the occasion. A handful of candidates from all parties thought the death was ultimately an irrelevancy to the campaign, but sizeable minorities in all parties saw it as a turning point in the flow of events.

Some Labour and Conservative candidates found that John Major's 'beggars' interview had provoked opposition or agreement (particularly in the South-West) respectively but, surprisingly, most did not sense that it had had any particular impact. Virtually all candidates of all parties mentioned the 'Blair effect' and the D-Day commemorative services as important factors in the campaign. In addition, some Labour candidates mentioned the threatened privatisation of the Post Office and dislike for John Major as doorstep issues. Several Labour candidates were particularly appreciative of Margaret Beckett's able handling of the leadership, and a number were thankful that the shadow boxing for the leadership contest had been mostly restrained and not at all vituperative. Some Conservative candidates mentioned taxes as an issue with which they had been confronted. Some had appreciated Central Office's handling of the OECD report, which they felt had given a handy boost on the eve of the poll. Several candidates in all parties were unhappy about 'by-election drain'.

Most candidates worked as many hours as they could on the campaign trail, though Conservative candidates were more likely to relax on Sundays. A few candidates mentioned long periods of full-time activity before the campaign got under way. The most extreme example of this was perhaps Eryl McNally in Bedfordshire and Milton Keynes (she won by an unexpected majority). Those who attended public meetings reported low attendance, generally from 20 to 100 people, though several Labour and Conservative candidates mentioned meetings of up to 300 and 400 people. The Liberal Democrats claimed a turnout of 1,200 in a public meeting in Eastleigh. A majority of Conservative candidates had given up organising their own meetings, and several mentioned that they had also refused to take part in joint debates. Labour candidates were similarly unenthusiastic about public meetings. Liberal Democrats were the keenest. The presence of Natural Law candidates on the platform was cited by several candidates as a reason to stay away from joint debates, but others found that they had provided light relief. Celebrity visits were, unsurprisingly, concentrated in marginal constituencies and target seats. The national media were only noticed in 'interesting' seats, such as Bedfordshire and Milton Keynes, and South Wales East. A large number of candidates complained about the local media, which was variously charged with largely ignoring the election and failing to take up press releases, or with excessive attention to trivia, and excessive devotion to the equal coverage provisions laid down for broadcasters.

Although there were exceptions, most candidates reported canvassing to be running at a very low level. In relevant areas, returns from the 1994 local government elections were usually used. Some seats had concentrated canvassing in marginal Westminster constituencies. Telephone canvassing was normal practice for the Conservatives and increasingly used by Labour. The Liberal Democrats used it far less. Several candidates mentioned that telephone 'knocking up' on polling day was a useful technique. In general, faxes and mobile telephones were becoming standard in serious contests, with Conservatives in a clear technological lead. However, some 'low-tech' Labour campaigns achieved high swings. Several candidates used 'admobiles', trailing posters around shopping areas. Most candidates were disappointed with polling day organisation, though Labour candidates were slightly more satisfied. Nearly everyone discriminated between good and bad areas in their constituencies, though in different ways; Labour candidates in strong Labour seats did not really need to. Targeting was sometimes the consequence of some areas being organised and others not, and sometimes a more strategic choice. This mostly meant concentrating on mobilising maximum support in good areas, although a few of the more confident candidates and some Liberal Democrats spoke about sending people into relatively bad areas to build up future support. Several Conservative candidates used a different sort of targetting by sending election material solely or mainly to known Tory voters through the heavy use of direct mail. There was also a noticeable trend towards targeting meetings, which would be held in sympathetic homes for small groups of sympathisers. Labour candidates gave aid to their neighbours in several northern Euro-constituencies, exporting workers to neighbouring marginals.

An inspection of the expense returns from the constituencies shows that, in contrast to Westminster elections, no one spent right up to the permitted maximum, which was about £42,000 in English seats. The 554 candidates spent £4,960,000, an average of £9 each. On average, the Conservatives spent £24,000 (57 per cent of the allowed maximum). Among those elected, Graham Mather in Hampshire North and Oxford West (97 per cent) and Bryan Cassidy in Dorset and East Devon (93 per cent) came nearest to the limit. The Earl of Stockton in Bristol (95 per cent) was the only challenger to spend more than £30,000. In the extreme case of a hopeless seat, Merseyside East, Conservative expenditure fell to £4,549 (11 per cent). Every Conservative incumbent spent over £20,000 and, except in Lincolnshire, where the sitting MEP spent only £15,763, £100 less than his successful Labour challenger, outspent his or her challenger, but only eleven Conservative challengers in the sample outspent the Labour incumbent.

On average, the Labour candidates in the sample spent £18,000 (43 per cent of the maximum). Pauline Green, defending her marginal London North seat, easily came top in England (85 per cent), but the two Welsh candidates under threat from Plaid Cymru exceeded that figure, with 91 per cent in North Wales and 97 per cent in Mid and West Wales. Except in two safe Scottish seats, every Labour incumbent spent at least £10,000 and every challenger spent at least £7,000, but none, not even those who gained seats, outspent the incumbent they were challenging.

Liberal Democrat expenditure was far more variable. Those in the sample averaged £9,000 (21 per cent). Their victor in Cornwall and West Plymouth spent £36,000 (88 per cent), and all of those with a serious chance spent over £20,000. But elsewhere £3,000 was common, falling to £850 in Merseyside East.

Table 8.1   Average expenditure by minor party candidates, 1994

Greens £1200;	Natural Law £1500;	Liberal £1600;	UKIP £2000

Dafydd Wigley, challenging for Plaid Cymru, spent £35,000 in North Wales, but Allan Macartney won North East Scotland for the SNP on only £21,000. For the other parties, Table 8.1 tells the story. The anti-Market independent in Worcestershire and South Warwickshire reported an outlay of £32,000, but no one else exceeded £8,000. There would appear to be little correlation between expenditure and votes won.

We wrote to all the successful candidates and a large number of the defeated and received a high response. The following pages are largely based on those responses.

Most candidates acknowledged that popular interest in the elections was low, but felt that it had increased during the campaign. Incumbents felt levels of knowledge were higher than in 1989. Similarly, party activity was considered to have been well below General Election levels. However, the Labour challengers in Lincolnshire and Humberside South (Veronica Hardstaff), London North West (Robert Evans), Bedfordshire and Milton Keynes (Eryl McNally), and Nottingham and Leicestershire North West (Mel Read), all reported very high levels of activity, and it is notable that these were all striking gains against prestigious Conservative candidates; respectively, Bill Newton-Dunn (Chairman of the British Section of the EPP Group in the European Parliament), Lord Bethell (an MEP since 1975), Edwina Currie (a former Conservative minister and sitting MP), and Martin Brandon-Bravo (a Conservative MP from 1983 to 1992). The Liberal Democrats reported high levels of activity in Herefordshire and Shropshire. At the other extreme, one of their northern candidates claimed he had a team of just four people. Overall, activity was felt to be reasonably high and, again, incumbents felt it compared favourably with the general level in 1989. Activity was lower in those areas where local elections had taken place in May, activist fatigue being particularly apparent where the results had been bad. Volunteers, central resources and party professionals were drained by the by-elections. London Labour MEPs felt the draw of the East London by-elections, and the Yorkshire contests competed with Bradford South. Eastleigh provided a major distraction for the Liberal

Democrats, but there was little evidence of any large influx into the south west of Liberal Democrat activists from the north of the country. Party morale was not a serious worry. For Labour it seemed particularly high in target seats and marginals. Surprisingly few candidates reported any problems with overall party organisation within their Euro-constituencies, and such problems as there were related more to disorganisation than hostility or indifference to the Euro-campaign. Boundary changes complicated matters for some candidates, mainly because of the lateness of the changes. There were three main organisational variants: a roving personal campaign team with small membership; a Euro-constituency council with representatives from each Westminster seat; and federalised structures in which local parties had a lot of discretion over campaign tactics. Some Conservative MEPs who felt particularly under threat developed highly detailed campaign plans.

Most candidates were unsurprised by the low turnout, but sixteen found it unexpectedly low, and five found it unexpectedly high. The bulk of the candidates claimed to have seen the result coming. None of the Labour candidates were surprised to have won, but several expressed astonishment at the size of their majorities and also at the size of the Labour vote in unlikely parts of their seats. Two Conservative candidates felt they had won but found they had lost, and three felt they had lost but actually won. Most Liberal Democrat candidates tried to mobilise tactical votes, but the majority admitted failure. One Conservative candidate felt that there had been tactical voting for the Liberal Democrats in that particular constituency. Nine Labour candidates felt that they had successfully mobilised tactical votes, and Plaid Cymru felt it had been successful with the tactical argument in North Wales. Little significant pressure group activity was reported. Those mentioned by candidates included: the Batheaston by-pass, other environmental issues, Manchester Airport, hunting, animal welfare, world development, the M25 motorway, the Channel Tunnel rail link, the railway service in general, motorbikes and farmers.

The attitudes of candidates towards the help provided by their party headquarters were markedly different. Conservative Central Office emerged with high marks from most Conservative candidates, many saying they had been impressed by the service, and only one candidate being unreservedly critical. Labour candidates had diverse opinions about Walworth Road. One candidate described it as 'the kiss of death'. Candidates in the north, particularly in Scotland, were generally unhappy. A dozen candidates said they simply ignored it and got on with their camapigns, but another dozen gave it high praise. Three Liberal Democrat candidates felt Cowley Street had been irrelevant, most were indifferent towards it, and only one or two gave unqualified praise.

Most Labour candidates were highly critical of their party's national campaign, describing it variously as being too negative, not sufficiently related to European issues, misdirected, and wasteful of the expertise and of the good record of Labour MEPs. Resentment about the domination of Westminster seemed widespread. As one incumbent put it, 'The campaign was totally Westminster oriented. There were always MPs on the television or in the press. Most of them knew nothing about the EU and the European Parliament, and it showed!' New candidates were less critical. A score of the Conservative candidates were appreciative of their party's national campaign, with some singling out the Prime Minister's interventions for particular praise. A dozen were critical, particularly about what they saw as an excessively Euro-sceptical tone, and others picked out different aspects for praise and blame. Several candidates specifically mentioned the poor quality of the campaign advertisements. Among Liberal Democrat candidates, few had a kind word for the national campaign, it being variously described as 'unfocused', 'negative', 'a confused mess', and 'a disaster'. Many resented the more Euro-sceptical tone adopted by Paddy Ashdown.

The national press conferences were despised or ignored by the vast majority of the candidates. Only two Labour candidates saw anything positive in them, compared with four Conservative candidates and just one Liberal Democrat candidate. They were considered irrelevant and useless for local campaigning, although one candidate asked pensively 'Who is more insular, the candidate swept up in a full-time local campaign, or the London media circus?'

The help provided by Brussels to the candidates was generally praised. About a third of Labour candidates said they had used PES or EPLP resources, and most who offered assessments of the material and advice given were appreciative. Some distributed general Euro-information documentation in their campaign material, and this information was said to have been particularly useful in the pre-campaign period. The PES manifesto, which was so freely available, was warmly praised by several candidates. There was a distinct divide between incumbents and new candidates. MEPs were far more likely to turn to the Brussels help desk, presumably because they were more aware of its potential worth. Ten Conservative candidates claimed to have used EPP facilities, but only in the pre-campaign. The ELDR was of help to most Liberal Democrat candidates, if only through the supply of the European manifesto.

THE SOUTH-WEST
JOHN FITZMAURICE

In modern politics, the expectations game is everything. By a dialectical process, pre-established hurdles become the accepted currency by which the media and the political class judge the performance of political parties at any given election. The European elections campaign and the result in the South West provide a textbook illustration of this phenomenon. This, more than any other part of the country, was Liberal Democrat territory. On 12 April, the *Daily Telegraph* published a map based on a *Times*/MORI poll which gave the Liberal Democrats eleven Euro-seats in a broad swathe across the South of the country, breaking out from the deep yellow of the South West. In the light of the Liberal Democrats' local elections successes and Eastleigh poll advantage, even the more sober media commentaries assumed that the Lib Dems would make a clean sweep of the farthermost seats in the South West.

When the votes were counted, the Liberal Democrats had won just two Euro-seats, Cornwall and West Plymouth, and Somerset and North Devon, and won a 'moral victory' in a third, Devon and Plymouth East, where the 10,203 votes of a spoiling 'Literal Democrat' candidate were alleged to have robbed the Liberal Democrats of an otherwise certain victory (the Conservatives took the seat by just 700 votes). There were also two 'near misses', Dorset and East Devon, where they came within 2,500 votes of victory, and Wiltshire North and Bath. Such results a year earlier would have been seen as a famous victory. In the event, the result was a disappointing anti-climax, seen almost as a defeat. The Liberal Democrats' gains had been discounted in advance. To be fair, Liberal Democrat strategists, well aware of opposition attempts to talk up their chances, had tried to play down expectations throughout the campaign. Tim Clement-Jones, their campaign director, authored a ditty which Paddy Ashdown often repeated: 'One's a break-through, two's a joy, three's fantastic, four

. . . oh boy!' But media hype, the local elections, good polls and expert Tory spin-doctoring conspired to set up heady expectations which, against their better judgement, many Liberal Democrats privately shared.

Since this was the only area where they had any real hope of winning seats, the Liberal Democrats concentrated their campaign efforts on the South-West (and the neighbouring Eastleigh by-election). Within the region, they focussed principally on the seats of Somerset and North Devon, and Cornwall and West Plymouth. In these two seats they spent over 90 per cent of the legal limit of £42,000, whereas in Bristol they spent only about £10,000. They concentrated on literature and some 'visibility' activities, such as stakeboards with posters. In Somerset and Devon, they circulated five different pieces of literature. They moved into telephone canvassing on a bigger scale, especially in very rural areas. Their visibility was helped by the fact that they had MPs and Liberal Democrat-controlled local councils in both key targets. A key element, they believed, was the early selection of their candidates. Graham Watson, candidate in Somerset and North Devon, had been in place since 1989, and Robin Teverson, candidate for Cornwall and West Plymouth, since 1992. Local issues, particularly water privatisation and water charges, figured largely in the contest.

Strategic decisions taken by the national leadership during the campaign proved more controversial. Paddy Ashdown, himself an MP in Somerset, had concluded that the party's traditional identification with Europe and positions that could be characterised as 'federalist' might, in the prevailing more sceptical climate (which affected Liberal Democrat voters as much as those of any other party), cost the party votes. (Some Liberal Democrat strategists had argued that close identification with 'Europe' might have cost the Party votes in the past; see, for example, Butt Philip, 1993.) He therefore opted for a purely national campaign, aiming to defuse Conservative attacks on the veto issue with his proposal for a possible referendum on the outcome of the 1996 IGC. As one Tory candidate put it, 'You would have needed a microscope to see any European content in their campaign'. Yet some Liberal Democrat candidates in the region were not wholly convinced by this line. Though not denying that national issues were central, they had found the public more knowledgeable and concerned on European issues than had previously been the case. For them, organisational, rather than political, problems explained the Liberal Democrats' traditional poor showing in European elections. The other principle thrust of the Liberal Democrat campaign was to encourage tactical voting – the so-called 'Heineken strategy' – in an election generally perceived as a referendum on the Conservative Government. This strategy generated several tabloid leaflets and a number of personalised letters from Paddy Ashdown to 'soft' Labour voters. But the Ashdown letters also attracted controversy, as the death of John Smith was thought to have firmed up softer Labour support and some activists claimed that the letters had caused offence.

Labour went into the campaign with the limited defensive objective of holding Bristol, an unexpected gain in 1989 and thought to be at risk from redistribution. But as the campaign advanced, Labour's objectives became slightly more ambitious. In addition to aiming for a good second place in the Eastleigh by-election, the party sought to increase its share of the vote across the region and to limit tactical voting for the Liberal Democrats. It achieved all of these objectives to some degree. It won in Bristol, and came second in Eastleigh. It secured a close second place in the Cotswolds seat and continued the modest reversal of the decline of its share of the vote in the region that had begun in 1987. However, it made no dramatic breakthrough. Even in its third-best seat (Wiltshire North and Bath, which includes Swindon) it only won 24.5 per cent, a poor third. On the other hand, around the coast it achieved a new basis for advance at the next General Election. Party morale in the area was high and the campaign was adjudged to have been balanced between national and European (mainly social matters such as the minimum wage, a key issue in the region) issues.

With the exception of Labour-held Bristol, the Conservatives were defending all of the seats in the region against the Liberal Democrats, which led some to see a distinct South West regional campaign. In Devon and East Plymouth, they had to select a new candidate, as the long-standing incumbent, Lord O'Hagan, had retired. Elsewhere, their outgoing MEPs all sought re-election. Candidates tried to fight their own campaigns in their own style. Only the relatively Thatcherite Brian Cassidy professed to be at home with the more Euro-sceptical slant of the Conservatives' national campaign. On the other hand, the defeated incumbents Margaret Daly and Christopher Beazley regarded the Euro-sceptical tone of the national campaign and, above all, the open party divisions as having had grievous negative effects. The Conservative candidates' election addresses and other literature were surprisingly specific about European issues and about their own achievements on behalf of their areas. The Conservatives brought many 'key campaigners' into the region; John Major in Bristol (where he gave his 'beggars' interview to the *Bristol Evening News*), Kenneth

Clarke, Mrs Bottomley, John Patten, and David Hunt, for example. Conservative MPs in the region were active in the campaign, with supporting localised mail shots.

For the Liberal Democrats, Paddy Ashdown was highly active in the area. Labour, on the other hand, brought in few key campaigners. Local media interest was surprisingly low, and the RPA seems to have acted as an inhibition, with newspapers and free papers offering only a standard 200–word platform to candidates. There were exceptions. For example, in Somerset and North Devon, local papers offered all candidates a weekly platform, with a picture.

Participation in the region as a whole (42.5 per cent) was slightly up on 1989. The best turnout was 46.7 per cent in Somerset and North Devon (second-best in the country). The lowest figure was 38.9 per cent in the Cotswolds. However, there were significant variations within Euro-constituencies. For example, in the Dorset and East Devon Euro-seat, turnout was measured at 47.8 per cent in West Dorset and only 35.6 per cent in Bournemouth East.

Labour's best result was 44.1 per cent in Bristol, giving the incumbent, Ian White, the largest majority in the region. Labour's poorest share was 14.2 per cent in Somerset and North Devon. In Cornwall and West Plymouth, a Liberal Democrat gain, the Labour vote fell, while in Labour-held Bristol, it was the Liberal Democrat vote that fell. Such figures belie the initial, unrefined Liberal Democrat claims that they had done less well than expected either because the Labour vote had held up or because tactical voting had failed to materialise on the usual scale. While the Labour vote did hold up, it did so selectively and modestly. (For example, Bryan Cassidy, incumbent Conservative MEP in Dorset and East Devon and under threat from the Liberal Democrats, believed that he owed his survival to the fact that the Labour vote did hold up.)

The Liberal Democrats were unable to win more than two seats in the South-West. This *was* a breakthrough, ending the party's European famine and sending British Liberals to Strasbourg for the first time since 1979. Membership of the European Parliament would bring with it valuable funds and secretarial assistance, which the Party could pump back into the region. Incumbency has its own strengths. Party activists argued that the European elections formed part of a continuum stretching back to the local elections and previous by-election victories (Eastleigh in 1994, Christchurch and Newbury in 1993) and forward to the next General Election. But therein lies the rub, the subject of much reflection at a Liberal Democrat seminar held soon after the elections; will the Party's European performance serve as a platform for future advantages, or as a regional cage?

LONDON AND THE SOUTH-EAST
LEWIS BASTON AND SIMON HENIG

London and the South-East has been disastrous territory for Labour in recent years. In General Elections in Greater London, Labour has lagged behind the Conservatives since 1974. In the surrounding commuter belt territory of the South-East, the situation has become almost apocalyptic; only one Labour MP was elected in 1983 and 1987, and only three in 1992. In terms of share of the vote, Labour had slumped to third party status in the South-East.

However, for some time prior to June 1994 the political scene had been changing. The 1989 European elections saw Labour win seven London seats to the Conservatives' three, and, while the Conservatives retained all the other seats, there was some indication that voters were more inclined to support Labour when the government of the country was not at stake. The pattern was repeated in the 1993 and 1994 local elections. In the county council elections of 1993 the Conservatives were reduced to control of just a single county, as hundreds of seats were lost across the South-East. In the borough elections in London in May 1994 the Conservatives forfeited control of six of their eleven London boroughs. These results augured badly for the Conservatives in the forthcoming Euro-elections. Both Labour and the Liberal Democrats were hopeful of making multiple gains throughout the region as the campaign began. Nearly half of the constituencies in the South-East could be classified as 'marginal' in some way; London and the South-East truly would be a major battleground.

But the campaign was a quiet, lacklustre affair. There was little physical evidence that an election was taking place. The number of windowbills displayed was very low in most of London and little canvassing was done except in selected areas within marginal seats. Party activity was running at a low level for various reasons. The fact that the elections were taking place just one month after the borough elections meant that London activists and voters were suffering election fatigue as well as the usual Euro-apathy.

The attention of party workers and the media was, more than in other regions, distracted by the by-elections taking place on the same day. Liberal Democrats throughout the region attached a high priority to Eastleigh. Labour officials were mostly concerned with the three 'District Line' by-elections in East London, and the diversion of party workers to them caused strains with the campaigns of some London MEPs.

The region was not without its share of colourful incident. The Conservative campaign in the Bedfordshire and Milton Keynes seat was run with exquisite showmanship by Edwina Currie, who at one point appeared dressed as a mediaeval queen and rode a hot air balloon. Her attempt to move from Westminster to Strasbourg, and the fact that she was by far the most best known and most quotable candidate in the region, drew media attention to the seat. Her ultimately successful Labour opponent, Eryl McNally, ran a more prosaic, but efficient, campaign; she had been working the seat for nearly a year. Alan Sked, leader of the UK Independence Party, chose to contest the seat because of the Currie publicity factor. Like Lord St Oswald in 1979, Currie performed a little worse than neighbouring Conservative candidates – perhaps a warning to those considering showbiz campaigns.

Suspicious Conservatives blamed Post Office workers opposed to privatisation for a strange bungle in London North-West, where a Conservative leaflet intended as a free postal delivery attracted surplus postal charges, so that voters had to pay to receive the unfortunate Lord Bethell's material. The campaign in Wight and Hampshire East received a sordid shock in the last week of the campaign, when the *Daily Star* printed allegations about the behaviour of Mike Hancock, the Liberal Democrat challenger. In a tight local race, the scandal may have cost the Liberal Democrats a potential gain. Another blow for the Liberal Democrats was the much-publicised (and Labour orchestrated) defection of Alec Kellaway, their candidate in the Newham North East by-election, to the Labour camp.

The South-East is a large and amorphous region, and there were few truly regional issues. The course of the Channel Tunnel rail link was an issue in Kent and the south and east sides of London. Improving transport and trade links with Europe was a low-key theme to the regional Euro-election and the Newham by-election. Labour's London MEPs produced a London manifesto which aimed to spell out the impact of the Party of European Socialists' manifesto on the London area. Labour MEPs also emphasised environmental matters more than the national campaign, conscious of the strong Green vote in the region in 1989 – and also demonstrating the differing priorities of the MEPs and the Westminster party.

The parties' campaign strategies diverged. The Liberal Democrats were very keen to claim second place in many seats outside London and gather Labour tactical voters, and their national campaign stressed this in the last week. Labour played the same card, sometimes in the same seats, such as the Thames Valley, but with more general success. Labour emphasised Conservative broken promises and leaflets featured local examples of the consequences of recession; for example, a businessman turning to Labour in London South Inner. In several seats the Conservatives tried new and noteworthy techniques. The standard pattern of free delivery to each household was varied, to allow two different leaflets to go to supportive households while sending none to opponents. 'Total targeting' was used in Sussex South and Crawley and Hampshire North and Oxford. Opponents of such new-style campaigns found them frustrating to counter because there was no sense of engaging in a debate of any sort.

Local media attention was not substantial outside the *Evening Standard*'s circulation area. Many newspapers contented themselves with small statements from each of the candidates, although the Portsmouth area papers displayed considerable interest in the Hancock story. The *Standard* concentrated more on the national cut-and-thrust than any regional campaign; on 7 June Lord Bethell was given a column to write a general recommendation for the Conservatives. The paper did its best to help its preferred party, for instance, trumpeting the Conservatives' interpretation of the OECD report (also on 7 June), but could not resist revelling in their misfortunes once the results were out; 'Essex turns red, Tories get blues' (13 June).

It rapidly became clear on 'declaration night' that Labour had performed better in London and the South-East than in any other area of the country. Eight seats were gained across the region, six in the Conservative heartland outside London. As generally predicted, Labour gained London North-West and London South-East. Their triumphs in Kent, Essex, Hertfordshire and Bedfordshire were perhaps more surprising, given Labour's total of just one Westminster MP in these four counties combined. Yet the Conservatives got off lightly. In no seat did their vote exceed 44 per cent, while majorities in Sussex South, East Sussex, Thames Valley and the three Hampshire seats were cut to wafer-thin margins. Several of the nine remaining Conservative MEPs could be grateful that large-scale 'tactical voting' had failed to materialize.

The six highest swings in Britain between the two main parties since 1992 were all in London and the northern Home Counties, headed by

London East (where the three London by-elections were held on the same day), Essex South (which includes Basildon) and London North (a personal triumph for Pauline Green). For the Liberal Democrats, the results were disappointing. No seats were gained, largely because the Labour vote held up, or even increased, in target seats. Near misses in East Sussex and the Hampshire seats were no consolation. An erroneous BBC result which temporarily suggested the Liberal Democrats had gained Surrey only added to the gloom. The Green Party vote predictably slumped from its 1989 peak, with a high of only 6.5 per cent for Jean Lambert in London North East. Their share of the poll was often exceeded by a collection of anti-Maastricht campaigners, who scored over 5 per cent in seven constituencies.

Labour's victories in the South-East outside London were of great psychological importance to the party, giving it confidence that this need not be barren territory, and that the Conservatives could be beaten even where they were strongest in 1979–92. The defeat of the Liberal Democrats in areas where they were competing with Labour for the anti-Conservative vote was perhaps of longer-term importance. Since 1992, the Liberal Democrat share of the vote fell in 17 seats and rose in eight – mostly seats where Labour had never been a serious proposition. The contrast with Liberal Democrat success in the local elections was stark.

MEPs bring money, which Labour had lacked in much of the South-East and, with luck, positive publicity. London's nine Labour MEPs assumed a special mission – aiming, in the absence of an elected tier of regional government, to become the voice of Greater London, giving it coherence in European and other policy forums. London North's Pauline Green was in herself an unusual phenomenon – a powerful socialist leader from the suburban South-East of England.

A low share of the vote and the loss of eight Euro seats was not the only Conservative worry arising from the 1994 election. The fabled electoral machine showed definite signs of rust in some previously safe areas. Bad organisation in critical areas was explicitly blamed by two defeated candidates and alluded to by others. One candidate, in speculative mood, suggested that the future of campaigning might lie in contracting literature delivery out to private firms, rather than relying on dwindling numbers of elderly workers. Though their ascendancy was severely damaged, the South-East remains the Conservatives' best region, returning nine of the party's current 18 MEPs. But the party would be foolish to ignore the threat from the abrupt changes in the political map of the South-East.

THE EASTERN COUNTIES
JOHN GREENAWAY

Over the last few decades the generally prosperous East of England has become an increasingly Conservative area. All five Euro-seats were previously comfortably held by the Conservatives. Nevertheless, Labour had a secure base in the large towns and cities of the region, possessed a good organisation (except in some rural blackspots) and had high expectations based on encouraging 1993 county election results. Norfolk was seventh, Lincolnshire eighth and Suffolk & South-West Norfolk tenth on Labour's national target list. On the day of his death John Smith had been due to address a rally in Ipswich and throughout the campaign Labour notables toured the region. Liberal Democrat strength was patchy. Their best hope was Essex North and Suffolk South; here they had made inroads into Colchester in the May District elections and an ex-Conservative independent was also standing.

Although the Eastern counties are geographically near to the Continent, the election campaign had no more of a European angle here than elsewhere in the country. The domestic record of the Government was the key issue. What local issues there were, like privatisation of the Forestry Commission in Thetford or Sizewell or fishing (Grimsby and Lowestoft) were too localised to have an impact on the large Euro seats. The only possible exception was controversy over the Trans-European Road Network, as many electors had strong views on road building, either for or against.

A feature of the campaign was the lacklustre coverage by the local media. Some local radio stations had 'election calls' to the candidates or set piece interviews; others did not go this far. The Representation of the People Act clearly inhibited the broadcast media, as they felt obliged to give the Natural Law Party candidates equality of coverage with the mainstream parties. Less explicable was the local press. None of the local newspapers made any active attempt to report the campaign. The coverage of the *Cambridge Evening News* was typical of the region. Apart from reporting the Prime Minister's day of campaigning, it offered four one-page reports throughout the campaign which consisted of a balanced coverage based on press statements from the five parties. Candidates from all parties subsequently felt deeply frustrated at their inability to get meetings, events or press releases taken up locally. Regional television tended to highlight certain seats, especially the Norfolk one, which was also featured in a

Newsnight eve-of-poll report. The considerable television coverage on this seat may have helped push up the turnout in Norfolk.

The Green Party felt particularly frustrated since neither the regional nor the national television offered them equal showing to the other three parties, despite their good vote last time. This greatly hampered the visibility of their campaign. Apart from this the Green Party was handicapped by both financial and organisational weakness: in Cambridgeshire the party could not afford the £1,000 necessary to produce the freepost leaflet. The party did best where it had pockets of local enthusiasm and support and used the elections to consolidate and build on these. Environmental issues as such were played down and emphasis put upon opposition to GATT, criticism of Maastricht and upon Green social and economic policy.

The Conservatives were on the defensive. A peculiarity of the region was the simultaneous existence of large numbers of ministers and of Euro-sceptic MPs. Motivating workers was not easy and in Lincolnshire the antipathy of Euro-sceptic MPs tended to rub off on to activists. In the Essex North and Suffolk seats the Conservatives concentrated almost entirely on targeting their own known supporters; in Norfolk Paul Howell attempted a more noisy and active campaign. The results suggest that sitting MEPs have little personal vote. In Cambridgeshire the unknown Yorkshireman, Robert Sturdy, who replaced Sir Fred Catherwood, did just as well as someone like Mr Howell, who had a high, though not always popular, local profile.

The Liberal Democrats also experienced problems in motivating workers, who were less keen on remote Euro-battles than on local skirmishes. Election-fatigue in areas like Norwich and Colchester affected them more than Labour and gave the impression of an overall slipping back. Some Liberal Democrats were frustrated at their national campaign. Andrew Duff, the candidate in Cambridgeshire, believed Mr Ashdown had been 'nobbled' by the party in the South West and had fought a regional and conservative campaign.

The Labour campaign was the best organised and was well-financed. In most areas the emphasis was on targeting the Liberal Democrat vote and on stressing that Labour was best placed to get rid of the Tories. But in Essex the party found it was making inroads into the previously Conservative skilled working-class vote.

The results clearly showed a degree of anti-Conservative tactical voting on the part of the electorate. In much of East Anglia Labour and Liberal Democrats engaged in a leaflet war, manipulating voting and opinion poll data to show that they were in second place. In

Lincolnshire, Norfolk, and Suffolk the Labour case was more credible, so the Liberal Democrat vote fell heavily and Labour captured the seats. The 20 per cent Liberal Democrat poll in Cambridgeshire allowed the Conservative to hold on. In Essex North and Suffolk South the Liberal Democrat campaign was strongest; the voters remained confused and, with all three main parties close, Mrs McIntosh clung on to the seat with the extraordinarily low poll of 33 per cent. Turnout was around the national average of 35 per cent except in Norfolk which, at 44.1 per cent, was the fourth highest poll in England. The Labour triumph here of an 11 per cent lead was achieved despite rural areas polling 10 per cent higher than urban areas with Labour, urban council house wards lowest of the lot: all proof of Labour's newfound appeal to middle-class, Southern Britain.

THE MIDLANDS
PAUL FURLONG

The 'Midlands' includes 16 European constituencies comprising 177 Westminster constituencies – about one-fifth of the UK total. It stretches from South Yorkshire in the north to the Cotswolds, almost touching the edges of Bristol, in the south west. This is a very diverse area. It encompasses England's industrial heartland in the West Midlands, the rust belt of the steel and coal towns around Doncaster and Sheffield, and some of the high technology growth areas along the M4 and M40 motorways. It has some of England's most intensively farmed and wealthiest agricultural counties, and some of its densest centres of population. It is a multi-cultural area, and yet one which also represents what some might regard as core English values. In recent Westminster elections, the West Midlands in particular has been regarded as an important battleground between Labour and Conservative, since in this traditionally Labour area the votes of skilled manual workers switched in significant proportions to the nationalist-populist appeal of Margaret Thatcher's blend of Conservatism. With the changing atmosphere of the 1990s, Labour clearly needed not only to win back support in areas such as Dudley and Wolverhampton (Midlands West Euro-constituency), but also to prove its capacity to appeal to 'Middle England' in the suburbs and smaller towns in the South and East Midlands.

At first sight, the campaign and the results gave some comfort to the Labour Party. Labour won 14 of the 16 seats, and the two

Conservative holds were won with majorities of 2.2 per cent (the Cotswolds) and 0.6 per cent (Worcestershire and South Warwickshire) respectively. This represented five Conservative losses, including the seat of the leader of the Conservatives in the European Parliament, Sir Christopher Prout (Herefordshire and Shropshire). However, it is difficult to interpret this as a resounding success for Labour's European strategy, or to draw conclusions about the implications for a future General Election.

The campaign followed closely on the heels of local government elections in many of the major towns, including Birmingham. Birmingham was particularly significant in this context because the City Council had been Labour-controlled since 1984 and was targeted by the Conservatives as an area they could win, both in the local elections and in the Euro-elections. However, the Prime Minister opened the Conservatives' local election campaign in Birmingham with a high-profile speech which was widely perceived to have misfired. In attacking the local Council's record, John Major was seen as attacking Birmingham itself. The campaign went badly wrong for the Conservatives, and they lost local seats in Birmingham in some surprising areas.

This was to have important consequences for the European elections for several reasons. First, the City Council had already adopted the slogan 'Birmingham – a European City' for its urban regeneration programme. The identification between local and European elections was therefore strong. Second, Conservative failures in the local elections in some high-profile council areas throughout the region made it difficult for them to appear as other than prospective losers unless they could force the campaign onto distinctly European issues. Third, the conduct of the campaign militated against this. What happened in the Midlands, as elsewhere, was to a considerable extent a dialogue between party organisations, in which the three main parties concentrated in getting out their support in their traditional areas, not seeking to win over converts for their European policies.

In doing so, the parties were responding to national priorities. Though there was a distinctive local flavour to the campaign in some parts of the region, the local campaign and the local candidates were to a considerable extent dominated by the national party leadership and driven by the national party organisation, with the consequence that European issues did not get a great airing. This could be seen most obviously in the conduct of the local campaigns, which were reliant on restricted groups of activists for all parties, and on the lack of sustained media interest. The Representation of the People Act was thought to have resulted in diminished coverage and was much resented by some incumbent candidates, who were eager to point out what they had achieved for their constituencies through Europe. Blunders and indiscretions which in a General Election might have excited attention went relatively unobserved by the non-participants. For example, the Conservative candidate for Birmingham East, Andrew Turner, declared categorically in his campaign leaflet that 'Conservatives oppose a single European currency', sentiments which had caused a furore when uttered by a Cabinet minister a month before. The lack of media attention and the effective kidnapping of the campaign by the national organisations was doubly galling to the candidates, particularly to the sitting MEPs.

Because of the weight of national campaigning and the low levels of public interest, it is difficult to identify special local factors in these elections. Suspicions of a sympathy vote for John Smith or the workings of the incumbent factor must remain speculative. A further reason for scepticism about the significance of the results was the generally low turnout, which fell below 25 per cent in some of the individual Westminster constituencies.

In many respects, Euro-elections are now an established feature of the political cycle, especially in the larger conurbations, where there are effective party organisations. This trend is helped by the priority now given by all the national party organisations to any election which has a national coverage, whatever the precise level of representation at issue. With the exception of 1979, the Euro-elections have most closely followed not the patterns of the Westminster elections, but those of the various local elections, whose number and complexity means that they currently occur every year across significant proportions of the region. Seen in this context, it is the Westminster election campaigns which are the anomaly, both with regard to the level of turnout and in the terms of voting patterns and the type of media interest.

In view of the diversity of the region, the results were strikingly homogeneous. In every constituency except one, Labour gained votes, both on the 1989 European elections and on the 1992 Westminster elections. The exception was Sheffield, where there was a swing to the Liberal Democrats. This did not affect the result there, however, since Labour still won the seat with a 38.4 per cent majority, one of its largest in the country. If the two Conservative seats are excluded, the majority varied from 0.9 per cent to Labour in Hereford and Shropshire to a massive 58.9 per cent in Yorkshire South. For Labour, therefore, the central message of the elections in this important region would seem to have been that the party gained most in the areas where it had previously been weakest. This was bad news for the Liberal Democrats. The Conservatives could take solace from the lack of similarity between these elections and Westminster contests. This was particularly true in the shires where, despite the loss of Euro-seats, many an uncomfortable Conservative backbencher was relieved to see the Labour vote up, safe in the knowledge that the far more insidious Liberal Democrat threat had been contained. However, the results were not completely reassuring for the Labour Party. As one experienced MEP put it, 'You cannot have it both ways. If you decide to run the campaign as a referendum on the government and John Major then you have to accept that seven out of ten people didn't participate in that referendum. People weren't switched on by having the elections turned into a referendum on the government or on John Major. You can't say you won on European issues if you deliberately turned your back on them. The way I see it, we should be anything but euphoric.'

THE NORTH WEST
STANLEY HENIG

It is yet another of the peculiarities of the British electoral system that the North West region, so critical to the outcome of any contemporary Westminster election, was of little real interest in the 1994 European elections. The region consists of 10 Euro-seats.

Cumbria and Lancashire North	Greater Manchester Central
Lancashire Central	Greater Manchester East
Lancashire South	Greater Manchester West
Merseyside East and Wigan	Cheshire East
Merseyside West	Cheshire West and Wirral

At the 1992 general election Labour gained an average of 45 per cent of the votes in these ten Euro-seats to the Conservatives' 38 per cent. Whilst this gave Labour 49 seats to 28, it can be characterised as a 'match-losing performance'. Based on the average scores in the previous European elections (52 per cent to 32 per cent) Labour could have expected to win another 14 parliamentary seats in 1992 – enough without any movement elsewhere in the country to deprive the Conservatives of their parliamentary majority. At the next Westminster elections the North West will again be a major battleground. The European election context was quite different. Labour's big lead in 1989 was enough to secure eight of the ten seats in the region. Only Cumbria and Lancashire North and Lancashire Central stood out – just – against the tide. These might have been expected to provide focus and excitement for the 1994 contest. However, even before it started the two seats were in effect 'allotted' to Labour by the impact of political slide-rules on boundary changes. Conservative Wyre was taken from the northernmost European seat which thus became the most marginal of Labour Euro-constituencies. The other two Lancashire seats were rejigged, with the old Lancashire East in effect disappearing. The new Lancashire Central took in Burnley and Pendle from the old Lancashire East seat as well as Wyre. It lost Chorley, South Ribble and West Lancashire to the new Lancashire South which replaced Lancashire East as a Euro-constituency. The revamped Lancashire Central thus became another 'Labour super-marginal'. With none of the other boundary changes likely to make any real difference to the parties' standing, Labour hence entered the European elections 'holding' all ten seats in the region. In the context of a national swing to Labour even compared to the 1989 European elections it seemed highly unlikely that there would be any change in the North West. Furthermore, with all ten seats essentially battles between the Conservatives and Labour there was little scope for third party interest.

In the circumstances it is perhaps hardly surprising that little of any genuine regional campaign could be discerned. Party activity was predominantly a sub-set of the national campaign. The 'big names' who campaigned in the region – John Major, Michael Howard, Michael Heseltine and Sir Leon Brittan on the Conservative side; Margaret Beckett, Tony Blair and Gordon Brown for Labour – paid their visits in a predominantly national context. John Major did address some potential regional/European issues during his visit to Merseyside, but in general the statements by the big names were concerned with broad national campaign issues. Coverage by the regional media was patchy. Local radio stations took a moderate interest – Radio Lancashire organised phone-ins with Mr Brown and Mr Major. Press coverage was variable. The *Lancashire Evening Post* gave a reasonable amount of space to local campaigning. The two

Liverpool newspapers gave a fair coverage of the European elections overall, but very little to the one-sided battle for the local seats. The *Manchester Evening News* had virtually nothing on any aspect of the elections. Activity by party workers was probably most comparable with local elections – leafleting and canvassing were both very muted compared to general elections. In the two marginal seats, despite their pre-election 'change' of allegiance, there was still a tendency for the Conservatives to campaign as incumbents and Labour as challengers. Most election literature sought some relevant link to Europe, but party workers had few illusions as to the real basis for voter choice.

The outcome – predictable from day one of the campaign – left Labour holding all ten seats with Lancashire Central its ninth most marginal seat and Cumbria and Lancashire North its thirteenth on a national basis. Labour's average score moved up to 55 per cent. There is an interesting contrast between the two seats in which incumbent Conservatives were defeated. In Cumbria and Lancashire North the turnout was just over 40 per cent. Based on Westminster constituencies within the Euro-seat the highest turnout – 46 per cent – was in Workington the home of the Labour candidate, Tony Cunningham. The swing from Conservative to Labour at just over 11 per cent since the 1992 general election and 5.6 per cent since the 1989 Euro-elections was slightly lower than the average regional swing, but almost spot on the national swing.

In Lancashire Central the turnout was just over 34 per cent and was lowest in the Labour strongholds of Burnley and Preston. The swing of 8.3 per cent since 1992 and 3.3 per cent since 1992 was lower than anywhere in the region except Merseyside West. There are varying potential explanations for this. The Labour candidate Mark Hendrick was of mixed race origin. He had been selected for the old Lancashire Central seat, not including Burnley – the most solidly Labour part of the new Euro-constituency. Hendrick's relations with the Burnley Labour Party seem initially to have been uneasy. However, the turnout in Burnley (28 per cent) was actually slightly higher than in Blackburn (26 per cent) which had the same Labour candidate as previously. Michael Welsh had been a Conservative MEP for fifteen years, much longer than Lord Inglewood in Cumbria and Lancashire North. He fought a vigorous campaign. Differential turnout suggests that he benefitted from an incumbency factor in the unchanged parts of the Euro-constituency.

Both Lord Inglewood and Michael Welsh campaigned as strong pro-Europeans. The former claimed 'we have to be in there wholeheartedly or not at all', whilst for the latter 'the bonds that unite us are stronger than those which divide us'. Clearly both found difficulties with their party's national stance. However, there is no evidence at all that the discrepancy between candidates and national party made any difference to the specific local outcomes.

In summary, there was no specific regional campaign in the North West in the 1994 Euro-elections and no significant deviation from the norm in the results. It was by no means clear that the 1999 Euro-elections would take place on the same electoral system. If they did, the Conservatives would hope to 'regain' their two lost seats. However, it is in any event hard to imagine national circumstances remaining as favourable to Labour. If Labour were to go into those elections as the party of government then the familiar oscillation in mid-term voting might also make Lancashire South and the two Cheshire seats potential marginals. Meanwhile, the North West would certainly be a key, and interesting, battleground at the general election in 1996 or 1997.

THE NORTH EAST
PHILIP NORTON

The campaign in the nine constituencies in the North-East was so uneventful as to pass almost unnoticed. There were no ultra-marginal seats, and the only seat under threat was the re-drawn Yorkshire North constituency of Conservative Edward McMillan-Scott. In the other eight seats, some boundary changes had not always helped the incumbent but given the Labour lead in the opinion polls, there seemed little likelihood of any of the eight Labour incumbents having to find new employment after the election.

The lack of interest in the campaign meant that candidates had to fight not only one another but also apathy among the electors. As the *Hull Daily Mail* commented at the start of the campaign, 'rarely has such a major test of party strength and loyalty been conducted amid such abject apathy by the electorate'. Coverage by the local and regional press, and by local radio stations, providing candidate profiles as well as campaign reports, appeared to have little impact. Candidates encountered little interest in the election when campaigning. 'I've been going about stirring up apathy,' commented one long-serving Labour MEP. There were few incidents during the campaign to raise the level of interest. Newsworthy events were rare and low-key. In Yorkshire

South-West, for example, a 12-foot tall trailer sign saying *Vote for Megahy* got stuck under a ten-foot-high bridge (*Yorkshire Post*). There were also few notables among the candidates. All enjoyed some visibility by virtue of being incumbents, but none that extended much beyond their own constituencies. Among challengers, some publicity flowed to the Conservative candidate in Yorkshire South-West for the simple reason that she was of French origin. In Leeds there was the added attraction of a challenge from the breakaway Liberal party in the shape of former MP Michael Meadowcroft. But there was nothing to engage the sustained interest of the electorate.

In campaigning, there was no central issue that emerged. Conservative candidates appeared more prone than Labour candidates to emphasise European issues but, given that Labour incumbents could – and did – stress their work in the European Parliament, the divide was not very great. Candidates of both major parties appeared willing to fight both a domestic and a European campaign. In Humberside the Labour candidate used his election address to stress his record in the European Parliament and his party's policy on European issues. During the campaign he used the publication of crime figures to attack the government's record on law and order. His Conservative opponent used his election address not only to emphasise the critical stance of the Conservative party in tackling European issues but also to record his own position on capital punishment and field sports. The Liberal Democrat approach was the more remarkable of the three. The candidate's election address in Humberside highlighted the party's success in the May local elections and declared 'Show the Government what you think'. 'These elections can't change the Government,' it went on, 'but they could send it a strong message.' The candidate of the Natural Law Party concentrated on the values of yogic flying and a universal message. 'I only wish people well. I genuinely want peace on earth,' she told a local newspaper.

On election day most electors stayed at home. The turnout in the nine constituencies averaged 33 per cent, ranging from 28 per cent in Tyne and Wear to almost 39 per cent in Yorkshire North – the only one to register a turnout above the national average. The swing from Conservative to Labour averaged 5.5 per cent but showed some significant variations. In Humberside, the swing in the redrawn seat was calculated at just under 8 per cent. In Yorkshire South-West it was less than 3 per cent. The swings made no difference to the outcomes, other than to consolidate Labour's position in eight seats and to render marginal the Conservative-seat of Yorkshire North – a seat made up of six UK parliamentary constituencies, five of which returned Conservative MPs in 1992. Edward McMillan-Scott's majority of 7,072 was less than the combined vote of the Green and Natural Law candidates. In a good year for the Conservatives, Humberside would have been lost by Labour. (In the seven UK parliamentary seats that comprise the constituency, the Conservatives got five-thousand votes more than Labour in 1992.) It was clear from the outset that it was not going to be a good year for the Conservatives. The Labour majorities in the eight Labour-held seats ranged from a low of 40,618 in Humberside to a high of 111,638 in Durham.

Apart from the Conservative hold in North Yorkshire, the results were notable for their similarities. In all nine seats, the Liberal Democrats came a reasonable or strong third in the polls, displacing the Greens. However, only in Durham did the Liberal Democrat come within 5,000 votes of catching the Conservative candidate. The Green candidates garnered between 4,000 and 7,000 votes (7,163 in Yorkshire South-West was their best result) and came fourth in six of the nine seats. In Yorkshire West, the New Britain candidate came fourth with 8,027 votes (several hundred votes ahead of the Green), in Northumbria the candidate of the UK Independence Party got 7,210 votes – almost 1,500 votes ahead of the Green – and in Leeds Michael Meadowcroft got 6,617 votes, just squeezing ahead of the Green candidate (6,283 votes). The only other Liberal candidate to stand in the region – in Tyne and Wear – competed with the Green for fourth place, the Green candidate just getting the edge. In every constituency the candidate of the Natural Law Party came bottom of the poll, in most cases with under or just over 1,000 votes.

The fringe candidates added a little colour to an otherwise colourless election. Candidates of the three principal parties dominated. Labour could take satisfaction from consolidating its majority position: it got 57.8 per cent of the votes cast in the nine seats. The Conservatives got 23.6 per cent but had the satisfaction of holding on to Yorkshire North, thus ensuring at least a splash of blue on the map north of the Humber. The Liberal Democrats trailed with 13.4 per cent of the vote but nonetheless had the satisfaction of establishing their position as the third party. Even so, protest votes appear to have gone more to Labour than to the Liberal Democrats. Other protest votes were mopped up by the fringe candidates, who between them took 5.3 per cent of the pool. Altogether, just over one-and-a-half-million people voted in the region (1,514,499). Three million stayed at home.

WALES
DUNCAN MITCHELL

The cinema hit in the summer of 1994 in Cardiff was *Four Weddings and a Funeral*; the European elections in Wales could be described as *Three Coronations and Two Lotteries*. The opportunity to hold a serious and badly-needed debate about Wales' constitutional status and future within a 'Europe of the Regions' was squandered by a short campaign which was virtually ignored by the Welsh media, and disrupted by the death of the Labour leader, John Smith. Depressingly, the second-order image of European elections seemed as strong in Wales as ever.

All the right ingredients for a genuinely distinct regional campaign were there. Wales is a nation with its own political, economic and administrative infrastructure. The existence of an indigenous nationalist party, Plaid Cymru, has forced mainstream parties to develop a distinct identity in Wales. Most parties acknowledge that European integration gives Wales not only the opportunity to develop a higher, more independent profile, but also creates a desperate need to demand a share of resources which will enable it to deal with the challenges of structural change and peripherality. The Welsh political parties, which are separate national organisations, with considerable financial and political autonomy, produced their own manifestos or election statements, addressing Welsh concerns, and indeed constitutional questions, directly. The European elections were therefore the ideal platform for politicians of all persuasions to promote their agendas for Wales in Europe.

To understand why the elections did not live up to such expectations, we must first look at the boundary changes necessitated by the award of an extra European Parliamentary seat to Wales, bringing its total to five. The committee appointed by the Home Secretary initially proposed that one of the new seats should cover much of the western seaboard. This bizarre contrivance could have produced one Conservative or Plaid Cymru victory, although Labour had won all four Welsh seats in 1989. The ensuing furore forced a reconsideration, leading to the creation of three totally safe Labour seats in South Wales, where the sitting MEPs, David Morris and Wayne David, and the well-known Glenys Kinnock's 'coronations' were a foregone conclusion, and seats in Wales North and Mid and West Wales which would be a contest between Labour and Plaid, given the likely collapse in the Tory vote. Conservative, Liberal Democrat and Green strategies consequently became more long-term, fighting not to win, but to prevent their party's electoral base being eroded. This did not help to focus on the immediate European issues. (In fairness, Welsh Liberal Democrats would have welcomed a full-blown constitutional debate, but recognised early on that this would not happen.)

The key seats were clearly Mid and West Wales, and Wales North. In such large, relatively unfamiliar constituencies traditional small-scale campaigning tactics were irrelevant. Welsh politicians were utterly dependent on their media colleagues. The latter appear unfortunately to have concluded that an already 'boring' election was as good as won for Labour: the only possible 'story' would be Plaid victories. This partly explains Welsh media coverage, which those involved in the campaign characterised as either non-existent, trivial, or biased in favour of Plaid Cymru. Voters were given little or no information about Welsh/European matters or the parties' subtly varied constitutional positions, and had no alternative to national (UK) coverage. The parties' best efforts to talk about Welsh issues were defeated by non-attendance at press conferences: party images, denied a truly Welsh context, became the bland adjunct to a referendum on the Major Government. The results in the two key constituencies were indeed a 'lottery' therefore, determined by the unpredictable extent and direction of the collapse in Tory and Green fortunes.

In Wales North, the sitting Labour MEP Joe Wilson campaigned hard to counteract the 'Wigley factor'. Wilson's Plaid Cymru opponent, Dafydd Wigley, was helped by his high profile as President of his party and as the MP for Caernarfon since 1974, and by what Conservatives and Labour saw as substantial media bias. The Conservative campaign rapidly foundered, to Wigley's advantage. Reports of growing 'dissatisfaction' with the Tory candidate appeared to be confirmed at Easter, when a senior Conservative figure in Caernarfon endorsed the Plaid candidate. Meanwhile, in Mid and West Wales Labour's Eluned Morgan, a 27-year-old former BBC researcher, was facing a vigorous campaign mounted by Marc Phillips of Plaid Cymru. Mr Phillips was backed not only by Cynog Dafis, who had won Ceredigion and Pembroke North in 1992 on a Plaid Cymru/Green ticket, but also by some local Green activists. During the campaign he was also endorsed by a leading Green figure, Jonathon Porritt. The unfortunate Green candidate, Chris Busby, bitterly attacked his erstwhile colleagues, but was helpless to prevent their 'betrayal'. While this was going on, Glenys Kinnock, with the aid of extensive local and national media coverage, was said to be campaigning in South Wales East as if it were a 'marginal', and not the safest seat in the UK.

The results appeared to prove sceptics right: Labour won all five seats, and took 56 per cent of the Welsh vote. Joe Wilson's majority in Wales North doubled, although Dafydd Wigley came a respectable second. Eluned Morgan's majority of nearly 30,000 was a blow to Plaid in Mid and West Wales, whilst in South Wales all three Labour candidates won thumping majorities, and Glenys Kinnock increased Llew Smith's old record majority by a further 10 per cent, to over 120,000. Plaid's disappointment at failing to win seats against a background of Conservative unpopularity mirrored Tory relief at having hung on to second place in the three South Wales seats. The Green collapse was confirmed – they secured only 2 per cent of the vote. For the Liberal Democrats, a share of 8.7 per cent was at least an improvement on the dark days of the Alliance split.

The high turnout (43.0 per cent, compared with 40.7 per cent in 1989, and a UK average of 36.8 per cent) gave the lie to those who might argue that media inactivity was merely a reflection of public apathy. It also left a question mark over Conservative claims that their supporters stayed at home. Instead, there seems to have been substantial 'lending' of Tory votes to Plaid in order to rebuke the government, because of the 'Wigley factor' in Wales North, or to prevent Labour winning. Plaid's position on constitutional issues appears to have played a secondary role. If this is the case, Plaid could take even less comfort from their two second places, and it undermines Plaid's claim to have become the 'second party in Wales', with 17 per cent of the vote. Whatever the message for the individual parties, voting patterns were determined not by Welsh and European issues, but principally by domestic UK factors. Those who would like to see a proper airing of the former would have to wait until 1999.

SCOTLAND
DAVID MILLAR

The scene was set for the European election campaign in Scotland by the surprising results of the regional council elections in Scotland. These were the last elections to be held for seats in the nine Scottish regional councils, due for replacement by unitary authorities in 1996.

The losers in these elections were Labour, whose percentage share of votes at 41.2 per cent showed a fall since the 1990 regional elections of 1.5 per cent, and the Conservatives with 13.7 per cent, a decrease of 5.8 per cent. The winners were the Scottish National Party (SNP), which scored 26.7 per cent, an increase of 4.9 per cent, and the Scottish Liberal Democrats (SLD), who won 12.3 per cent, an increase of 3.7 per cent. More startling were the gains in seats, the SNP adding 30 to the 43 already held, and the SLD adding 20 to the 42 held before the election.

There was only one change among the retiring Members of the European Parliament standing for election: in the Glasgow constituency the veteran Janey Buchan was replaced as Labour candidate by Bill Miller. The Scottish Green Party and the Natural Law Party entered candidates in each of the eight Scottish constituencies, and sundry other parties entered the field in some areas. The candidate with the highest profile was Winnie Ewing (SNP), seeking a fourth election mandate in the European Parliament and defending a 44,000 majority over the Conservatives in 1989. In the event, claiming that there was scarcely a shop which she had not visited from Muckle Flugga in Shetland to the Mull of Kintyre, Dr Ewing increased her majority by 6.8 per cent to 58.4 per cent of the vote, her nearest rival being the Labour candidate with 15.6 per cent. The most effective candidate turned out to be Dr Allan Macartney, who won the North-East Scotland seat from Henry McCubbin (Labour), improving his 1989 vote of 62,735 to 92,892, an increase of 13.4 per cent.

The campaign, launched on 9 May, was critically affected by events within and without Scotland. Of these the most substantial was the death on 12 May of the leader of the Labour Party, John Smith, a Scot sitting for a Scottish constituency. As a mark of respect, public, open campaigning ended immediately in Scotland, to be resumed only on 23 May. This moratorium probably disadvantaged the SNP and the Liberal Democrats, which relied on vigorous campaigning to compensate for their lack of funds compared to the two large parties. The funeral and interment of Mr Smith, and media speculation about his successor kept the Labour Party before the electors' attention during the remainder of the European campaign, even though the latter remained the priority issue in public for the party leaders.

Three other issues competed for the electors' interest during the campaign. The first, which dominated the media in the last week, was the commemoration of the D-Day landings on 6 June 1944, which was widely reported in the press, and in broadcasts. The second issue was the extraordinary attack by the Prime Minister on street beggars, which dominated the media, even in Scotland, from 28 to 30 May and eclipsed front-page coverage of the election campaign.

The third external issue which exerted some influence was the Eastleigh by-election, perceived as a referendum on the policies of the Government and reported in Scotland as such. While the apparent likelihood of a Liberal Democrat victory may have encouraged that party's campaigners in Scotland, the Eastleigh battle (and those for Euro-seats in South-West England) denied the Liberal Democrats' Euro-campaign the services of its Scottish MPs for many days.

The SNP, using the slogan 'SNPower for Change' and emphasising the power of the voter to change Scotland and to make Europe work for Scotland, linked Scottish independence firmly to membership of the European Union. Photographs of Dr Ewing featured prominently in SNP election literature. Meanwhile, the Scottish Liberal Democrat leader, Jim Wallace MP, claimed that his Party was 'the only consistently European Party in Scotland'.

The Conservatives launched their campaign on 11 May in Inverness, with the Foreign Secretary advocating a 'multi-track, multi-speed, multi-layered Europe', a theme to which the Prime Minister returned in England on 31 May. Ian Lang, the Secretary of State for Scotland, surprised many who had assumed him to be at least mildly pro-European when on 23 May he came out for 'Euro-realism', speaking of the EU as 'the self-serving Empire in Brussels'.

At a rally in Glasgow on 2 June organised by the Scottish Council of the European Movement, the issues which aroused most passion were the veto in EU decision-making and Scotland's role in Europe.

As an example of the interest of television broadcasters in the election, each candidate in the South of Scotland seat was offered one minute by Border TV in which to make a formal policy statement and 20 seconds by BBC Scotland, with brief additional silent coverage of each candidate speaking to electors. Local papers in the six seats assumed to be 'safe' for the Labour Party showed little interest; in the Highlands and Islands Dr Ewing's charisma and in North-East Scotland the SNP challenge to Labour secured greater media interest however.

The protest vote against the government was expressed in a surge of support for the SNP, which culminated in the expected gain from Labour in North-East Scotland. Based on the regional election results, one commentator at least predicted on 23 May that Conservative voters in the area would vote SNP to defeat Labour. In fact the drop in the Conservative vote of 8 per cent was second only to that in South of Scotland (9.5 per cent), where the SNP's share increased by 5 per cent. Anecdotal evidence indicates that the latter figure included some dissident Tories voting SNP as an anti-government protest. The SNP probably also benefited from the passiveness of Labour and the Liberal Democrats since the April 1992 general election as regards the issue of Scottish Home Rule. Scottish politics has followed a divergent path from English politics since the early 1970s, a trend confirmed in the European election of June 1994.

NORTHERN IRELAND
PAUL HAINSWORTH

Northern Ireland's three MEPs are elected by a different system – proportional representation by single transferable vote (STV) – from the majority system in place for the rest of the United Kingdom. From the outset, the intention has been to enable a wider representation than would have existed across a highly polarised society and, thereby, facilitate the election of a representative from the minority Catholic/ nationalist community.

European elections in Northern Ireland are rather predictable occasions: since the first direct elections in 1979 only four individuals have been elected and always from the same three political parties. In 1994, therefore, no serious observers expected anything other than the return of the three incumbents: the Rev. Ian Paisley, Democratic Unionist Party (DUP); John Hume, Social Democratic and Labour Party (SDLP); and Jim Nicholson, Ulster Unionist Party (UUP). Nevertheless, the predictability of the result did not deter a record number of candidates from coming forward. In 1994, there were 17 candidates (1979: 13; 1984: 8; 1989: 10), including one from the centrist Alliance Party, three from Sinn Fein (SF), three representing the Natural Law Party, four Ulster independents, and three assorted left-wing candidates.

The candidacies of the leading contenders were established well before the election but the campaign only really began in earnest about a month before the vote, with the regional press – *Belfast Telegraph*, *Belfast News Letter* (Unionist), *Irish News* (Nationalist) – then giving the campaign daily coverage and urging voters to use their vote rather than abstaining.

Arguably, the main interest in the campaign was upon the split between the two main Unionist parties, the UUP and the DUP. Intermittently allied, these two parties had diverged for about eighteen months and the effect of Euro-campaigning was to exacerbate divisions. The DUP leader, Ian Paisley, now accused the UUP of being 'soft' on opposing Anglo-Irish political initiatives, notably the December 1993 Downing Street Declaration on Northern Ireland. In effect, Paisley's campaign was a de facto referendum on this document, with regular front page 'ads' urging voters to 'Stop Dublin Interference' or 'Give Dublin Your Answer'. The UUP's more accommodating stance here provoked the DUP leader to equate UUP leader James Molyneaux with Judas Iscariot. According to seasoned reporter on Northern Ireland, David McKittrick (*Independent*, 8 June 1994), this jibe enlivened 'a low-key and generally lacklustre' campaign.

Unsurprisingly, the UUP rejected the DUP's accusations and the party's Euro-manifesto, *Europe: Making it Work for Ulster*, included a defensive riposte from Mr Molyneaux: 'Against intense opposition Ulster Unionists continue to defend the integrity of the United Kingdom. Unionists should beware of those whose negative attitude plays into the hands of the IRA (Irish Republican Army) and the (Irish) Republic's Government by permitting them to exploit any suggestion of defeatism.'

As the campaign entered the final days, Mr Nicholson accused 'other candidates' of contributing to an 'orchestrated campaign' to discredit the UUP. Jim Nicholson saw the electorate (presumably Unionist) as faced with 'a stark choice': 'it can abstain, it can vote for empty bombast or it can vote for positive Ulster Unionism which is delivering' (*Belfast Telegraph*, 7 June 1994).

The UUP concentrated upon Nicholson's record in Europe and upon their agenda of 'positive progress', citing such examples as the setting up of a House of Commons' Select Committee on Northern Ireland – seen widely as a reward for tactically supporting John Major on Maastricht – and the reform of the legislative procedure for Northern Ireland business at Westminster. Mr Nicholson also warned that Ulster needed a full-time MEP – an undisguised criticism of Ian Paisley's and John Hume's dual mandate. In turn, Mr Paisley reminded voters that Mr Nicholson belonged to a Euro-group that supported Maastricht (i.e. the European People's Party) and contained Irish MEPs. Moreover, the DUP leader placed much emphasis on his anti-Maastricht and independent credentials.

The struggle for nationalist votes was less intense than that within Unionist circles. John Hume had effectively dominated the European arena in the eyes of nationalist and Catholic voters and Sinn Fein's novel strategy of fielding three candidates was an exercise in damage limitation. SDLP/Sinn Fein rivalry, intense in previous years, was defused by the ongoing dialogue between John Hume and Sinn Fein president, Gerry Adams. Without doubt, the dialogue provided a backcloth to the Euro-elections, with Unionists attacking a perceived 'pan-nationalist front'. John Hume's dogged pursuance of talks, however, was intended to explore all avenues towards peace in Northern Ireland.

The main thrust of Sinn Fein's campaign was to project peace in Ireland and partition as European issues. More subtly – and from the stance of constitutional nationalism, rather than support for 'the armed struggle' – John Hume's agenda was also to relate European integration and reconciliation to the need for such processes in all-Ireland. However, Mr Hume's campaign, under the banner of *Towards a New Century*, capitalised on his European record and front-bench membership of the leading EP party grouping, the Party of European Socialists. The SDLP manifesto prioritised support for the European social charter, a Europe of the regions, anti-poverty measures, environmental protection, integrated rural development and, above all, unemployment redress.

In fact, virtually all candidates claimed that unemployment was the principal issue even if their campaigns suggested otherwise. Lobbying and a questionnaire from the Euro-conscious Northern Ireland Council for Voluntary Action (NICVA), too, had injected a broader emphasis on social issues into the campaign. Equally, a women's forum had attempted to stress an alternative agenda and it was significant perhaps that a quarter of the Euro-candidates were women. Untimately, though it was traditional, local issues and divisions which dominated the campaign.

At 49.4 per cent, the turnout was marginally better than in 1989 (49.0 per cent). As expected, there was little by way of surprise. Ian Paisley topped the poll as usual with slightly more votes but a slightly lower share of the vote than in 1989. John Hume again came second, only 1,250 behind, but at 28.9 per cent, achieved the highest ever SDLP share of any major poll, narrowed the gap – 79,000 votes in 1984 – between himself and Ian Paisley and widened it further between his party and Sinn Fein, taking 75.0 per cent of the nationalist vote in the process. Both Ian Paisley and Mr Hume were elected comfortably on the first count.

On the second count, Mr Nicholson was duly elected, taking over two-thirds of Ian Paisley's second preferences and thereby indicating that divisions on high did not translate seriously into Unionist disaffection at the base. However, an appreciable proportion (22 per cent) of Ian Paisley's transfers went to an independent Ulster candidate, thus providing a rough guide to separatist (UDI) leanings within DUP voters.

Amongst the unsuccessful candidates, Sinn Fein's tactic of fielding three geographically dispersed candidates (including one woman) managed to increase both the total and the share of the party's vote. Sinn Fein therefore was not 'punished' for its delayed response to the Downing Street Declaration although John Hume's success tended to dwarf Sinn Fein's steady performance. Mr Hume interpreted his success as a significant endorsement of the peace process and, clearly, engaging with Sinn Fein had not harmed the SDLP leader. In fact, the Sinn Fein candidate Tom Hartley suggested that regular SF voters had switched to Mr Hume this time.

For all other candidates, the election was disheartening since all except the three MEPs lost their deposits. Over four in every five voters supported the incumbent MEPs. The Conservative Party declined badly from 25,000 to 5,000 votes following the resignation of its local leader and discontent with Government policies, while Alliance candidate Mary Clark-Glass, despite an active campaign, witnessed the decline of her party's vote and share of the poll.

Understandably, the three leading candidates could all claim to be winners. However, the results basically confirmed the status quo of Northern Ireland politics (see Table 8.2). The British and Irish governments continued to affirm their commitment to the peace process and dialogue over Northern Ireland and ruled out the veto of any single party while the DUP's vote especially, but also the UUP's, served as a warning to both governments against moving too dramatically with political initiatives. Equally, John Hume's success pointed in the other direction illustrating that the Euro-election had simply confirmed the polarised status of politics in Northern Ireland. As Sydney Elliott pointed out: 'The broad political situation was not materially changed by this result' (*Fortnight*, July – August, 1994).

Table 8.2   European election results, Northern Ireland, 1979–89

Electorate	1,162,344
Valid vote	559,867
Spoiled votes	9,234
Percentage poll	49.2%
Quota	139,967

	1979		1984		1989	
DUP	170,688	29.8	230,251	33.6	160,110	29.9
SDLP	140,622	24.6	151,399	22.1	136,335	25.5
UUP	125,169	21.9	147,169	21.5	118,785	22.2
SF	–	–	91,476	13.3	48,914	9.1
AP	39,026	6.8	34,040	5.0	27,905	5.2
CONS	–	–	–	–	25,789	4.8
Others	92,316	16.1	22,264	3.2	16,973	3.2

First Count

J. Anderson (Natural Law)	1,418	(0.25%)
M. Boal (Conservative)	5,583	(1.00%)
J. Campion (Peace Coalition)	1,088	(0.19%)
M. Clark-Glass (Alliance)	23,157	(4.14%)
N. Cusack (Labour)	2,464	(0.44%)
T. Hartley (Sinn Fein)	21,273	(3.80%)
J. Hume (SDLP)	161,992	(28.93%)
M. Kennedy (Natural Law)	419	(0.07%)
D. Kerr (Independence for Ulster)	517	(0.10%)
J. Lowry (Workers Party)	2,543	(0.45%)
D. McGuinness (Sinn Fein)	17,195	(3.07%)
F. Molloy (Sinn Fein)	16,747	(2.99%)
R. Mooney (Constitutional Independent, NI)	400	(0.07%)
J. Nicholson (Ulster Unionist)	133,459	(23.84%)
I. Paisley (DUP)	163,246	(29.16%)
H. Ross (Ulster Independence Movement)	7,858	(1.40%)
S. Thompson (Natural Law)	454	(0.08%)

Elected: Ian Paisley (DUP) and John Hume (SDLP)

Second Count (Distribution of Paisley surplus)

J. Anderson	(+75)	1,493
M. Boal	(+524)	6,107
J. Campion	(+39)	1,127
M. Clark-Glass	(+219)	23,376
N. Cusack	(+55)	2,519
T. Hartley	(+5)	21,278
M. Kennedy	(+25)	444
D. Kerr	(+306)	877
J. Lowry	(+36)	2,579
D. McGuinness	(+44)	17,239
F. Molloy	(+10)	16,757
R. Mooney	(+56)	456
J. Nicholson	(+16,082)	149,541
H. Ross	(+4,717)	12,575
S. Thompson	(+80)	534

Elected: Jim Nicholson (Ulster Unionist)

9 The Outcome

The United Kingdom went to the polls quietly on Thursday 9 June, together with the voters of Ireland, Holland and Denmark. The polling booths opened at 7.00 a.m. and closed at 10.00 p.m. The weather was mild, with only a few showers in the north. Polling was said to be sluggish. Nothing untoward happened. There was not a single prosecution for personation, intimidation or rowdyism around the polling station or any of the other offences that so characterised British elections a century before.

The BBC was on strike again, and election day coverage suffered as a result. All of the broadsheet newspapers and a large number of the tabloids ran front page stories about President Clinton's visit to Oxford, with large photographs of him in his academic gown outside the Sheldonian Theatre. Several newspapers ran in-depth pieces on the European Court of Justice's ruling on the Acquired Rights Directive of the previous day, but the issue remained confused. Alec Kellaway's defection to the Labour Party in Newham was covered in depth: 'ASHDOWN'S CHOICE DEFECTS TO LABOUR' (*Daily Mail*); 'PADDY'S MAN RATS ON VOTERS' (*Daily Express*); 'ASHDOWN ROCKED BY DEFECTION ON EVE OF POLL' (*Independent*). During the day, a minor story broke about desertions from Hackney South Conservative Association, but this turned out to be a damp squib. The pundits put on their psephological hats. Conservative voters were reckoned to be less likely to turn out. The Conservative Party, which could only hope for a late swing, was reported to be steeling itself for the worst, and a MORI poll in the *Times* showed the Conservatives at their lowest point yet, sparking the headline 'LABOUR HEADS FOR LANDSLIDE VICTORY'.

Five by-elections were also held on 9 June. It was one of the curiosities of the Euro-election that, while counting in the by-elections began immediately after the polling booths closed, counting in the European elections could not begin until the last polling booth in all the EU Member States had closed on the evening of Sunday 12 June, a provision laid down in the 1976 Community Act Concerning the Election of the Representatives of the European Parliament by Direct

Universal Suffrage. The Liberal Democrats saw this as a sort of consolation for the late moving of the Eastleigh writ, since they were generally expected to win there, and this would give them a weekend of positive media coverage.

There were delays in the by-election counts. The differently-coloured local and European election ballot papers had to be sorted, and it was not until 1 a.m. on Friday morning that the first result was declared. The initial evidence was bad news for the Conservatives. They came third behind the Liberal Democrats in Bradford and in two of the three East London seats. Only in Newham North-East, where the apostate Mr Kellaway lost his deposit, did they keep a second place. In the key contest in Eastleigh, the Conservatives fared disastrously. In a seat which they had held with a 17,000 majority in 1992, they came third. Only in Rochdale in 1958 and in Brecon in 1985 had they suffered such a humiliation (see Table 9.1).

Psephologists were quick to point out that, were the Eastleigh result to be repeated nationally, the Conservatives would lose even their safest Euro-seat, Buckinghamshire and Oxfordshire East, by 10 per cent. However, shrewd officials in Central Office rejoiced to see the Labour vote holding up in a southern seat. On this basis, a split opposition vote might enable them to survive the Liberal Democrat challenge threatening them in at least a dozen southern Euro-seats. Anthony King wrote in the *Daily Telegraph* that 'the real winners came second in Eastleigh'. The next day, the media was predicting the worst for the Conservatives: 'TORIES FACING ROUT IN EURO-POLL' (*Daily Telegraph*), 'MAJOR'S POLL ORDEAL BEGINS' (*Independent*), 'MINISTERS HOPE TO SALVAGE MAJOR'S AUTHORITY IN FACE OF HUMILIATION' (*Guardian*), 'UK CONSERVATIVES FEAR DISASTER' (*Financial Times*).

Table 9.1   The June 1994 by-election results

	Conservative		Labour		Liberal Democrat		Other
	%	+/−	%	+/−	%	+/−	%
Bradford	17.8	−20.6	55.3	+7.7	23.9	+10.2	5.5
Barking	10.4	−23.5	72.1	+20.5	12.0	−2.5	3.0
Dagenham	9.9	−26.4	72.0	+19.7	8.4	−3.1	9.9
Newham N.E.	14.6	−15.9	74.9	+16.6	4.2	−7.0	6.3
Eastleigh	24.7	−26.6	27.6	+5.9	44.3	+16.3	3.4

The Euro-elections did not only have to compete with the by-elections for coverage. On Friday 10 June, nominations for the Labour leadership and deputy leadership at last opened. Margaret Beckett, John Prescott, and a surprise candidate, Denzil Davies, announced their candidatures (though it was doubted whether Mr Davies would get enough signatures). Tony Blair was said to be biding his time. Amid the punditry there was some linkage between his ascendancy and Labour's strong second showing at Eastleigh.

Not even the Eastleigh rout could compete with the Saturday morning's principal piece of news: Bobby Charlton, a popular sporting figure and a member of England's 1966 football World Cup-winning team, was knighted in the birthday honours list, and virtually every single front page in the land sported a large photograph of a grinning Sir Bobby. (Perhaps more ominously, Sir Christopher Prout was made a Privy Counsellor.) Nevertheless, the newspapers dwelt heavily on two waiting games in their inside pages; the Euro-results on the Sunday evening but, as important, Tony Blair's expected announcement of his candidature. Recriminations and splits within the Conservative party started to reappear. Friday's papers carried stories of a potential backbench rebellion, said to be orchestrated by Bill Cash, and on Saturday Norman Lamont returned to the vexed issue of the single currency. 'I think we should be prepared to say we won't participate,' he said. Sir Edward Heath riposted that 'Now the time has come when we shall openly put forward the case for the EU and its further development,' and later in the same programme Michael Portillo found himself in an unaccustomed position of regretting 'this public opening of wounds'. But the big story of the day, expected for so long, was Tony Blair's announcement to his Sedgefield constituency that he would be standing for the Labour leadership.

On Sunday 12 June the remaining eight Member States went to the polls, but the British media remained primarily concerned with the Labour leadership issue. It transpired that Mr Blair was being backed by 13 out of 19 Shadow cabinet members and 135 out of the party's 268 MPs. Ken Livingstone announced his intention to enter the fray. Speculation on the probable result of the previous Thursday's voting was the second main story in the broadsheets. An ICM poll for the *Daily Express* (published in the sister *Sunday Express*) suggested that the Conservatives might hold onto just 15 of their 32 seats. The *Independent on Sunday* ran a story, 'TORIES DOWN TO 10 SEATS', based on an exit poll of London seats conducted for the Electoral Reform Society. The *Sunday Telegraph* ran with its own Gallup poll; 'THIRD OF

TORY VOTERS WANT MAJOR TO GO'. The *Sunday Times* was already speculating on how the Conservatives could reverse their apparent decline 'TORIES PLANS TAX CUTS TO RESCUE BESIEGED MAJOR'. But more perceptive political commentary saw a close link between Mr Blair's ascendancy and the forecast Euro-results; for example, 'ELECTION SUCCESS SIGNALS RISE OF THE LABOUR SOCIAL DEMOCRATS' (*Sunday Telegraph*).

The BBC was the only national television channel to provide non-stop coverage of the results. If its journalists had carried out their plans for another one-day strike then there would have been no television coverage of the elections in the United Kingdom apart from news bulletins. The last polling station closed in Italy at 10 o'clock local time, 9 o'clock in the United Kingdom. The first result to come in was from Sheffield, where the incumbent Labour MEP, Roger Barton, was returned with a massive 50,288 vote majority. But the commentators were quick to spot potential significance in the second place won by the Liberal Democrat, Sylvia Anginotti, whose 26,109 votes pushed the Conservative candidate into third place. From the outset, the Liberal Democrats had predicted significant gains in Sheffield, but it remained an isolated pocket of support in the north. Could any significance about the Liberal Democrats' performance in the south be derived from it? Calculating swing was a tenuous affair. Turnout was markedly down. Based on the 1989 Euro-election figures, there had been a 7.1 per cent swing from Labour to the Liberal Democrats. But if the benchmark was the 1992 General Election, then there had been a 3.5 per cent swing from Liberal Democrat to Labour.

A striking feature of this election was that it remained difficult accurately to predict the probable result until late into the counting process, but some general trends soon became clear. The Labour Party was doing better than it had expected, with surprising wins in former Conservative strongholds, particularly in the South-East. But the Conservatives were also doing slightly better than expected, principally because, despite some close calls, the Liberal Democrats were not doing as well as had been predicted.

As with previous Euro-elections, the European Parliament had set up a media centre to cover the elections in all 12 Member States. A giant screen, with a series of smaller screens around it, reproduced the television coverage from the many different companies involved, including the BBC. Labour's European Affairs spokeswoman, Joyce Quin, visited the centre during the night, as did the Labour member of the Commission in Brussels, Bruce Millan, but no other British politicians appeared. BBC coverage of the results in other countries was also limited, as the election team concentrated, at times almost exclusively, on what the results would mean if reproduced in a General Election, with a computerised 'virtual reality swingometer' and an energetic Peter Snow much in evidence. The fourth Euro-elections in the United Kingdom were to remain a resolutely domestic affair.

By 4 a.m. on the Monday morning, 76 constituencies had reported. Northern Ireland and eight mainland seats waited to count until the next day. The Monday counts begun at 9.00 a.m., with most declarations occurring before the lunchtime news bulletins. The results, in any case incomplete, came too late for the Monday morning newspapers, which were obliged to run speculative stories based on early results. The European election coverage had in any case to compete with another major news story. Stella Rimington, the head of MI5, had given an unprecedented public speech on the role of her organisation, and this quasi-constitutional departure much exercised the media.

By midday most of the results were known. The Conservatives had survived in 18 seats, but in 15 the margin was very slim. The party had won its lowest ever share of the vote, 28 per cent. The Liberal Democrats had to be content with just two, while the SNP doubled their representation from one to two seats. But the Labour Party surged from 45 to 62 seats (see Table 9.2, Table 9.3 and Figure 9.1).

In the afternoon, a defiant John Major called a press conference in the garden of 10 Downing Street. The weather was fine, and the Prime Minister was in his shirt sleeves. The garden press conference was deliberately reminiscent of the White House and received coverage in its own right. The Prime Minister signalled that a reshuffle of his government would soon take place, and this, rather than the election results which had inspired it, was the main news in the early evening bulletins. It was joined in the later bulletins by news of a debate which had taken place at the GMB trade union's general assembly between the three principal leadership contenders; Margaret Beckett, Tony Blair, and John Prescott.

On Tuesday 14 June the House of Commons returned from its Whitsun recess. The Prime Minister's garden press conference and his open hints of a reshuffle had largely succeeded in drawing the sting of the results themselves, which were already mostly confined to the inner pages of the morning's newspapers. The Labour leadership was clearly of more interest to the media than the Conservative leadership, although there was much speculation as to who would benefit or suffer

Table 9.2 European election results, by constituency, 1994

	Winner	Turnout %	Con %	Lab %	LD %	Grn %	Anti %	Other %	Swing 92/94	Swing 89/94	MEP
LONDON											
London Central	Lab	32.4	31.4	47.0	12.5	4.4	**2.6**	2.1³	−8.6	−4.6	*S Newens
London E	Lab	33.1	24.2	57.8	9.1	2.5	**3.5**	2.7²	−21.6	−9.5	*Ms C Tongue
London N	Lab	33.8	29.2	55.5	8.6	3.1	**2.8**	1.0²	−18.7	−11.8	*Ms P Green
London NE	Lab	26.4	17.9	62.1	7.9	6.5	**1.6**	4.1⁴	−13.3	−5.2	*A Lomas
London NW	**LAB**	34.9	37.1	47.4	11.2	2.8	—	1.4³	−12.9	−7.2	R Evans
London S & Surrey E	Con	34.1	38.8	33.5	19.2	4.2	—	4.3³	−14.3	−6.4	*J Moorhouse
London SE	**LAB**	35.1	36.4	41.0	14.5	3.7	—	4.5³	−14.7	−5.9	S Spiers
London S Inner	Lab	27.2	18.6	61.0	14.9	4.7	—	0.8	−12.0	−7.3	*R Balfe
London SW	Lab	34.1	30.9	49.7	11.4	3.3	**3.0**	1.7³	−15.9	−6.5	*Ms A Pollack
London W	Lab	35.8	28.7	51.9	11.8	3.4	**2.5**	1.7²	−17.2	−8.2	*M Elliott
SOUTH EAST											
Beds & Milton Keynes	**LAB**	38.4	30.3	46.6	13.8	3.3	5.6²	0.5	−19.1	−11.1	Ms E McNally
Bucks & Oxfordshire East	Con	37.0	42.3	25.5	23.5	4.6	—	4.0²	−12.8	−6.8	*J Elles
East Sussex & Kent S	Con	41.6	38.6	16.4	35.8	3.5	**4.2**	1.6²	−11.2	−8.1	*Sir J Stewart-Clark
Essex N & Suffolk S	Con	40.9	33.2	31.5	25.6	3.2	6.0	0.4	−14.8	−7.3	*Ms A McIntosh
Essex S	**LAB**	32.8	31.3	44.6	16.2	2.9	—	4.9²	−20.1	−10.6	R Howitt
Essex W & Herts E	**LAB**	36.1	34.5	36.2	19.5	3.1	6.2²	0.6	−16.8	−9.4	H Kerr
Hampshire N & Oxford	Con	38.0	35.8	24.1	31.3	3.6	**4.2**	1.0²	−10.8	−4.4	G Mather
Hertfordshire	**LAB**	39.8	34.1	39.1	18.6	3.7	3.1	1.4³	−15.3	−10.5	P Truscott
Itchen, Test and Avon	Con	41.5	35.4	22.8	32.4	3.5	**5.4**	0.6	−9.8	−4.1	*E Kellett-Bowman
Kent E	**LAB**	40.0	34.2	34.6	22.1	3.6	**4.7**	0.9	−13.9	−6.9	M Watts
Kent W	**LAB**	37.0	32.1	41.0	17.9	3.0	**5.2**	0.8	−17.6	−9.4	P Skinner
South Downs W	Con	39.1	43.6	16.8	32.7	4.0	—	2.8²	−10.8	−3.2	J Provan
Surrey	Con	37.2	43.2	16.0	29.2	3.7	6.4²	1.4	−9.6	−2.5	*T Spencer
Sussex S & Crawley	Con	37.4	33.9	33.0	22.3	5.0	5.2²	0.5	−14.3	−8.0	B Donnelly
Thames Valley	Con	34.5	37.3	36.9	17.5	3.2	—	5.1³	−16.4	−7.5	*J Stevens
Wight & Hampshire S	Con	36.9	34.9	22.3	32.1	3.7	6.7	0.4	−12.9	−4.1	R Perry

cont. overleaf

	Winner	Turnout %	Con %	Lab %	LD %	Grn %	Anti %	Other %	Swing 92/94	Swing 89/94	MEP
SOUTH WEST											
Bristol	Lab	40.6	29.6	44.1	19.6	3.5	**2.8**	0.4	−12.9	−4.9	*I White
Cornwall & W Plymouth	LD	44.5	28.3	19.7	41.8	2.0	**3.0**	5.1[4]	−6.1	−6.0	R Teverson
Devon & E Plymouth	Con	44.7	31.7	20.1	31.4	4.7	−	12.0[4]	−10.3	−7.3	G Chichester
Dorset & E Devon	Con	40.9	37.2	15.9	36.2	3.9	6.3[2]	0.5	−9.1	−4.6	*B Cassidy
Somerset & N Devon	LD	46.7	34.3	14.2	43.6	4.5	2.9	0.5	−7.0	−3.2	G Watson
The Cotswolds	Con	38.9	34.5	32.3	22.7	4.2	5.7	0.6	−11.9	−7.1	*Lord Plumb
Wiltshire N & Bath	Con	41.1	34.9	24.5	30.6	2.9	**2.8**	4.3[3]	−9.4	−2.6	*Ms C Jackson
EAST ANGLIA											
Cambridgeshire	Con	35.6	37.6	35.4	20.3	3.2	−	3.5[2]	−14.5	−8.5	R Sturdy
Norfolk	**LAB**	43.9	33.6	45.2	17.2	3.5	−	0.5	−14.1	−9.9	C Needle
Suffolk & SW Norfolk	**LAB**	38.1	33.7	40.5	20.7	4.2	−	0.8	−14.1	−9.2	D Thomas
EAST MIDLANDS											
Leicester	**LAB**	37.3	34.4	44.9	14.9	4.6	−	1.2	−12.9	−6.7	Ms S Waddington
Lincolnshire & Humbs N	**LAB**	36.0	35.4	42.4	13.9	4.4	−	3.9[3]	−13.0	−7.9	Ms V Hardstaff
Northants & Blaby	**LAB**	39.0	33.5	46.1	13.4	4.4	−	2.6[2]	−17.0	−9.7	Ms A Billingham
Nottingham & NW Leics	Lab	38.7	29.1	49.8	12.5	3.7	4.5[2]	0.5	−13.9	−8.7	*Ms M Read
Notts N & Chesterfield	Lab	35.4	21.0	63.1	12.1	2.8	−	0.9	−12.2	−8.1	*K Coates
Peak District	Lab	38.7	28.3	53.1	15.0	2.8	−	0.8	−16.5	−9.7	Ms A McCarthy
WEST MIDLANDS											
Birmingham E	Lab	29.5	22.7	58.2	12.5	4.0	−	2.5[2]	−13.3	−4.7	*Ms C Crawley
Birmingham W	Lab	28.3	26.6	53.7	10.1	3.0	3.6	3.1[2]	−13.3	−4.5	*J Tomlinson
Coventry & N Warks	Lab	32.3	26.8	52.5	10.2	2.6	5.5	2.3[2]	−15.5	−8.8	*Ms C Oddy
Herefordshire & Shrops	**LAB**	38.4	35.8	36.7	21.3	5.6	−	0.7	−11.8	−6.6	D Hallam
Midlands W	Lab	31.0	26.6	59.4	7.3	2.6	−	4.0[2]	−14.4	−5.7	S Murphy

Staffordshire E & Derby	Lab	35.7	27.2	55.6	9.5	2.3	**3.8**	1.5²	−16.5	−8.9	P Whitehead
Staffs W & Congleton	Lab	31.3	27.8	53.1	15.4	2.9	–	0.9	−13.4	−7.8	M Tappin
Worcs & S Warwicks	Con	37.7	35.1	34.6	21.1	4.4	4.0	0.7	−11.9	−5.7	J Corrie
YORKSHIRE											
Humberside	Lab	32.1	27.8	51.9	17.1	–	2.5	0.7	−12.7	−7.9	*P Crampton
Leeds	Lab	29.9	23.0	56.9	11.2	–	4.0	4.8²	−13.7	−5.5	*M McGowan
North Yorkshire	Con	38.4	38.0	34.2	23.5	–	3.8	0.5	−10.9	−6.1	*E McMillan-Scott
Sheffield	Lab	27.3	17.1	58.3	19.9	–	3.6	1.0²	−7.7	−1.7	*R Barton
Yorkshire S	Lab	28.4	13.8	72.7	7.9	**2.6**	2.5	0.5	−10.6	−3.1	*N West
Yorkshire SW	Lab	28.8	21.7	59.2	13.6	–	4.5	1.1	−11.6	−2.9	*T Megahy
Yorkshire W	Lab	34.4	25.0	53.4	12.1	4.7	4.2	0.5	−14.0	−5.3	*B Seal
NORTH WEST											
Cheshire E	Lab	32.2	29.6	53.7	12.6	–	2.2	1.9²	−13.6	−8.1	*B Simpson
Cheshire W & Wirral	Lab	36.5	29.8	53.6	10.5	3.1	2.6	0.5	−12.7	−8.1	*L Harrison
Gtr Manchester Central	Lab	28.9	23.2	53.4	16.4	–	3.5	3.5²	−11.6	−6.5	*E Newman
Gtr Manchester E	Lab	27.0	19.3	60.4	15.1	–	4.3	0.9	−13.2	−5.4	*G Ford
Gtr Manchester W	Lab	29.5	23.3	61.8	9.0	–	2.6	3.3²	−14.2	−6.6	*G Titley
Lancashire Central	Lab	34.0	35.4	42.4	14.9	4.0	2.5	1.0	−8.2	−3.3	M Hendrick
Lancashire S	Lab	32.9	30.0	54.3	10.0	2.0	2.8	0.9	−12.7	−6.6	*M Hindley
Merseyside E & Wigan	Lab	24.5	14.0	72.0	6.9	–	2.6	4.5²	−9.8	−5.5	*T Wynn
Merseyside W	Lab	26.0	20.0	58.4	14.1	–	3.4	4.1²	−7.6	−5.2	*K Stewart
NORTHERN											
Cleveland & Richmond	Lab	35.0	26.0	58.7	12.2	–	2.5	0.6	−15.2	−7.2	*D Bowe
Cumbria & Lancs N	Lab	40.5	36.7	48.0	11.9	–	2.6	0.7	−11.1	−5.6	A Cunningham
Durham	Lab	35.3	13.2	72.1	11.0	–	3.0	0.6	−15.3	−6.5	*S Hughes
Northumbria	Lab	33.4	21.2	59.3	11.6	**4.1**	3.3	0.4	−12.8	−3.8	*G Adam
Tyne & Wear	Lab	27.8	13.3	74.4	6.0	–	3.0	3.3²	−12.6	−4.3	*A Donnelly

cont. overleaf

	Winner	Turnout %	Con %	Lab %	LD %	Grn %	Nat %	Other %	Swing 92/94	Swing 89/94	MEP
WALES											
Mid & West Wales	Lab	47.6	16.4	40.5	12.3	25.3	2.0	3.4²	-10.2	-8.5	Ms E Morgan
North Wales	Lab	45.0	15.5	40.8	6.9	33.8	1.3	1.8²	-11.9	-10.7	*J Wilson
South Wales Central	Lab	39.1	15.6	61.4	9.8	10.0	2.1	1.1²	-9.6	-5.9	*W David
South Wales E	Lab	42.7	12.6	74.0	5.1	4.9	2.3	1.1²	-11.6	-7.3	Ms G Kinnock
South Wales W	Lab	39.6	12.2	66.1	9.8	7.8	2.6	1.4²	-8.2	-6.5	*D Morris
SCOTLAND											
Glasgow	Lab	34.3	6.8	52.6	4.6	25.6	1.4	9.0⁴	-2.4	-0.5	W Miller
Highlands & Islands	SNP	38.7	12.3	15.6	10.1	58.4	2.4	1.3²	-4.7	-3.1	*W Ewing
Lothians	Lab	38.4	16.6	44.9	8.9	26.5	2.6	0.5²	-8.9	-5.3	*D Martin
Mid Scotland & Fife	Lab	38.0	13.5	45.8	8.2	30.8	1.4	0.3	-9.7	-3.6	*A Falconer
North East Scotland	SNP	37.4	18.6	28.4	8.3	42.8	1.2	0.8³	-10.3	-2.9	A Macartney
South of Scotland	Lab	39.8	22.7	45.2	6.6	22.4	1.2	1.9²	-9.2	-7.4	*A Smith
Strathclyde E	Lab	36.9	7.6	58.0	3.5	29.5	1.0	0.4	-5.8	-2.9	*K Collins
Strathclyde W	Lab	39.7	14.5	44.4	7.5	31.6	1.5	0.5	-7.4	-4.5	*H McMahon

If the winner is indicated in **bold** this denotes a gain relative to the notional result on new boundaries in 1989.

Official candidates of the UKIP are marked in **bold** in the 'Anti' column. Starred shares in this column are the combined vote of two Euro sceptic candidates – not including the NF, Third Way and various very minor Independent candidacies. In Scotland and Wales the only identifiable Antis were UKIP candidates in Mid & West Wales and Highlands & Islands who scored 2.9% and 0.9% respectively and are counted under the 'Other' column.

The number of 'Other' candidates is given in superscript. The Natural Law Party stood in every seat. 20 candidates stood for the Liberal Party, whose highest share of the vote and only saved deposit was in Devon & E Plymouth with 6.2%. In the same seat a 'Literal Democrat' won 4.3%. In Glasgow Scottish Militant Labour obtained 7.6%.

'Swing' is Butler swing, positive indicating a swing to Conservative.

Incumbent MEPs are indicated with a star.

Constituencies are allocated to the standard region containing the largest part of their population in this table. For the purposes of the regional chapters in this book Itchen, Test and Avon is discussed in the South-West and Essex N & Suffolk S in East Anglia.

Table 9.3 Regional summary of results, 1994

	Turnout %	Change in % turnout since		% share of vote 1994					Change in % vote since 1992				Change in % vote since 1989			
	%	1992 %	1989 %	Con %	Lab %	LDem %	Nat %	Oth %	Con %	Lab %	LDem %	Nat %	Con %	Lab %	LDem %	Nat %
London	32.7	−41.3	−3.4	29.8	50.3	12.1	—	7.8	−16.0	+13.9	−3.3	—	−5.9	+8.4	+6.9	—
South East	38.0	−42.2	+3.5	36.0	30.3	24.7	—	9.1	−18.4	+9.5	+1.2	—	−9.3	+4.8	+16.1	—
South West	32.9	−38.6	+3.2	32.9	23.9	32.7	—	8.6	14.4	+4.3	+1.5	—	−9.3	+0.4	+19.7	—
East Anglia	39.2	−40.7	+3.7	34.9	40.8	19.2	—	5.1	−16.2	+12.6	+0.1	—	−8.3	+10.3	+13.2	—
East Midlands	37.5	−42.6	+1.6	30.4	49.7	13.6	—	6.2	−15.9	+12.6	−2.0	—	−8.0	+8.5	+9.1	—
West Midlands	33.0	−45.4	−2.0	29.0	49.5	13.9	—	7.5	−15.8	+10.7	−1.1	—	−6.5	+5.4	+9.5	—
Yorks. & Humberside	31.2	−44.1	−3.8	24.4	54.5	15.2	—	6.0	−12.7	+9.2	−1.6	—	−.9	+2.5	+10.0	—
North West	30.2	−46.9	−5.9	25.7	56.0	12.0	—	6.2	−11.6	+10.3	−3.3	—	−5.7	+5.6	+6.4	—
Northern region	34.4	−42.2	−1.6	22.7	61.8	10.8	—	4.7	−12.3	+13.3	−5.2	—	−4.3	+5.0	+6.1	—
Wales	42.8	−36.9	+2.8	14.6	55.9	8.7	17.1	3.8	−13.8	+6.1	−3.6	+8.3	−8.9	+6.9	+5.4	+4.2
Scotland	37.9	−37.6	−2.9	14.5	42.5	7.2	32.6	2.4	−11.2	+3.6	−5.9	+11.1	−6.4	+0.7	+2.9	+6.9
Great Britain	35.9	−42.0	−0.6	27.9	44.2	16.7	4.2	6.9	−14.8	+8.9	−1.5	+1.9	−6.8	+4.1	+10.5	+0.9

The regions used in this table are based on the Registrar General's standard regions. Seats which cross regional boundaries are assigned to the region within which the majority of their electorate lives.

Figure 9.1   Result of 1994 European election

in a reshuffle. On Wednesday the national railway signalmen went on strike for the first time in what was to become the first protracted industrial dispute since the miners' strike. Although some trains still ran, the media devoted intense coverage to the story of the strike, which was linked up with an underlying story about forthcoming rail privatisation. In the evening Kenneth Clarke delivered an upbeat speech at Mansion House. On Thursday Sir Norman Fowler announced his resignation as Chairman of the Conservative Party. On Friday the Liberal Democrats announced a reshuffle of their Westminster front bench, and Michael Heseltine pre-emptively rejected the reputedly poisoned chalice of the Conservative Party Chairmanship. On the Saturday the forthcoming Monklands East by-election in John Smith's former seat hove into view. The Sunday papers reconsidered events of the past week, including the European election results, but also John Major's hints of a reshuffle, Sir Norman Fowler's departure, Michael Heseltine's manoeuvring, Kenneth Clarke's speech, Stella Rimington's speech, the Liberal Democrat reshuffle and, perhaps above all, the Labour leadership contest. By Monday 20 June the 1994 European elections in the United Kingdom had completely faded from view.

There had been an altogether unprecedented number of close contests, which was perhaps particularly surprising considering that each Euro-constituency contained around half a million voters. Recounts were demanded in more than a dozen constituencies. The Conservatives won five, and Labour won two, seats by margins of under 1 per cent of the total vote (see Tables 9.4–9.6).

In 14 of the 18 seats where the Conservatives survived they would have lost on a further swing of a mere 2 per cent. John Major had escaped the threatened wipe-out by a very narrow margin, but he *had* escaped it.

Table 9.4 Narrow majorities, 1979–94

	2%–5%			1%–2%		Under 1%		
	Con.	Lab.	SNP	Con.	Lab.	Con.	Lab.	Total
1979	3	2	1	2	2	1	–	11
1984	3	4	–	3	–	–	–	10
1989	2	2	–	3	3	–	1	11
1994	8	3	–	1	–	5	2	19

Table 9.5   The seven smallest majorities, 1994

Euro-constituency	Winner	% Majority	Second place	Majority
Devon and East Plymouth	Conservative	0.3	Liberal Democrat	700
Kent East	Labour	0.3	Conservative	635
Thames Valley	Conservative	0.4	Labour	758
Worcestershire and South Warwickshire	Conservative	0.6	Labour	1,204
Herefordshire and Shropshire	Labour	0.9	Conservative	1,850
Sussex South and Crawley	Conservative	0.9	Labour	1,746
Dorset and East Devon	Conservative	1.0	Liberal Democrat	2,264

The postal vote in Devon & E. Plymouth (2.3%), in Thames Valley (2.4%) and in Worcs. & S. Warwick (2.4%) could have been decisive in the Conservative victories. Nationally the postal vote amounted to 325,185 (1.8% of the valid vote).

Table 9.6   The Liberal Democrat challenge in the south, 1994

Somerset and North Devon	9.2% Liberal Democrat gain
Cornwall and West Plymouth	13.5% Liberal Democrat gain
Devon and East Plymouth	0.3% Conservative hold
Dorsct and East Devon	1.0% Conservative hold
Wight and Hampshire South	2.8% Conservative hold
East Sussex and Kent South	2.9% Conservative hold
Itchen, Test and Avon	3.0% Conservative hold
Wiltshire North and Bath	4.3% Conservative hold
Hampshire North and Oxford	4.6% Conservative hold
South Downs West	10.9% Conservative hold
Surrey	16.8% Conservative hold

The Liberal Democrats had much reason to be disappointed. As expected, they won Cornwall and West Plymouth (13.5 per cent majority) and Somerset and North Devon (9.2 per cent majority) in some comfort. They came very close in Devon and East Plymouth, where the Conservative candidate squeaked in with an 0.3 per cent majority (700 votes). The Liberal Democrats were infuriated by the spoiling action of the 'Literal Democrat', Richard Huggett, who took 10,203 votes. The party later decided to go to court, claiming that the returning officer should have rejected so misleading a label. But, after a three-day hearing in November, the judges ruled against the Liberal Democrats, though indicating that they regarded the legal situation as unsatisfactory. However, in the same seat David Morrish, a candidate for Michael Meadowcroft's breakaway Liberal Party, won 14,621 votes, and the Green candidate, Paul Edwards, 11,172 votes. In five seats, the Liberal Democrats missed victory by 4 per cent, and in two by under 1 per cent. In Dorset and East Devon they failed to unseat the Conservative incumbent by 2,264 votes. In Wight and Hampshire South, notwithstanding a bad press for their candidate, they were only 5,101 votes behind. It truly was a case of 'so near and yet so far'. The Liberal Democrats could rue the lack of resources which had perhaps prevented them from persuading more Labour supporters to cast a tactical vote, but shrewder tacticians sensed an underlying reason, summed up in a headline after the Eastleigh by-election: 'LIBS IN A PADDY AS LABOUR STEALS POLL THUNDER' (*Independent on Sunday*).

One unexpectedly elected candidate declared that Labour had fared 'better than its wildest dreams'. As was described in Chapter 5, the party had initially been forecasting a fairly lacklustre result, assuming a poor showing in the May local elections. It played down its prospects in the Euro-elections, and privately did not expect to do better than win a few more seats on aggregate, since at least two of the seats it had won in 1989 remained highly marginal. But as the results came in it became clear that Labour had made inroads in the most unlikely places; Bedfordshire and Milton Keynes, Essex South, Essex West and Hertfordshire East, Herefordshire and Shropshire, Hertfordshire, Lincolnshire and Humberside South, Norfolk, Suffolk and South-West Norfolk. The shires of classic Conservatism and the seedbeds of the Thatcherite revolution seemed equally vulnerable to Labour's advances. Moreover, in unseating the Conservatives' leader and its chairman in Strasbourg Labour had taken two psychologically important scalps. Glenys Kinnock was returned in South Wales East with a massive 61.4 per cent majority, and throughout the Midlands and the north Labour majorities were consolidated. The Labour leader at Strasbourg, Pauline Green, almost doubled her vote in what had been considered a marginal seat. It was not all good news. Henry McCubbin's defeat in Scotland North East was the first Euro-seat that Labour had ever lost since Euro-elections began in 1979, and represented the most visible aspect of a growing threat. Nevertheless, in winning 62 seats Labour ironically found itself in exactly the same position the Conservatives, with 60 MEPs, had enjoyed in 1979.

For the Conservatives, the result was a disaster, but not an unmitigated one. Ten of the 14 Conservative Euro-MPs who lost their seats had first been elected in 1979. The casualties included their leader, Sir Christopher Prout, and their Chairman, Bill Newton-Dunn, and a number of former committee chairmen and party spokesmen. Edwina Currie's high-profile candidature in Bedfordshire and Milton Keynes was unsuccessful, and the Earl of Stockton saw his Labour opponent's vote increase in Bristol. On the other hand, although the Conservatives lost Somerset and North Devon and Cornwall and West Plymouth, and although they had retained a number of other seats by slender majorities, they had not succumbed to the 'yellow peril', the much-touted Liberal Democrat threat. Ironically, the 'Blair effect' had lost them some seats, but it had also safeguarded others. The key was the squeezing of the Liberal Democrat vote in the closing days of the campaign. This may in part have been due to Conservative targeting, but was mostly due to the increasing attractiveness of Mr Blair. Where Labour was strong, it grew stronger. But where the Conservatives were threatened by the Liberal Democrats, the Labour vote held up enough for the incumbent to hang on in all but two seats. As we shall see, the Greens may also have helped the Conservatives avoid a rout (see below). On the other hand, two incumbent Conservative MEPs, Patricia Rawlings in Essex West and Hertfordshire East, and Christopher Jackson in Kent East, also fell foul of a new menace, the spoiling votes of anti-Maastricht candidates (see Table 9.7). The defeat of two other sitting MEPs, Ben Patterson in Kent West and Michael Welsh in Lancashire Central, could in some part be attributed to the same phenomenon, as could Philip Jenkinson's near miss in Hertfordshire. In all five cases, Labour was the beneficiary.

Unsuccessful Conservative candidates could do little but lick their wounds, hope that anti-Maastricht candidates were a temporary phenomenon, and console themselves that there would inevitably be a downturn in Labour's fortunes in 1999, but for the Prime Minister the Euro-elections result represented a sort of triumph. Despite the media expectation that it could only hasten his fall, he had adopted a high profile in the campaign, deliberately making his own running, and thereby associating himself with the result. By any objective standards, that result was an abject disaster, one of the two major parties in the country having been reduced to a rump of just 18 out of 87 seats. Yet so low had the spin-doctors played expectations, with talk of the Prime Minister being obliged to stand down if the Conservatives won less than *ten* seats, that the 1994 Euro-elections could be presented as a

Table 9.7   The spoiling votes of anti-Maastricht candidates, 1994

Conservative candidate	Lost by (votes)	Anti-Maastricht candidate	Polled (votes)
Christopher Jackson (Kent East)	635	Colin Bullen (UK Independence Party)	9,414
Patricia Rawlings (Essex West and Hertfordshire East)	3,067	Bryan Smalley (Britain)	5,632
Philip Jenkinson (Hertfordshire)	10,304	Malcom Biggs (New Britain Against New European Union)	6,555
Michael Welsh (Lancashire Central)	12,191	David Hill (British Home Rule)	6,751
Ben Patterson (Kent West)	16,777	Craig Mackinlay (UK Independence Party)	9,750

success. As one cartoonist cruelly put it, they represented the Conservatives' 'best defeat in 30 years'.

The claim that, in 1989, the Green Party had usurped the traditional role of the Liberal Party as repository of the protest vote was confirmed by their poor performance in 1994. Nowhere in the country could their candidates achieve anything better than fourth place, and nowhere did they come ahead of a Liberal Democrat candidate. The existence of nationalist candidates pushed them down to fifth place in ten of the 13 Scottish and Welsh seats and sixth place in the remaining three. In the 21 English seats where, discounting very minor candidates, the Greens found themselves in straightforward four-corner fights with the three major parties, they were never less than 10,000 votes behind the third-placed candidate and mostly very much more. The Greens did not only have to contend with the Liberal Democrats. In eight of the 17 seats where Liberal Party or other Liberal tradition candidates stood, the Greens were pushed into fifth place. In 20 of 35 seats where anti-Maastricht candidates stood, the Greens were pushed into fifth place, in 13 cases by UK Independence Party candidates, and in the other seven by a collection of anti-federalist and Home Rule independents. The only good news for the Greens was that they had saved three deposits, their best individual performance coming from their leader, Jean Lambert, who polled 6.5 per cent of the vote in London North East.

The Times (14 June 1994)

'This is our best defeat in thirty years'

Some claimed the Green Party might have played another role. Speculating as to where votes might go, if they go anywhere at all, in the theoretical absence of any particular candidate, is an improbable exercise but, as Table 9.8 shows, Green Party votes far outstripped Conservative majorities in six seats where Labour was challenging strongly. Tactical voting in these seats by Green voters would have paid handsome dividends for the Labour Party.

For the Scottish nationalists, the 1994 Euro-elections were a great success. With the exception of the South of Scotland, where the opposition vote was split almost equally between the Conservatives (45,595) and the SNP (45,032), the SNP came either first or second in every Scottish seat. Winifred Ewing's Highlands and Islands constituency was transformed into an SNP stronghold, with an impregnable 42.8 per cent majority over Labour, and the SNP could be proud of its 31,227 majority (14.4 per cent) in Scotland North East – a first, highly symbolic defeat of a sitting Labour MEP. Both seats had special features: Mrs Ewing had the largest area in Britain and the lowest electorate; Dr Macartney had the highest electorate. Ominously for the Labour Party, in every other Scottish seat there was a swing in votes from Labour to the SNP, whether calculated on the basis of the 1989 Euro-election or the 1992 General Election.

For the Welsh nationalists, the result was not so heartening. Plaid Cymru came second in the two northern seats. In North Wales the Plaid jumped from 13 per cent to 34 per cent, and Dafydd Wigley almost came within striking distance (15,142 votes adrift) of the Labour incumbent, Joe Wilson. In Mid and West Wales they went

Table 9.8   *The spoiling votes of Green Party candidates, 1994*

Seat	Conservative majority	Green Party vote
Thames Valley	754	6,120
Worcestershire and South Warwickshire	1,204	9,273
Sussex South and Crawley	1,746	9,348
Essex North and Suffolk South	3,633	6,641
Cambridgeshire	3,942	5,756
Cotswolds	4,268	8,254

from 17 per cent to 25 per cent. They came a poor third in South Wales Central, just beating the Liberal Democrat candidate into fourth place by 386 votes. But Plaid came a very distant fourth in South Wales East (just saving a deposit) whilst in South Wales West they just lost their deposit. However, in Wales as a whole they came second with 17 per cent to the Conservatives' 15 per cent, and this might augur well for future general elections.

Although a distinct entity, the UK Independence Party was part of a broader, anti-federalist phenomenon. The UK Independence Party was proud of its own performance. Claiming to have been starved of publicity by 'pro-Maastricht forces', it polled an average of 3.5 per cent in the seats it contested, and it bested the Greens in 15 seats. Its candidates saved their deposits in the Itchen, Test and Avon and Kent West seats, although nowhere did the party win more than a fourth place. Its best performances are set out in Table 9.9.

However, the UK Independence Party's performance is only part of the picture. A number of other anti-federalist candidates did well (Table 9.10).

There were also five seats where a combination of anti-federalist candidates won relatively high percentages of the vote. In four of the five seats, the combined anti-federalist vote would have been enough for a single candidate to save his/her deposit (see Table 9.11).

It is clear anti-federalist parties and candidates did touch a popular, if minority, chord among the electorate. It is a moot point as to whether they were simply a temporary phenomenon. Alan Sked spoke after the elections of making a determined membership drive with a view to the next General Election, but independent candidates may simply have felt that their point had been made. However, ratification

Table 9.9   *The UK Independence Party's best performances (over 4 per cent of the vote), 1994*

Constituency	Percentage	Votes
Itchen, Test and Avon	5.4	12,423 (saved deposit)
Kent West	5.2	9,750 (saved deposit)
Dorset and East Devon	4.8	10,548
Kent East	4.7	9,414
Sussex East and Kent South	4.2	9,058
Hampshire North and Oxford	4.2	8,377
Northumbria	4.1	7,210

Table 9.10 Other anti-Federalist candidates' best performances (over 4 per cent of the vote), 1994

Constituency	Percentage	Votes
Essex North and Suffolk South (Independent Anti-European Superstate)	6.0	12,409 (saved deposit)
Cotswolds (New Britain – Britain Not Brussels)	5.7	11,044 (saved deposit)
Essex West and Hertfordshire East (Britain)	5.6	5,632 (saved deposit)
Coventry and North Warwickshire (For British Independence and Free Trade)	5.5	9,432 (saved deposit)
Yorkshire West (New Britain Against New European Union)	4.7	8,027
Worcestershire and South Warwickshire (National Independence Party)	4.0	9,273
Lancashire Central (British Home Rule)	4.0	6,751

Table 9.11 Combined anti-federalist votes, 1994

Seat	First party	Percentage	Second party	Percentage
Bedfordshire and Milton Keynes	UK Independence Party	3.7	New Britain Against New European Union	1.9
Dorset and East Devon	UK Independence Party	4.8	Conservative Non-Federal Party	1.5
London East	UK Independence Party	3.5	Third Way Independence Party	2.0
Nottingham and Leicestershire North West	UK Independence Party	3.1	Independent Out of Europe	1.4
Surrey	UK Independence Party	4.0	Independent Britain in Europe	2.4

of the results of the next IGC, scheduled to open in 1996, may well occur in the period before the 1999 European elections. Should the IGC embark on further far-reaching constitutional reform, anti-federalist candidates may well stand again in the subsequent European elections.

The Liberal Party significantly saved a deposit in the critical Devon and Plymouth East seat, and polled over 4 per cent in Essex South and Leeds (where its leader, Michael Meadowcroft, was the candidate). It polled over 3 per cent in the two Merseyside seats but was otherwise a negligible force. The Natural Law Party just topped 1 per cent of the poll in nine seats, but its vote was generally derisory. The most remarkable independent vote went to the Scottish Militant Labour candidate in Glasgow, Tommy Sheridan, who came third behind Labour and the SNP, having polled 12,113 votes (7.6 per cent).

The turnout, at 36.2 per cent, was marginally below the record high of 36.8 per cent in 1989. It ranged from 47.2 per cent in North Wales to 24.3 per cent in Merseyside. It varied remarkably within Euro-constituencies (see Chapter 8), and Labour majorities were consolidated by differential turnout, particularly in the north. In Northern Ireland, with PR and high profile candidates, it was 49.2 per cent, slightly higher than the 48.8 per cent recorded in 1989. Although turnout was objectively disappointing, Britain had the consolation of rising from the bottom place it had occupied in the European turnout league in the previous three European elections, with the Netherlands and Portugal recording about 35.5 per cent. Turnout also fell sharply in Ireland and Greece. The Europe-wide figure (56.8 per cent), declining with each election, was at its lowest since 1979.

In terms of opinion polls, the European elections were different from a general election. Turnout was less than half that of a general election. There were many fewer polls conducted during the campaign, and only one (by ICM) was conducted wholly within four days before the election. The apparent closeness of the 1992 contest may have affected electors' behaviour or their responses to interviewers, but as the outcome of the 1994 European election was never really in doubt this factor would have been absent. Four surveys were carried out within the last nine days of the campaign – ICM, MORI, Gallup, and NOP, although none could properly be considered to be an 'eve-of-poll prediction'. NOP's telephone poll for the Labour Party, deliberately leaked, produced a result that was almost identical with the final results for both the Conservatives and Labour, while ICM was one per cent out in each case. Both MORI and Gallup reported shares that proved to be higher than the final Labour vote and lower than the final Conservative vote. All the polls correctly identified regional variations in support for the parties. However, none of the polls indicated a strong showing by the minor parties nor the net effect that this would have on the Liberal Democrat share.

A clear lesson reiterated by the 1994 European election polls was that electors were very poor predictors of whether or not they would vote. In ICM's poll, 55 per cent said that they were 'certain to vote'; in MORI's, the percentage was 45 per cent, and in Gallup's, 54 per cent – all way above the actual turnout of 36 per cent. In its post-election survey, ICM also found considerable 'overclaiming' – a much higher proportion of respondents claimed to have voted than actual turnout (see Table 9.12).

The long-term pattern of change presented by European election results is striking. The Conservatives have lost 13–15 seats at each European election. However, the Conservatives were the beneficiaries of a freak result in 1979 when, the Euro-elections following hard on the heels of the 1979 General Election, most Labour voters stayed at home,

Table 9.12 *Unadjusted opinion polls during the 1994 European election campaign*

Poll	Field-work	Con.	Lab.	Lib Dem	Other	Con. lead	Sample
ICM/ Daily Express	17 May	27	46	22	5	−19	1,019
ICM/ Guardian	20–21 May	26	47	23	5	−21	1,420
MORI/ Times	19–23 May	27	47	22	4	−20	1,929
Gallup/ Daily Telegraph	25–30 May	23	53.5	19	4.5	−30.5	1,042
MORI/ Times	2–6 June	23	51	20	6	−28	2,669
NOP/ Labour Party	4–5 June	28	44	19.5	8.5	−16	c.1,000
ICM/ Daily Express	6 June	27	45	22	6	−18	1,050
Gallup/ unpublished	1–7 June	24.5	49.5	18	8	−25	2,939
Result	*9 June*	*27.8*	*44.2*	*16.7*	*11.2*	*−16.4*	

enabling the Conservatives to capture 60 seats. The phenomenon of the Conservatives' constant decline in numbers is also explained by the fact that the Conservatives have been in government in the United Kingdom throughout the fifteen year period since the first direct elections were held, and have thus been more vulnerable to mid-term unpopularity (see Tables 9.13 and 9.14).

Mid-term unpopularity was a feature of the 1994 elections in some other EU Member States, although anti-government votes did not necessarily go to the main opposition parties. It was otherwise impossible to spot a general trend in Europe. There was no overall swing to the left, nor any overall swing to the right. Far right parties did well in Belgium, kept their ground in France, and fell foul of the 5 per cent threshold in Germany. In Italy, the right-wing *Alleanza Nazionale* won 11 seats. The Greens unexpectedly won two seats in Ireland and, less unexpectedly, a seat in Luxembourg, but elsewhere they did not do particularly well. In France their vote declined and, as has been seen, in Britain it shrunk drastically. Anti-European parties

Table 9.13   Adjusted figures in the final polls, 1994 European slections

Poll	Fieldwork	Con.	Lab.	Lib Dem	Other	Con. lead	Sample
MORI/ Times	2–6 June	27	47	20	6	−20	2,669
ICM/ Daily Express	6 June	29	43	20	8	−14	1,050
Gallup/ unpublished	1–7 June	28	44	19.5	8.5	−16	2,939
Result	9 June	27.8	44.2	16.7	11.2	−16.4	

Table 9.14   Percentages and seats in European elections, 1979–94

| | Percentages | | | | | Seats | | | |
	Voting	Con	Lab	(Lib)	Other	Con	Lab	Lib Dem	Other
1979	32.1	50.1	33.1	13.1	3.8	60	17	–	1
1984	31.8	40.8	36.5	19.5	3.3	45	32	–	1
1989	36.6	33.5	38.7	6.2	21.6	32	45	–	1
1994	36.2	27.9	44.2	16.7	11.2	18	62	2	2

did very well in Denmark, capturing a fourth of the vote, and in France (12.3 per cent of the vote and 13 seats), but made little ground in Germany and, as was seen, remained a minor phenomenon in Britain. The Liberals did not make expected gains in Belgium and fell below the 5 per cent threshold in Germany, but made gains in the Netherlands and in Britain. In Spain and Britain, opposition parties gained at the expense of unpopular governing parties (socialist and conservative respectively), but in Germany the long-incumbent Christian Democrats did well, and in Greece and Italy freshly-elected governing parties (PASOK and Forza Italia) saw their positions strengthened. Populists did well in France (Bernard Tapie) and Italy (Silvio Berlusconi) but were otherwise absent. The left did poorly in Spain and France, but well in Portugal and Britain. In short, there were few common trends.

However, in terms of political balance in Strasbourg, there were discernible overall consequences. A first was a general fragmentation of political representation within the Parliament, as new political forces, such as Bernard Tapie's *Energie Radicale*, Philippe de Villiers *Majorité pour l'autre Europe*, Silvio Berlusconi's *Forza Italia*, and the far right *Alleanza Nazionale*, cast around for new coalitions and groups. However, it should be noted that this did not lead to any increase in the overall number of political groups; there were nine in the old Parliament and nine in the new. A second consequence was that representation on the right tended to be more fragmented than representation on the left. On the one hand, there were more centre-right groupings and, on the other, the PES Group confirmed its position as the major grouping of the left. A third consequence was that the two main political families, the Christian Democrats and the socialists, confirmed their numerical and political pre-eminence. The PES group now had 198 members, and the EPP group 157. Crucially, neither was able to muster an absolute majority (284 votes), so vital to the legislative functioning of the Parliament. Hence the fourth consequence, which was a revival of the old, 1989–94 loose coalition between the EPP and PES groups, with the PES group as the dominant partner. The overwhelming power of this coalition was further enhanced by the restructuring of Parliament's managerial machinery that had taken place in the wake of the implementation of the Maastricht Treaty. Hence, the leadership of the PES group was easily the most powerful political position within the Parliament (see Table 9.15).

Within the PES group before the 1994 elections, the two pre-eminent groupings were the EPLP (45 members), and the German SPD

Table 9.15 Political groups in the European Parliament after the 1994 European elections

	Belgium	Denmark	France	Germany	Greece	Ireland	Italy	Luxembourg	Netherlands	Portugal	Spain	UK	Total
PES	6	3	15	40	10	1	18	2	8	10	22	63	198
EPP	7	3	13	47	9	4	12	2	10	1	30	19	157
LDR	6	5	1	0	0	1	7	1	10	8	2	2	43
EUL	0	0	7	0	4	0	5	0	0	3	9	0	28
FE	0	0	0	0	0	0	27	0	0	0	0	0	27
EDA	0	0	14	0	2	7	0	0	0	3	0	0	26
Greens	2	1	0	12	0	2	4	1	1	0	0	0	23
ERA	1	0	13	0	0	0	2	0	0	0	1	2	19
EDN	0	4	13	0	0	0	0	0	2	0	0	0	19
Ind	3	0	11	0	0	0	12	0	0	0	0	1	27
Total	25	16	87	99	25	15	87	6	31	25	64	87	567

(31 members), and there was some rivalry between the two for power and influence. Both parties were in opposition, and both were expected to do well in the Euro-elections as a result. As the elections approached, one of the chief ways in which this rivalry manifested itself was in manoeuvring for the post-election PES group leadership, and for the Presidency of the Parliament itself (a position which would be in the PES group's gift if it remained the largest group within the Parliament). As was seen in Chapter 5, at the Labour Party's Glasgow European Conference John Smith had confirmed both that the party would be claiming the position of leader of the PES group, and that Pauline Green would be the party's candidate, but her candidature would obviously depend upon her re-election. The SPD's prime candidate was Klaus Hänsch, an MEP since 1979, and an influential figure within the party and the Parliament.

Everything depended on the relative performance of the two parties at the polls. Here, the SPD was considered to be at a potential advantage, since Germany would return 99 Euro-MPs to the UK's 87 and, with Chancellor Kohl's government in mid-term, the SPD was hoping to capture a larger proportion of the new seats. In the event, the SPD did do well, capturing nine new seats and taking its overall tally of MEPs to 40, though this was hardly a proportional increase. However, the CDU/CSU did better than expected, together capturing 47 seats. The clinching blow was Labour's extraordinarily good performance, taking its representation from 45 to 62 MEPs. As was seen, in her own seat Pauline Green had managed to transform what had been a marginal Labour gain in 1989 into a solid 26.3 per cent majority in 1994, and so her candidature seemed virtually assured. The leaders of the European Socialist parties, meeting in the margins of the 23 and 24 June Corfu European Council, duly agreed that Pauline Green should be the leader of the PES group in the European Parliament. On 6 July Pauline Green was elected leader by the PES group, with 179 votes in favour, two votes against, and two abstentions. Her chief potential rival, Klaus Hänsch, became the PES group's candidate for the Presidency of the Parliament and on 19 July was duly elected President at the first plenary session in Strasbourg. Pauline Green's election as PES group leader was an unprecedented step. It was the first time ever that a Briton had been elected leader of one of the two principal political groupings within the European Parliament and was in itself powerful symbolic evidence of the Labour Party's new European policy.

The 62 Labour MEPs found themselves in an enviable position in the new Parliament. They had fought the election on the common PES manifesto, they formed the largest and most influential national contingent within the PES group, and one of their number was PES group leader. The position bore immediate fruit. Ken Collins, an MEP since 1979, was re-elected Chairman of the powerful Committee on the Environment, Stephen Hughes (1984) was elected Chairman of the politically important Committee on Social Affairs and Employment, and Eddie Newman (1984) became Chairman of the Petitions Committee. In an unprecedented step, Terry Wynn was reappointed as rapporteur of the 1995 Budget, having served in the previous Parliament as rapporteur on the 1994 Budget. (British MEPs have made the politically important budgets rapporteurship into something of a speciality – five in 15 years.) When, later in July, Parliament decided to create a temporary committee on employment, Ken Coates (1989) was appointed rapporteur.

Pauline Green's election to the PES group leadership had liberated the post of leader of the European Parliamentary Labour Party. On 6 July, the EPLP held hustings and elections for all of its leadership positions. All 62 members were present, and it immediately became apparent that the 23 new members, who knew little about the past activities of incumbent Labour MEPs, would form an important block of votes. It was decided that nominations for all posts should be taken before the elections began, and this prevented the traditional 'slippage' of unsuccessful candidates from one post to another. Wayne David (1989) was elected leader of the EPLP on a second ballot. The other contenders had been Terry Wynn and a former EPLP leader, Glyn Ford (1984).

Once nominations to the various posts had closed, it was realised that, in all, there were only two women candidates, and it was therefore decreed (in line with a general policy of positive discrimination) that the women candidates would be considered as the only valid candidates in their respective competitions. There had originally been three nominations for the position of Deputy Leader: Christine Crawley (1984), Gary Titley (1989) and Brian Simpson (1989). Christine Crawley was ruled to be the only valid candidate, and was subsequently elected by 48 votes in favour, eight against, one abstention, and four spoiled ballot papers. Two nominations had been received for the position of Chair; Mike Hendrick (1994) and Veronica Hardstaffe (1994). Following the decree, Veronica Hardstaffe was deemed to be the only valid candidate and was duly elected by 55 votes in favour, three against, three abstentions, and one spoiled ballot paper. Mike Tappin (1994), Eddie Newman (1984) and Alex Smith (1989) were elected unopposed as EPLP Secretary, Treasurer and Whip respectively. At a later meeting, the EPLP chose David Martin (1984) as its candidate for a Vice-Presidency of the Parliament, and Richard Balfe (1989) as its candidate for the position of quaestor of the Parliament. Subsequently, Mr Martin was elected (343 votes) Vice-President on 19 July, and Mr Balfe quaestor (257 votes) on 20 July by the Parliament.

In contrast with Labour's rising fortunes, the Conservative MEPs found themselves in a much reduced position. In the party's more numerous heyday, it had formed the third-largest group in the Parliament, provided the chairmen of several important committees, and even, from 1987 to 1989, the President of the Parliament itself (Lord Plumb). The 18 Conservative MEPs first met on 17 June 1994 and after some debate decided formally to reapply for allied membership of the group of the European People's Party within the European Parliament. A new MEP, Giles Chichester, told the BBC he had argued against such a move but would abide by the decision. The EPP group subsequently met on 4 July and voted, by a majority of 76 to 11, to grant the Conservative MEPs allied membership. Certain Belgian and Dutch MEPs, said to have been angry at Mr Major's Euro-sceptical remarks during the Euro-campaign, were among those who voted against. Thus the contingent of British Conservative Euro-MPs once more became formally known as the 'British section of the EPP group'. Other MEPs admitted to the EPP group as allied members included James Nicholson, the Official Ulster Unionist, the Danish Conservatives and certain French UDF members.

The move to rejoin the EPP group came perhaps surprisingly early and was also surprisingly free of political opposition or controversy. It was reported largely without comment in the British media, and the Conservative Euro-sceptics at Westminster – rumoured to be plotting a rebellion in that very period – did and said nothing. The earliness of the move was in part the result of practical considerations; the share-out of committee chairmanships and rapporteurships traditionally took place at the beginning of the legislature, and it would have made little sense to join the EPP group after this had occurred. But the earliness was also the result of an argument, advanced by Sir Christopher Prout, that opposition to the move might grow within the EPP group, and that the offer might not exist for much longer. Indeed, the move to rejoin was largely inspired by the outgoing leader of the British Conservatives.

Although deprived of his seat, Sir Christopher remained an important influence in the early days of the new Parliament. Technically, defeated MEPs retained their official position until midnight, 18 July, and he was present at the new Conservative MEPs' 17 June meeting and was invited to address it. He advanced five arguments. First, a move to rejoin the EPP as allied members would be consistent with the views of the Prime Minister and his predecessor. After all, he pointed out, Mrs Thatcher had wanted the British Conservatives to team up with their Christian Democrat counterparts as early as 1976, and it was only the opposition of the Dutch Christian Democrats which had obliged the Conservatives to form their own group. Second, the alliance had worked extremely well in the British Conservatives' interest. Third, allied membership was an excellent formula, providing the opportunity to shape and influence policy without the obligation of accepting *faits accomplis*. Fourth, if the Conservatives did not rejoin the Christian Democrats there was a great risk that the right within the Parliament would fragment further and render the inherently more cohesive left even more powerful. Last, and perhaps most importantly, it was critical for the British and the Germans to work as closely together as possible. Sir Christopher's arguments were not contested.

The Conservatives' 17 June meeting also discussed possible contenders for the leadership of the Conservatives in the European Parliament. There were a large number of initial contenders, but these ultimately boiled down to two; Lord Plumb, an MEP since 1979, a former President of the Parliament, and a former leader of the British Conservatives, and Edward McMillan-Scott, an MEP since 1984. Mr McMillan-Scott later withdrew his candidature, and at a second meeting on 4 July Lord Plumb was elected unopposed. At the same meeting Tom Spencer, an MEP for ten years, was elected as Chairman of the British Section of the EPP group. Mr Spencer had to beat off opposition from three other candidates, Bryan Cassidy, James Elles and Caroline Jackson, all MEPs since 1984. In a first ballot, Mr Spencer received eight votes and the other three candidates three votes apiece. The three then withdrew their candidatures, and Mr Spencer was elected unopposed on a second ballot.

The distinction between, and terminology of, the two Conservative leadership positions is potentially important. The leader of the British Conservatives in the European Parliament, Lord Plumb, is responsible for relations with the EPP group and with the British government, and the latter role would clearly be of less significance if the Conservatives were in opposition. The Chairman of the British Section of the EPP group is responsible for relations with the Conservative Party, the operation of the Information Campaign Fund, and the internal organisation and administration of the Section. Relations with the domestic party would clearly become relatively more important were the Conservatives to be out of government.

A number of other elections took place at the 4 July meeting. Edward Kellett-Bowman, an MEP for eleven years, was returned as Treasurer of the British Section of the EPP group. He and John Stevens, an MEP since 1989, both obtained nine votes in two successive ballots. The new Leader then drew lots to determine the victor. Anne McIntosh, an MEP since 1989, was elected as the one non-office-holding Member of the British Section Bureau, obtaining a majority against John Stevens and Caroline Jackson on a single ballot. Sir Jack Stewart-Clark, an MEP for fifteen years, was elected unopposed as the British Conservative candidate for a Vice-Presidency of the Parliament, a position he had held in the outgoing Parliament. Sir Jack was duly elected, with 308 votes in favour, on 19 July. James Provan, an MEP between 1979 and 1989 and re-elected in 1994, was appointed jointly by the Leader and the Chairman as Whip of the British Section. Mr Provan was also nominated as the Conservatives' candidate for the position of Quaestor of the Parliament, a position he had held between 1979 and 1989, but the contingent lacked sufficient numerical weight to be able to obtain the position. Gone, too, were the days when the Conservatives had been able to command several important committees. They had to be satisfied with one Vice-Chairmanship, of the Environment Committee, for Caroline Jackson.

One of the new leadership's early acts was to follow up a proposal first made by Edward McMillan-Scott by establishing a committee of inquiry into the 1994 European elections campaign. Lord Plumb and Tom Spencer jointly appointed Geoffrey Moorhouse, an MEP since 1979, as the Chairman of the Inquiry Committee, with Edward McMillan-Scott, Anne McIntosh and Caroline Jackson as members, and Anthony Teasdale as Secretary. The Committee, which first met in September, sent out a questionnaire to all Conservative candidates. The intention was to feed the results of the inquiry back into preparations for the 1999 European elections. The Moorhouse Report was never published, but was rumoured to have highlighted a number of positive and negative aspects of the campaign, and to have made specific recommendations for the 1999 campaign, mostly relating to giving MEPs a higher profile in the party's campaign and structure.

On 5 July the EPP group elected Wilfried Martens as its new President, replacing Leo Tindemans, also a Flemish Belgian Christian Democrat and former Prime Minister. Mr Martens, an avowed federalist, had previously been mentioned as a potential candidate for the Presidency of the European Commission and had been President of the pan-European People's Party federation. Mr Martens received 118 votes out of 136 cast, with some British Conservatives among those who did not vote for him.

The two new British Liberal Democrat MEPs, Robin Teverson and Graham Watson, joined the ELDR group, bringing its membership to 43. Graham Watson became a member of the Bureau of the group, the third-largest group within the Parliament.

Allan Macartney joined Winifred Ewing in the 19-member Group of the European Radical Alliance, together with members of Bernard Tapie's *Energie Radicale* list and Marco Panella's Italian Radical Party MEPs.

Back in Britain, the Euro-election results had led to a profound rethink within the Liberal Democrat Party. The party had put a brave face on its electoral performance; it had won two seats, perhaps lost out on a third because of spoiling tactics, and a fourth by under 1 per cent. Its leaders knew that the failure to break through was linked to the 'Blair effect', with the full ramifications becoming more apparent as the Euro-election receded. On 17 June the party announced a reshuffle of its front bench team, and in September it shifted former shadow Treasury spokesman Alan Beith to Home Affairs and appointed the former shadow Trade and Industry spokesman, Malcom Bruce, to the shadow Treasury post. However, in private party personnel were readily prepared to admit that the party's problems went deeper than matters of presentational style. Indeed, the party was faced by a quandrary which was to run on into the autumn conference season and beyond, for what, in brutal terms, could differentiate its product from that of a rapidly-modernising Labour Party? On 14 June Paddy Ashdown wrote an article for the *Independent* entitled 'Not a split opposition, but an alternative'. But the next day the Labour Party Shadow Cabinet's discussions ignored his suggestions of cooperation, endorsing the party's anti-Liberal Democrat stance in the south.

On the day of the Liberal Democrat front bench reshuffle, nominations for the Labour leadership closed. Tony Blair had received 154 out of a possible 264 nominations; John Prescott had received 46, and Margaret Beckett 42. Mr Blair, the newspapers trumpeted, was virtually at the winning post, and so it proved to be. On Thursday 21 July he was elected leader of the party, with 57 per cent of the vote in the electoral college – more than his two opponents combined, having won outright majorities in all three sections (61 per cent among parliamentarians, 58 per cent among constituency members, and 52 per cent among trades unionists). In the deputy leadership contest, John Prescott beat Margaret Beckett (56.5 per cent to 43.5 per cent), thus establishing the 'dream ticket' which the media had predicted would best enhance Labour's electoral chances.

Already, as a candidate, Mr Blair had established strongly pro-European credentials. In a 6 July interview with the *Times*, he declared that 'it is tremendously important for us to be a party that is pro-European'. He described the Conservative shift in position as 'a big mistake for the medium and long term. It may bring them short-term advantage, but it is a big mistake. We need to be a major player in Europe in partnership with other countries.'

In a 30 August interview with the *Independent*, John Prescott revealed that he would not be taking up a departmental portfolio at Westminster, but that he would have 'integrated responsibility' for the party's European policy. 'We are having a major shift in thinking,' he said, 'away from treating European policy as a sub-division of the Foreign Office. We are giving it a major boost in our organisation.' The 'Blair effect' reached its apogée in the last week of August, when three different polls (ICM in the *Guardian*, Gallup in the *Daily Telegraph*, MORI in the *Times*) gave Labour an unadjusted opposition lead of between 32 and 33 per cent. 'Support for John Major's administration', reported the *Guardian* (26 August), 'has dropped to the point where there is no historical precedent for a government coming from so far behind in the polls to win a general election.'

Nevertheless, John Major, if not his party, was a clear winner in the 1994 Euro-elections. Most talk of his replacement had gone. With skilful spin-doctoring before, and reshuffle talk after, the elections had effectively deflected attention from the poorness of the results themselves. (The reshuffle, which was ultimately announced on 21 July, the same day as Tony Blair's election, was anti-climactical, with Jeremy Hanley a suprise choice to replace the retiring Sir Norman Fowler as Chairman of the party and none of the major departments of state changing hands.) The more Euro-sceptical tone he had adopted during the campaign had won him the approbation of Lord Tebbit and, if the Prime Minister had not succeeded in fully mobilising the core Conservative vote, he could at least plausibly claim that he had staved off the worst. European affairs were shortly to enable him to consolidate his position further.

On 24 and 25 June the Heads of State and Government of the Member States met on the Greek island of Corfu for the traditional end-of-presidency European Council. One of the more important items on the agenda was the nomination of the person to replace Jacques Delors as President of the European Commission at the beginning of 1995. Candidates had to meet a series of informal requirements. Since the previous occupant had come from one of the larger Member States, candidates from smaller Member States would be preferred, and since the previous occupant had been a socialist, Christian Democrats would be preferred. In addition, it was rumoured that, at the December 1991 Maastricht European Council, the Heads of State and Government had agreed among themselves that the candidate should ideally be a Prime Minister in office; that is, one of themselves. Since unanimity was required, the successful candidate would have to be acceptable to all twelve Member States. However, since the implementation of the Maastricht Treaty, a new condition had come into force; whoever was nominated would have to be approved by the European Parliament.

For a long time the Dutch Prime Minister, Ruud Lubbers, had been slated as the front-runner for the nomination, but as the date for the decision came nearer he was rumoured to have lost French and German backing. At the 30–31 May Franco-German summit at Mulhouse the French and German governments announced that they would be supporting the candidature of the Belgian Prime Minister, Jean-Luc Dehaene. The candidature of Mr Dehaene, a committed European federalist, and the apparent manner of his appointment (described by one irate backbencher as 'Franco-German diktat') were unacceptable to the Conservative Party's Euro-sceptics, and they began to insist that Mr Major should veto the nomination. Britain's senior Commissioner in Brussels, Sir Leon Brittan, had meanwhile announced his candidature for the nomination, and he became the British government's official nominee.

As the Corfu summit approached, apparently contradictory impressions came from the Foreign Office and Downing Street, and it seemed that there was a genuine diplomatic misunderstanding about Mr Major's determination not to accept Mr Dehaene. By the end of the summit, Mr Lubbers had reluctantly withdrawn his candidature, and eleven Member States had announced that they were prepared to support the nomination of Jean-Luc Dehaene. Sir Leon withdrew his candidature, but John Major refused to agree to Mr Dehaene's nomination, and the summit broke up in some acrimony with no decision taken. The incoming German presidency was obliged to organise an extraordinary European Council in Brussels on 15 July and there the twelve Member States were ultimately able to agree on the compromise candidature of the Luxembourg Prime Minister, Jacques Santer. John Major's obstinacy had won him few friends on the continent and had further damaged his already strained relations with the German Chancellor, but it had greatly endeared him to the Eurosceptics within his party. As one Central Office official said, 'He has banished all doubts. He will lead us into the next general election.'

The new European Parliament heard Mr Santer and voted on his nomination at its first plenary session in Strasbourg (19–22 July). Mrs Green, in her new role as leader of the PES group, was one of the key speakers against Mr Santer's nomination. It was, she argued, nothing to do with the individual, but the manner of his nomination, and she insisted that the British government had abused its veto powers in refusing the candidature of Jean-Luc Dehaene. Mr Santer's final approval was a close-run thing; 260 to 238 – a majority of just 22, with all 18 Conservative Euro-MPs voting in favour, and all Labour members voting against.

The European Parliament bared its new Maastricht teeth once more during its first plenary session. On the recommendation of the Labour MEP Mel Read, the Parliament rejected on consumer protection grounds a proposal for the liberalisation of telephony by 373 votes, far surpassing the required absolute majority of 284 votes. It was a powerful display of the new Parliament's resolve.

As 1994 drew to a close, Labour MEPs were much in evidence in the Parliament. Terry Wynn shepherded Parliament's opinion on the 1995 budget through its complicated political and procedural hurdles. Ken Coates was an active inquirer in the temporary Committee on Employment. Ken Collins took the Environment Committee on into fresh institutional battles with the Council. Labour's highest-profile new member, Glenys Kinnock, eagerly took up her new duties in the Development Committee, drafting the committee's opinion on the 1995 budget.

Conservative MEPs found themselves in a far more awkward position, both in the Parliament, where their small numbers denied them any major policy roles, and in relation to themselves, their own party and their EPP allies. Over the summer of 1994 a row broke out between Britain and its partners over the likely nature of constitutional reform at the 1996 IGC. A German CDU policy paper and a policy paper released with the authority of the French Prime Minister, Edouard Balladur, both asserted the need for a hard core of European countries to forge ahead with further integration. Less enthusiastic countries would be consigned to slower, outer lanes. On 7 September

Mr Major gave a speech at the University of Leiden in which he set out his vision of the European Union's future development. Reminiscent of Mrs Thatcher's September 1988 Bruges speech in its setting, the Prime Minister's speech rejected the CDU 'hard core' model, and asserted the need for a wider and looser Europe. To the dismay of Conservative MEPs and Euro-enthusiasts, the Prime Minister was dismissive of the European Parliament. 'The European Parliament is not the answer to the democratic deficit,' he said, 'as the pitiably low turnout in this year's European elections so vividly illustrated.' Tom Spencer, the leader of the British Section of the EPP group, wrote a letter to the Prime Minister protesting about his language, and Lord Plumb could not conceal his disagreement.

In the week before the Conservative Party's October Conference at Bournemouth, Mr Martens gave a speech to the EPP group in which he underlined the disadvantages of the British government's stance. 'What room for manoeuvre is there', he argued, ' . . . when its current majority in the Commons is only 17 and it has more than 30 hardline anti-Europeans in its own ranks who will make the government's survival dependent on its policy in Europe?' Mr Martens went on to say that 'There is one thing which no member state can escape: if it wants to be in the front rank in Europe, it must . . . not run after the pseudo-popular Euro-sceptics.' Two weeks earlier, in a parliamentary vote on the CDU proposals, the EPP had enthusiastically voted in favour, but the British Conservative members had been split three ways, with some following their EPP colleagues, but others abstaining and still others voting against. The more Euro-sceptical Conservatives included Giles Chichester (who had opposed allied membership of the EPP on 17 June), Bryan Cassidy (a noted Thatcherite), Graham Mather and Edward McMillan-Scott.

The Conservative conference was to underline how deep and enduring were the party's divisions on Europe, with Norman Lamont raising the possibility of the UK leaving the European Union and Michael Portillo taking a Euro-sceptical stance, while some of the party's older statesmen – Douglas Hurd, Geoffrey Howe and Leon Brittan – urged a less radical line. Mr Major stayed on the middle ground.

The parallels with the position of the British members of the 1979 European Parliament were striking. Then too, there had been one abnormally large group of fairly united members and a smaller group of MEPs who were internally divided over European policy and who, as a result, experienced stormy relations with the larger political group to which they were allied. Then, the smaller group had been Labour; now it was Conservative.

Until his defeat in the 1992 General Election, the former Conservative Party Chairman, Chris Patten, had believed that British Conservatism could find its place in the mainstream of continental Christian Democracy. Two years later that vision seemed an unlikely prospect. The 1994 European elections had consolidated a process which had begun in 1987 with Neil Kinnock's policy review, and in 1988 with Margaret Thatcher's Bruges speech. The Conservatives chose to vacate the positive and mainstream European policy position they had occupied for so long. In retrospect, the Conservatives' negative 1989 European elections campaign was a key moment in this process, enabling Labour to consolidate its positive position on Europe almost by default.

10 Questions

To the 'founding fathers' of the European Community, the establishment of a directly-elected European Parliament was a key element in the development of a democratic and federal European structure. The first direct elections were expected to take place soon after the Rome Treaties entered into force, but resurgent intergovernmentalism effectively postponed them by over twenty years. Yet, if anything, expectations about the effects of direct elections increased as the probability of their taking place decreased. European federalists saw them as the missing link, believing that a directly-elected European Parliament would establish popular legitimacy for the Community and link the European institutions to the peoples they served. Academics foresaw the rapid evolution of true, popular, political parties at the Community level.

Perhaps inevitably, the first direct elections in 1979 proved an anticlimax and a disappointment. Where voting was not compulsory, or combined with national elections, turnout was low, and it declined with each succeeding election. There was no sudden appearance of European political parties and there were no European campaigns. Although the newly-legitimated Parliament mustered the political energy to reject the 1980 budget, it was not transformed into a major force on the European political scene and, despite its best endeavours, it remained a distant and obscure institution to most Europeans. With each European election, hopes were raised and dashed. European elections obstinately refused to become anything other than a collection of relatively low-key national elections. This was as true of 1994 as it had been of 1979.

A German political scientist has argued that European elections should be seen as what he termed 'second-order national elections' (Reif, 1980, 1985). First-order elections, such as national presidential or parliamentary elections, are primarily concerned with power distribution and government formation and are characterised by high levels of electoral participation and high-profile campaigns. In first-order elections political parties are well established and devote a large proportion of their resources to the struggle. Second-order elections form a residue. They do not involve national power distribution or

288

government formation. Turnout levels and popular interest are lower. Campaigns are much lower-key (party organisations attach less importance and devote less resources to them, and the national media are less interested). Because no national level power is at stake, voters who do bother to turn out are more likely to feel 'liberated'. Smaller, less traditional, and more peripheral parties tend to benefit and, depending on the stage in the national electoral cycle, mid-term disaffection with governing parties may be exaggerated. The vote is expressive rather than instrumental.

The 1994 European elections in Britain clearly corresponded closely to this definition. No national government was at stake. The British Conservatives tried to argue that the distribution of power at Strasbourg mattered, but their arguments were not taken up in the electoral debate. Turnout and popular interest were low – very low by general election standards. The campaign was low-key. The political parties devoted far fewer resources to the European elections than they would habitually do in general elections. The national and regional media showed low levels of interest and were frequently distracted. Some smaller and some more peripheral parties drew appreciable support, and the Conservative government suffered from exaggerated mid-term unpopularity. In short, the 1994 European elections in the United Kingdom were very much second-order national elections.

Reif argued that European elections would remain second-order national elections for as long as they were perceived to be subordinate to national elections. The European Parliament has made huge constitutional advances since 1979 and is likely to see its powers further enhanced by the 1996 IGC. The Maastricht Treaty has created a new, more equal role for the Parliament in its relations with the Council, and granted it important appointment powers over the Commission. But it will be a long time before national parliamentary elections are perceived by the Member States' electorates as being subordinate to elections to the European Parliament. Indeed, such a change in perceptions could not begin to occur until a clearly discernible European executive emerged.

Because European elections remain second-order national elections, they are looked to primarily for what they say about national politics. But part of Reif's argument would still apply even if national elections were to become subordinate to elections at the European level. He pointed out that, whatever their perceived importance, European elections had always to find a place in the context of national electoral cycles. European elections occur at discrete, five-year intervals. As matters now stand, the European Parliament cannot be dissolved, and so the five-year European electoral cycle is a rigid given. But, with the exception of Luxembourg, which has synchronised its national elections with the European elections for reasons of economy, Member States' national electoral cycles are completely independent and frequently random.

This is particularly true of Britain, where the length of parliaments vary considerably. In turn, the moment at which the European elections occur relative to the national electoral cycle will affect their significance. In 1979, for example, the European elections came barely a month after the Conservatives' victory in the 3 May General Election, and in 1989 they came almost half-way through the life of the 1987–1992 Conservative government. Thus, in 1979 the European elections confirmed the government's recent success whereas, in 1989, they confirmed the government's mid-term unpopularity.

European elections and their consequences must also interact with other parts of the national electoral cycle. In Britain, European elections now habitually occupy a regular niche, since they occur one month after local elections and six weeks before the Westminster summer recess. In the struggle for political significance, this cycle 'condemns' the European elections to constant competition with the preceding local elections which, despite their partiality, are now regularly interpreted by the media as a nationwide test and indicator of the political parties' standing. And, where the European elections *are* considered significant, the ensuing summer recess and growing speculation about the autumn conference season condemns that significance to a short shelf-life.

If European elections must always take their place within national electoral cycles, this does not mean that they cannot be about European issues. One of the more striking findings in this study was the deap-seated frustration of many of the candidates from all three of the major political parties about the absence of a European dimension to the campaign. As was seen in Chapter 8, this was especially true of incumbent Euro-MPs, who felt they had been able to achieve much for their constituencies and that the advantages of Europe should have been stressed more. Why should 'Europe' have been so absent from the campaign?

The Conservative Party maintained that it did try to fight the campaign on European issues. But as one candidate put it, the issues were 'more about Britain and Europe than about Europe and Britain'. Another candidate was more forceful: 'The campaign had nothing to do with the European Parliament.' It was true that such issues as the veto, the single currency, and the 1996 IGC were largely irrelevant to the European Parliament, which had little power or influence in relation to any of them. But it is also true that other issues of more relevance to the European Parliament were raised. For example, all three parties released major policy statements on the Social Chapter and on reform of the Common Agricultural Policy. Yet these topics were hardly touched upon in the campaign itself. To some extent, the Conservatives' choice of 'European' issue was dictated by internal political concerns. In particular, the Prime Minister seemed as determined to woo the growing ranks of the Euro-sceptics within his party as he did to capture the patriotic vote among the electorate. But political parties alone cannot determine the political agenda, and the media's important role is considered below.

Labour candidates were equally frustrated by their national party's determination to campaign primarily on domestic issues. 'What an irony,' moaned one candidate, 'for once we are united on Europe and yet we choose largely to ignore it.' When confronted with such complaints, party officials pointed out that the party did try to run on European issues. Like the Conservatives, MEPs were always on the national press conference platforms. The Labour Party launched major policy initiatives on the reform of the CAP and on cutting down on fraud within the Community, but these apparently fell on deaf ears. However, Labour's apparent emphasis on the government's record was not only a result of media disinterest in its European policies. As one sceptical candidate put it, 'Do not forget that more Labour MPs voted against the Maastricht Treaty than did Conservative MPs. The Labour Party would be as split as the Conservatives but for the fact that it has the luxury of opposition.' Labour's policy noticeably hardened on such issues as the veto and taxation, particularly after early Conservative successes in attacking John Smith over the PES manifesto; the Union flag was as much in evidence in the Transport House press room as the European flag.

Liberal Democrat candidates were perhaps the most disillusioned with their national party's chosen emphasis. 'We should be proud of our policy on Europe,' said one candidate, 'and not ashamed of it.' Yet Paddy Ashdown was not alone in sensing that there had been a sea change in popular attitudes towards the European Union. In part, this may have arisen out of growing disquiet over the Maastricht Treaty, compounded by the blocking minority row and exacerbated by the impending row over Jean-Luc Dehaene's candidature. In part, too, the public's concern reflected the Conservatives' success in setting such matters as the veto squarely in the middle of the agenda. But many candidates sensed a genuine change. As one Euro-enthusiastic Labour candidate put it, 'We have gone too far too fast. We must go back and pick up the people.'

The national media plays a crucial role in setting the agenda of election campaigns. As Chapter 7 showed, the media increasingly became convinced that the outcome of the European elections would determine John Major's future. This was its primary interest, and when John Smith's death removed the immediate threat to the Prime Minister's position, the European elections lost much of their allure. The Labour leadership contest then became the major story, but the NEC's decision to open nominations on 10 June effectively postponed the dénouement until long after the European election results. The truncation of the campaign was a further reason for lower levels of media interest. In addition to the pronouncements of potential contenders for the Labour leadership, the campaign was punctuated by a number of newsworthy distractions; John Major's response to Sinn Fein's request for clarifications of the Downing Street declaration, the Chinook helicopter crash, the D-Day commemorative ceremonies and President Clinton's visit. But the campaign was also punctuated by a number of 'silly' stories, from the 'killer virus' to the alleged antics of the former Conservative minister Alan Clark. Above all, the media's search for a story was revealed in the selective attention it gave to the pronouncements of the Prime Minister and other Conservative politicians.

Although the results of the European elections did matter in terms of the composition and distribution of power within the new European Parliament, relatively little media attention was paid to these aspects of the campaign. An important reason for this disproportionate focus upon the national aspects of the campaign is bound up in the structure of the media. In the first place, there are few genuine 'European Community politics' journalists. Many newspapers and television and radio channels have Brussels-based correspondents, but most are expected to cover not only the European Community but the other Brussels-based international organisation, NATO, and events in Belgium and surrounding countries. In the second place, Brussels-based correspondents are in direct competition with correspondents based in other national capitals. A London-based editor may well consider that, for example, an article from a Bonn-based correspondent about, say, the implications of the Euro-elections for the German

Chancellor will be of more interest to a newspaper's readers than a general piece from a Brussels-based correspondent about the likely composition of the new Parliament.

Above all, Brussels-based correspondents must compete with the Westminster lobby. Lobby journalists are considered, and consider themselves, to be the *créme de la créme*. Within newspapers and television and radio companies, the lobby journalists take pride of place. When European elections come along once every five years, they are primarily covered by the lobby journalists, who otherwise spend the vast proportion of their time and energies covering purely national politics. Thus for most lobby journalists 'Europe' is not a topic in itself, but an exogenous factor which is primarily of interest because it can have considerable consequences for the careers and fortunes of Westminster politicians.

The pre-eminence of Westminster journalists largely explains the neglect of Euro-MPs on the platform at the parties' national press conferences. Lobby journalists did not know them and were largely ignorant about their role and activities. On the other hand, lobby journalists were very familiar with the Westminster politicians on the platform, individuals with whom they constantly interact in the national political process. This familiarity was reflected in the sorts of questions asked, which concentrated heavily on domestic politics. As one wistful Euro-candidate put it, 'We need a new breed of lobby journalist, who is specialised in Westminster *and* Brussels and Strasbourg.' Another, more disillusioned, candidate put matters another way. 'The lobby has a vested interest in playing down the importance of the European Parliament,' he said. 'To acknowledge the importance of Strasbourg would be to acknowledge a diminution in the importance of the institution they cover – Westminster.'

Virtually all incumbent MEPs saw the media's interpretation of the Representation of the People Act as a 'villain of the piece', particularly at the local level. MEPs who had been acting as the spokesmen of their party and group within the European Parliament felt particularly aggrieved that the media refused to grant them the same coverage it accorded to the spokesmen of the national parties. The effect was further to mute the European aspects of the campaign since, not unnaturally, national party spokesmen tended to place most emphasis on the national aspects of any issue. (The Conservatives' post mortem Moorhouse Report was rumoured to have demanded in particular that the party should negotiate a modification of the broadcasting authorities' agreement so that MEPs could be recognised, for the purposes of the Representation of the People Act, as 'national party spokesmen'.)

How much did the Euro-elections matter to 'Europe'? The landslide in seats for the Labour Party helped the PES Group to consolidate its pre-eminence and cohesiveness within the European Parliament, but the left is far from enjoying an absolute majority. In practical terms, this means that the two largest groupings, socialist and Christian Democrat, will continue to exercise the loose, oligopolistic political arrangement they perfected in the previous Parliament. An early example of this arrangement came with the easy election of Klaus Hänsch as President (365 votes out of 452 cast). In the previous Parliament, a mutual agreement between the two groups had seen the Presidency 'rotate' from a Spanish socialist, Enrique Baron Crespo, to a German Christian Democrat, Egon Klepsch, and the large majority for Klaus Hänsch suggests that a similar arrangement has been agreed this time. The fundamentally consensual working method of the Parliament may also partly explain why Conservative claims about a left-dominated Parliament fell flat.

Some German SPD MEPs privately expressed the fear that the existence of a large British Labour contingent within the PES group might have consequences for the group's overall policy stance on European issues in the run up to the 1996 intergovernmental conference. But these fears were balanced by Tony Blair's European policy statements and the realisation that there had been a considerable shift towards Euro-scepticism within the Conservative Party (likely to consolidate Labour's more pro-European stance). Apprehensions were also offset by the knowledge that David Martin, a Vice-President of the Parliament and a former rapporteur on the Maastricht intergovernmental conference, would play an important role as rapporteur in the context of the 1996 intergovernmental conference.

Notwithstanding the consequences of the European elections for the European Parliament and the institutional balance in Brussels, their greatest significance remained domestic. This significance can best be illustrated by posing a number of hypothetical questions.

In the first place, what would have happened if John Smith had not died? Could Labour's tally of Euro-seats have been even higher? If, as he seems to have intended, Mr Smith had spearheaded a strongly pro-European campaign, would this have won the party more votes, or were the instincts of the Beckett–Cunningham–Straw campaign leadership team more attuned in the end to the tenor of public opinion?

On the Conservative side, Mr Heseltine would have maintained his threat to the Prime Minister, but how many seats would the Conservatives have needed to lose before a challenge to the leadership was triggered? Many Conservative candidates claimed that an extra week's campaigning would have enabled them to get more of their core vote out, but the climactic media coverage of the Prime Minister's plight would have gathered momentum. As pertinently, with Mr Smith still alive there would have been no 'Blair effect' to sap the Liberal Democrat vote. With Mr Smith and Mr Major to choose between, would hesitant voters have been more inclined to vote tactically for Paddy Ashdown?

In that context, what would have happened if the Liberal Democrats had won more than two seats? At what number would Conservative backbenchers' panic have begun? Presumably, Mr Major could have withstood the additional loss of Devon and East Plymouth, and perhaps also of Dorset and East Devon, but what if the Conservatives had lost Wight and Hampshire South, or East Sussex and Kent South?

Did Labour miss out on a trick by not placing more emphasis on its green credentials? Four thousand more votes would have given it three more seats from the Conservative heartlands (Thames Valley, Worcestershire and South Warwickshire, Sussex South and Crawley), and another three seats (Essex North and Suffolk South, Cambridgeshire, and even the Cotswolds) were all realistically within its grasp. On the other hand, bearing in mind the distinction between instrumental and expressive voting, perhaps the rump Green Party vote would always have been beyond Labour's reach.

Did the Prime Minister strike a sufficiently Euro-sceptical tone to ward off the worst of the anti-Maastricht threat, or could a few more judiciously-chosen phrases have saved the seats of Christopher Jackson and Patricia Rawlings? Did the Prime Minister's shift towards Euro-scepticism absorb the anti-Maastricht threat, or did it encourage it to reappear at the next general election and the 1999 European elections?

In overall terms, did the parties get their campaign tactics right? Several Labour and Conservative Euro-candidates pointed to the similar paradoxes that both party leaderships faced. On the Labour side, a majority would probably agree that the party was correct to aim for the jugular vein of the government's poor domestic record on tax and economic management but, by squeezing down the Conservative's Scottish vote, this strategy may well have helped the SNP to strengthen its vote and in particular to capture Henry McCubbin's marginal seat. In other words, a strategy that won the party votes and seats in England may have lost it votes and a seat in Scotland.

The Conservatives faced a very similar dilemma. A majority within the party would probably agree that the leadership was right in its identification of the Liberal Democrat surge as the principal threat, particularly with a view to the next general election. By squeezing the Liberal Democrat vote in the south the party may well have saved seats in the south west, but it may also have helped Labour to win Kent East and Kent West in the south east, and contributed to other Labour victories north of the Thames estuary. 'We probably got the balance about right,' said one party official, 'but as much by luck as by judgement.' However, other officials were more sceptical about the party's ability to ward off the consequences of the 'Blair effect'.

These strategic dilemmas raise a more general problem. In particular, is it possible for national parties to run a differentiated campaign? The Liberal Democrats have encountered a similar problem in their avowed strategy of fighting the Conservatives in the shires and Labour in the inner cities, for the question can be reasonably posed as to whether this does not require two different sorts of party. More disturbingly for the party, the Euro-election results would seem to show that what works in the south west need not work in, say, the north east. The Liberal Democrats had to tailor their campaign to the West country but, in so doing, they may have lessened their appeal to voters elsewhere. As Chapter 6 showed, the SNP, which was also traditionally composed of a coalition of very different forces, depending on the region and the identity of its principal opposition, was able to escape this dilemma in Scotland North East in 1994 through its local election coalition with Labour, thus distancing itself from any association with conservatism in the electorate's eyes.

How well did the parties and their leaders perform? As in 1992, the Prime Minister took a leading role and, as in 1992, he confounded the Cassandras, but in 1994 his apparent success owed more to the cabalistic skills of the spin-doctors than it did to objective performance. Nevertheless, the party ran an efficient and competent campaign. There were few mistakes and there was no repeat of the internecine warfare of 1989. Above all, the party's different factions mostly managed to keep their differences under wraps for the duration of the campaign. By any objective standards, the Conservatives easily out-performed Labour and the Liberal Democrats, both in terms of the national press conferences and the broader agenda-setting function. But, as Chapter 7 showed, the national, predominantly London-based campaigns led a curiously detached existence from the mood in the country, leading the *Times* to report 'MAJOR LEFT TO RUE DEFEAT AFTER WINNING THE CAMPAIGN' (13 June).

In the immediate aftermath of the Euro-elections, the EPP group commissioned a Harris poll. The results were never published, but some of the major findings leaked out. They made worrying reading for the Euro-enthusiasts within the Conservative Party. Those who voted tended to be more pro-European than the electorate in general, and Labour and Liberal Democrat identifiers and voters were decisively more pro-European than the electorate as a whole. A majority of Conservative supporters found the tone of the Conservative campaign about right, but the general electorate, particularly in London and the south east, believed the Conservatives' European policies were too negative. Here, then, was evidence of the sea change in British politics. There had been a shift in Conservative attitudes towards Euro-scepticism, and this had been matched by a simultaneous shift in Labour attitudes towards a more pro-European stance; a reversal in the two parties' historic roles.

Labour had to contend with the loss of its leader on the eve of the campaign. Even her sternest critics would admit that Margaret Beckett assumed the role of interim leader with great ability, dignity and efficiency. She was hampered by two factors. The first was that the media insisted on regarding her as an interim leader only. This situation was exacerbated by the Westminster Whitsun recess. Mrs Beckett met the Prime Minister in Question Time just once, and was adjudged to have been highly successful, but then Parliament went into recess and she was no longer able to meet Mr Major on equal terms. The second factor was that Mrs Beckett was regarded as a potential candidate for the leadership, an expectation confirmed by her resignation of the deputy leadership.

Together with all of the other potential leadership contenders, Mrs Beckett's ability to run a successful Euro-election campaign was hampered by another factor; the media insisted, not unnaturally, in interpreting the pronouncements of all of the potential leadership contenders as coded personal campaign messages. Other political parties – particularly the Liberal Democrats – complained that Labour had benefitted from a disproportionate amount of publicity. The downside of this disproportionality was that the media had difficulty in accepting that the Labour leadership was fighting the election as a team. In fact, with the exception of Gordon Brown's withdrawal from the race and backing for Tony Blair, the Labour leadership's discipline was extraordinarily good.

Nevertheless, at the organisational level the Labour Party fought a poor campaign. Although morale was swift to re-establish itself, the party suffered badly from the loss of its leader, and precious time was lost in organisational introspection. The party put on a united but sorely limited campaign. It only once managed truly to capture the initiative, when Gordon Brown was swift to pounce on the VAT story, but otherwise it found itself reacting to an agenda effectively set by the Conservative Party and the Prime Minister.

John Smith's death exacerbated a traditional weakness of the Labour Party; its fragmented leadership. On rare occasions, it seemed as though Conservative Central Office and Downing Street were not running completely coordinated campaigns, but for the most part the Conservative Party's organisational machine functioned seamlessly. Labour, on the other hand, had a multitude of potentially competing power centres – the leader's office (Margaret Beckett), the campaign manager (Jack Straw), the shadow Foreign Secretary (Jack Cunningham), the shadow Chancellor (Gordon Brown), Transport House, and Walworth Road – and each played an active but not altogether coordinated role in the election campaign. This tendency was no doubt exaggerated by the forthcoming leadership contest, but the underlying structural problem was already there.

Labour activists were privately prepared to admit that the campaign had been poor. 'Thank God it didn't matter,' said one. But others were more bemused by the irony of the situation. 'We fought good campaigns in 1987 and 1992,' said a Walworth Road official, 'and yet we lost. Nobody could be proud in 1994, and yet we won.' There was a strong backstage feeling that there should have been an aggressive European theme to the campaign, and that the party could have pre-empted some of the early Conservative attacks. 'Labour knew for a long time where the attacks were going to come from,' said one party official. 'As early as March policy papers were circulating warning us that we had quickly to confirm a European position that would rebut, attack and neutralise the Tories' European campaign, and yet we didn't.'

Paddy Ashdown got off to a poor start, becoming entangled in a constitutional policy difference with some of the more Euro-enthusiastic party elders. Tony Blair's early lead in the Labour leadership stakes left Mr Ashdown struggling with a problem he could not have expected. It is a moot point as to whether he won more votes by subjecting himself to a gruelling round of tours and visits or whether he would have been better advised to keep a higher London profile. In addition, the party suffered from severely strained resources, frequently leaving its ill-attended national press conferences to party officials.

There were many dogs that did not bark in the 1994 Euro-elections. An example was the absence of PR as a campaign issue. By tradition, it is the prime victims of the first-past-the-post system who argue the strongest case, but on this occasion the Liberal Democrats chose to put more emphasis on other elements of their agenda for constitutional change. Despite the recommendations of the Plant Report, Labour completely avoided the issue. A probable explanation in both cases was the parties' anticipation of substantial gains under the current system. Indeed, an irony of the Liberal Democrats' small gains is that these have undermined the purity of its argument about the iniquities of the system. (The decision of the Italian 'second republic' to introduce an element of plurality into its electoral system had already suggested that continental satisfaction with PR had its limits.) The Liberal Democrats' decision to soft pedal on PR was perhaps particularly surprising, given that the party had only recently tried to bring a case before the European Court of Justice on the issue.

Another striking aspect of the 1994 Euro-elections was the low visibility of both the Conservative and the Labour anti-marketeers. The one exception was Lord Tebbit, but he played a positive role by endorsing Mr Major's Euro-sceptic line. Enoch Powell's pronouncements, which might once have caused headlines, went largely unreported.

According to her private office, Lady Thatcher was in the United Kingdom throughout the election campaign and fulfilled 'a normal round of engagements'. She was almost completely absent from the campaign, and the media, hungry for stories of Conservative disarray, were unable to print a single story about her. This was a far cry from the high-profile critical remarks she had made throughout the Maastricht Treaty ratification process.

There are a number of possible explanations for Lady Thatcher's silence. The first is simple party loyalty – an instinct not to rock the boat during a difficult election.

A second explanation is the Euro-sceptics' long game. Earlier in the year Margaret Thatcher had let it be known that she would not favour an early leadership crisis. This, the pundits averred, was not because she believed that her chosen successor, John Major, was a faithful carrier of the Thatcherite flag, but because the Euro-sceptics did not yet have a potential winning candidate in place, and she did not want to enhance the prospects of the man who had brought her down, Michael Heseltine.

Baroness Thatcher and the Conservative Euro-sceptics probably also had another long game in mind; the 1996 intergovernmental conference. As one backbencher put it, 'Battle must be joined, but in 1996 and not in 1994.' A Thatcherite insider gave another potential explanation. The slogan the Conservatives chose to use for the Euro-election campaign, 'A Strong Britain in a Strong Europe', had been partly drafted by her in 1989, and the choice of this theme and the Euro-sceptical tone Mr Major adopted throughout the 1994 campaign were generally satisfactory to her.

Lady Thatcher was not the only prominent Euro-sceptic to keep her own counsel during the campaign. Peter Lilley, Secretary of State for Social Security, and one of the prime Euro-sceptics within the Cabinet, took the extraordinary step of absenting himself from the campaign altogether (he was rumoured to be holidaying in France), despite the call of the Prime Minister and the Party Chairman that all ministers should play an active role. Labour were not slow to capitalise on this very public display of mutiny, using Mr Lilley's absence to undermine Conservative claims of unity. Privately, Central Office was said to be 'furious' with Mr Lilley, particularly when a Labour policy gaffe in his field of responsibility had to be exploited by other ministers. Publicly, Central Office counted back to before the campaign had begun in order to be able to claim that Mr Lilley had played an active role. Much pressure was brought to bear on the errant Secretary of State until, on the eve of the elections, he briefly appeared (though in Yorkshire rather than London) at a candidate's press conference. Rumours abounded that Mr Lilley would be punished for his disloyalty, but in the July government reshuffle he was left at his post.

Michael Portillo, who had emerged as the Euro-sceptics' best future leadership hope, rocked the boat over the single currency issue during the May local elections but thereafter played a relatively high profile and impeccably loyalist role throughout the Euro-elections campaign, on occasion even acting as a calming influence. He performed ably at press conferences, sidestepping trick questions and refusing to be drawn on EMU or any of the other potentially divisive policy stances with which he had become associated. The Secretary for Wales, John Redwood, and the Home Secretary, Michael Howard, were equally loyal in respecting the party line. Mr Redwood became embroiled in a dispute about quangos in Wales, but Mr Howard played an agenda-setting role in the campaign, particularly through his speech on immigrants and asylum.

With the exception of George Gardiner's *Way Forward* article at the very beginning of the campaign, backbench Conservative Euro-sceptics also largely refrained from rocking the boat. Again, party loyalty during a critical election campaign and the Euro-sceptics' long game go some way towards explaining this silence. But another potential explanation was the forthcoming government reshuffle; clearly, the Whips would look more kindly upon conscientious campaigning than they would upon trouble-making, no matter how principled the stand.

The Labour Party was similarly free of anti-market dissent. The party was on a roll and, among the potential leadership candidates, Tony Blair's pro-European Union stance was clearly more popular than Margaret Beckett's sceptical line. Bryan Gould had left Parliament and nobody else had yet entirely adopted his anti-Maastricht rallying cry.

The lack of dissent on all sides can be explained in more general political terms. Boat-rocking only makes sense if it pays clear dividends (as, for example, populist dissent at party conferences may do). Boat-rocking during election campaigns may be dangerously counter-productive, since votes and seats may be lost and the boat rocker will almost certainly get the blame.

The Euro-elections provided a few examples of cases where candidates did have a personal effect on the vote. The prime example was provided by Winifred Ewing's pre-eminence in the Highlands and Islands. The personal popularity of Dafydd Wigley produced a large swing to Plaid Cymru in North Wales, and Militant Labour Tommy Sheridan won over 12,000 votes in Glasgow.

The 1994 Euro-elections raised two more general questions; why was turnout so low, and why did the 'feel good factor' not work?

Many Euro-candidates were surprised that turnout was not higher, confounding expectations based on the impressions they had got from canvassing. The opinion polls also predicted much higher popular participation than had previously been the case, and none of the classic explanations for lower turnout were present; the weather was dry and, even if they did not concentrate on European issues, all of the political parties ran basically positive campaigns and explicitly urged people to turn out and use their vote. Why then, in the end, did so few turn out? The question can be put the other way around. Why, given the apparent lack of consequence of Euro-elections, had so many turned out? Since European elections changed little or nothing, it could be argued, voters would be entirely rational in not making any effort to turn out. Euro-elections in the United Kingdom were, if anything, of less political consequence than local elections and indeed drew a lower turnout.

The answer must be connected to the distinction made earlier between instrumental and expressive elections. The Euro-elections were primarily expressive, and those who turned out did so in order to express approval or discontent. Viewed from this perspective, some former Conservative voters sanctioned the government by voting Liberal Democrat or Labour, but others sanctioned the government by simply staying at home. As one Labour candidate, quoted in Chapter 8, pointed out, this interpretation is not particularly reassuring for the Labour Party. If it had wanted to transform the Euro-elections into a referendum on the Prime Minister and his government, then it should be concerned that it had been unable to mobilise or motivate a larger proportion of the electorate. Some Labour candidates argued that, in running a critical campaign on domestic issues, the party had come perilously close to repeating the Conservatives' 1989 mistake of running a negative campaign.

Other important contributory factors to the low turnout probably include 'electoral fatigue' after the May local elections (there were turnout differentials between those areas where local elections had and had not occurred), low Conservative activist morale in safe Labour seats (particularly those whose majorities were consolidated by the boundary changes), and a sense of anti-climax after the death of John Smith.

The most likely answer as to why the 'feel good factor' didn't work is bound up in the overall economic fortunes of Britain's middle classes. By 1994 the core middle classes, known to the advertising and polling worlds as ABC1s, accounted for 44 per cent of the electorate, compared with 33 per cent in 1979. They consisted of households with professional or managerial staff as the main income earner (the ABs), together with other white-collar staff (the C1s). These middle classes have traditionally made up the bedrock of Conservative support. In the 1987 General Election, 52 per cent of AB electors supported the Conservatives, against only 15 per cent voting Labour. By the April 1992 General Election, Conservative support among the AB group had increased to 56 per cent (although Labour support had also increased, to 19 per cent). However, a September 1994 MORI poll showed that support for the Conservatives among the ABs had slumped to 38 per cent, while Labour enjoyed 37 per cent. Such figures went beyond mid-term unpopularity. In particular, unemployment among professionals and managers had risen more sharply than in any other section of the workforce. In addition, the Labour Party was seen to have disqualified itself in 1987 and 1992 through its promises to raise the National Insurance contribution ceiling and to increase the top rate of income tax, but even before the leadership elections had taken place, Gordon Brown had made it clear that Labour's 'traditional' reliance on tax increases would be abandoned, thus diminishing this disincentive.

The views of the larger component of the middle classes, the C1s, had shifted even more remarkably. In the 1992 General Election, Conservative support among white-collar workers was 52 per cent, against 25 per cent for Labour. But by September 1994, the Blair-led Labour Party enjoyed 44 per cent support, with 33 per cent for the Conservatives. The C1s had also suffered disproportionately from unemployment, but they had been particularly badly hit by the tax increases announced by Norman Lamont and his successor, Kenneth Clarke. Without any social security protection from VAT on gas and electricity bills, and without the additional salary cushion enjoyed by the ABs, the C1s were much more exposed to the impact of higher taxes.

Some analysts argue that the middle classes now comprise a much larger group than that covered by the ABC1 definition and in particular should include all householders and owner-occupiers. In this context the spread of owner-occupation, enhanced by the sale of council houses to former tenants under the right-to-buy legislation, was a boon to the Conservatives in the 1980s, but had become a drag in the 1990s, with an estimated one million households caught in the 'negative equity' trap, whereby the value of a property was less than the value of the mortgage initially taken out to buy it. In addition, Conservative Chancellors of the Exchequer had cut mortgage tax relief, and further reductions had been announced for the following year. Taken in the round, therefore, the all-important middle classes did not feel as good as the economic indicators might have suggested.

Many candidates sensed a more general malaise among the electorate, perhaps bound up with a general, post-Cold War disillusionment with western political institutions and processes, but specifically linked to the Maastricht Treaty ratification process. As one candidate put it, 'the political elites can no longer build Europe alone.' In 1996 a new intergovernmental conference will open. An intergovernmental working group will be established in the summer of 1995 to prepare for the IGC. Opinions differ as to what the scope of the 1996

IGC will be, but a number of major constitutional issues have been pre-programmed into the conference by the provisions of the Maastricht Treaty. In addition, the timetable for Economic and Monetary Union set out in the Treaty means that some countries could move to irrevocably fixed exchange rates and a single currency as early as 1997. As a senior politician commented, 'We have had a European election devoted to British politics and now it seems likely that we will have a General Election devoted to European politics.'

One of the most striking consequences of John Smith's death was the way in which it transformed the whole political situation, including the significance of the European elections, overnight. Until 12 May the Euro-elections were largely expected to bring about the Prime Minister's downfall, with some commentators speculating that the Conservative Party might even replace its leader before the summer recess. With the Labour leader dead, it became increasingly clear that John Major would not be replaced and thereafter the Euro-elections became a means of consolidating his leadership. After the local elections, most commentators expected the Liberal Democrats to surge out of the west country into the Conservatives' southern underbelly. But after Mr Smith's death it was Labour that won seats in Kent, Hertfordshire, Suffolk and Essex.

The 1994 Euro-elections were a curious affair. The Conservative Party was a clear loser, but John Major was seen as a clear winner. The Liberal Democrats won seats for the first time but were perceived as having fared badly. Tony Blair won an election before he became leader (no other national election this century has been fought with one of the major parties leaderless). The Labour Party won Euro-seats by focussing on national politics, and the Conservatives lost Euro-seats by focussing on Europe. Still deprived of power at Westminster, Labour became stronger in Strasbourg. But as the Euro-elections faded rapidly from view, Europe remained firmly on the British political agenda.

Appendix: An Analysis of the Results

*John Curtice and Michael Steed**

A SECOND-ORDER ELECTION

European elections were intended to stimulate a common political debate. In practice, they have been low-key affairs dominated by domestic issues; in short, second-order elections (for discussion of this concept see Chapter 10). The 1994 European election in Great Britain was no different. All three distinguishing characteristics of a second-order election were evident: low turnout, an anti-government swing and a relatively high level of support for small parties.

The Euro-election attracted even less interest than a typical local election. At 35.9 per cent, turnout in Great Britain was actually 0.7 per cent lower than in 1989, although still nearly four points higher than in 1979 and in 1984. Even in the metropolitan districts where local election turnout tends to be lowest, turnout has averaged nearly 39 per cent since 1973 (Rallings and Thrasher, 1993).

Participation in British Euro-elections tends not only to be low by local election standards but also by those of Euro-elections in other countries. The lowest turnout recorded in any of the other eleven countries between 1979 and 1989, 47.4 per cent in Denmark in 1989, was well above that recorded in any of the equivalent elections in Britain. But in 1994 turnout was down on the level five years ago in no less than eight of the other eleven member states. And in both the Netherlands (where, following a general election the previous month, turnout was just 35.5 per cent) and in Portugal (where the elections came in the middle of a public holiday and just 35.7 per cent participated) turnout fell to just below that in Great Britain, while the Irish Republic was only just ahead (37.0 per cent).[1] The indifference of British voters to the European Parliament may not have changed but it no longer seems to be unique.[2]

Those voters who did bother to turn out certainly used the election to cast an adverse mid-term judgement on the government of the day. The Conservatives secured just 27.9 per cent of the vote, down 14.9 per cent on its vote in the general election just two years previously. Indeed, by domestic historical standards this result was a disaster. Their support was as much as 6.8 per cent down on the last European elections which also took place when they were two years into their period of office. It was the lowest share of the vote ever recorded by the party in a nationwide election. And it was a worse performance than even Labour's debacle (28.3 per cent) in the 1983 general election, a result from which the party was still struggling to recover in 1992.

Yet the government's fate was far from exceptional compared with the rest of Europe. As Table A.1 shows only in Italy did the government coalition do better in the Euro-elections than in the previous general election. But there the previous general election which had swept the old Christian Democrat dominated order from power had only been held three months earlier, and recently elected governments commonly benefit from a 'honeymoon effect' in second-order elections (Reif, 1984; Reif, 1985)[3]. In the remaining nine countries where the relevant calculation can be made governments not only suffered losses, but in seven of them they experienced, just like the British Conservatives, a much greater reversal of fortune than their predecessors did in 1989. Indeed, as we can see in Table A.1, the Conservatives come but half way in the league table of government losses.

Thus the British election followed a wider European trend in exhibiting a stronger anti-government tide than ever before. But what of Labour's performance? Was it exceptional? Governments may invariably do badly in Euro-elections, but oppositions do not necessarily do well (Curtice, 1989). Yet

Table A.1   Government reverses, 1989 and 1994

	Change in % share of the vote for government parties since previous national election	
	1989	*1994*
Italy	−2.4	+ 6.8¶
Netherlands	−3.8	#
Belgium	−3.7	−3.2
Spain	−4.0	−8.1
Greece	*	−9.3
Germany	−6.5	−12.1
Great Britain	−8.6	−14.9
Portugal	−16.3	−16.1
Ireland	*	−16.7
Denmark	−5.1	−22.0
France	−13.9	−27.4

Notes: * General Election held on same day as European Election.
         # New government not yet formed following previous month's General Election.
         ¶ Comparison made with votes cast in national party list contest section of the General Election.

Sources: *1989*: J. Curtice, 'The 1989 European Election: Protest or Green Tide?' *Electoral Studies*, 8, (1989), 217–30. *1994*: Calculated from information in BBC Political Research Unit, *European Election Guide '94* (London: BBC); *El Pais*, 14 June 1994; *Financial Times*, 14 June 1994.

with 44.2 per cent of the vote Labour secured its highest share of the vote in any nationwide election since 1966 (which indeed was the last time it secured a safe overall majority). And in adding 9.0 per cent to its share of the vote in the 1992 general election, it outperformed all of the principal opposition parties in Europe. Even so, this performance was not unprecedented. For Labour was the best performing opposition party in Europe in 1989 as well, as Table A.2 shows, but still went on to lose the 1992 general election.[4] It would be rash to assume Labour's performance constituted a significant new breakthrough.

At first sight, the final feature of second-order elections, support for small parties or parties that did not contest the previous General Election, has been less apparent in Britain than in the rest of the European Union. In 1979 just 3.3 per cent of the vote was cast for candidates other than those standing for the Conservative, Labour or Liberal parties, and in 1984 just 3.2 per cent. But much of the reason for this was a lack of opportunity. Apart from the Scottish and Welsh Nationalists, just 23 other candidates fought the European Election in 1979 and 26 in 1984. Those who stood did in fact tend to fare better than similar candidates in general elections (Curtice, 1981; Curtice, 1985).

Table A.2. Opposition performances, 1989 and 1994

	Change in % share of the vote for principal opposition party since previous national election	
	1989	*1994*
Great Britain	+8.6	+9.0
Portugal	+7.1	+5.4
Spain	−4.5	+5.4
Denmark	−6.6	+4.5†
Ireland	*	+2.0
Belgium	−3.1	+0.3
Netherlands	−2.6	#
Italy	+1.0	−1.3¶
Germany	+0.3	−1.3
Greece	*	−6.6
France	−0.4	−15.3

Notes: * General Election held on same day as European Election.
  # New government not yet formed following previous month's General Election.
  ¶ Comparison made with votes cast in national party list contest section of the General Election.
  † Performance of Liberal and Conservative parties combined as both parties vie for the position of principal opposition party.
  § Performance of Francophone and Flemish Liberals combined.
Sources: as Table A.1.

In 1989, however, the Greens fielded candidates in all 78 constituencies and secured a spectacular breakthrough, winning no less than 14.9 per cent of the vote. But in addition a further 4.1 per cent went to 41 further candidates and the two nationalist parties. In 1994, voters were given plenty of opportunity to experiment with small parties. The Natural Law Party contested every constituency as did the Greens, while a further 105 other candidates also stood. Although this time the Greens only managed to secure 3.2 per cent, the total vote cast for small parties was at 11.1 per cent well above the 3.8 per cent secured in the 1992 General Election, or indeed the record general election high of 4.3 per cent in October 1974.

So the 1994 European Election was on all three counts quite clearly a second-order election. Indeed, if anything it was even more so than its three predecessors. But one change from previous elections should be noted. Following adjustments to the composition of the European Parliament agreed at the 1992 Edinburgh summit in the wake of the reunification of Germany, the United Kingdom was granted an additional six MEPs (see Chapter 3). The government rejected calls that these additional MEPs should be elected by some form of proportional representation and instead allocated five extra seats to England and one to Wales to be elected by the traditional single member plurality system. This required that the Euro-constituency boundaries be redrawn throughout England and Wales to accommodate these extra seats (see Chapter 3). This means that when we compare the 1994 result with the 1989 results for individual Euro-constituencies, we have to use estimates of what the 1989 result would have been on the 1994 boundaries.[5]

THE GOVERNMENT

The coincidence of low turnout and a poor Conservative performance inevitably led to the suggestion that Conservative voters had been more likely to stay at home. This was quickly grasped by Conservative commentators who argued it showed that, while voters might be disenchanted with the government, they were still reluctant to support the opposition. In a general election, they would be open to persuasion to return to the Conservative camp.

Support for this proposition came from an ICM poll conducted immediately after polling day which found that 51 per cent of those who claimed to have voted Conservative in 1992 said they did not vote in the European elections (ICM, 1994). In contrast amongst those who claimed to have supported Labour in 1992, only 36 per cent said they did not vote, while the equivalent figure amongst 1992 Liberal Democrats was 43 per cent.

However, if differential turnout were the main cause of the Conservatives' problems we would expect to discover that, when compared with 1992, turnout fell most in those seats where there were most Conservative voters in the first place. But this was far from being the case. In England turnout fell most in safe Labour seats, and especially in those seats wholly or partly in a metropolitan county.[6] This was despite the fact that the difference in the average level of turnout between Labour and Conservative seats had already widened considerably in the 1992 General Election (Curtice and Steed, 1992). When compared with the last Euro-elections in 1989 the pattern is even more striking.

As a result, as the regional summary of the results in Table 9.3 (p. 261) shows, turnout in the South of England outside London was markedly higher than in the three northernmost regions of England. In 1989, in contrast, turnout had varied little from one part of England to another.

Does this mean that those who voted Conservative in 1992 were in fact more eager rather than less eager to turn out and vote? Probably not. The most likely explanation lies in voters' perceptions of the marginality of their seat. Opinion polls during the campaign had fuelled speculation that the Conservatives might lose a large proportion of their seats and in particular that the party could be vulnerable to a Liberal Democrat breakthrough. Thus, voters in all but the safest of Conservative seats were encouraged to think the result in their constituency would be close, and for many and especially those living in seats where the Liberal Democrats were challenging, this was a novel experience which might have encouraged them to vote.

The argument is supported by the evidence displayed in Table A.3, which shows that turnout rose most in those seats where, when the results in the component Westminster seats were added up, the Liberal Democrats had come a good second to the Conservatives in the 1992 general election. In contrast it rose by a little less in the very safest Conservative seats.

However, if the results are looked at in another way there would appear to be some evidence of differential turnout. In the thirteen seats where turnout fell by 46 per cent or more compared with 1992, the Conservative vote fell by 16.0 per cent. In contrast, in the thirteen seats where turnout fell by 38 per cent or less, support for the Conservatives fell by just 13.4 per cent.

Table A.3   Variation in turnout in England

Political history of seat	Change in % turnout since		
	1989	*1992*	
Lab. first 1989 and 1992	−5.3	−44.3	(20)
Lab. first 1989, Con. first 1992	−2.0	−43.6	(17)
Con. first 1989 and 1992; Lab second 1992 and less than 26% behind	+2.6	−42.0	(12)
Con. first 1989 and 1992; Lab. second 1992 but more than 26% behind	+2.1	−43.6	(7)
Con. first 1989 and 1992; LibDem. second 1992 and less than 30% behind	+4.6	−39.1	(11)
Con. first 1989 and 1992; LibDem. second 1992 but more than 30% behind	+1.0	−42.4	(4)

Notes: Lab. first 1989: Labour won seat on basis of estimate of 1989 result on new boundaries.
Lab. first 1992: Labour ahead in seat on basis of aggregated votes in the component Westminster constituencies in the 1992 general election.
Et simile for remaining rows.
(Table based on seats in England only.)

But this needs to be treated carefully. No less than seven of the thirteen seats where turnout fell by less than 38 per cent are in Scotland and Wales in both of which the Conservative vote was already much weaker in 1992 than it was anywhere in England. Of the remaining six seats, four were ones where the Conservatives were being challenged by the Liberal Democrats. And in all of these the below average fall in turnout was indeed accompanied by a slightly below average fall in Conservative support given their geographical location.[7] But when we look at the rest of the seats in England very little relationship between the fall in turnout and the fall in Conservative support remains. Thus it may be that Conservative voters were particularly stimulated to make the journey to the polling station because of the novelty of political competition in those seats where the Liberal Democrats were challenging, but that elsewhere differential turnout was not an important influence on the outcome.

Conservative apologists also took comfort from the fact that the party had avoided the dire fate held out for it by projections from votes cast in the local elections in May and from some opinion polls published during the campaign. These projections had suggested the party could win less than ten seats and perhaps even fewer than the Liberal Democrats. Disaster was only narrowly averted. No less than 15 of the 18 Conservative MEPs were elected with majorities of less than 6 per cent (while only five seats were lost by that margin). If the party's vote had been but 2 per cent lower in each constituency and each of the two main opposition parties' votes just 1 per cent higher, the Conservatives, while still winning as much as 25.9 per cent of the vote, would have been left with just seven seats, the same as the Liberal Democrats.

The Conservatives avoided the anticipated meltdown primarily because the Liberal Democrat vote was much lower than in the local elections and opinion polls. However, there was still plenty in the pattern of Tory performance to worry party strategists. For party support proved to be most fragile in its heartlands. In those Euro-seats where the Tories won more than 50 per cent of the vote in 1992, their vote fell on average by as much as 17.7 per cent; in contrast in those seats where they started off with 35 per cent of the vote or less, their share fell on average by just 12.0 per cent.

It might seem common sense that a party losing ground at an election should lose most votes in those seats where it had more support to start with. However, this expectation can be shown to rest on weak logical ground (see McLean, 1973). And in practice it is very unusual for it to happen in British elections. While party performance often varies markedly from one part of the country to another, only rarely does a party systematically lose most votes in its heartlands. The causes and consequences of this pattern at the 1994 European Election are thus central to our understanding of the government's performance.

One clear consequence was a sharp regional variation in Conservative performance. Only four of the 24 seats where the Tories began with less than 35 per cent of the vote lie in the six regions in the South and Midlands of England,[8] and only one of the 25 where they had over 50 per cent in 1992 is in the North of England, Scotland or Wales. And as Table 9.3 (p. 261) shows, Conservative support fell more in the South and Midlands than in any of the five regions elsewhere. Indeed, Conservative support fell most (−18.4 per cent) in the party's strongest region (South East) and least (−11.2 per cent) in its weakest (Scotland).

But differences in the experience or character of the regions themselves do not appear to have been the principal cause of the variation in Conservative performance. If we take the twelve seats where the 1992 Conservative vote was closest to their national performance (that is between 40 and 45 per cent), we find that the fall in Conservative support in the six in the South and Midlands (−14.8 per cent) is identical to that in the six in the North (−14.8 per cent). There are, though, three minor exceptions to this general absence of clearly regional variation.

First, the Conservatives' vote held up consistently better in the three seats in the North of England where they started off strongest (−11.0 per cent). Secondly, their support also stood up a little better along the western edge of England; in a string of six Euro-seats running from Shropshire to Cornwall, it fell on average by just 13.8 per cent. Finally, the largest fall in Conservative support (−20.8 per cent) was in a cluster of seven Euro-seats, comprising the five in Bedfordshire, Essex and Hertfordshire together with the two adjacent London seats, East and North. These three exceptions will prove useful to us in trying to account for just what did cause the variation in Tory performance.

Previous elections have suggested that one important potential reason for geographical variation in party performance is that voters respond to the state of their local economy (see, for example, Curtice, 1988; Curtice and Steed, 1992; Johnston et al., 1988; Spencer et al., 1992). For example, the variation in change in Conservative support between 1987 and 1992 was clearly related to the geography of the recession. And in general, trends in unemployment between 1992 and 1994 were rather more favourable than the national average in parts of Scotland and the North of England and rather worse in London, a pattern not dissimilar to that of Conservative performance at this election.[9]

Yet the fit between the two factors is surprisingly weak. For example, in the twenty seats where unemployment rose most markedly[10] between 1992 and 1994, Conservative support fell by 15.8 per cent, virtually the same as in the 42 Euro-seats where the recent trend in unemployment was little different from the national average.[11] Further, within the south-eastern corner of England, unemployment rose most between 1992 and 1994 in London, East Anglia, Kent and East Sussex, not in the area centred on Bedfordshire, Essex and Hertfordshire where the Tories suffered their biggest losses. Equally, recent trends in unemployment were not relatively favourable in the western strip from Shropshire to Cornwall where the Conservatives' performance was rather better. In short, the results confirm the evidence of econometric research that the voters' loss of faith in the Conservatives since 1992 cannot simply be accounted for by the state of the economy (Spencer and Curtice, 1994).

Seats where the Conservatives are traditionally strong are those where there are more middle-class people. Thus, another possible explanation for the pattern of the Conservatives' performance is that the election witnessed a revolt against the government's performance by its core middle-class constituency. They might, for example, have become disillusioned because of negative house price inflation, tax increases or the rising incidence of unemployment in the service sector. And some recent evidence from both opinion polls and local elections suggests Conservative support has fallen more heavily amongst middle- than amongst working-class people (*British Public Opinion*, 1994, p. 5; *Economist*, 1993; *Economist*, 1994). But the evidence of the European Election does not point straightforwardly to such an explanation. In the ten most middle class constituencies[12] in the country, all of which are in London and the South East, the average fall in Conservative support was, at 16.5 per cent, actually below the average for that region as a whole.

Another difficulty faced by the government for nearly two years before the 1994 European Election was the adverse coverage it received in the traditionally Tory tabloid press. Further, there is a striking regional pattern to the pattern of newspaper readership.[13] In Scotland readers of the Labour supporting *Daily Mirror* and the *Daily Record* outnumber the combined readership of the *Daily Express, Daily Mail, Daily Star* and the *Sun* . In Wales and the North of England readers of the Tory tabloid press outnumber readers of Labour papers by only around two to one. But as we move south, the ratio increases to around 2.5:1 in the typical Euro-seat in the Midlands and over 3:1 in the South East. So, if the steady stream of criticism in the Tory tabloid press has had any impact on its readers, then we would expect just the contrast in Conservative performance between South East Britain and North West Britain that actually occurred in the Euro-election.

The association between Conservative performance and the incidence of Tory tabloid readers also proves to be closer than it is between Conservative performance and the middle-class character of a constituency. Take, for example, the two sets of seats where – given their geographical location and 1992 Conservative vote – there had been an above-average Conservative performance (combined average drop, −12.9 per cent); that is, the three most Conservative seats in the North of England and the six along the western strip from Shropshire to Cornwall. All of these seats have a relatively low level of Tory tabloid readers given the size of the Conservative vote. On average the Conservatives won 47.2 per cent of the vote in 1992 but Tory tabloid readers outnumber Labour ones by 2.4:1. In contrast, amongst the remaining ten Euro-seats where the Conservatives won between 45 and 50 per cent of the vote in 1992, the average ratio of Tory tabloid readers to Labour ones is 2.8:1 and the fall in the Conservative vote as high as 17.2 per cent.

The association we have found may be spurious. The geography of newspaper readership is highly correlated with distance from London and may well be picking up other cultural influences on a core–periphery dimension. Further, the theory cannot account for the worst cluster of Tory performances in the seven Euro-seats centred on Essex. On the other hand, this was an area where the Conservatives both made most electoral headway in the 1980s and resisted the general drop in Conservative support in the South between 1987 and 1992 (Curtice and Steed, 1992, pp. 330–1), and so Tory support there could in any case be considered to have been particularly vulnerable. The possibility that the attacks of the Tory tabloid press have had some impact on support for the Conservative government cannot be discounted.

Despite the uncertainties, one conclusion seems clear. The Conservatives' disastrous performance in its southern heartlands cannot be regarded as an immediate response to short-term economic difficulty but rather points to more profound problems of political disenchantment. Many of the party's most symbolic gains under Mrs Thatcher, 'Essex man' and '*Sun* woman', appear to have shown a particular reluctance to stay with the party. Indeed just how systematically Mrs Thatcher's electoral gains have been lost since her demise can be seen if we compare the 1994 Euro-election result with that of the 1979 General Election when Mrs Thatcher first came to power.[14] As Table A.4 shows, measured over this longer period, Conservative support has fallen more or less evenly across the country as a whole. The Conservatives' General Election successes in the 1980s were notable for their increasing concentration of support in the southern half of the country. But the 1992 General Election and 1994 European Election have resulted in the complete disappearance of those gains.

Table A.4   Long-term trends in party support

	Mean change in % vote compared with 1979 General Election		
	Con.	Lab.	Lib.Dem.
London	−16.8	+ 11.3	+ 0.1
South	−18.8	+ 2.6	+ 7.7
Midlands	−17.3	+ 10.4	+ 1.3
North	−16.7	+ 12.6	−0.8
Wales	−18.1	+ 8.9	−2.2
Scotland	−17.3	+ 1.4	−2.5
Great Britain	−17.5	+ 8.0	+ 1.8

Personal reputation proved to be of little use in stemming the tide of anti-government protest. True, the vote for the leader of the Tory MEPs, Sir Christopher Prout fell rather less in Herefordshire & Shropshire (-12.3 per cent) than in similar seats, as did that for Lord Bethell (-13.5 per cent in London North West), Margaret Daly (-11.4 per cent in Somerset & North Devon), Lord Inglewood (-10.0 per cent in Cumbria & Lancashire North) and Michael Welsh (-9.9 per cent in Lancashire Central) but they all lost their seats nonetheless. Amongst the 20 remaining seats defended by Tory MEPs the Conservative vote fell on average by 16.6 per cent, which though a little better than in the eleven seats the Tories were defending with a new candidate (-17.8 per cent) was still rather worse than the national average.

THE OPPOSITION PARTIES

At first sight, the fortunes of Labour and the Liberal Democrats were very different. While, as we have already seen, Labour achieved its highest share of the vote since 1966, at 16.7 per cent the Liberal Democrats were unable even to match their General Election performance just two years earlier. Indeed, as in the three previous Euro-elections the Liberal Democrats' share of the vote was lower than their standing in the opinion polls in the period immediately before polling day or indeed their performance in the local elections the previous month.

It seems that, for the Liberal Democrats at least, European elections are not simply second-order elections where votes are won and lost on national issues. Indeed, a poll conducted by ICM immediately after polling day suggested that if voters had been voting in a general election the Liberal Democrat vote might well have been as much as five points higher (ICM, 1994, Tables 4 and 11; also Franklin and Curtice, 1995). In previous Euro-elections it might be argued that, because the party appeared to have little or no chance of winning a seat, some of its supporters were reluctant to waste their votes. But in 1994 most commentators confidently expected the party to win at least the two seats it eventually secured. The party's weak performance this time around suggests more serious problems of image may be at stake. Much Liberal support has been built up over the past three decades, especially at local elections and parliamentary by-elections, by projecting a strongly localist appeal. It may be this appeal is undermining the Liberal Democrats aspiration to be seen as a serious national party. We also cannot discount the possibility that the party's pro-European stance is unacceptable to some of those who might otherwise vote for it in Euro-elections.

The fortunes of the two opposition parties were also very different from one part of the country to another. Despite the nationwide fall in its support compared with the General Election, as Table 9.3 shows, the Liberal Democrat vote clearly rose in both the South East and the South West. In contrast, Labour's vote rose least in the South West and in some parts of the South East. In short, it would seem that where the Liberal Democrats prospered, Labour did less well, and vice versa.

Why was this so? All of the seats that the Liberal Democrats hoped to win were in the South of England. One obvious possibility is that some voters in the South of England who had not previously done so opted to vote tactically for whichever of the two main parties was best placed to defeat the Conservatives. This is indeed part, but only part, of the explanation. There was also a genuinely regional component to the variation in the opposition parties' performance, though it was not one that simply followed the standard regional boundaries used in Table 9.3.

Let us look first of all at the evidence of tactical voting. For the voter who was inclined to do so, voting tactically was by no means necessarily easy. Both parties could find evidence to support the claim that they had the best chance of winning in a particular constituency. Labour, for example, could use the results of the last European elections to show that it was ahead of the Liberal Democrats everywhere except in Cornwall & West Plymouth and was close to victory in many Conservative-held seats. Meanwhile, the Liberal Democrats could point out that if the 1992 general election results were added up in each Euro-constituency they started off second to the Conservatives in no less than fifteen seats. But the national opinion polls showed a striking Labour advance since 1992 (and only a modest Liberal Democrat one) which theoretically meant that Labour could be better placed to win even where they were third in 1992. To this the Liberal Democrats could counter with calculations derived from the 1993 county council election results which put them in first or second place in no less than 21 seats (Electoral Reform Society, 1994)

The better option was not always obvious even if a voter could acquire accurate local information. For example, over two-thirds of the electorate in the newly-formed Herefordshire & Shropshire Euro-seat lived in constituencies where Labour had been third at each of the previous three general elections. But on the basis of the total votes cast in 1992 Labour were marginally ahead (0.2 per cent) of the Liberal Democrats.

In practice however, a clear pattern can be discerned. There were eight European constituencies where on any reasonable test[15] the Liberal Democrats appeared the better placed to win. On average the Liberal Democrat vote rose by 3.2 per cent in these eight seats and the Labour vote by 3.6 per cent. Many commentators have argued that, because Labour's vote advanced in these seats, this meant that it did not suffer a tactical squeeze. But this is to miss the point. Voters vote tactically if, because of their perception of the tactical situation in their constituency, they vote for a party different from the one they *would otherwise have voted for at that election* – who they voted for at a previous election is irrelevant. Thus what matters is that in these constituencies Labour's vote rose by considerably less than the national average while the Liberal Democrats bucked the national fall in their support.

Only in one of these eight seats, Wight & Hampshire South, was there no evidence of additional tactical voting. Here, Labour's vote rose by 8.6 per cent and Liberal Democrat support fell by 0.8 per cent. One possibility is that the outcome here was influenced by unfavourable publicity about the Liberal Democrat candidate's personal life. The result was one of the first to declare and it led the Liberal Democrat President, Charles Kennedy, to complain on television that Labour's rise was stopping his party winning more seats. In the event, this was the only seat where this proved to be true. The main reason why the Liberal Democrats failed to pick up more than the two seats that they would have won, even in the absence of any new tactical voting, was that their overall national performance was simply too weak for them to profit from the local boost they received in most of their target seats. To compound their ill fortune, in the one seat which they might still have secured through tactical voting, Devon & East Plymouth, they suffered from the confusion created by an independent candidate who stood as a Literal Democrat (see Chapter 9).

In up to a dozen further European constituencies it was more arguable as to who was better placed to defeat the Conservatives, and where voters must have received conflicting information.[16] It is here that region also seems to have made a difference. For in four seats adjacent to the eight clear cases discussed above, the Liberal Democrats did consistently better than they did in seats with a similar tactical situation elsewhere.

Two of the four seats neatly illustrate the point. The first is Itchen, Test & Avon. Here the Liberal Democrats were only 4.9 per cent ahead of Labour in 1992, but their vote increased by 6.8 per cent and Labour's by only 2.1 per cent. By contrast, in The Cotswolds, where the Liberal Democrats had been 4.3 per cent ahead in 1992, Labour surged by 9.5 per cent while the Liberal Democrat vote fell back by 4.5 per cent.

The second example is Sussex South & Crawley. This was a seat where Labour started off 1.5 per cent ahead of the Liberal Democrats. Their vote rose by 9.7 per cent while the Liberal Democrats only rose by 0.7 per cent. But even so, this was a distinctly less good result for Labour than in four other constituencies[17] where Labour started off 2 per cent or less ahead of the Liberal Democrats but where on average the Labour vote rose by 12.4 per cent and the Liberal Democrat vote fell by 2.4 per cent.

Two important implications follow from this analysis. First, further to the extension of tactical switching between Labour and the Liberal Democrats in the 1992 General Election (Curtice and Steed, 1992; Evans, 1994), in the 1994 European Election the non-Conservative electorate proved even more willing to vote for the opposition party better placed to defeat the Conservatives. In previous Euro-elections in contrast, additional tactical voting was largely absent (Curtice, 1981; Curtice, 1985). The fortunes of the opposition parties may have diverged but the result suggested that it made more sense to think of their combined vote as a single 'opposition vote' than ever before.[18] If this behaviour were to carry through to the next General Election, it could do significant damage to the Conservatives' chances of re-election.

Second, despite the claims made by Labour spokesmen as they were announced, the results did not herald a Labour breakthrough in the south of England. Rather, the election revealed there were two 'souths'. One, the 'deep south', consists of all the eight Euro-constituencies along the south coast west of Kent, together with a block of four, from Somerset to Surrey, lying immediately to their north. It contains all of the counties where the Liberal Democrats were the largest party following the 1993 county council elections, and largely coincides with the area where the Liberal Democrat vote held up best in 1987 and 1992 (Curtice and Steed, 1992). This is where the Liberal Democrats were able to convince voters that they were the stronger challengers to the Conservatives – or, in the case of Sussex South, to frustrate Labour's claims.

Just how far Labour was from making a breakthrough in the 'deep south' can be seen if we compare the result of the European Election with that of the 1979 General Election. Labour's vote was on average actually 1.5 per cent lower than when it last lost power. In contrast, the Liberal Democrat vote in the region was no less than 11.4 per cent higher than fifteen years previously, despite the fact (see Table A.4 above) that nationally its vote was less than 2 per cent higher. Far from becoming Labour territory, the election result confirmed the evidence of the last two general elections that the 'deep south' offers the Liberal Democrats their best chance yet of establishing a significant geographically concentrated bridgehead of support.

Labour's breakthrough was in a different south, the 'semi-south'. This consists of the eleven Euro-constituencies in the South of England, from Bristol in the west to Kent and Essex in the east, which lie immediately to the north and east of the 'deep south', together with the three seats in East Anglia. Labour was severely battered in this zone during the 1980s, lying third in no less than 70 of the 94 Westminster seats in 1987. Now, seven years later, it managed to win no less than 10 of the 14 Euro-seats, and came third nowhere. Labour's vote was on average 12.5 per cent higher than in 1992, a performance which it bettered only in London.

Even so, Labour's success in the 'semi-south' should not be exaggerated. On average, its vote was up by only 7.2 per cent compared with 1979, lower than in any other part of England and Wales apart from the 'deep-south'. In contrast Labour's performance in the North of England was undeniably impressive. Its 56.8 per cent of the vote was an all-time record, better even than in 1966. True, the party's advance appears to have been stemmed in Scotland by the success of the Nationalists, but, compared with much of the post-war period, Labour's vote still has a distinctly northern bias.

The Liberal Democrats also did relatively badly in Scotland which provided nine of the twenty seats won by the party in 1992. Some of this fall in support may be accounted for by the failure of personal votes cast for some of the party's Westminster MPs to transfer to the party's relatively unknown European candidates (especially in the Highlands & Islands). But as Table 9.3 shows, the party's Scottish result is still clearly the worst in Britain if compared with the last European Election in 1989 rather than the 1992 General Election. The party's southern tilt may provide it with new opportunities but it also threatens one of its traditional parliamentary bases.

The result was also an emphatic repudiation of the Liberal Democrats' boast to be the main opposition to Labour in Labour's heartlands. This had received some substance in the May local elections when the Liberal Democrats had outpolled the Conservatives in a majority of the main northern cities (*Economist*, 1994), and they came well ahead in parliamentary by-elections in Rotherham on 5 May and in Bradford South on the same day as the European Election. Yet they came third or fourth in every single seat won by Labour except one, Sheffield. Even in Sheffield the result was a pale reflection of what the party had achieved there in the local elections in May, when it had succeeded in outpolling Labour.

MINOR PARTIES

Easily the most successful of the remaining parties were the nationalists in Scotland and Wales. Both parties succeeded in achieving their highest ever share of the vote in their respective countries. But just what significance should be attached to this is unclear. As Table A.5 shows, both parties clearly benefited from the greater willingness of voters to vote for smaller parties in second-order elections; indeed, this seems to have become more true with each succeeding Euro-election. Further, Plaid Cymru in particular has done better in every single European election than it has in any general election.

Even so, neither party's 1994 achievement can be dismissed lightly. Both parties achieved a substantial advance on their previous European Election performance in 1989. Plaid Cymru won overall second place for the first time ever in a nationwide election in Wales. However, the party's advance was far from uniform, but rather emphasised further the concentration of the party's support in the Welsh-speaking northern and western parts of the country. Thus, its support rose by 20.4 per cent in North Wales (where the party's cause was probably helped by personal support for the party leader and Caernarfon MP, Dafydd Wigley) and by 7.7 per cent in Mid & West Wales, but by an average of only 2.9 per cent in the three South Wales seats. There is little doubt

Table A.5   Nationalist performances, 1979–1992/4

| | Scotland | | Wales | |
	General Election (per cent)	European Election (per cent)	General Election (per cent)	European Election (per cent)
1979	17.3	19.4	8.1	11.7
1983/4	11.8	17.8	7.8	12.2
1987/9	14.0	25.6	7.3	12.9
1992/4	21.5	32.6	8.8	17.1

that Plaid Cymru might have been able to secure its first ever MEP if the redrawing of the Welsh Euro-boundaries had followed the lines of the original (provisional) recommendations of the European Boundary Committee which had included a seat combining the Welsh-speaking counties of Dyfed and Gwynedd.

The SNP did more than win extra votes; it also captured a second seat, Scotland North-East, thereby inflicting on Labour its only reverse of the election. Alan Macartney's achievement in capturing Scotland North-East with a 16.0 per cent increase in support is much more significant than Winnie Ewing's success in holding Highlands & Islands at every Euro-election since 1979, even though this time she secured her highest vote yet (58.4 per cent). Her continued election has clearly been based on a personal vote in a highly rural and remote area where personal votes for Westminster MPs are common and where the Liberal Democrats lead in a general election.

In contrast, personal voting is considerably less important in Scotland North-East, which includes the cities of Aberdeen and Dundee. The SNP's capture of the seat followed the party's success in the May local elections in gaining control of one of the two regional councils covered by the seat (Tayside) and in becoming the largest party in the other (Grampian). Not only does the seat contain two of the party's three existing Westminster seats but it also includes two of its best prospects. Together, the European and local results strongly suggest that the party's best prospects for further gains lie in this area.

The SNP's success in Scotland North-East also helped to reinforce the party's claim to be the principal challenger to Labour in Scotland. In Scotland as a whole it easily managed to win more votes than the Conservatives and the Liberal Democrats put together. But if it were ultimately to achieve its aim of displacing Labour in Scotland it would have to win over Labour voters in the central belt, and in the five Euro-seats covering that area the party was on average more than twenty points behind.

In winning nearly half a million votes, or 3.2 per cent of the total, the Greens' performance was only disappointing in comparison with the 14.9 per cent it secured in 1989. The 15 candidates who had stood under the old Ecology Party label in 1984 only managed an average of 2.7 per cent of the vote, while the 253 candidates who stood in the last general election only averaged 1.3 per cent. Green candidates standing in recent local elections have also commonly secured on average around 4 per cent of the vote. It would seem that for every two people willing to vote for the Greens in a Westminster election another three are prepared to do so in a second-order election when the government of the country is not at stake.

In 1989 the Greens had done best in areas where traditionally the Liberal Democrats' predecessor parties had been stronger. This time, apart from Scotland, where it secured just 1.6 per cent of the vote, its support was remarkably even. Only one candidate (in Wales North) in England and Wales polled under 2 per cent, while just three saved their deposits by winning more than 5 per cent[19]

Some of the more unpopular small parties were also able to do a little better than in general elections. Five National Front candidates averaged 1.5 per cent compared with the equivalent figure of 0.8 per cent in 1992. Even the most unpopular of small parties demonstrated they could perform more successfully in second-order elections. The Natural Law Party stood in every constituency (including three candidates standing in Northern Ireland); it won just 0.6 per cent of the vote but this was still 0.2 per cent higher than the average vote for its candidates in the 1992 general election[20]. Eleven candidates standing as either Communists or Socialists also only averaged just 0.6 per cent, making Tommy Sheridan's vote of 7.6 per cent for Militant Labour in Glasgow all the more remarkable.

ANTI-EUROPEAN CANDIDATES

Not least of the reasons why it is difficult for European elections to be about Europe is that the three main British parties only differ in their degree of enthusiasm. All, for example, supported the Maastricht Treaty. But for the first time in a European election, voters were widely given the opportunity to vote for minor party candidates who either opposed the Maastricht Treaty or even Britain's continued membership of the European Union (see Chapter 9 for a detailed discussion of this phenomenon).

Most attention was claimed by the UK Independence Party (UKIP). This was formed in August 1993 by Dr Alan Sked, who had polled 1.0 per cent in the Newbury by-election in May 1993 and 1.6 per cent in the Christchurch by-election the following June. His 24 candidates secured a total of 155,488 votes or an average of 3.3 per cent where they stood. Dr Sked himself argued that his party's performance owed much to the party election broadcast which he fronted (Sked, 1994, p. 113). However, his candidates did less well than 19 other independent candidates who stood under various anti-Brussels or pro-British independence labels (particularly 'New Britain' or 'Home Rule'). Their average vote in the 17 constituencies where they stood (in two seats two of them stood against each other) was no less than 4.0 per cent of the vote, enough to give them 127,148 votes across the country as a whole.

In other words the UKIP vote was more than a response to a party broadcast; rather it was part of a wider anti-European sentiment which lacked a single national focus. With nearly three hundred thousand votes in less than half the seats, this force secured hardly any attention during the campaign.

Even making allowance for the fact that anti-European Union candidates were more numerous where they were more successful – in the South (outside London) and the Midlands where they won an average of no less than 4.8 per cent of the vote[21] – such candidates could well have achieved some 3.7 per cent or around 600,000 votes if they had contested every seat. That puts the anti-European Union vote ahead of the Greens.[22]

If the elections had been fought across the whole country by one or more anti-European parties, the credibility of and support for anti-European candidates would probably have been boosted further. It may be that the use of the single-member plurality electoral system and the absence of any referendum on the Maastricht Treaty together played a vital role in insulating Britain's main parties from more widespread anti-European voting. In the two countries where a referendum had revealed widespread opposition to Maastricht and where national party list systems were in force, Denmark and France, anti-European parties achieved considerable success. In the former, where an anti-European list has always played an important role in European elections, support for such lists was eight points higher than in 1989. In the latter, major anti-European lists appeared for the first time and between them secured nearly 15 per cent of the vote.

Some of the untapped anti-European votes in Britain appear to have been garnered instead by the twenty candidates who stood under the banner of the Liberal Party, formed in 1989 under the leadership of Michael Meadowcroft by Liberals who disliked the Liberal Democrats, and which stood on an anti-Maastricht platform. On average they won 2.9 per cent of the vote, but only 2.2 per cent where they faced competition from an anti-European candidate.[23]

It might have been anticipated that the Liberals would do most harm to the Liberal Democrats where they stood.[24] But it is difficult to find any systematic evidence that they did, except perhaps in some northern cities. However, their best vote and only saved deposit, 6.2 per cent for David Morrish, the former Alliance leader on Devon county council, may have just been the final blow to the Liberal Democrats' hopes of winning Devon & East Plymouth.

It might also have been anticipated that, given that Tory voters were least enthusiastic about Europe, anti-European candidates would have done most harm to the Conservatives. But, for example, if we take the 29 seats fought by anti-European candidates in the South and Midlands, the Conservative vote fell by 17.1 per cent compared with 15.9 per cent where they did not fight. This 1 per cent difference is no more than one would expect if anti-European candidates had in fact taken their vote equally from all three main parties.

THE ELECTORAL SYSTEM

The first-past-the-post electoral system is widely regarded as having been favourable to the Conservatives since 1979. On four consecutive occasions the party has been enabled to win overall majorities at Westminster despite winning no more than 42–3 per cent of the popular vote. But this election gave the party little reason to be grateful to the electoral system. Rather, the result revealed the highly contingent nature of the benefit the Conservatives have derived from it.

The Conservatives failed to secure no less than a quarter of the seats they might have expected to win given their share of the national vote. If the change in party support had been uniform, that is, the same in each constituency as it was across the nation as a whole, the Conservatives would have won 24 seats, six more than they actually secured. This is true irrespective of whether change is measured from 1989 or 1992. Mr. Major may have been relieved to avoid meltdown, but in truth the electoral system denied him what would in the circumstances have been regarded as a substantial triumph.

Instead of losing support uniformly, as we have seen, the Conservatives lost support most heavily in their heartlands. In other words they lost votes where it could most cost them dear. Labour meanwhile put in its best performances in the 'semi-south' and the Midlands, where it was best placed to turn extra votes into extra seats; it avoided wasting votes either pursuing hopeless causes in the 'deep south' or defending safe seats in Scotland and Wales. Equally the Liberal Democrats did best where their hopes were already strongest.

The Conservatives' problems were exacerbated by a second pattern. Compared with 1989, turnout tended to fall in the Labour half of Britain but rose in the Conservative half. This helped to boost the Conservatives' share of the national vote but, of course, did nothing to help them win any seats.

One thing that did not go wrong for the Conservatives was the boundary review undertaken to accommodate the six extra Euro-seats granted to the United Kingdom. Estimates of what the 1989 results would have been on the new boundaries suggested that the Conservatives would have secured two of the extra seats and Labour four, roughly what one would expect given that Labour was over five points ahead of the Conservatives in votes. Indeed, by updating the constituency boundaries the review helped the Conservatives by counteracting the tendency for population shifts gradually to make Labour seats smaller.[25]

But this was little compensation for a dramatic change in the electoral geography of Conservatism. A rule that had endured since the advent of the existing two-party system failed to apply. It has become a cliché in commentary on British politics to point out that the Liberal Democrats are disadvantaged by the first-past-the-post electoral system because their vote is geographically evenly spread. But at the 1994 European election this was not the case. The standard deviation of the distribution of Conservative support across constituencies was virtually identical to that of the Liberal Democrats. As Table A.6 shows, it was Labour's vote that looked exceptional for being unusually strongly geographically concentrated.[26]

The scale of this disadvantage can be seen if were to assume the Conservatives secured the 8.2 per cent swing they would need to have the same share of the vote as Labour at the next Euro-election. We assume that this same swing occurs in every constituency while the vote for the Liberal Democrats and other parties remains at its 1994 level. Despite having the same number of votes as the Conservatives, Labour would still be comfortably ahead in terms of seats by no less than 44 to 35.

Perhaps of more immediate interest is an examination of the possible implications of the electoral geography of the 1994 Euro-election for the next

Table A.6   Geographical variation in party support, 1979–94

| | Standard deviation of constituency vote | | | |
	1979	*1984*	*1989*	*1994*
Conservative	10.3	12.1	11.0	8.9
Labour	11.5	14.0	13.9	15.2
Liberal Democrat	5.0	5.5	3.7	8.7

general election. We can explore this by assuming that each party's vote in each Westminster constituency changes in line with the change between 1992 and 1994 in the Euro-constituency of which it is part. If this were to happen the Conservatives would be left with just 146 Westminster seats. In contrast, if each party's vote in each constituency were to move in line with the overall national change in support between 1992 and 1994, the party would win as many as 175 seats, a difference of 29.

Even more striking is what would happen if the Conservatives were to recover, so that the election result in terms of overall national votes cast were to be the same as in 1992, but each party's support rose or fell uniformly from the new 1994 baseline we have just created. In other words, we examine what would happen if the 1992 election result were to be repeated on the 1994 electoral geography. The Conservatives would win just 307 seats, well short of an overall majority, instead of the 336 they actually secured in 1992.[27]

Britain is, of course, the only country in Europe to use the single-member plurality electoral system. In no other country could a party succeed in securing 74 per cent of the seats on the basis of 44 per cent of the votes as Labour did in 1994, thereby ensuring that it had the largest single delegation of any national party in the European Parliament. Yet even if a supposedly proportional system had been in use, the outcome in seats could still have been significantly disproportional.

In Table A.7 we estimate what the outcome in seats would have been if the original proposals for a regional list system contained in the 1977 European Assembly Elections Bill had been used in this election. The key elements of this proposal were that each standard region should form a separate constituency and that seats would be allocated within each constituency using the d'Hondt or 'highest average' method of allocation (for further details see Carstairs, 1980). In Table A.7 we have calculated what the outcome in votes was within each standard region in 1994; in contrast to the other regional tables in this book, the votes in those Euro-constituencies which cross a standard region boundary have been allocated to the relevant standard region using the results of the last general election to estimate how each party's vote should be divided.[28] Having performed this calculation we have then applied the d'Hondt formula to allocate seats.

Labour would clearly have been much less well off and the Liberal Democrats much better off than under the existing system. Even so, in winning

Table A.7 The Result under Regional PR

	% share of vote					Seats			
	Con. %	Lab. %	Lib. Dem. %	Nat. %	Other %	Con.	Lab.	LDem.	Nat.
London	29.4	51.0	11.8	—	7.8	3	6	1	—
South East	36.1	30.5	24.2	—	9.2	7	5	4	—
South West	33.0	23.3	33.3	—	10.4	2	2	3	—
East Anglia	34.6	40.4	19.6	—	5.4	1	2	—	—
East Midlands	30.2	50.0	13.5	—	6.3	2	3	1	—
West Midlands	29.1	49.4	14.0	—	7.5	2	5	1	—
Yorks. & Humberside	25.1	53.8	15.1	—	6.0	2	4	1	—
North West	26.3	55.3	12.4	—	6.0	2	6	1	—
Northern region	21.1	63.9	10.2	—	4.8	1	4	—	—
Wales	14.6	55.9	8.7	17.1	3.8	1	3	—	1
Scotland	14.5	42.5	7.2	32.6	3.2	1	4	—	3
Great Britain	27.9	44.2	16.7	4.2	6.9	24	44	12	4

Notes: The regions in this table are the standard regions as specified by the 1977 European Elections Assembly Bill. In those Euro-constituencies which cross a standard region boundary, the number of votes won by each party in each relevant region has been estimated using the results in each Westminster seat in the 1992 general election.

44 seats, Labour would still secure just over half the seats despite winning less than half the vote.

There are two reasons. The first is the high threshold created by allocating seats within regions rather than across the country as a whole. None of the minor parties is strong enough to win a seat within any of the individual regions. Even in the largest constituency, the South East, which would have 16 seats, a party would still need to secure nearly 6 per cent of the vote to win one seat. None of the minor parties came close to that, even if we assume that all of the anti-European candidates would have stood on the same list.

In contrast, if the three component nations of Great Britain had each been treated as a single constituency the result would be very different. With 71 seats to be allocated in a single English constituency, a party would need just 1.4 per cent of the vote to secure a MEP. Further small parties would be able to appeal for votes across the whole country with just a single slate of candidates rather than only in those constituencies where they could find candidates. But even ignoring the latter point, under this system the Greens would have had enough votes to secure two MEPs and an anti-European list one. Labour's tally would be down to just 39 seats, only two more than its strict entitlement based on share of the vote.[29]

The second reason why this system would give Labour a majority of the seats is that the d'Hondt method of allocating seats is more favourable in the way it operates to large parties than most other methods (Carstairs, 1980, Chap. 3). Repeated over eleven separate regional constituencies, this feature means that Labour would be allocated up to six more seats than it might receive under alternative methods.

The 1994 European election result thus not only shows that the first-past-the-post system does not always behave as it is widely thought to, but neither also do proportional representation systems. Both advocates and critics of electoral reform too readily assume that proportional electoral systems necessarily ensure that a party can only win over half the seats if it manages to win over half the votes. Our calculation of what would have happened under the 1977 proposals shows that this is far from the case. Systems which use relatively small constituencies can produce significantly disproportional results. In the context of the continuing debate within the Labour and Liberal Democrat parties about electoral reform, it is clear that the particular choice of proportional system can matter.

Britain's continued use of the first-past-the-post electoral system to elect its MEPs is of far more than domestic concern. It had great impact on the political character of the European Parliament. In particular, it helped ensure that the total number of MEPs belonging to the broadly-defined left in the parliament (268) was nearly the same as the number belonging one of the right-wing groups (272),[30] thus reinforcing the Socialist–Christian Democrat oligopoly that has come to characterise the parliament (see Westlake, 1994, pp. 184–7). If the Labour party had only secured the 44 seats it would have won under a regional party list system rather than the 62 it actually secured under first-past-the-post, the right would have had a much clearer majority. The threat the first-past-the-post system poses to the Conservatives' chances of winning a domestic election may be no more than hypothetical, but the damage it has done to the political influence of itself and its allies in Europe is already real.

CONCLUSION

For the most part the outcome of the 1994 European Election in Britain was determined by domestic considerations. The electorate took the opportunity to express their reservations about the performance of the Conservative government and gave a significant boost to the political credibility of the Labour opposition. Only at the margins, most notably in the success of anti-European candidates, did attitudes towards Europe have any discernible influence.

The election result contained clear warning signals for the Conservatives' domestic prospects. Not only did they record their worst election result ever, but the outcome saw the emergence of an electoral geography which is potentially damaging to the government's chances of re-election. But the result should not be regarded as a death sentence. By the standards of other European elections neither the Conservatives' misfortune nor Labour's success is particularly remarkable. And if the Conservatives can stage a political recovery they can hope to regain some of their particularly heavy losses in their heartlands.

But if Europe had little to do with the way people voted, this does not mean that the outcome is without consequence for Britain's future relations with Europe. The majority of Conservative MEPs are, unsurprisingly, on the Europhile wing of their party. The virtual halving of their number helps to weaken yet further their party's ties with Europe at a time when the party is adopting an increasingly hostile stance towards closer European integration. In contrast, Labour's success strengthens the party's ties with Europe. The party provides no less than one-third of the MEPs belonging to the Group of the Party of European Socialists, including its new leader.

European elections were originally designed to help integrate Europe's citizens into a new political structure. In practice their role in Britain at the last two elections has been very different. They have enabled voters to register a mid-term protest whose impact has been exaggerated by the first-past-the-post electoral system. In so doing they have helped integrate the opposition Labour Party into Europe. But at the same time they have encouraged the isolation of the Conservative government. True, Labour's support for Europe may help to strengthen the European Union in the long-run if it can ever win power at Westminster. In the short term, however, it is the reinforcement of Conservative scepticism which is of greater import. The hoped for benefits of European elections are still far from being realised.

---

*   The authors are deeply grateful to Martin Range of the Social Studies Faculty Centre, Oxford for his invaluable computing support.

1.   Note, however, that the turnout figures usually quoted for other European countries include invalid votes whereas they are excluded from the figures usually quoted for Great Britain and Northern Ireland. See Curtice (1989). Invalid votes typically constitute 1 to 2 per cent of the vote in the Irish Republic.

2. Turnout continued, however, to be lower than in Northern Ireland (49.4 per cent). For an analysis of the result in Northern Ireland, see the contribution by Paul Hainsworth in Chapter 8.
3. In the 1979 European Election, the Conservatives themselves added 7.1 per cent to their General Election vote of the previous month. See Curtice (1981).
4. Labour's lead over the Conservatives (16.3 per cent) was also less than the Conservatives achieved over Labour in the 1979 European Election (17.6 per cent).
5. These estimates were calculated by Colin Rallings and Michael Thrasher of Plymouth University for the broadcasting organisations. We are grateful to the BBC for making these available to us. Because Westminster constituencies are used as the building blocks in constructing Euro-constituencies, we are able easily to compare the 1994 Euro-election results with those of the 1992 general election by simply aggregating for each Euro-constituency the results in the component Westminster constituencies.
6. However, turnout in Wales and Scotland failed to follow the English pattern. Despite the fact that Labour was defending all of the seats in Wales, turnout fell by only 36.9 per cent compared with 1992, and was even up by 1.7 per cent on 1989. Similarly, in Scotland, where Labour were defending seven of the eight seats, turnout fell by only 37.6 per cent compared with the General Election and by just 2.9 per cent compared with the last European Election. Within England, the fall in turnout compared with the General Election was also relatively low in London (−41.3 per cent) given the predominance of Labour-held seats. The fall in turnout compared with the previous General Election in London was also relatively low at the three previous Euro-elections.
7. The eleven seats where the Liberal Democrats started off less than 30 per cent behind are all in the South of England. The Conservative vote fell on average by 15.8 per cent in these seats whereas across the South of England as a whole, the Conservative vote fell on average by 16.8 per cent.
8. That is London, South East, South West, East Anglia, East Midlands and West Midlands.
9. Unemployment figures by constituency are published monthly in the *Employment Gazette*. Our calculations are based on the figures for January 1992 and March 1994.
10. These are seats where total unemployment as a percentage of the electorate rose by 0.5 per cent or more.
11. That is seats where unemployment as a percentage of the electorate was up by less than 0.5 per cent or fell by less than 0.1 per cent.
12. As measured by the percentage of economically active head of households who are employers and managers (socio-economic groups, 1, 2, 13) in the 1991 Census.
13. Data from the 1991-2 National Shopper Survey kindly supplied by Richard Webber. See also Webber (1993).
14. The 1979 General Election was fought on different constituency boundaries from those used in 1994 to construct Euro-constituencies. But notional results for that election on the existing boundaries are

available (BBC/ITN 1983). We have constructed Table A.4 by comparing the 1994 result with those 1979 notional results aggregated up to the existing Euro-constituencies.

15. That is, the Liberal Democrats were more than ten points ahead of Labour across the whole Euro-constituency in 1992 and where 70 per cent or more of the electorate lived in Westminster constituencies where Labour were third in 1992. The seats are Cornwall & West Plymouth, Devon & East Plymouth, Dorset & East Devon, Somerset & North Devon, South Downs West, Surrey, Sussex East & Kent South, and Wight & Hampshire South.

16. And sometimes inaccurate information. For example, *The Sunday Times* (8 May 1994) published a map based on the results of that month's local elections which showed the Liberal Democrats first in five European constituencies where in the event they came third and in two of which Labour came first.

17. Essex West & Hertfordshire East, Herefordshire & Shropshire, Kent East and Thames Valley.

18. This conclusion receives added weight from the results of a NOP opinion poll conducted a few weeks after polling day in which a majority of voters said that there were 'big differences' between the Conservatives and the Liberal Democrats but only 'small differences' between Labour and the Liberal Democrats. In 1992 by contrast as many voters thought the Liberal Democrats were closer to the Conservatives as thought they were closer to Labour. In addition, twice as many Liberal Democrat supporters in the NOP poll said they would support Labour in the absence of a Liberal Democrat candidate as said would support the Conservatives. In contrast, in 1992 slightly more Liberal Democrat voters said that the Conservatives were their second choice party as said that Labour were. See Kellner (1994b); Heath et al. (1994).

19. These candidates stood in three very different constituencies, London North-East (contested by Jean Lambert, one of the party's best-known candidates and one of the very few personal votes (6.5 per cent) evident at this election), Herefordshire & Shropshire (5.6 per cent) and Sussex South & Crawley (5.04 per cent). The vote in the latter two was secured despite the contests being marginal; tactical considerations apparently did not deter Green voters except where a nationalist was standing.

20. Easily their most successful candidate was Judith Thomas in Surrey, who won 1.4 per cent. She clearly profited from coming ahead of Susan Thomas, the Liberal Democrat, on the ballot paper.

21. Tables 9.7, 9.8 and 9.9 above list the 18 constituencies where the anti-European Union vote was more than 4 per cent; 14 of them are in the South (outside London) or the Midlands.

22. It also suggests that anti-European sentiment now is stronger than anti-common market sentiment was in 1979 when only five anti-EC candidates stood, winning on average 3.0 per cent of the vote.

23. In contrast the Greens' performance was unaffected by the presence or absence of an anti-European Union candidate.

24. Indeed, some commentators have suggested that the Liberal Democrats' disappointing national performance could be accounted for by the large

vote for small parties in general. Yet if we take the eleven seats where the vote for small parties (other than nationalists) rose most between 1992 and 1994 (in each case by 8.0 per cent or more) we find that the Liberal Democrats' performance (+ 0.2 per cent) was actually slightly better than the national average. See Kellner (1994a); Waller (1994).

25. This can be seen by comparing the mean Conservative share in 1989 of the two-party vote (that is the vote cast for Conservative and Labour combined) under the new and old boundaries. The mean two-party vote under the old boundaries was 46.8, but under the new boundaries 47.3. For further information on the utility of this measure in understanding the operation of the first-past-the-post electoral system see Curtice and Steed (1992); Soper and Rydon (1958).

26. We can also measure the Conservatives' disadvantage another way by examining the efficiency of the distribution of its support compared with Labour. This can be measured by comparing the mean and the median Conservative share of the vote cast for Conservative and Labour combined. In 1994 the Conservative share of the vote in the median constituency was as much as 2.5 per cent lower than the mean whereas in 1989 the two were equal. For further details see Curtice and Steed (1992) and Soper and Rydon (1958).

27. One might be tempted to argue that this potential disadvantage can be ignored because the Conservatives will benefit from the review of parliamentary boundaries currently being undertaken. But the review of parliamentary boundaries looks unlikely to be of sufficient benefit to the Conservatives to overcome it. Rather, even after allowing for the impact of the review, the Conservatives might need an overall national lead over Labour of as much as nine points in order just to secure an overall majority of just one if the electoral geography of the next general election were to resemble that of the 1994 European election.

28. Note that on this calculation it seems likely that the Liberal Democrats were marginally ahead of the Conservatives in the South West standard region. The result clearly underlines the fears that have even been expressed by Tory MPs about the strength of the Liberal Democrats in the area.

29. The Liberal Democrats would also benefit with 15 seats while the Conservatives would continue to secure 24.

30. Calculation based on figures of EP group membership published in Morgan (1994). The following have been counted as left-wing groups: Party of European Socialists, Europe United Left, Greens and European Radical Alliance. Right-wing groups comprise European Peoples' Party, Liberal Democrat and Reformist Party, *Forza Europa*, the European Democratic Alliance, and Europe des Nations. Note that there are a further 27 members, mostly on the extreme right-wing, who do not belong to any group.

Bibliography

Alderman, R. K. and Carter, N. (1993) 'The Labour Party Leadership and Deputy Leadership Elections of 1992', *Parliamentary Affairs*,

Anderson, B. (1991) *John Major: the Making of a Prime Minister* (London: Fourth Estate).

Baker, D., Gamble, A., and Ludlam, S. (1993a) 'Whips or Scorpions? The Maastricht Vote and the Conservative Party', *Parliamentary Affairs*, vol. 46.2.

Baker, D., Gamble, A., and Ludlam, S. (1993b) '1846 . . . 1906 . . . 1996? Conservative Splits and European Integration', *Political Quarterly*, vol. 64 no. 4.

Baker, D., Gamble, A., and Ludlam, S. (1994) 'The Parliamentary Siege of Maastricht 1993: Conservative Divisions and British Ratification', *Parliamentary Affairs*, vol. 47, no 1.

Boyce, B, (1993) 'The Democratic Deficit of the European Community', *Parliamentary Affairs*, vol. 46, no 4.

BBC/ITN (1983) *BBC/ITN Guide to the New Parliamentary Constituencies* (Chichester: Parliamentary Reference Services).

British Public Opinion (1994) 17 April (London: MORI).

Butler, D., and Jowett, P. (1985) *Party Strategies in Britain: A Study of the 1984 European Elections* (London: Macmillan).

Butler, D., and Kavanagh, D. (1992) *The British General Election of 1992* (London: Macmillan).

Butler, D., and Marquand, D. (1981) *European Elections and British Politics* (Harlow: Longman)

Butt Philip, A. (1993) 'Europeans First and Last; British Liberals and the European Community', *Political Quarterly*, vol. 64, no 4, pp. 447–61.

Carstairs, A. (1980) *A Short History of Electoral Systems in Western Europe* (London: Allen & Unwin).

Castle, B. (1993) *Fighting All the Way* (London: Macmillan).

Corbett, R. (1994) *The Maastricht Treaty* (Harlow: Longman).

Corbett, R. (1994) 'The elected European Parliament and its impact on the process of European integration', doctoral dissertation, University of Hull.

Curtice, J. (1981) 'An Analysis of the Results', in D. Butler and D. Marquand, *European Elections and British Politics* (Harlow: Longman).

Curtice, J. (1985) 'An Analysis of the Results', in D. Butler and P. Jowett, *Party Strategies in Britain* (London: Macmillan).

Curtice, J. (1988) 'One Nation?', in R. Jowell, S. Witherspoon and L. Brook, *British Social Attitudes; the 5th Report* (Aldershot: Gower).

Curtice, J. (1989) 'The 1989 European Election: Protest or Green Tide?', *Electoral Studies*, vol. 8, pp. 217–30.

Curtice, J. and Steed, M. (1992) 'The Results Analysed', in D. Butler and D. Kavanagh, *The British General Election of 1992* (London: Macmillan).

'Tories out', *Economist* (1993) 15 May.

'The Tories revolt', *Economist* (1994) 14 May.

Electoral Reform Society (1994) *The 1994 European Parliamentary Constituencies: Projected Results* (London: Electoral Reform Society).

Eurobarometer, published monthly, Brussels.

Evans, G. (1994) 'Tactical Voting and Labour's prospects', in A. Heath, R. Jowell and J. Curtice, with B. Taylor (eds), *Labour's Last Chance? The 1992 Election and Beyond* (Aldershot: Dartmouth).

Franklin, M. and Curtice, J. (1995) 'Britain: Opening Pandora's Box', in C. van der Eijk and M. Franklin, *The European Electorate on the Eve of Union* (Ann Arbor: University of Michigan Press).

George, S. (1990) *An Awkward Partner: Britain in the European Community* (Oxford: Oxford University Press).

George, S. (1992) (ed.) *Britain and the European Community* (Oxford: Oxford University Press).

Guardian (1992) 'Black Wednesday Massacre' (Tuesday, 1 December).

Heath, A., Jowell, R. and Curtice, J. (1994) 'Can Labour win?', in A. Heath, R. Jowell and J. Curtice with B. Taylor, (eds), *Labour's Last Chance? The 1992 Election and Beyond* (Aldershot: Dartmouth).

Herman, V., and Hagger, M. (1980) *The Legislation of Direct Elections to the European Parliament*, (Aldershot: Gower).

Hix, S. (1994) *History of the Party of European Socialists*, PES Group (draft), (Brussels).

ICM (1994), *Results of a Poll Conducted after the European Elections* (London: ICM Research).

Johnston, R., Pattie, C. and Allsopp, J. (1988) *A Nation Dividing: The Electoral Map of Great Britain 1979–87* (London: Longman).

Kellner, P. (1994a) 'Scale of protest vote takes Major into uncharted territory', *The Times* (14 June).

Kellner, P. (1994b) 'Party's image shifts to the left', *The Independent* (20 September).

Ludlow, Peter (1993) 'The UK Presidency: A View from Brussels', *Journal of Common Market Studies*, 31, (2).

McLean, I. (1973) 'The problem of proportionate swing', *Political Studies*, 21.

Morgan. R. W. (1994) (ed.) *Times Guide to the European Parliament June 1994*, (London: Times Books).

Rallings, C. and Thrasher, M. (1993) *Local Elections in Britain: A Statistical Digest* (Plymouth: Local Government Chronicle Elections Centre).

Reif, K. (1984), 'National Electoral Cycles and European Elections 1979 and 1984', *Electoral Studies*, 3.

Reif, K. (1985) 'Ten Second Order Elections', in K. Reif (ed.), *Ten European Elections* (Aldershot: Gower).

Reif, K. and Schmitt, H. (1980) 'Nine Second Order National Elections', *European Journal of Political Research,* (1).

Scalingi, P. (1980) *The European Parliament: The Three-Decade Search for a United Europe* (London: Aldwych Press).

Sked, A. (1994) 'The Fifth Biggest Party in Britain', *Parliamentary Brief*, 2 (June/July).

Soper, C. and Rydon, J. (1958) 'Under-representation and Electoral Prediction', *Australian Journal of Politics and History*, 4.

Spencer, P., Beange, R. and Curtice, J. (1992) *The 1992 Election and the North-South Divide* (London: Lehman Bros).

Spencer, P. and Curtice, J. (1994) *The Economy and the Opinion Polls* (London: Kleinwort Benson Research).

Waller, R. (1994) 'Labour Triumph, Lib-Dem Setback, Tory Relief', *Parliamentary Brief*, 2 (June/July).

Watkins, A. (1991), *A Conservative Coup: the Fall of Margaret Thatcher* (London: Duckworth).

Webber, R.(1993), 'The 1992 General Election: Constituency Results and Local Patterns of Newspaper Partisanship', in D. Denver, P. Norris, D. Broughton, and C. Rallings (eds.), *British Elections and Parties Yearbook 1993* (London: Harvester Wheatsheaf).

Westlake, M. (1994a), *A Modern Guide to the European Parliament* (London: Pinter).

Westlake, M. (1994b), *Britain's Emerging Euro-Elite? The British in the Directly-Elected European Parliament, 1979–1992* (Aldershot: Dartmouth).

Wood, A. (ed.) (1989) *The Times Guide to the European Parliament: June 1989* (London: Times Books).

Young, H. (1991), *One of Us* (London: Macmillan).

Index